This comprehensive analysis traces Sam Shepard's career from his experimental one-act plays of the 1960s through the 1994 play *Simpatico*. Concentrating on his playwriting, this book charts Shepard's various developments and shifts of direction, and the changing contexts in which his work has appeared.

Engaging, informative, and insightful, *The Theatre of Sam Shepard* is the definitive source on the works of this original writer.

The Theatre of Sam Shepard

The American theatre and its literature are attracting after long neglect the crucial attention of historians, theoreticians, and critics of the arts. Long a field for isolated research yet too frequently marginalized in the academy, the American theatre has always been a sensitive gauge of social pressures and public issues. Investigations into its myriad shapes and manifestations are relevant to students of drama, theatre, literature, cultural experience, and political development.

The primary intent of this series is to set up a forum for important and original scholarship in and criticism of American theatre and drama in a cultural and social context. Inclusive by design, the series accommodates leading work in areas ranging from the study of drama as literature to theatre histories, theoretical explorations, production histories, and readings of more popular or paratheatrical forms. While maintaining a specific emphasis on theatre in the United States, the series welcomes work grounded broadly in cultural studies and narratives with interdisciplinary reach. Cambridge Studies in American Theatre and Drama thus provides a crossroads where historical, theoretical, literary, and biographical approaches meet and combine, promoting imaginative research in theatre and drama from a variety of new perspectives.

Books in the series:

1. Samuel Hay, *African American Theatre*
2. Marc Robinson, *The Other American Drama*
3. Amy Green, *The Revisionist Stage: American Directors Re-Invent the Classics.*
4. Jared Brown, *The Theatre in America during the Revolution*
5. Susan Harris Smith, *American Drama: The Bastard Art*
6. Mark Fearnow, *The American Stage and the Great Depression*
7. Rosemarie K. Bank, *Theatre Culture in America, 1825–1860*
8. Dale Cockrell, *Demons of Disorder: Early Blackface Minstrels and Their World*
9. Stephen J. Bottoms, *The Theatre of Sam Shepard*

The Theatre of Sam Shepard

States of Crisis

STEPHEN J. BOTTOMS

University of Glasgow

CAMBRIDGE
UNIVERSITY PRESS

PU   THE UNIVERSITY OF CAMBRIDGE
Th   mbridge CB2 1RP, United Kingdom

CAMBRIDGE UNIVERSITY PRESS
The Edinburgh Building, Cambridge CB2 2RU, United Kingdom
40 West 20th Street, New York, NY 10011-4211, USA
10 Stamford Road, Oakleigh, Melbourne 3166, Australia

First published 1998

Printed in the United States of America

Typeset in New Caledonia Roman

Library of Congress Cataloging-in-Publication Data
Bottoms, Stephen J. (Stephen James), 1968–
The theatre of Sam Shepard : states of crisis / Stephen J.
Bottoms.
p.   cm. – (Cambridge studies in American theatre and drama)
Includes bibliographical references and index.
ISBN 0-521-58242-3 (hb). – ISBN 0-521-58791-3 (pb)
1. Shepard, Sam, 1943–   – Criticism and interpretation.
I. Title.   II. Series.
PS3569.H394Z63   1998
812'.54 – dc21   97–11991
                       CIP

*A catalog record for this book is available from
the British Library*

ISBN 0 521 58242 3 hardback
ISBN 0 521 58791 3 paperback

Transferred to digital reprinting 2000
Printed in the United States of America

Do I contradict myself?
Very well then, I contradict myself.
(I am large, I contain multitudes.)

– Walt Whitman

IN THE END WE WERE NOT CERTAIN! WE COULD MAKE
NEITHER HEAD NOR TAIL OF THE PREDICAMENT!

– Pablo, *Suicide in B$^\flat$*

this is for my family.
because they function.

Contents

Illustrations

Preface

Sam Shepard said: right smack in the centre of a contradiction –
that's the place to be. That's where the energy is, that's where the heat is.
– Paul "Bono" Hewson, *Zoo Radio*, BBC Radio 1, 1 January 1993

Sam Shepard has today achieved the status of a kind of American cultural icon, so much so that the lead singer of the hugely successful rock band U2 felt justified in citing him as a guru to explain their global stadium tour, *ZooTV* (Hewson's comments are a rather loose paraphrase of remarks made in *Interview* magazine in 1988). Yet it is one of the supreme contradictions of Shepard's career that he has reached such dizzy heights on the strength of playing supporting roles in a collection of films, few of which are more than mediocre, and writing a somewhat larger collection of plays, few of which are even remotely familiar to the general public. Another contradiction is that even the academic sector, one of the few areas where the importance of those plays is widely recognized, has produced remarkably little of critical substance to explain *why* they are worthy of attention.

This book attempts to rectify that situation somewhat, by advancing a sustained critical argument in relation to the development of Shepard's playwriting over the course of his career. This argument has a lot to do with the kind of paradox Hewson is talking about, by insisting that Shepard's work is dominated, and indeed distinguished, by patterns of internal tension and contradiction, by loose ends and uncertainties, which – far from obstructing the plays' creation of meaning – operate to generate a plethora of possible readings. More specifically, I suggest that the tensions at work in Shepard's writing can often be seen as representing an unresolved conflict between modernist and postmodernist perspectives on such issues as the nature of self-identity, the search for coherence and meaning in late capitalist culture, and the creative process itself.[1]

None of this, however, should be seen as offering conclusive answers to, or final judgments on, Shepard's work. He is, after all, still writing, and although there may be a temptation (after a decade during which his once-prolific output has tailed off markedly) to try to draw a line under his work and add it up, I believe and hope that he will yet surprise us further. Moreover, those plays which we already have are by no means fixed entities: they lend themselves to any number of potential stage treatments and may radically change meaning – chameleon-like – according to when, where, and how they are presented. For me, their fascination as theatre stems precisely from the fact that it is so often so difficult to pin down what they are "about." I take seriously Shepard's own warning that dramatic criticism can be "a very dangerous area" because "it takes away from the simple reality of the play." The assignation of a totalizing interpretation, he suggests, can create a frame of reference which "becomes more important than the play," since it preconditions the way in which others subsequently look at it.[2]

The similarity of this position to the one outlined in Susan Sontag's famous essay "Against Interpretation" is no coincidence: both were members of the Greenwich Village bohemia of the 1960s; Sontag's essay was first published in 1964, the same year that Shepard's first plays appeared onstage. Sontag's solution to such critical reductiveness was to propose a form of criticism which sought to apprehend art rather than comprehend it ("to show *how it is what it is*, even *that it is what it is*, rather than to show *what it means*"),[3] and no doubt there is a full-length phenomenological study to be done on Shepard's playwriting, a detailed assessment of how it is that his strange language and stage imagery so often seem to lodge themselves in the spectator's imagination with such peculiar force. However, although an examination of the formal qualities of the plays is central to my discussion, my approach is based on the premise that everything (and form above all) *means* something, and that most things mean lots of things – however unstable the processes of signification. I have therefore applied what is in many ways quite a traditional interpretative approach, in order to map out some of the many fields of meaning which seem to me to be brought into play by Shepard's open-ended dramaturgical style, partly because I believe that this is necessary for the richness of his work to be fully appreciated, but also partly because I believe that to avoid doing so is to abdicate critical responsibility. There are, for example (as has been pointed out by a number of critics to whom the Sontagian pieties of the 1960s mean little), legitimate political questions to be asked of Shepard's work, with respect to the representation of gender, the treatment of violence, and so forth. I make no apology for my generally admiring treatment of these plays, but nor do I apologize for asking a few awkward questions.

That said, I underline again that the approach here is a provisional one, which seeks simply to posit certain lines of inquiry, and to follow through the logic of that starting position. The chronological structure of the analysis is aimed at elucidating certain threads of development (simultaneously continuous and discontinuous) in both Shepard's writing and his approach to performance over a thirty-year period – a development which both reflects and contends with numerous broader issues that have arisen in American culture in these years. Yet if what follows reads as a fairly consistent narrative, it is also true that other, equally valid narratives could be written by other storytellers. As Shepard's plays seem forever to be reminding us, the structures by which we choose to interpret the world and our place in it are our own subjective ones, not final truths. Ultimately, this book seeks simply to encourage readers to engage afresh with Shepard's plays for themselves, rather than simply buy into received "wisdom." If it thereby contributes to their continued exploration, whether in print or – most important – onstage, it will have succeeded in its aim.

I have drawn on a broad range of resources, and where appropriate have referred (in addition, obviously, to the published plays) to Shepard's various nondramatic writings, to the surprisingly large number of interviews he has granted over the years, and to some of the unpublished notebooks, diaries, and unfinished or abandoned plays held in the Shepard archive at Boston University. I have also referred to various performances of Shepard's work, to the insights of some of those who have created them, and to my own experience of directing five of the plays between 1990 and 1994: *Red Cross, Melodrama Play, Angel City* (still my personal favorite), *Buried Child,* and *Fool for Love.* The lessons of these productions, in adding so much to my own understanding of the plays' dynamics, are reflected more in the overall thrust of the argument than in specific production details. I would, however, like to express my eternal gratitude to all those who participated in these projects. You all know who you are: you don't know how much I owe you.

I would also like to acknowledge here the invaluable advice, assistance, and encouragement of the following people, at various times: at the University of Glasgow, Greg Giesekam and John Caughie; at the University of East Anglia, Chris Bigsby, Tony Frost, and Allan Lloyd-Smith; at the

University of Bristol, Christopher Robinson and John Adler; at Cambridge University Press, Don Wilmeth, Vicki Cooper, and especially Anne Sanow. Thanks also to Jackie Jones, John Peel, Don Shewey, Sarah Teale, Christine Krolik at the Magic Theatre, and the staff of the Department of Special Collections at Boston University's Mugar Memorial Library. I am particularly grateful to Sam Shepard himself, and his agent, Judy Boals, for permission to print quotations from unpublished material held in that archive, and also to the following friends and colleagues of Mr. Shepard, who agreed to speak with me in relation to this or other projects, and whose insights have proved important to this book's development: Maria Irene Fornes, John Lion, Nancy Meckler, Tom O'Horgan, and, most inspirationally of all, Joseph Chaikin.

Introduction

States of Crisis

WHEN SAM SHEPARD'S ONE-ACT PLAY *States of Shock* premiered in New York in 1991, the title, if not the piece itself, seemed almost to summarize the author's entire output. The phrase, which recurs elsewhere in his work, is an apt description for the arresting, disturbing atmospheres which Shepard's plays so often create onstage. While the subtitle of this book expands the frame of reference somewhat ("shock" being only one of the forms of disorientation experienced by the plays' characters and, indeed, by their audiences), this is nevertheless its starting point. The tensions and contradictions generated by Shepard's writing – whether overt or, in much of his later work, more covert – tend to disrupt any possibility of the theatrical event's being experienced smoothly, and so throw up all kinds of unresolved questions. Although Shepard's work has gone through many phases since he first began writing for Off-Off-Broadway venues in 1964, this instability has been a distinguishing feature throughout.

One way to begin to look at Shepard's theatre is to contrast his approach with that of another major American dramatist of recent years, David Mamet. The two share certain superficial similarities in their concerns which have led to frequent comparisons, but there is a fundamental difference in their approaches. Mamet's is a very taut, precise writing style in which every scene is pared down to the bone, in the belief that "every time the author leaves in a piece of nonessential prose (beautiful though it may be), he weakens the structure of the play. . . . Everything which does not put forward the meaning of the play impedes the meaning of the play."[1] Shepard, however, does not share this conviction that the elements

1

of a play must all be made to serve a dominant, preconceived meaning or "ruling idea." Whereas Mamet rigorously avoids random impulses and linguistic excess, Shepard's writing tends to be dominated by such characteristics, and even his most controlled work defies linear dramatic logic. His is a theatre of fragments, and often of verbal and visual glut, in which disparate elements butt up against each other in abrupt or unsettling juxtapositions, and in which intense, disturbing confrontations are inextricably entwined with a certain wild playfulness and madcap comedy (Shepard's plays are nothing if not funny). This inclusive approach often makes the plays seem unwieldy or somehow incomplete, yet onstage it is also this very "flaw" – the lack of structural or thematic resolution – which makes his best work so provocative. Take, for example, the lingering impact of some of his startling stage images, which so stubbornly resist submitting themselves to unidirectional interpretation as symbols for dramatic themes: green slime dripping from a medicine bundle, a phalanx of popping toasters, a chair hurled across stage on the end of a lasso, a butchered lamb, manic swimming on beds against an all-white background. Similarly, Shepard's musically inspired use of language rhythms can operate to seduce or even bombard audiences, even as the reception of exact syntactic meaning is problematized. The overall effect is neatly summarized by one of Shepard's former collaborators, director Robert Woodruff:

> The plays are almost assaultive, without being hostile, and they're full of holes and contradictions that you just can't fill in. . . . When an audience leaves one of Sam's plays, they're probably really confused. They've just had several hundred images thrown at them – flash, flash, flash! – and they can't synthesize it all. [2]

However, far from impeding the production of meaning, the plays' roughness tends to open up a proliferation of possible ways in which the individual viewer can read meaning into them. In being unable "to synthesize it all," audience members are required to fill in the gaps for themselves, to draw their own conclusions. As Shepard himself has pithily put it: "Ideas emerge from plays – not the other way around."[3] This is not to say, of course, that Shepard never feeds "ideas" into his writing: indeed, his work is packed with concerns and allusions which reward detailed examination. Yet crucially, these ideas are rarely, if ever, worked through schematically or as a thesis. Rather, they are fed into the work as hints and momentary implications which gradually coalesce into a kind of poetic density. Ideas are thrown up, prompting responses which are frequently contradictory, and this in turn leads to further tensions and ambiguities. Shepard's emphasis is on exploring the way these various thematic fragments relate to and are created by emotional conditions, and he treats each new thought less as an object for intellectual scrutiny than as a trigger for exploring hopes and anxieties. Each of his plays thus represents the fruit of a kind of ongoing dialogue the author seems to be having with himself. The intensity of that dialogue may vary, from agonized, near-hysterical extremes in his most overtly unstable work, to a subtler probing and questioning in his more measured pieces. In each case, though, these texts create such a range of conflicting voices and connotations that they defy any attempt to understand them conclusively according to a single interpretative perspective.

My sense that Shepard is, in various ways, exploring questions which remain unanswered, or even unanswerable, informs my choice of the term "states of crisis." For while elements of crisis, schism, and conflict have always been the staple elements of dramatic action, they have classically been presented within structured narratives. An audience empathizes with the protagonists, looking forward to the ultimate resolution of their struggle while following a through-line of cause-and-effect action, in which each moment is seen to be directly relevant to the past and future of the play and of the characters' lives. This continues to be the most common form of drama, one championed by writers like Mamet, who is (however idiosyncratically) a confessed neoclassicist. Shepard, by contrast, is an experimentalist whose plays largely ignore such conventions. While they may make use of narrative plots, these are sketchy and unstable at best, their premises frequently lifted directly from familiar sources as if to ironize the idea of plot itself. Likewise, characters tend to be opaque and erratic: their motivations are shrouded in confusion, and such goals as they have almost invariably remain unfulfilled. The plays end not in resolutions but with abrupt anticlimaxes, unexplained images, or the suggestion of tensions continuing indefinitely into the future. They do not restore equilibrium, because in adopting an open-ended, exploratory approach to the writing, Shepard has placed himself in a state of disequilibrium and refuses to depict an arbitrary recovery of balance simply for the sake of convention. "I never know when to end a play," he commented in a 1984 interview: "A resolution isn't an ending; it's a strangulation."[4]

In short, Shepard's plays tend to be structured less as chains of events than as collages or patchworks of colors, sounds, and confrontations: the focus is on what is happening on stage *in the moment*, rather than on the explication of some fictional past or future (although the very uncertainty which consequently surrounds the past is often exploited as a further source of anxiety in the present). And in any given moment, the plays may simultaneously suggest a whole range of immediate tensions. There are relational crises (why are these people stuck with each other? how are they supposed to function together?), identity crises (who am I? how do I create or express myself? do I *have* a self?), existential crises (does it all mean anything anyway?), ontological crises (where are we? what is this reality?), national and cultural crises (what is America? what, if anything, defines us as a nation and can we live with that?), and any number of others. In the following sections of this introduction, I outline the points of tension which are treated with particular emphasis in the subsequent chapters, using this discussion to return, finally, to perhaps the most vital issue of all: the crisis of reception. Confronted with the uneven concoctions that Shepard throws at his audiences, just how is one to respond?

Crisis in Writing

I want to begin unpacking some of the factors which inform Shepard's bewildering aesthetic by proposing that there are at least three different Sam Shepards vying for ascendancy in his writing: the "high" or "romantic" modernist, the "late" modernist, and what I will call the reluctant postmodernist. No doubt there are others too, but the key fault lines seem to me to lie between these positions. Nor should this be surprising, given that Shepard's key formative years as an artist were during the 1960s, a period of cultural upheaval he himself has described as "seething with a radical shift in the American psyche."[5] In the avant-garde atmosphere of the Greenwich Village in which he lived between 1963 and 1971, the last American wave of high modernism (swept in by the '50s innovations of abstract expressionist artists and beat poets) coexisted with the impact of recent European imports like Sartrean existentialism and the theatre of the absurd (often classified in hindsight as late modernism), and with the new depthlessness, repetition, and fragmentation of pop art and its literary equivalents (now seen as the beginnings of postmodernism). The philosophical conflicts among these contending aesthetics also reflected wider cultural changes, as American society began finally to fragment beyond repair into competing subcultures and interest groups, while the traditional faith in the basic decency of the nation and its leaders was fatally undermined by revelations of conspiracies, assassinations, war atrocities, and so forth. Shepard's writing represents an arena in which numerous aspects of the cultural and philosophical upheaval of this and subsequent decades can be seen being played out at the immediate level of personal experience.

Shepard's debt to the lessons of existentialism, and its theatrical manifestation in absurdism, is immediately obvious, and one he continues to acknowledge. As recently as 1994 he was quoted as saying that however unfashionable existentialist thought might now be, it remains a vitally necessary tool for asking fundamental questions about the human condition.[6] The sense that his characters are adrift and alone in a universe which is essentially without meaning or rationale is one which recurs as either dominant theme or underlying factor in virtually all of his plays, and points to the continuing influence of the work of Samuel Beckett, one of the very few theatrical examples whom Shepard has acknowledged as important to him. Indeed, without Beckett – and *Waiting for Godot* in particular, which first inpired Shepard as a teenager in California – he would never have begun developing as a playwright in the way he did. It was Beckett who had revolutionized theatre by abandoning wholesale the classical model of dramatic narrative, and established instead the idea of presenting a drama of the existential present which consciously resists conclusive rationalization. Beckett's is perhaps the original dramaturgy of crisis-in-the-moment, evoking on stage an immediate sense of fear or emotional paralysis in the face of life's futility. Shepard followed his example in creating stage figures who are fractured victims of inexplicable circumstance, and who fill the voids of their lives with games, confrontations, and blocks of rhythmic, imagistic language. Moreover, as with *Endgame* or *Waiting for Godot,* Shepard's figures are usually imprisoned spatially as well as temporally, trapped in more or less claustrophobic stage spaces which, for one reason or another, they either cannot or dare not vacate.

Yet where Beckett's work tends to suggest the stark austerity of a sensibility on the edge of self-erasure and silence, Shepard's plays seem characterized by a very American brashness, a yearning for freedom, for wild self-release. Such desires almost invariably prove unrealizable: indeed, the specific inability of America to deliver on its promises of liberty and self-fulfillment is one which Shepard's work exposes in myriad different ways. That does not, however, quench the desire, and the frustration generated by its lack of fulfillment seems central to the sense of entrapment and nightmarish hysteria which informs so many of these plays. Accordingly, Shepard's use of both language and image is more extreme and erratic than Beckett's carefully modulated, muted style. The desire for expansive freedom, moreover, has always been central to Shepard's actual writing process: far from accepting the stark nihilism of Beckett's outlook,

he has tended (somewhat contradictorily) to ascribe to the more romantic, high modernist belief that the act of creativity itself might somehow
be a source of both liberation and redemptive meaning.

In this respect, the early lessons of nontheatrical influences, including
action painting, beat writing, and especially jazz music, have been crucial.
Shepard has continued to cherish their key principle of unrestricted
spontaneity in the creative process, of pursuing the expression of one's
immediate impulses rather than trying to submit oneself to preconceived
ideas of structure and content. This kind of free-form creativity has often
been seen as offering a way both to express underlying feelings of alienation and angst in relation to the everyday world, and also perhaps to
break beyond these to unlock hidden truths from the depths of the psyche. In accordance with this, Shepard has cultivated the use of stream-of-
consciousness writing in which the present state of the writer's mind is in
some sense the subject of the work. As he told *Time Out* in 1972: "I never
know what to say when somebody says what are the plays about. They're
about the moment of writing."[7] Shepard's free-form technique is evident
in its most raw, undeveloped state in his very earliest plays, but he has
continued to practice it, with modifications, throughout his career. He
claims, for example, that *True West* (1980) went through thirteen different drafts before he was happy with it, and that each of those drafts was
not merely an adjustment of the previous one, but a complete rewrite. He
finally stumbled over the inspiration he was searching for "when I heard
the voice of Lee speaking very clearly, and then I heard Austin's response.
The more I listened, the more the voices came. . . . *True West* felt like a
total improvisation, spinning off itself."[8]

Shepard gave his fullest public account of this improvisational
approach in his article "Language, Visualization and the Inner Library,"
written for *The Drama Review* in 1977, in which his language is saturated
with the romantic terminology of high modernism. The writing of each
play begins not with a concept, he explains, but with an image or a
"voice," often recalled from a state of half-sleep or daydream, which
serves as a starting point for a journey into the unknown: "the picture is
moving in the mind and being allowed to move more and more freely as
you follow it." He equates the process with a state of waking sleep, which
helps explain why almost all of his plays, to one degree or another, evoke
something of the chaotic randomness of dreams. Shepard even goes so far
as to reject the traditional definition of craftsmanship as indicating an
ability consciously to shape and hone raw material into a finished product, redefining it instead as the ability to resist the temptation to censor
the spontaneous creative impulse: "The extent to which I can actually fol-

low the picture and not intervene with my own two cents worth is where inspiration and craftsmanship hold their real meaning."[9]

Shepard's struggle to ensure that his work is genuinely spontaneous is also evident from various of the unpublished notes and draft material held in archive at Boston University. Take, for example, the self-recriminations which end many of the numerous unfinished (often barely begun) typescripts dating from the mid- to late 1970s. One such, titled "White Slavery," ends after just one page and one line of typed dialogue, beneath which, in handwriting that gets steadily more rapid and illegible, are five repetitions of the same frustrated phrase: "writing's not fast enough." Apparently he felt that his conscious mind was being allowed too much time to intervene with its "two cents worth." Another such piece is aborted after a mere four lines, as a "CENSOR enters in black mortician's suit" and announces, "You're painting yourself into a corner and you haven't even started."[10] (Note the use of painterly terminology: for Shepard, the visual and the verbal are inextricable.)

In the modernist tradition, this desire to open oneself up to free-flowing impulses has often been equated with an attempt to tap into imagery which is universally resonant, on some primal or prerational level of experience, and Shepard has expressed a passionate commitment to this idea. For example, in a revealing 1984 interview with Amy Lippman, he clearly alludes to the Jungian notion of a collective unconscious, the repository of mythic archetypes, which lies at a deeper substratum of the psyche than one's personal unconscious, and which it is the task of the artist to locate:

> Hopefully in writing a play, you can snare emotions that aren't just personal emotions, not just catharsis, not just psychological emotions that you're getting off your chest, but emotions and feelings that are connected with everybody. Hopefully. It's not true all the time; sometimes it's nothing but self-indulgence. But if you work hard enough toward being true to what you instinctively feel is going down in the play, you might be able to catch that kind of thing. So that suddenly you hook up with feelings that are on a very broad scale, [moving] in a direction we all know, regardless of where we come from or who we are. . . . Those, to me, are mythic emotions.[11]

The word "mythic" is worth highlighting as one of the most overused and underdefined words in Shepard criticism. Reviewers in particular frequently deploy it as a conveniently vague adjective which suggests a certain profundity without actually requiring the writer to explain what he or she means by it. As a result it often also becomes confused with "myth,"

as in *lie*, and "popular mythology," as in American folk culture. To avoid
such confusion, I use such terms sparingly in this book, but it is significant
that Shepard's own use of the word is consistent with the high modernist
notion of seeking to create art that can generate the kind of unifying
human experience which – in the skeptical twentieth century – social
conventions and religion are no longer able to provide.

Shepard's concern with achieving some kind of universal resonance in
his work also helps explain his fascination with the musicality of language.
The idea of using language to approximate something of the rhythmic,
sensuous quality of music is a commonplace in modernist writing, largely
because music too has been seen as representing a symbolic expression of
subconscious desires. In the 1960s, in particular, this idea was pushed to
extremes: jazz and rock music were seen by many as having the potential
to awaken their listeners to another dimension of experience, to "break
on through to the other side" (as The Doors' Jim Morrison famously put
it). Shepard was again sympathetic to such notions: in his 1975 journal
The Rolling Thunder Logbook, he compared Bob Dylan's music with
shamanistic rites in which driving rhythms are used to conjure up the
spirit world. Shepard's descriptions of his own work are more modest, but
this has not stopped others from making similar claims on his behalf, particularly in respect to his earlier work. In Jack Gelber's 1976 article "The
Playwright as Shaman," for example, Shepard is credited with using his
emphasis on the immediacy of the theatrical moment to create a form of
metaphysical drama, which generates ecstatic states akin to a drug trip or
a primitive religious rite.

The problem with such hyperbolic claims is that they entirely ignore
the many elements of Shepard's writing which openly contradict them.
Over the course of his career, his work has increasingly gravitated toward
the postmodernist suspicion that the redemptive impulses of high modernism, the desire to create new unities as a focus for a formless universe,
might in fact be futile. Indeed, even as he has continued to pursue his
free-form writing technique, Shepard has periodically admitted that
this creative process – far from resulting in liberating expressions of
the collective unconscious – has all too often led him toward weary self-
repetition ("You suddenly find yourself doing the same thing over and
over again"),[12] or to the dredging up of personal neuroses which should
have been left well enough alone: "A lot of those things aren't even worth
looking into," he has remarked: "they're like devils. You're causing yourself more trouble . . . indulging in thought forms that are destructive."[13]
Still more pertinent is his awareness that the very idea of using improvi-

sation to liberate the imagination is to some extent a delusion, since the writer is always constrained within the preexistent, culturally determined structures of thought which he or she has been shaped by. Thus, in *The Rolling Thunder Logbook* he questions the assumption of personal heroes like Dylan and Allen Ginsberg that creativity is a purely instinctive quality – "a God-given stamp at the moment you come sliding from your Mama's thighs." Instead, he insists it is "a worked-at process," and that as one learns, one is being conditioned: "we're not born with any word language to begin with, [so] there must be a kind of system of thought which a poet gears himself into. Over years."[14]

The logical extension of this is the fear – recurrently visible in the plays themselves – that the instinctive material explored through improvisation might simply be the random regurgitations of an imagination entirely shaped by the culture within which it operates. Often largely composed of fragments of imagery and language drawn from American popular culture, Shepard's writing suggests a sensibility acutely aware of its own colonization by a flashy, violent, and spiritually bankrupt society. This kind of cultural specificity openly contradicts the idea of the plays being equally accessible to "everybody . . . regardless of where we come from or who we are." (It also, incidentally, diverts from the strictly nonspecific, solipsistic landscapes of Beckettian absurdism.) On occasion, Shepard gone still further than this, exhibiting a patently postmodernist skepticism toward the idea that "mythic" expressions of common human experience are in any way possible in the current cultural climate. In a 1992 interview with Carol Rosen (in which he also refuted Jack Gelber's description of him as a shaman), he stated bluntly:

> Myth in its truest form has been demolished. It doesn't exist anymore. All we have is fantasies about it. Or ideas that don't speak to our inner self at all, they just speak to some lame notions about the past. But they don't connect with anything. We've lost touch with the essence of myth. . . . The same with the Native Americans – they were connected to their ancestors through myth, through prayer, through ritual, through dance, music – all of those forms that lead people into a river of myth. And there was a connecting river, not a fragmented river.
> ROSEN: And that's gone.
> SHEPARD: It's gone, yes.[15]

This apparent contradiction of the sentiments expressed in the Lippman interview seems to be less the result of a loss of romanticism in the intervening years (the same interview has him pontificating about the

existence of angels) than simply a rare case of Shepard's allowing himself
to talk publicly about the bleaker, more skeptical side of his outlook. This
side, however, finds plentiful expression in the actual texts of his plays, in
which his sense of life as a "fragmented river" (a bizarre but curiously apt
term in his case, given his use of alternately flowing and disjointed
rhythms) is powerfully expressed. Indeed, if Shepard's is a theatre of the
present moment, this is a present which has less to do with the ecstatic
celebration of metaphysical immanence (which would rely, paradoxically,
on a stable sense of one's location in time) than with Fredric Jameson's
definition of postmodernity as a schizophrenic condition in which existence seems to have dissolved into a series of fractured presents without
coherent relation to past or future.

Yet the deracination of human life and society which this perspective
implies offers little to be celebrated, and Shepard is clearly acutely
uncomfortable with it. Indeed, his doubts over the validity of his spontaneous approach, and its gravitation toward fragmentation, have periodically led him to seek a greater degree of conscious shaping for his work.
For example, in direct contradiction to the scribbled exhortation in
"White Slavery" to write faster, Shepard wrote just months later that he
felt his freewheeling approach was just too random: "improvisation – in
my case – trying to find music through stumbling around. I need more
head – I need to bring my head into it more."[16] One manifestation of this
desire to create a more reliable structure through greater conscious fore-
thought has been his growing interest in storytelling, an attempt to create
a sense of more ordered narrative. This impulse, visible as early as 1967,
becomes especially evident in some of his later, more realistic plays. And
yet even here, the stories told by the characters, usually in the form of
monologues, function simply as isolated fragments within overall narrative structures which remain conspicuous for their lack of stability. There
is, to be sure, a degree of deliberate subversion at work here: *True West*,
for example, seems quite self-conscious in the way it relates Lee's wildly
contrived ideas for a movie scenario to the workings of the play itself. And
yet there seems little doubt that Shepard would *like* to find a "story" he
could believe in, be it for his plays or for life in general. The problem is
that such attempts seem doomed to failure: Aristotle is just too far away.
In the past, he noted in a 1984 interview,

> storytelling was a real form, that people felt fit their lives in a way: this
> long thing – beginning, middle and ending – really meant something in
> their lives, and maybe now we're in a time where that doesn't fit any-

more . . . because everything's so fragmented and broken . . . And it's a
hard pill to swallow, because I really still migrate toward that old classical form, although I can't do it. I've tried over and over again to make
this kind of sweeping thing, and it just doesn't . . . [trails off into
silence][17]

Shepard's, then, is a reluctant postmodernism: his work displays a profound unease with contemporary American culture (its slick artificiality,
its loss of centeredness, its abandonment or corruption of basic human
values), while also demonstrating an awareness that it is not possible to
transcend or step outside that cultural condition in order to adopt a critical distance. Moreover, I would suggest that – whether by accident or
design – the plays have become gradually more sophisticated in their
handling of the kind of disruptive, unresolved formal qualities typical of
postmodernist art. As the early, relatively simple stream-of-consciousness
playfulness gave way to an increasingly jagged, agitated style, a mounting
fear of the total absence of reliable structures became visible. By the mid-
1970s, Shepard had grown adept at stealing and subverting the familiar
conventions of filmic or dramatic genres so as to undermine the comforting assumptions underlying them: the introduction of detective figures, in particular (reprised as recently as 1994 in *Simpatico*), allowed for
mockery of the very notion of piecing the "clues" of experience together
into some kind of comprehensible narrative. In the later 1970s and '80s,
while based at San Francisco's Magic Theatre, Shepard then began developing an idiosyncratic form of stage realism in a series of family dramas.
And while this new interest in conventional form may – to some extent –
have been another manifestation of the desire for more stable grounding,
it also led him toward an increasingly subtle *de*stabilization of the cozy
assumptions of the domestic genre. His is a realism which, in the words
of the Magic Theatre's founder, John Lion, confronts the "reality" of "a
world that doesn't make sense, can never make sense, will never make
sense."[18]

The profound ambivalence of Shepard's writing, his simultaneously
romantic and deeply skeptical outlook, is perhaps exhibited most clearly
in his periodic tendency to draw on the imagery of traditional myth narratives. In *True West*, for example, his portrayal of complementary but
eternally feuding brothers, a pairing whose genealogy runs all the way back
to Cain and Abel, reads as an almost too deliberate *quotation* of the Jungian scheme of conscious ego and repressed shadow side which such duos
supposedly represent. More ambivalent still is *Buried Child*, with its

exploitation of a variety of different myth schemes, from Oedipus to Osiris. As with his use of pop-cultural sources, there is something of the self-con- sciousness of postmodernist pastiche in these instances, the ironic manip- ulation of the redundant fragments of ancient stories which have lost their power to affect us in their original form. Yet there is also the sense that these stories might contain lingering truths, that the fragments might still resonate, that such myths – however compromised they may be – are all we have. And that contradiction, suggests John Lion, "is the source of the wild humor in Shepard: this romantic impulse versus the conscious intel- lectual sense that it's *hokum*. Which of course leads us back to the exis- tential dilemma."[19]

Shepard has continued, throughout his career, to search for new images of coherence, but this struggle to establish some sense of stability seems constantly to be undermined by his own tendency toward doubt, irony, even an implicit self-ridicule. This instinct for self-subversion is perhaps most paradigmatically visible in his ongoing inclination toward setting up binary oppositions within the plays as possible, provisional sources of structure, which are then blurred, contradicted, or even dis- mantled altogether. In effect, the project on which poststructuralist the- orists and some more intellectually oriented postmodernist artists have consciously embarked (see, for example, Jacques Derrida's writings, or Thomas Pynchon's novel *Gravity's Rainbow*, which mercilessly ridicules binary oppositions of all sorts) has been roughly paralleled by Shepard's more instinctive approach. Inside versus Outside, civilization versus nature, subjective versus objective, reality versus fantasy, hero versus villain, exterior personality versus essential self, and even, finally, mascu- line versus feminine: each of these distinctions is proposed and then problematized in Shepard's work. Structure, grounding, certainty remain helplessly inaccessible.

Crisis of Identity

The creative tensions generated by Shepard's open-ended writing style find a localized focus in the tortured question of personal identity, which is arguably his most insistent thematic thread. Nor is the importance of this issue surprising, given that so much of his writing derives from an urge toward exploring the inner self. Crucial to the high modernist con- cern with spontaneous creativity is the conviction that it enables a pure, authentic self-expression, freed from the censoring tendencies of the

conscious personality. By sidestepping the rationalizations and deceptions of the ego, and so confronting – as honestly and unflinchingly as
possible – one's subconscious fears and desires, many modern artists have
sought to arrive at a kind of true personal speech, a statement of unique
identity. Here again (alongside his more universalizing aspirations) Shepard has followed suit: indeed, his entire output can in one sense be seen
as representing a kind of Whitmanesque "Song of Myself" as he has
sought to explore what he once described as the "huge, mysterious and
dangerous territories" within his own psyche. Moreover, this fact in itself
appears to be one of the key sources of the sense of crisis which his work
so often evokes. The earliest plays, for example, combine a liberating
sense of playful freedom with the exploration of an acute underlying fear-
fulness. And if, as he says, those initial sketches were a means of "breaking the ice with myself," then the later progression of his work often
displays something little short of mental warfare. "When it comes right
down to it," Shepard has stated, "what you're really listening to in a writer
is . . . his ability to face himself."[20]

The urge toward full self-expression, of course, is predicated on the
assumption that there is indeed an authentic inner self to find expression,
as distinct from the exterior, socially conditioned personality. By his own
admission, Shepard's work periodically appeals to an almost religious
sense of some inner essence which one has to discover by stripping away
the artificial layers of the everyday persona, or perhaps (in the Jungian
formulation) by "individuating" the fractured parts of the mind into the
true whole. In a 1984 *New York Times* interview, he explained his conviction that "personality is everything that is false in a human being . . .
everything that's been added onto him and contrived. It seems to me that
the struggle all the time is between this sense of falseness and the other
haunting sense of what's true – an essential thing that we're born with and
tend to lose track of."[21] In an apparent attempt to counteract such amne-
sia, various of his plays posit fleeting utopian images of the divided mind
being made whole, or of old, dead roles being purged through an assortment of rituals.

These gestures, however, never survive unquestioned. For there is also
a recurrent fear in Shepard's work that the depth model of interior self
within exterior appearance might in fact be a fallacy. Indeed, this is one
of the binary oppositions which the plays problematize most insistently.
What if there really is no inner self to be "true" to, only roles to invent?
What if the very idea of a personal essence is merely a fiction concocted

by the surface personality to give itself the stabilizing illusion of depth?
The plays repeatedly betray a suspicion that personal identity might con-
sist of no more than the sum of one's culturally imposed layers, and that
only through the outward performance of a desired self-image can one
achieve any sense of distinct being. Such performativity apparently constitutes the *only* "truth" in a postmodern culture which – according to
Jean-François Lyotard – now functions entirely according to the interplay of self-legitimating, self-perpetuating "language games."

Much of Shepard's writing seems driven by the tortured and ultimately
unresolvable conflict between these incompatible depth and surface
models of personal identity, a fact which also sheds an entirely different
light on the idea of "facing oneself" through the writing process. For the
impression created in these plays is often less that of a writer boldly nav-
igating the depths of his psyche than of someone attempting to make
himself up: the fragments of autobiographical detail that so frequently
find their way into Shepard's writing are incorporated in much the same
way as the borrowings from pop culture – scraps of personal experience
which might somehow be rendered meaningful by their reification as art.
And while it is always a risky business ascribing the nature of a writer's
work to the details of his or her biography, the details of Shepard's pecu-
liarly unsettled background are hard to ignore when considering the
plays' recurrent sense of a search for personal stability amid rootlessness
and drift. The postwar generation of which he was a part grew up during
a time of upheaval in almost every aspect of American life. In his case this
was compounded by the fact that his father was a military pilot who was
constantly being relocated to different postings. Born at an air force base
in Illinois in 1943, Samuel Shepard Rogers VII was moved, as a small
child, to places as diverse as South Dakota, Utah, Florida, and even the
Pacific island of Guam. His family finally settled near Los Angeles, just as
he was due to start high school, but this too only added to Shepard's sense
of dislocation: he has spoken of his sense of southern California as a "sort
of temporary society . . . where nothing is permanent, where everything
could be knocked down and it wouldn't be missed. [There's] a feeling of
impermanence that comes from that – that you don't belong to any particular culture."[22] As John Lion has pointedly remarked: "Sam did not
'deconstruct' personality as some would claim: he was a deconstructed
personality."[23]

In this light, Shepard's fascination with the notion of self-invention –
which has been as obvious as his simultaneous and somewhat contradictory pursuit of the more traditional notion of self-expression – seems no

mere game. At several stages in his career, he has abruptly abandoned an established style of playwriting in favor of something new and untried, and this practice has been mirrored by his tendency to invent new roles for himself in life. From his early gesture of renaming himself on becoming a playwright, through his attempts in the late 1960s to turn himself into a rock star, to his now widely recognized persona as a strong-and-silent-type movie actor, he has demonstrated a certain restlessness with himself, and a determination to use new experiences to turn himself into something new. While he denies any active attempt to manipulate the way he is perceived by the world at large, it is also clear that any writer who publishes a book of ostensibly autobiographical sketches – *Motel Chronicles* – which includes a memoir of his own birth ("I lurched off the bed and dragged my pudgy body toward those two windows") must have a highly developed sense of irony about his public image.[24]

The clearest evidence of Shepard's concern with self-invention is the plays themselves, in which characters relentlessly seek to create and re-create their personal appearances. Many of these figures manipulate an ever-shifting series of roles and masks, thereby suggesting the absence of any underlying sense of self, a kind of schizoid instability. Time and again, they fall back on the fact of their immediate, physical presence on stage, and perform for grim survival: it is as if, by placing other characters in the position of receptive observers, they hope to gain some fragile, exterior confirmation of their existence, and so establish themselves as coherent characters. Yet this very reliance on exteriors, this insistent urge for attention, tends to problematize any more "sincere" search for truth which the characters purport to pursue. If there is a Pirandellian dimension to these figures – characters "in search of an author" to give meaning, direction, and coherence to their lives – they tend inexorably toward the performative alternative wittily described by Shepard in one frustrated but telling note to himself: "Six Egomaniacs in Search of an Audience."[25]

From the blurry-edged inhabitants of his earliest plays (who are little more than ciphers, vehicles for the author's wordplay), through the kaleidoscopic fragmentation of the figures in *Angel City* (1976), to the more consistent but obsessively performance-oriented family members in *A Lie of the Mind* (1985), Shepard's plays consistently depict characters with a profound lack of clear direction or "rounded" identity. Moreover, their need constantly to perform themselves into existence meets a further complication in that, far from having an endless multiplicity of possible roles from which to choose, they seem trapped within a distinctly limited range of potential options, victims of deterministic influences which, try as they might, they cannot shake off. This is one of the most vexed and recurrent issues which Shepard's work raises: how much of an independent identity can one ever claim to have, if one's fate is being shaped and channeled, even before the moment of one's birth, by forces entirely beyond one's control? The characters in these plays are plagued by an ongoing terror of "unseen hands" (from government to family to the manipulating control of the author himself), which seem to be conspiring to shape their every action, stripping them of any pretense at autonomy. And yet there is a recurrent sense that their ongoing struggle for self-definition – however futile – is also, paradoxically, its own fulfillment. For Shepard, it seems, we are *both* the victims of determinism *and* the inventors of our selves: another of his key existential questions is how to balance these incompatible "truths."

Crisis of Masculinity

The contradictions inherent in Shepard's treatment of the theme of identity are perhaps made most starkly apparent in his depiction of gender roles, since the urge towards self-exploration has led him to an obsessive fascination with the question of what it means to be an American male. Many different types of masculine behavior are depicted in these plays, from the adolescent mischievousness of the trickster figures in the earliest plays, through the posturing "heroism" of cowboys and rock stars, to the fathers, sons, and lovers of the family plays: in each case, Shepard appears to be working out some anxiety with regard to the adequacy or acceptability of the masculine attitudes depicted. In particular, the plays repeatedly return to the depiction of a violent and arrogant machismo, which is implicitly located as the source of America's tendency toward personal and societal self-destruction. Through their dramatization of tycoons, gunfighters, drifters, visionary artists, and modern-day Fausts, the plays suggest that the still-prevalent frontier myth of the heroic "rugged" individual, demanding independence at all costs, lies at the very root of the ruthless self-aggrandizement which still holds sway at every level of American culture.

As Shepard himself admits, this concern with male violence represents an attempt at a kind of exorcism, at confronting and dealing with attitudes which had been inculcated into him from a very young age: "Machismo may be an evil force," he notes, "but what in fact is it? . . . I know what this thing is about because I was a victim of it, it was part of my life, my old man tried to force on me a notion of what it was to be a 'man.' And it destroyed my dad. But you can't avoid facing it."[26] Nor was his father the only source of such indoctrination during his youth. The 1950s was, in America at least, probably the most chauvinistic decade of the century, thanks to a concerted national attempt to reestablish rigid social gender roles after a war which had seen women working in "male" industries, while men were fighting abroad. The popular culture of the period was saturated with strong, dominant men and passive, domesticated women, in western serials, superhero comics, Mike Hammer-style detective fiction, and so forth. Shepard's work owes a great deal to such imagery, as he refracts and distorts it through his ironic and at times self-lacerating perspective.

Yet even as he implicitly critiques such dominant attitudes to gender roles, Shepard himself frequently seems trapped within this same limiting view of masculinity. This seems to be largely because of his continuing insistence on seeking to apprehend certain underlying universals, which results in the contradiction of his own suggestion that machismo is a socially constructed phenomenon. Any definition of "essential maleness" is likely to include many of the characteristics Shepard exposes as potentially dangerous, and indeed at times his work appears to imply that male brutality (and, by extension, female victimization) is an inescapable biological given, repeating itself cyclically through the generations. Thus, while he almost invariably ironizes his portrayal of stereotyped masculinity, via pop culture parody, or the more or less gleeful exposure of his characters' personal inadequacies, he rarely seems able to envisage any kind of serious alternative. Moreover, while his determination to write about what he knows and feels most intimately is entirely understandable, his tendency to focus on the problems of straight white male Americans to such an obsessive extent (provocative as this may be in many respects) means that other character types are almost always marginalized and peripheral figures, when they appear at all. Consequently, they can voice little or nothing that might be seen as positing a way out of the trap that Shepard depicts.

A similar problem has also, incidentally, been evident in the construction of Shepard's public image as a movie star. His playing of roles such as the pioneer test pilot Chuck Yeager in Philip Kaufman's *The Right Stuff* (1983) indicates a certain ironic self-consciousness with regard to his representation of masculinity.[27] So too does his willingness to be photographed in 1984 by Annie Leibovitz (the *Rolling Stone* photographer

famed for depicting stars in self-mocking poses) in full "Marlboro Man"
cowboy regalia, leaning proudly against a horse. Yet the difficulty with
such ironic poses, as has often been pointed out in the fields of film and
gender studies in recent years, is that even while placing the traditional
role "in quotes," one effectively acknowledges its lingering authority by
once again reinscribing it in the popular imagination. This is especially
the case if the irony is overlooked.

Shepard seems to have recognized this, and it is notable that after his
Oscar nomination for *The Right Stuff*, and the concomitant celebration of
him as the "New American Hero," he backed away from playing macho
film roles, despite numerous offers. Indeed, between 1983 and 1990 he
played only minor supporting roles in films dominated by female stars,
often as a mild-mannered husband or boyfriend (the exception being his
appearance in the film of his own play, *Fool for Love*, in 1985). During the
same period he finally brought female characters to the foreground in his
writing, in a visible attempt to rethink gender division and escape the trap
of binary opposition. This was a goal he came closest to realizing with *A
Lie of the Mind*, which goes some way toward proposing a kind of
utopian-postmodern vision of gender identity as to some extent fluid,
another form of role play. According to this logic, the performing self is
perhaps able to reconstruct an ideal identity from a range of possible
attributes, both "masculine" and "feminine." Even this play, however, has
been attacked for portraying most of its female characters (subjected to
various forms of violence by the men) as brain-damaged or a-rational.
Shepard's writing since then, even while idealizing feminine attributes,
has continued to suggest a more or less polarized view of gender division
(especially in his 1992 film *Silent Tongue*). It seems, moreover, that brute
masculinity, for all his evident abhorrence of it, continues to exercise a
powerfully seductive influence over Shepard, as it does over American
culture at large. His exploration of gender identity remains fundamentally ambiguous and unresolved.

Crisis in Performance

If Shepard's writing style and thematic preoccupations have suggested a
gradual, if seemingly reluctant, shift toward a postmodernist perspective
over the course of his career, much the same could also be said of his attitude toward the realization of his texts in performance. At the outset of
his career, he initially sought a strict degree of control over the way in
which his work was performed. The introductions to four of his earliest

pieces by their original directors in *Five Plays* (1967) afford pointed testimony to his tendency to interfere in the rehearsal process if he disagreed with their decisions, and to insist on getting his own way. The idea of the director and production crew having a degree of creative autonomy themselves, a role in the "authorship" of the final performance, was not one he seemed willing to consider at this point. This attitude was entirely consistent with his early adherence to modernist aesthetics, since for a play even to come close to being a pure expression of the writer's unique, personal vision, the possible distorting influences of actors, directors, and designers must be strictly monitored. Samuel Beckett, as director of many of his own plays, sought to restrict the actor's room for individual initiative to the point, in *Not I*, of having only a single mouth, spotlit on a stage otherwise shrouded in total darkness, jabbering away at a speed which prevented the actor's coloring the delivery with any personal inflections.

The very extremity of such gestures, however, also points up the limitations involved in seeking completely to control the production process from a single authorial standpoint: this is to attempt to deny the fundamentally collaborative nature of theatre as an art form. Shepard's steadily more exploratory attitude to the production process indicates his increasing awareness of this fact. From the late 1960s, far from seeking to follow the Beckettian example of stripping the drama down to bare essentials which he could more easily control, he began playing with a greater variety of elements, often using large casts and adding live music and extravagantly theatrical effects. Simultaneously, he became less belligerent about enforcing his own prescriptions on productions. As his comments at the time make clear, he still had very specific ideas about the kind of impact his plays should have on audiences, but this new openness indicated that he was no longer nearly so cocksure about how that could best be achieved: "I've laid myself open to every kind of production for my plays," he told Richard Schechner in 1973, "in the hope of finding a situation where they'll come to life in the way I vision them. Out of all these hundreds of productions, I've seen maybe five that worked."[28] That year Shepard granted Schechner's Performance Group the rights to present the American premiere of *The Tooth of Crime*, despite severe personal misgivings about what Schechner might do with the play. (While experimenting freely with most other elements of the theatrical event, Shepard has always adhered to the traditional model of frontal staging and a clear separation of stage and audience, and is skeptical about the value of the more overtly avant-garde uses of theatre space pioneered by contemporaries like Schechner.)[29]

In 1974, Shepard made his first tentative attempt at directing one of
his own plays, *Geography of a Horse Dreamer*, apparently in the hope of
learning more about the dynamics of theatrical rehearsal and performance, so that in the long term he could indeed make his plays "work" in
the way he envisioned. This experience, however, taught him that the
challenges of the production process itself are far greater than he had
previously realized. Subsequently, from the mid-'70s through the early
'80s, while playwright-in-residence at the Magic Theatre (which, with its
small auditorium and proscenium stage, ideally suited Shepard's prefer-
ence for an intimate but still separate relationship between stage and
audience), he acted almost as an apprentice to Robert Woodruff, who
directed most of his major plays during this period, while experimenting
with directing some of his own lower-profile pieces. Having finally
assumed full directorial control of his plays during the 1980s, he used this
position not to reinforce the playwright's authoritarian position as creator-
auteur, but to play down the sanctity of his own text, to de-privilege its significance by treating it as simply one element in an interplay of multiple
creative inputs. Refusing to provide anything but the loosest instructions
to actors, designers, and musicians, he actively encouraged them to bring
their own ideas to the production, and functioned more as a facilitator for
this collaboration than as director per se. He would even make amend-
ments to the text in response to the way the piece was developing through
rehearsal. In effect, the modernist desire for pure authorial presence had
by this stage been shed in favor of a more open, dialogic process in which
text and performance form a dynamic tension, informing and feeding off
each other without either one claiming ultimate precedence.[30] This kind
of playful exchange of ideas, in which no prescriptive, singular vision is
imposed on the production, represents a distinctively postmodernist
directorial approach.

These questions over how best to approach the production process
have been mirrored quite closely by arguments about how best to respond
to Shepard's work as an audience member. Parallel to the notion of assert-
ing total authorial control over the stage image, there is the high modernist tendency to view the artist as a visionary whose work must be treated
as sovereign, rather than being submitted to critical authority and scrutinized for interpretation. That attitude has been bound up with responses
to Shepard's work from the beginning: Edward Albee, with a degree of
skepticism, noted of *Icarus's Mother* in 1965 that "if we have to ask ourselves what it is [about], then it becomes nothing."[31] Jack Gelber again
provided a more evangelical take on the same idea by insisting, in his 1976

article, that the metaphysical qualities of Shepard's work can only be appreciated fully by those willing to surrender themselves to its effects: "One must not ask him to answer questions he hasn't asked."[32] The objections to this attitude are obvious: just because these plays refuse to submit themselves to unidirectional interpretation, is one therefore required to leave one's brain at the door in order to appreciate them? Does this mean that those who do not experience ecstatic release in the plays' presence have somehow spoiled it for themselves by thinking too much?

Interestingly, if Shepard himself ever shared such attitudes, he shed them quite quickly. As is evident from a short article written during his time in England in the early 1970s, in which he reflects on his experience of two very different English audiences, his own attitude to the audience reception of his work is considerably more sophisticated and open-minded than Gelber's. After attending a concert given by the rock group The Who, he describes both his love of the music and his vague sense of discomfort that "everyone looks ecstatic and hypnotized as though the same emotion has put everyone out to lunch." Conversely, he speaks of his worry that *The Tooth of Crime* will not be received well at the Royal Court Theatre, with its tradition of earnest, socially concerned dramas, where audiences, he believes, are conditioned to expect "'significant overtones.' . . . Somehow it's got to be analyzed and put in the right perspective." Ideally, he notes, a viewer of his plays would react with neither mindless emotionalism nor reductive intellectualizing: "Somewhere between the Who concert and the Royal Court there must lie another possibility."[33]

It seems to me that Shepard's desire for something "in between" these poles suggests a genuinely progressive position on his part, indicating the need for an *active* engagement with plays which cannot be neatly understood, but should not just be unthinkingly absorbed. The relationship of audience and stage, in other words, is itself a dialogic and nonhierarchical one: the spectator may not be able to interpret a clear statement from the play, but is nevertheless liberated to respond to it in his or her own way, questioning it, perhaps mentally arguing with it in a manner not dissimilar to that pursued by Shepard in the writing process itself. And while he stresses that people should feel free to come at his work "any way they can," it is certainly the case, in my own experience, that the audience members who seem to have drawn most from Shepard's work are those who have actively grappled with the contradictory thoughts and emotions the plays elicit in an attempt to discover their own understanding of their significance.

This is not, however, to suggest that the possible range of audience responses is left as wide open as it is in, say, the visually oriented abstraction of performance art. It seems to me that Shepard's work – alongside that of a few contemporaries such as Maria Irene Fornes – occupies a richly fertile but still relatively unexplored no-man's-land in American theatre, between the normative standards of conventional drama and the almost entirely subjectivized territory of experimental performance. Shepard's use of fragmentary narratives, and his borrowing from familiar generic conventions, means that in most cases audiences are able – and sometimes actively encouraged – to form certain assumptions or expectations about where one of his plays might be going. Yet these are invariably subverted, or thwarted entirely, as the free-flowing style of the work leads off in fresh, unexpected directions. This, in turn, requires the spectator to reconsider his or her perspective, possibly only to have that new position problematized. The resulting sense of crisis, the lack of conclusive resolution, can be distinctly unsettling for audiences. But the necessity to find one's own way through what is happening can also be strangely liberating. Whatever the other problems or shortcomings of his playwriting, this ability to prod and cajole audiences into uncomfortable, exploratory spaces gives Shepard's work a peculiar vitality in a theatre culture where the expected is all too often championed as the correct.

1

Working Out

The Early Plays, 1964–1967

In OCTOBER 1964, a double bill of Sam Shepard's first two plays, *Cowboys* and *The Rock Garden*, opened at Theatre Genesis, a small Off-Off-Broadway venue based at St. Mark's-in-the-Bouwerie, a church in Manhattan's East Village. The string of short, one-act pieces which followed in the period up to March 1967 (when his first two-act play, *La Turista*, opened) make up a fairly distinct grouping within the overall development of Shepard's work. Although they represent his writing at its most embryonic and unrefined, they are worth examining in some detail because they form the foundation of all the work that followed, in their exploration of the potential of theatrical language and their use of simple but striking stage imagery. There is also a raw dynamism about these plays which demands attention: as the earliest and purest expression of Shepard's concern with mining subconscious impulses, they create an immediate impression of unresolved emotional tension, combining an exhilarating, free-form playfulness with an acute sense of underlying anxiety. This anxiety is particularly bound up with the questions of identity and self-definition which have continued to haunt his work ever since. The writing style and, indeed, the influences which feed it place these plays firmly in the modernist tradition, but one can also see in them some of the tensions which later precipitated significant shifts in Shepard's approach.

Beginnings

One of the ongoing contradictions in Shepard's writing is immediately evident in these earliest plays, suggesting as they do both a concern with

the authenticity of spontaneous self-expression, and an interest in the
potential of performative self-invention. The latter was particularly
clearly expressed in that first double bill of plays, perhaps because the
decision to begin writing plays in the first place was symptomatic of Shepard's need to create a new identity for himself. When he arrived in New
York in 1963, it was as a nineteen-year-old with little direction in life other
than the desire to get as far away as possible from his family home in California. Abandoning a prospective career in animal husbandry, he had
joined a small repertory company, the Bishop's Players, and traveled
across the country with them playing one-night stands in churches. Abandoning them, in turn, on reaching New York (acting appears to have been
more a means of escape than a serious career move), he found work as a
busboy at the Village Gate nightclub in Greenwich Village, and it was
from this accident of fate that his subsequent playwriting career sprang.
The Village Gate's head waiter, Ralph Cook, had recently been desig-
nated St. Mark's Church's "minister to the arts" by the pastor, Michael
Allen, in which capacity he had set up Theatre Genesis, with himself as
artistic director. Cook had dedicated this project "to the new playwright,"
but lacked any new playwrights to realize this goal. Shepard, who at that
stage was simply scribbling in notebooks in his spare time, offered his ser-
vices, and *The Rock Garden* and *Cowboys* were mounted as Genesis's
second production.

Shepard thus found himself clambering onto the back of the accelerating Off-Off-Broadway bandwagon. There was a growing number of
such small, ad hoc theatre venues in Lower Manhattan, which had taken
their cue from Joe Cino's Caffe Cino, Al Carmines' Judson Poets' Theatre
and Ellen Stewart's Cafe La Mama (founded in 1958, 1961, and 1962
respectively), and had set up in basements, lofts, coffeehouses, and
churches. An enthusiastic underground theatre movement was forming,
of which Genesis became an integral part, and for Shepard the resulting
sense of community came as a kind of salvation. St. Mark's, he says,
became "literally home" to him, and the many other artists who used the
premises (dancers, poets, painters), a surrogate family. He frequently
slept and ate there, adopting the place as a much-needed focus for his life
in New York. This sense of having a new home, a new identity, was also
signaled very openly by his change of name, from Samuel Shepard
Rogers the seventh (as a boy he had been known as Steve, to distinguish
him from his father, Sam the sixth) to Sam Shepard. This abandonment
of "Steve Rogers" (the alter ego of the star-spangled superhero Captain
America) in favor of a name which – as he well knew – he now shared

with alleged Ohioan wife-murderer Dr. Sam Sheppard was a typically demonstrative act of self-reinvention, which dissociated him from generations of family tradition.

Shepard's need to shake off the influence of his family was clearly enunciated in one of those first two plays. *The Rock Garden*, as he has bluntly acknowledged, "is about leaving my mom and dad."[1] Just as the play's central meaning is, for Shepard, uncharacteristically obvious, so its form is uncharacteristically restrained. Marked not by excitement but by deliberate tedium, *The Rock Garden* presents a nightmarish vision of life in a dull, repressive middle-American family, in the shape of three carefully demarcated scenes, first at the breakfast table, second between mother and son, and finally between father and son. This neat, schematic structure reflects the stifling conformity of the environment, in which the parents drone on to themselves and the children barely speak: the spilling of a glass of milk becomes a major disruptive event. Yet the muted tone is suddenly dispelled when, with a jarring shift of gears, the play concludes with the Boy delivering an uncompromisingly frank monologue celebrating his nascent sexuality: "When I come, it's like a river."[2] At the end of this speech, the Boy's father abruptly falls off his chair, but does not get up again. While the image remains unexplained, it is difficult not to see the Boy's sudden role-switch from quiet passivity to verbal excess as a gesture of open rebellion, and as a kind of performative act of patricide: his father collapses from shock at the graphic details of the speech. Certainly this reading is one which, in hindsight, neatly parallels Shepard's real-life divestment of his father's name.

Having liberated himself, for the time being at least, from his family, Shepard began to revel in his newfound freedom in New York. He and his roommate, Charles Mingus III (son of the famous jazz musician), whom he had also known at high school in California, became a recognizable double act around the city, by running around "playing cowboys." This involved, they claim, riding on the hoods of taxis, dodging buses, and introducing themselves to total strangers in adopted comic voices: they would play any character or attitude which came to mind, in a kind of ongoing improvisation game. Mingus has stressed that this manic child's-play had a very serious side to it, that it represented a common search for identity in the big city, a need to try out roles as if they were new clothes. It was this partnership which became the basis of *Cowboys*, the play which attracted most attention at the opening double bill, and which set the tone for the writing that followed. The piece seems to have been an almost verbatim transferral of Shepard and Mingus's playful antics to the

stage – so much so that Mingus's father reportedly threatened to disown
his son for not claiming joint authorship. Although unavailable in print,
the play was apparently very similar to its 1967 rewrite, *Cowboys #2*, and
was described in detail by Jerry Tallmer in his review for the *New York
Post*. Two young men pass the time near a highway, talking to each other
in

> various dialects from Country Western to Walter Brennan to Haughty
> British and Plain American. They wait for rain. It rains. They grovel in
> the mud . . . They are attacked by Comanches. . . . They describe lov-
> ing, imaginary breakfasts. They have a falling out over an imaginary
> lost canteen. They drive away from police sirens. . . . They practice
> baseball . . . [3]

As Tallmer's blunt tone implies, he was unimpressed with the piece, seeing it as a collection of fragments strung together without regard for conventional dramatic structure, plot, or characterization. Yet this freewheeling playfulness was precisely what attracted admiration from many
others. Most vocal among these was Michael Smith, whose enthusiastic
Village Voice review ("a pair of provocative and genuinely original plays")[4]
gained Shepard his first positive press exposure. As a result of this review,
sufficient interest was generated in the Off-Off-Broadway community
that Shepard found his work in demand. He embarked on writing a string
of one-act plays, which appeared at a variety of venues over the next couple of years, gaining him something of a cult following.

Shepard wholeheartedly embraced this new idea of being a writer,
seizing on it – as he later put it – as "a way to inhabit a life."[5] Role-playing games continued to be a key feature of his material, and yet if these
early plays were, in one sense, a form of ongoing self-invention, they were
also a means to self-discovery. He began to delve deep into a creative
imagination which had previously gone unexplored: "I can remember
being dazed with writing," he notes in his 1986 Introduction to *The
Unseen Hand and Other Plays*, "with the discovery of finding I actually
had these worlds inside me. These voices. Shapes. Currents of language.
Light. . . . I wrote all the time. Everywhere" (ix). Each of the pieces which
followed *Cowboys* pursues the same basic technique of taking an image
derived from Shepard's everyday relationships and experiences, and
using it as a trigger to release these spontaneous energies. *4-H Club*, for
example (1965), is again based on life with Mingus, this time inspired by
events in the kitchen of the all-male apartment they shared. Conversely,
Chicago (1965), *Red Cross* (1966), and *La Turista* (1967) – set respec-

tively in abstracted versions of a bathroom, a vacation cabin, and a Mexican hotel bedroom – all begin with depictions of male-female couples, based loosely on Shepard's relationship with his girlfriend of the time, the actress Joyce Aaron. *Icarus's Mother* (1965) clearly takes its inspiration from a Fourth of July picnic outing.

As director Jacques Levy notes, Shepard took these sketchy opening premises and "expanded and changed, off-slanted, exaggerated, whatever. He would just start with a group of characters with only a vague idea of where he was going."[6] Thus a play might start out with a representation of a recognizable environment, but if one of the characters dreams up a situation – rain, for example, in *Cowboys* – then this immediately becomes their "truth," sending the play spinning into offbeat fantasy. These pieces develop into loose but provocative conglomerations of image-filled speeches and erratic behavior – often in the form of games or physical exercises. Yet their mundane origins are evident in the simple names of their characters (Stu, Jim, Howard, Carol, Joe), which stand in marked contrast to the flashy "handles" of so many of Shepard's later characters. At this stage Shepard was simply "working out," using simple images drawn from everyday life as the starting point for stream-of-consciousness writing games. He seems, moreover, to have been somewhat embarrassed by some of the results of this playful experimentation: not all of these early plays now survive in print, largely because, once his work was finding publishers, he chose to hold some of it back. *Up to Thursday*, for example, produced by Edward Albee's Playwrights' Unit in 1965, and reportedly the best of a sizable stack of plays that Shepard had presented to Albee for consideration, can now only be found in manuscript form in Boston University's Shepard archive. Shepard also chose to consign the double bill *Rocking Chair* and *Dog* to oblivion, and another piece, *Three and Melons*, was given only a rehearsed reading before being hastily withdrawn. It is clear that, from an early stage in his career, Shepard matched an uninhibited writing approach, avoiding self-censorship in the creative process itself, with a canny awareness of the need to monitor both his output and his public profile.

Early Influences

Shepard has claimed that "the so-called originality of the early work just comes from ignorance. I just didn't know."[7] While there is no doubt a degree of truth in this assertion, in that he was clearly not attempting to follow any preconceived ideas of playwriting as a craft, the remark also seems somewhat disingenuous. His high school education had introduced him to some of the established landmarks of dramatic literature (he had, for example, read O'Neill's *Long Day's Journey Into Night*, and even confesses to having written a "very bad" Tennessee Williams-style melodrama, *The Mildew*, for the school magazine), and his subsequent decision to ignore conventional notions of linear plot development and consistent characterization was in all likelihood quite deliberate. Indeed, his apparently naive early style was in large part a response (albeit idiosyncratic) to certain avant-garde influences prevalent at the time. *Cowboys*, for example, like many other recent American theatrical experiments (Jack Gelber's *The Connection* and Edward Albee's *The Zoo Story*, to name but two of the most noteworthy), clearly owed a great deal to Samuel Beckett. Shepard has admitted to having been greatly struck by reading *Waiting for Godot* while still a teenager in California, and this connection was immediately apparent to Jerry Tallmer: as he disparagingly implied in his review (and *Cowboys #2* corroborates this), the time-filling antics and word games of Shepard's young men were highly reminiscent of those of Beckett's Vladimir and Estragon. Various critics have also pointed to marked similarities between some of Shepard's early work and other plays loosely grouped under the "absurdist" label, such as those of Albee and Harold Pinter.

Another important influence on these pieces was the emerging Off-Off-Broadway theatre scene itself, an experimental environment which legitimized the abandonment of conventional, set-based realism in favor of formal innovation and minimalistic staging. This approach, it should be noted, was a response not only to recent European experiments but also to practical necessity. Constrained by tiny operating budgets (most shows had no admission charge and were financed simply by passing a hat around the audience), and largely staffed by untrained actors and directors, these new (non)theatres could not and did not wish to adhere to the kind of elaborate staging practices which still dominated commercial theatre. Minimalism was as much an economic necessity as an aesthetic principle (the story of Shepard and Mingus carrying their own bathtub to Theatre Genesis to use on the set of *Chicago* was characteristic of the period), and the use of rapid, cinematic cuts between scenes, wildly energetic language, and an emphasis on the physicality of the actors were all vital to compensate for technical limitations. Off-Off dramatists were actively encouraged to develop dynamic, individual styles which would make virtue of necessity: anything went, so long as it seemed new, exciting, and

cheap to put on. Read alongside some of the other plays of this period –
such as Maria Irene Fornes's *Promenade* (1965), the scenes of which were
built around locations randomly picked from sets of shuffled cards, or Paul
Foster's *Balls* (1964), in which two Ping-Pong balls swing back and forth
to the sound of taped voices – Shepard's early work appears somewhat less
gnomic and extraordinary than it might seem at a first glance.

Nevertheless, his was also a distinctive voice even in this whirlpool of
creative activity. The *New York Times* noted as early as December 1965
that, at just twenty-two, he had become "the generally acknowledged
'genius' of the OOB circuit."[8] One difference was Shepard's unique facil-
ity with language; another was his ability to absorb in a more playful, intuitive fashion than most the lessons of the experimental milieu he was
moving in. Some of his Off-Off colleagues were rather too self-conscious
or derivative in taking their inspiration from a grab bag of avant-garde
theatrical sources: Foster's *Balls*, for instance, was accused by *Voice* critic
Arthur Sainer of virtually plagiarizing both the style and spirit of Beckett's
Embers and *Play*. By contrast, Shepard was not attempting to mimic
Beckett so much as respond to the possibilities he had opened up. By his
own account, his initial, teenage reading of *Godot* had left him with a
sense of simple delight at its innovative use of free-flowing rhythm ("I
thought, 'This is amazing. I don't understand it at all, but the words and
language amaze me'")[9]: it interested him chiefly because of the license it
seemed to grant writers to find their own way, regardless of conventional
strictures. In this respect, the influence of Vladimir and Estragon on
Cowboys was probably not significantly different from that of Laurel and
Hardy, the personal heroes of Shepard and Mingus, and the model for
their double act. The fact that Shepard could so seamlessly marry the
twin influences of absurdism and Hollywood shows that, even at this early
stage, he was drawing on whatever sources attracted him, regardless of
their status as "high" or "popular" art.

This playful eclecticism eventually led Shepard towards a distinctly
postmodernist use of style-quotation and pastiche, but in these plays he
adheres to the modernist convention of absorbing borrowed fragments of
language or imagery within the distinct, personal style of the individual
artist. Shepard's early writing suggests sources as diverse as movie westerns (the cowboys-and-Indians role-play) and high school science lessons
or gym classes (they are littered with both mock-technical disquisitions
and physical exercises – "Move it! Keep it going! Work it out!"). Yet in
each case the quotation is seen to be in some way part of the characters'

Nicole Moretti and Steve Bottoms in *Red Cross*, performed by Flexible Deadlock at UEA, Norwich, 1991. (Photo: Andy Wisher)

game-playing, which remains the consistent thread throughout these pieces.

Shepard's eclecticism is also evident in the way he drew inspiration from a range of nontheatrical artistic innovations. "Everything influenced me," he has said, stressing that one reason he turned to playwriting in the first place was that theatre struck him as "a form where you could amalgamate all the arts."[10] That idea was again key to what was happening in Greenwich Village: at Judson Church, in particular, one could see the rich potential for combining poetry, music, dance, painting, and film in unusual ways, and Shepard actively participated in some of their workshops to devise cross-disciplinary "Happenings." His playwriting, though, was generally more in tune with Theatre Genesis's orientation toward translating into dramatic form the raw, subjective expressionism of action painters like Jackson Pollock and Willem de Kooning, and of beat writers like Allen Ginsberg and Jack Kerouac (it is no coincidence that *Chicago* opened at Genesis in a double bill with *The Customs Collector in Baggy Pants*, a monologue by beat poet Lawrence Ferlinghetti).[11] In particular, Shepard idolized Pollock, a man whose background was remarkably similar to his own. While – again – there was probably an element of Shepard's need to invent a role for himself involved in this (the tough, virile cowboy-artist persona that Pollock had adopted seems to have been something Shepard sought to emulate),[12] his interest in the artist went far beyond a concern with his public persona. This much is clear from his notes for an unfinished play, *Jackson's Dance* (1972), which indicate a fascination with the intuitive, impulsive, and visually dynamic quality of Pollock's work: the play was to "dive into the dreams behind his painting," and to depict the artist as "a mythic figure, played on by forces beyond his control and understanding."[13] Such romantic imagery is highly revealing in terms of Shepard's personal preoccupations: Beckett may have helped break barriers, but he was an Irishman with a distinctly European worldview, whereas Pollock, Kerouac, and company were Americans whose energy and passion was seen as having opened up new frontiers. In a sense they and their imitators were inheritors and revivers of the American transcendentalist tradition of Emerson, Thoreau, and particularly Whitman, whose slogan "Unscrew the locks from their doors! Unscrew the doors themselves from their jambs!" was taken by Allen Ginsberg as the epigraph for *Howl and Other Poems* (1956), and so set the tone for a generation.

This new wave of young American artists, which had originated in San Francisco and had reached New York by the late '50s, was in revolt against a dominant conservatism in the arts, which was seen as valuing a sterile formalism over raw creativity. When in 1946, after years of battling with his materials, Jackson Pollock had finally abandoned brushwork altogether in favor of dripping and splashing his paint straight onto the canvas, he was seen – in Willem de Kooning's famous phrase – as having "broken the ice." The idea of creating a seamless flow between artist and artwork, of somehow expressing one's very essence in the act of creation, became crucial to the new generation: the abandonment of conscious attempts to structure art was seen as a kind of guarantee of the primal authenticity of the work. Jack Kerouac, for example, believed that the first draft of a piece of writing was invariably the truest, and regretted his own attempts at even the most cosmetic rewrites. Shepard was clearly heavily influenced by this holy art attitude, and even as a virtual unknown was remarkably belligerent in defending his work against directors who sought to modify it. If those early plays did spring from "ignorance," he seems to have been uninterested in being educated. He claims that not a word of any of his plays was rewritten until *La Turista* in 1967 (his tenth), and even then he did it his own way, rewriting the entire second act from scratch.

It is easy to see why this do-it-yourself ethos of pure self-expression appealed to so many young people at this time, as they sought to find a value in themselves and in their abilities. It should be stressed, however,

that Shepard and his contemporaries were not seeking merely to vomit
the contents of their unconscious minds onto an unsuspecting public.
The aim, rather, was to achieve a new kind of consciousness, by concentrating on the primacy of existing in the present moment, of "is-ness."
Influenced by an often indistinguishable mix of existentialist philosophy
and Zen Buddhism, the new generation sought to break past the formal-
izing and censoring tendencies of the conscious mind, using elements of
chance and flux as a means to celebrate the random reality of each
moment, even in its passing. Immediacy was everything, and anything
which brought greater awareness of the fact of living – from John Cage's
entirely silent piano composition, 4'33" (which obliged the audience to
listen to the air, to their own breathing), to Barnett Newman's massive
canvases of pure color (in which the viewer's sensory experience
becomes, in effect, the subject of the painting) – was regarded as legitimate and authentic. In a sense, Shepard's real innovation in theatre was
in seeking to transfer this idea to the process of playwriting. Looking back
in 1977, he noted that "the single most important idea" of the 1960s was,
for him, "the idea of consciousness":

> How does this idea become applicable to the theatre? For some time
> now it's become generally accepted that the other art forms are dealing
> with this idea to one degree or another. That the subject of painting is
> seeing. That the subject of music is hearing. That the subject of sculp-
> ture is space. But what is the subject of theatre which includes all of
> these and more?[14]

Ultimately, as Shepard has acknowledged, there is no simple answer to
this question. At the time, however, he seems to have sought to answer it
by emphasising the freedom which theatre gave him to cut loose with his
imagination, to indulge in games, leaps of fancy, to create images and toy
with the sounds of words purely for their own sake. The subject of a play,
in other words, was playing: "the reason I began writing plays," Shepard
has written, "was in the hope of extending the sensation of play (as in 'kid')
on into adult life."[15] Here again, Shepard was very much in tune with the
temper of a time in which Susan Sontag was calling for a new, erotic attitude toward art, and psychologist Norman O. Brown's paean to the indulgence of the pleasure principle in *Life Against Death* (1959) was attracting widespread interest. Shepard seems to have drawn particular
inspiration from attending Joseph Chaikin's workshops for the Open Theatre (founded in 1963), in which actors were determinedly attempting to
break down the overrationalized conventions of their craft and simply

play. In the so-called transformation exercise, for instance, actors would spontaneously react to each other and to their own subliminal impulses to change the dynamic of the improvisation at will: "Transformation frees the actor to be the child . . . now I'm the grass, now I'm the king of the mountain, now I'm the cloud."[16] The idea of transformation – of freely and fluidly shifting a character from one state of mind or body to another – became central to Shepard's playwriting.

Jazz Writing

Of all the inspirations Shepard drew on, however, the most important and intensely personal was his love of music. Many artists of this period, including those that Shepard idolized, like Pollock and Kerouac, saw the quest for playful, Dionysian freedom as being epitomized in the playing of improvisatory jazz music. The act of pouring one's spirit into the trumpet or saxophone until the breath runs dry was seen as *the* truly authentic art of the moment. But Shepard did not need to have this explained to him by others. As a child, his father had brought him up to appreciate jazz music, and had taught him the basics of jazz drumming (somewhat ruthlessly, if the exchange on the subject between Pop and Ice in Shepard's 1969 play *The Holy Ghostly* is to be seen as autobiographical). Shepard became an accomplished drummer, but he was less interested in the traditional jazz his father played than in the bebop style which came to prominence as he was growing up in the 1940s and '50s. Bop drummers such as Kenny Clarke had revolutionized the form by abandoning pure time-keeping in favor of a more unpredictable approach, using cymbals to mark the rapid tempo, and giving the drums themselves free rein to interrupt the music with sporadic rhythmic patterns both on and off the main beat. Shepard thus grew up listening to, and playing, music which was constantly challenging the boundaries of its own form, reinventing itself through improvisation.

By the late 1950s and early '60s a further development was taking place in New York, as free jazz demolished the few structural limits that bop had left in place, in its pursuit of unrestricted musical self-expression. One of the key innovators in this direction, with Ornette Coleman, was Charles Mingus, who was renowned for building into his compositions sections in which his entire band would improvise simultaneously. Shepard's friendship with Mingus's son secured him frequent free access to the band's concerts at clubs such as the Five Spot, and the pair were even roommates for a time with the band's drummer, Dannie Richmond, a personal hero of theirs. The influence of all this on Shepard's writing cannot be overstated. Mingus's band – which blended elements as diverse as Dixieland jazz, Mexican carnival music, black gospel, and even the European classical tradition – spoke directly to both his drummer's instinct and his eclectic streak, and its lessons were permanent:

> [I] was stunned by his sense of polyrhythm – rhythm on top of rhythm on top of rhythm. I was fascinated by the idea of merging that with writing, seeing if there was a way of evoking the same kind of collage in the writing of plays.
>
> I started thinking about the kind of structure jazz has, the kind of life it implies, and I decided to see if I could be a playwright myself with what I'd learned from them.[17]

Shepard's talk of transferring rhythmic patterns to his writing was no mere rhetoric. Ellen Stewart, for example, has reminisced about him jamming on drums all night in La Mama's basement, to get himself into the mood to hit the typewriter at dawn. The immediacy of the connection between Shepard's music and his writing has been stressed by no less a light than legendary jazz composer Max Roach (for years the drummer in Charlie Parker's band), who in 1984 was drafted in to score music for a retrospective Shepard season at La Mama. "I had no idea of the profundity of the man," Roach told the New York *Daily News*: "He thinks like a drummer."[18]

Shepard's sense of rhythm is immediately evident in the patterns of the dialogue in these early plays: indeed, he frequently allows his fascination with the rhythmic potential of words to take precedence over all other considerations. This is apparent, for example, in the plays' sudden changes of pace, which mirror Mingus's tendency to shift tempo with bewildering rapidity. The language may have a slow, contemplative rhythm to it, as, for example, in many of the longer speeches, and then, without warning, suddenly erupt into juddering, rapid-fire exchanges. The wild-boys-at-play sections of *Cowboys #2* and *4-H Club*, and the frantic swimming sequence in *Red Cross*, are particularly good examples of the fast approach. Like verbal drum patterns, one character provides a phrase, which is then responded to with a taut, often monosyllabic response:

CHET: Some of 'em's Comanches, Clem!
STU: Fire!
CHET: Good boy, ya' got 'im!

STU: Fire!
CHET: Got 'im again. One shot apiece, Clem.
STU: Get 'em, Mel.
CHET: Fire! Got me a brave! Got me a brave!
STU: Good boy!   (148)

The effect in such exchanges is very much like the accents which Shepard's various percussion instruments provided to Joseph Chaikin's monologue years later on their collaborative piece, *Tongues* (1978). And the percussionist's dexterity with patterns of sound is also evident in Shepard's indulgence of rhyme in these plays. At the end of the exchange cited above, for example, when Stu imagines himself shot (CHET: "Bloody blood."), the response (STU: "Mud.") is one which recalls an earlier incident in the play, and is prompted not by any rational linkage but simply by the coincidence of sound. Similarly, in *Chicago*, Stu's singsong opening speech, as he splashes in the bathtub, uses rhythm and rhyme to demonstrate clearly the idea of play both "as in kid" and as in music: "Biscuits in the sun. And ya' run. And it's fun. Ya' have a gun. It's yer own. Ya' don't care. You can even shoot a bear. If ya' have any hair. If ya' don't. Ya' don't. If ya' do. It's true. And yer through anywho" (47).

In terms of content, this nonsense poem is entirely self-reflexive, pointing to nothing beyond its own verbal texture. Shepard's writing is at its most effective, however, when the rhythms and textures of his language contribute directly to the buildup of an emotion which is also expressed in the meaning of the words themselves. This method is seen most clearly in the long, self-contained monologues which litter these early plays. A good example is Carol's speech in *Red Cross*: her account of skiing downhill gathers momentum as she goes. Initially the description seems leisurely, full of incidental detail, but gradually the speed builds up:

> Then I'll start to feel a throb in the bridge of my nose. Then a thump in the base of my neck. Then a crash right through my skull. Then I'll be down. Rolling! Yelling! All those people will see it. I'll be rolling with my skis locked and my knees buckled under me and my arms thrashing through the snow. (125)

The impression of rapid motion is created here by the recurring pattern of pounding, monosyllabic words (throb, thump, crash), which set up an urgent rhythmic pattern, leading into the climactic moment of Carol's fall. Once she is down, the speed increases further with the loss of control: Shepard uses a single long sentence with a rapidly repeating pattern of personal pronouns, and sudden angular, violent sounds (locked, buckled, thrashing). From here the speech resolves into a fast, rhythmic sequence of observations leading up to the moment when Carol imagines her head blowing up. At the end of the speech, motion finally ceases as the tumbling stops, and the words too lose their urgency. Instead, Shepard sets up a cooler, more whimsical mood by using a lot of additional adjectives to pad out his phrases, and softer sounds (note the recurring sibilant "s"):

> It'll start to snow a little bit. A very soft easy snow. The squirrels might come down to see what happened. It'll keep snowing very lightly like that for a long time until my whole body is covered over. All you'll see is this little red splotch of blood and a whole blanket of white snow.
>
> (125)

Shepard's monologues have often been compared to operatic arias, and it is easy to see why, although the solo jazz break provides a better analogy: each speech contains its own internal dynamic of shifting tempos, crescendos, and diminuendos. "You could throw yourself into the passage, and then you could calm down, then you could ride this thing, then you could throw yourself in again," Shepard recalled of the joy involved in this approach: "You could move into all these emotional territories, and you could do it with passion."[19] The "aria" has remained a facet of Shepard's work throughout his career, yet nowhere is the technique so persistently and uncompromisingly used as in these early plays, where they form the most distinctive stylistic feature.

The driving force behind the imagistic content of the speeches is a kind of random visual thought-association, with Shepard relying upon each new image to spark yet another in response, or doubling back to reconnect with previously established images ("Mud"). Moreover, close examination shows that this technique, which itself suggests a kind of intuitive, jazz-collage approach, is also utilized as the principle for the plays' overall construction. This fact is most obviously visible in *Chicago*, since the entire piece is effectively one long monologue by Stu, an extended solo with only minor interjections by other characters. Sitting half dressed in a bathtub, Stu allows his imagination free rein, converting Joy's notion of his bath being a boat into a bizarre description of a nocturnal fishing trip. This he then links up with the fact that Joy is going away, so as to create a lengthy account of her traveling by train to take a fishing holiday. On "arriving" at the sea, Stu extends his vision into ever more surreal territory, building toward a climax as he imagines the fishing boats being deserted by sailors who are "screwing young virgins" up and down the beach.

This stringing together of image after image provides Shepard's means of continuing the a-logical narrative of these plays, and frees him from considerations of plot. Each play is marked by a fairly distinct collection of recurrent visual motifs which are played upon in much the same way that Mingus would latch onto and work around certain moods or environments in his music, as with the multiple Mexican flavors which make up *Tijuana Moods* (1957). These linking motifs are often signaled by the title. *Red Cross*, for example, revolves around ideas of health and sickness. Carol has a headache which she imagines developing into a full-blown hemorrhage; her boyfriend, Jim, suffers from an infestation of crab lice, but throws himself around the room in a succession of keep-fit exercises to try to take his mind off it. The dialogue is littered with double-edged references to "catching" things, breathing deeply, and so on. Similarly, the title and some of the central speeches of *4-H Club* evoke images of neat, traditional small-town Americana, but the play starkly juxtaposes these against a dominant tone of sweaty, anarchic, urban chaos. *Icarus's Mother* recalls the Greek myth of the winged youth crashing in flames, through its recurrent references to fire and to flight: lit throughout with flaming yellow, the play opens with a barbecue and smoke signals, and goes on to "jam" around the images of the firework display that the characters are ostensibly waiting for, and an airplane they see overhead.

In more conventional drama, a spectator's attention is held by the story or situation which the play establishes, and which sets up certain possibilities for an eventual plot denouement: the audience is drawn in and wants to see what will result. But Shepard's early plays offer their audiences no such footholds, existing – like improvised music – from moment to moment. The viewer has no way of postulating any possible future outcome, and the plays retain attention only through the surprise value of the ways in which imagery and language are varied and developed. As with jazz improvisation, unpredictability is vital: Shepard needs to be able constantly to surprise his audience with new variations on his themes. Also as with jazz, the plays seek to reintegrate previously introduced motifs, providing audiences with the thrill, or relief, of recognition when this occurs. The best of these plays are distinguished by the ingenious ways in which their conclusions achieve a drawing together of their key motifs. *Red Cross*, for instance, ends with a neat and alarming reversal of the characters' ailments, as Carol catches Jim's crabs and Jim falls victim to a hole in the head (a gruesome exteriorization of Carol's headache). *Icarus's Mother* draws together its two key threads of fire and flight in Frank's climactic speech: he describes the crash of the skywriting airplane, and the spectacular display of pyrotechnics which results.

This tendency in the early plays to try to assemble diverse, fragmentary impulses into a collage of recurrent motifs, to rescue a structure of sorts from the jaws of incoherence, is one of the features that places them most firmly in the modernist tradition. Indeed, though Shepard would have been unaware of it at the time, his approach bore marked resemblances to that which August Strindberg had employed in *A Dream Play* (1901):

> Everything can happen, everything is possible and probable . . . a mixture of memories, experiences, free fancies, incongruities and improvisations. The characters split, double, multiply, evaporate, condense, disperse, assemble. But one consciousness rules them all; that of the dreamer. [20]

Yet if the goal for Shepard, as for Strindberg, was to depict something of the depth and complexity of the author's consciousness – thereby suggesting an expression of authentic inner self, a center around which the fragments of experience can be assembled – these early pieces also display a contradictory propensity toward a *decenteredness* which to some extent anticipates his later, more overtly fragmented, more postmodernist work. The irony is that this tendency, too, stems from his spontaneous writing approach, which leads toward utter randomness as often as it does toward the reintegration of motifs. A brief comparison with another young New York playwright of this period, who was also building plays on the basis of musical collage techniques, underlines this point. Adrienne Kennedy's *Funnyhouse of a Negro* (1964) and *The Owl Answers* (1965) are both constructed from densely layered, multiple repetitions of phrases and images, which coalesce to form haunting, expressionistic visions of personal alienation. Yet these pieces read like carefully arranged symphonies in comparison with Shepard's loose, improvisatory jazz. And the very looseness of Shepard's plays means that, in comparison with the solidity of Kennedy's work, the collage effect is a very fragile one, which often seems in danger of collapsing under the weight of all the incidental tangents the writing veers off on. Indeed, at times the sense of random input in Shepard's early material pushes it close to the condition of "aleatory art" – the term being applied at the time to some of the experi-

ments of composer John Cage and others, whose use of chance proce-
dures (like Cage's rolling of dice to select notes) often stripped their work
of even the most tenuous sense of internal structure. While Shepard's
plays, at this stage, at least maintained a certain consistency in their linguistic style, even this was soon to begin breaking down, with his writing
increasingly problematizing the very notion that the author's controlling
vision is able intuitively to arrange the fragmentary products of its subconscious.

A related point is that these plays also render the idea of celebrating
the "is-ness" of the moment highly problematic. For Shepard's pursuit of
his speed-writing technique, though seemingly intended to capture the
immediacy of present consciousness, actually results in an inescapable
sense of *slippage*. Automatic writing, after all, is a process of chasing a
train of thought which is constantly receding in front of you, and in these
plays that effect is evident in the way that the significance of each
moment of the dialogue is perpetually being displaced onto the next.
Since every phrase or image in these plays relies upon its relationship to
all the others – either in terms of its similarity to them (recurring motif),
or difference from them (surprise value) – no one moment is actually
self-contained or intrinsically self-present. The fact that Shepard could
only bring these pieces to an end by imposing arbitrary climaxes – which
either refer back to previously established imagery, or simply come to an
abrupt stop – provides further illustration of this point. His own discomfort with endings results partly from an awareness that the "essence" of
what he was seeking to express has always remained elusive. The fundamental ungraspability of the present was something which Shepard
began to face and exploit more directly in subsequent work.

Fear

The structural instability of the early plays is mirrored by an underlying
sense of emotional disturbance. There is a desolation lurking beneath the
exuberance, as epitomized by the bathtub in *Chicago*, which sits
marooned in the middle of an otherwise bare stage, or by the hollow artifice of the pale blue scrim which stands as an almost sarcastic representation of sky in *Icarus's Mother*. These boldly simple visual statements
function in counterpoint to the character's playful antics, which – in such
chillingly detached settings – smack of a willful effort to paste over the
gaping void. Again, there is obviously a certain debt here to Beckett and
his use of simple, carefully distilled stage images of existential desperation, yet it is important to stress that, at this stage, Shepard's take on such

dislocation owed less to the kind of philosophical nihilism usually associated with absurdism, than to the immediate emotional pressures of his
own situation. His escape from his unstable family background, after all,
had not led him into an appreciably more reassuring environment: for all
the excitement of life in New York in the early '60s, it was still a huge and
frightening city. This period, moreover, was dominated by a series of
national crises, subsequent to the Cuban missile crisis and assassination
of Kennedy in 1963, which created a mounting and paranoid fear of
imminent apocalypse among many Americans. Shepard's early plays powerfully suggest something of that mood, but avoid any reference to temporal and cultural specifics. Set in hermetically sealed worlds of individual, psychic terror, these are – in effect – stage nightmares which
foreground the *threat* to the individual self of a world which makes no
sense.

   This enclosed, solipsistic writing style, foregrounding the expression of
intense emotional states, is again typical of the American modernist tradition within which Shepard was locating himself, a curiously narcissistic
tradition in which any source of personal anxiety – from the collapse of
relationships to the specter of nuclear war – tends to be viewed from the
same perspective of individual survival. Barnett Newman, for example,
famously stated that Hiroshima had been a crucial influence on his
abstract painting, because it concretized his own underlying fear of death.
A similar tendency is visible in Shepard's work: in *Icarus's Mother*, for
example, the nuclear threat, which is clearly implied in the pilot's
reported skywriting of the letters "$E = MC^2$," becomes simply another
dimension of the dominant fire imagery, and is finally crystalized in very
personal terms, in Frank's apocalyptic account of the death-by-incinera-
tion of that single pilot. Likewise, in *Red Cross*, Carol's speech about her
head blowing up while skiing points not to this event's danger to others
(the head becomes a huge snowball and "kills a million people," but this
is incidental), but to the fear of the reduction of the self to insignificance:
"All you'll see is this little red splotch of blood and a whole blanket of
white snow" (125). The final image of Jim's bleeding forehead in the all-
white set confirms this as the play's central motif, actualizing the verbal
fear as a stage picture. According to Carol, to Frank in *Icarus*, and to Chet
in *Cowboys* #2, personal obliteration via accident or disease hangs perpetually in the air like a Damoclean sword: "one day it just pops up, and
there you are . . . you fall over" (Chet, 144).

   A glance at any of the plays of this period underlines the fact that Shepard's exploitation of this kind of paranoia frequently provided him with

much of the fuel for his practice of imagistic snowballing. Indeed, he often began writing by simply picking on some minor anxiety, and then pursuing and expanding it, to the point of paralyzing terror. *Icarus's Mother*, for example, originated with Shepard's fear of flying, as he explained to director Nancy Meckler when she was preparing her London production of the play in 1971:

> He gave me an example, from the few times he'd tried to fly. You're sitting on a plane, and you suddenly get this flash of all these bloody bodies lying on a hillside. You get this flash, and then you stop it. But if you didn't, if you actually allowed yourself to look at it, and started to describe what you saw, you'd get so frightened that you'd start seeing the most ghastly things.[21]

In the play, Howard describes this fear of flying most graphically in his monologue about looking out of an airplane cockpit and becoming aware of the horrifying extent of the empty space on all sides: "You can't look up now or around or from side to side or down. You're straight in front straining not to see with peripheral vision" (70). More broadly, though, the play's predominant imagery of fire and flight, coming together in the pilot's crash at the end, can be seen to stem from this same basic fear. Comparable instances of this fear-expansion technique are apparent everywhere in these plays. In *4-H Club*, for instance, John's paranoia about the apartment's becoming infested with rats eventually mutates into an image of being eaten by savage, man-eating mandrills. In each case, niggling fear escalates into apocalyptic horror.

It is worth noting that the extreme emotional intensity of these pieces may well have been partly a result of Shepard's frequent use at this time of amphetamines: the term "speed-writing" perhaps carries a double meaning. He had been taking the drug in various forms, like benzedrine, since adolescence, and by the mid-'60s, he recalls ruefully, "crystal meth was a three-square diet with 'yellow jackets' and 'black beauties' for chasers."[22] His pronouncements on whether or not he used drugs while writing have been somewhat self-contradictory, but certainly it was common practice at this time for musicians and artists to stimulate their work via amphetamine use. Moreover, Shepard's creation of those characteristic, aria-like screeds of language would seem to be entirely consistent with speed's distinctive effect – that of intensifying mental activity, and radically amplifying the underlying mood of the user, be it excitement, joy, fear, or depression.

Whatever the factors involved in the writing process, the plays' success onstage depends largely on exploiting to the full their bizarre combination of playful energy and paranoia. Indeed, it seems that Shepard's vociferous arguments with directors during this early period stemmed at least partly from their failure to grasp this basic dynamic. Yet his attempts to enforce prescriptive ideas onto productions so that they coincided with his original vision succeeded only in creating more difficulties, since he remained oblivious to the very real practical problems which these plays pose for actors and directors. The sheer length of some of the monologues, for example, makes them – as Shepard has subsequently admitted – "a bitch to produce." The actors speaking them have to vocalize at length without any clear motivation for corresponding physical action, while the nonspeakers are marooned onstage waiting for their next line. Such problems are compounded by the fact that actors are provided with precious few clues by which to understand their parts psychologically, and thereby extrapolate appropriate action. The plays invest their characters with neither background history nor consistent, rationally comprehensible behavior, since Shepard, in projecting his own fluctuating consciousness directly into the plays, was not creating individual characters so much as vehicles for the expression of an immediate sense of emotional crisis.

An interesting illustration of the practical difficulties posed by these plays is provided by comparing two very different productions of *Icarus's Mother*. Michael Smith, in directing the 1965 premiere at Caffe Cino, sought to overcome the lack of apparent rationale in the play by imposing a Method-style psychological interpretation on the characters' behavior, which might give the actors something to fall back on when not speaking. But Smith's endeavors – by his own rueful account – worked against the fluidity of the text and resulted in an awkwardly restrained, stilted performance, as the actors continued to hunt in vain for their "motivation." Unsurprisingly, Shepard too was unhappy with the production, and it was not until Nancy Meckler directed *Icarus* in London in 1971 that he saw the play presented in a manner he felt was successful. The key to Meckler's approach (which also received considerable praise from critics) was that she sought not to rationalize the individual characters' behavior, but to create an underlying emotional atmosphere for the play as a whole. Rightly seeing Shepard's work as a form of subjective expressionism, she sought simply to foreground the sense of primal fear which, she felt, was the real subject of the play. This enabled her to solve even the problem of what to do with the silent actors during the long monologues, as she encouraged them to find some very simple physical obsession – such as the compulsive biting of nails – with which to occupy themselves when not speaking. In so doing, they acted to enhance further the fearful mood of the whole. The actors in the production, Shepard noted admiringly, succeeded by "playing *outside* the characters," treating their parts not as rounded, fictional persons to be internalized, but as externalizations of raw emotion.[23]

My own experience working on *Red Cross* in Norwich, England, in 1991, provided independent corroboration of Meckler's insights. Yet where she had apparently placed her emphasis on the spiraling fears conveyed in *Icarus*'s major monologues, *Red Cross*'s visceral sense of an immediate threat to the self seemed to us to manifest itself even more powerfully in the direct character confrontations – probably because the play is written as a triptych of one-on-one duologues. In particular, it became clear that the language battle between Jim and the Maid is no mere game, even if no simple, rational motivation is apparent. There is a vivid sense that the other character, a stranger, represents a potential threat, and Jim especially seems driven by a frantic need to establish his control over the stage space in order to assert himself and feel safe. Like many other characters in these plays, he appears to be literally performing for his life, prowling about the stage with violent, jerking physical exercises, and seeking verbally to bludgeon the innocuous-looking Maid into the position of receptive audience. Yet she resists this onslaught, initially by attempting simply to get on with her job of changing the beds, and ultimately by turning the tables on him with an astonishing verbal performance of her own which reduces him to helplessness. In confrontations of this sort, Shepard establishes a concern which becomes dominant in much of his subsequent work: language contains the potential not only for pleasurable play, but for use as a weapon, a tool of power or menace (it is in this respect that these plays most resemble those of Pinter or Albee).

Moreover, if Shepard feeds an implicit fear of the potentially threatening Other into the bizarre behavior of these characters, that fear also seems to be compounded by their inherent lack of "roundedness." Remaining as flexible tools for the author's paranoid wordplay, and lacking any kind of consistent identity, the characters' desperate performativity takes on the appearance, onstage, of a kind of urgent search for clear self-definition. There is another interesting parallel with the abstract expressionists here. Over the course of many years the key artists in that movement had been engaged in burying the subject figure ever deeper within the background of the painting, to the point where, in Pollock's drip paintings or Newman's color-fields, the two are indistinguishable. The boundaries between self and environment are blurred into nonexistence. Just so, by obliging each of the characters in these early plays to speak with much the same basic linguistic style, and placing them on permanently shifting ground, as their status and roles swap or double back on themselves, Shepard deprives them (whether by accident or design) of the very distinctiveness and control they simultaneously appear to crave. In his premiere production of *Red Cross*, Jacques Levy actualized this disintegrative element of the writing by dressing his actors in all-white costumes, thus merging them into the background of the all-white set. Delighted by this color-field effect, Shepard wrote it into the permanent text of the play.

Wildness and Civilization

Yet another dimension of the sense of identity crisis which these plays recurrently suggest is apparent in the struggle for independent *masculine* identity which seems inherent in Shepard's recurrent use of mischievous young male characters. These figures (Jim, Stu, Howard, Bill, and all the boys in *4-H Club* and *Cowboys #2*) may not be distinct, rounded characters, but they display a number of common traits suggestive of an impulse toward anarchic freedom – a disregard for morals and taboos, a preoccupation with the erotic and scatological, and a kind of solipsistic omnipotence (seen in their apparently godlike ability to transform the "reality" of their environment simply by reimagining it). Significantly, these traits are also the ones which epitomize the mischievous, childlike abandon of the trickster character-type which – according to Jungians – appears in similar forms in mythologies worldwide. This archetypal figure is said to represent the creative exuberance of male childhood, a fact which casts an entirely different kind of light on Shepard's stated concern for rediscovering a sense of play "as in kid." Indeed, his characters' obsessive fascination with basic physical functions is at times suggestive of a kind of "polymorphous perversity" – Freud's name for the way in which children derive erotic pleasure from every part of their anatomy. The boys in both *4-H Club* and *Cowboys #2*, for example, share lengthy exchanges about the erotic delights of eating, and indeed about alternative uses for food, from throwing it at people to wiping the floor with it. Similarly, *Icarus's Mother* begins with a chorus of belching, before following that up with numerous jokes on wind, indigestion, and urination. In *Red Cross*, by contrast, Jim's dialogue is loaded with sexual references, and he even goes as far as to extract a crab louse from his pubic hair and hand it to the Maid for inspection. Yet it is Stu, in *Chicago*, who takes this kind of wild sensuality to the most bizarre extremes, as he analyzes everything from the doughy texture of the biscuits Joy makes him, to the ravenous appetites of fish. His description of an overnight train journey to the sea becomes an odyssey through every kind of physical peculiarity, with people spitting, farting, vomiting, making love, and so forth. The stream-of-consciousness tale eventually climaxes with an orgy on the beach: "A mound of greasy bodies rolling in sperm and sand sticking to their backs" (56).

This approach does not simply represent a gratuitous disregard for conventional taboos. Just as the Boy in *The Rock Garden* had lingered on the subject of orgasm in an apparent attempt to assert his own sexuality and escape his father's influence, so these other young male characters seem to focus on the immediate reality of the body as a means of performative self-affirmation. The paradox, however, is that these trickster figures, however self-assured they might be in their madcap inventiveness, seem almost pathologically afraid of the unexplored territory lying beyond the scope of their world-creating imaginations. Take, for example, Stu's repeated refusal to step outside the safety of his bathtub into the empty space beyond it, or Jim's insistence on remaining in his vacation cabin/asylum all day, every day, never going out. The fact that their female companions seem happy to move about freely only exacerbates the tricksters' sense of paralysis: in *Icarus*, Howard and Bill find themselves frantically making up excuses for why they will not go "down the beach" (offstage) to get a closer view of the fireworks display: "the air is denser above sea level and the flak and shrapnel and – well, it's just safer up here" (73). This avoidance of the unknown is illustrated most vividly in *4-H Club*, which was first presented at the Cherry Lane Theatre by Albee's Playwrights' Unit, and so takes advantage of using a larger stage area than was available in most of the ad hoc Off-Off spaces. The text specifies that the tiny kitchen set be placed in the "extreme upstage left" area of an otherwise deserted stage space. The whole stage is to be lit with equal brightness, and the audience is thereby constantly aware of an unexplored expanse beyond the flimsy walls that the characters inhabit. The action of the play is crammed into a corner, and though the men come and go through a door at the back of their set, they never venture out into the space beyond it. They remain turned in on each other and away from the wild world and its savage, man-eating mandrills.

This fear of the outside world is entirely consistent with the Jungian analysis of tricksterism, which represents not only the playfulness but also the self-absorption of childhood. (Such figures are attractive because "something in us wishes to remain a child, to be unconscious, or, at most, conscious only of the ego; to reject everything strange.")[24] This kind of "primary narcissism," moreover, goes hand in hand with a continuing dependence on the protection afforded by the symbology of the mother and her womb, and here again Shepard's characters follow suit. *The Rock Garden* establishes this pattern from the first, presenting not only the Boy's apparent escape from subjection to his parents, but also a conflicting sense of the comforting security of Mom's smothering presence. The Boy's initial position of passive submission to the Woman, demonstrated by his being dressed only in underwear and lulled in a rocking chair, is subsequently recalled by similar images of somnolence and nakedness which recur throughout the other early plays. The unpublished *Rocking Chair* and *Up to Thursday*, for example, respectively reprised the images of the rocking chair and a sleepy young man dressed only in his underwear. In *Red Cross*, Jim is dressed only in his underwear throughout his confrontation with the "old and fat" Maid (a stereotypical earth mother figure: "I make the beds and cook the meals"), while *Chicago* presents Stu – half naked – playing games and singing baby rhymes in his bath while remaining dependent on Joy for food, towels, and attention. She thus takes on an unmistakably motherly role despite her ostensible function as his partner. The bath itself, even given the absence of water in it, can be read as connoting the safety of the womb, which Stu stubbornly refuses to leave.

The maternal feminine also seems to function to protect the young male from himself. For while the tricksters fear the threatening outside world, they also create danger for themselves. Their manic behavior, however creatively liberating, is so unfocused and untethered that it frequently steers events toward precisely the kind of chaotic instability they seem to fear. The most violent of ideas are often expressed in frighteningly casual terms: "They spurt [blood] when you step on them," muses Joe in *4-H Club*, on the subject of "squishing" mice: "Especially the babies" (97). By implying that casual brutality is endemic in the male psyche (a theme which becomes central in his later work), Shepard also implies the need for control; a control which the plays' maternal females appear to exert over their charges. Stu is periodically chastised by Joy for his excesses, and when the Maid confronts Jim with the horror and guilt of his having made her "drown" in their imaginary swimming lesson, he reacts like a scolded child, with desperate apologies and denials. In *Icarus's Mother*, there are no actual mother figures to scold Howard and Bill, but the title itself perhaps suggests the threat of maternal reprimand. Just as Icarus came crashing down in flames, so the two tricksters are confronted at the last with the results of their overreaching imaginations. When their story of the plane crash – invented to intimidate the women – comes "true," they stand in paralyzed horror as Frank's speech, and the sound and light around them, actualize their lies.

The unresolvable crisis for these tricksters is that while craving the safety and needing the civilizing control of maternal power, they are equally aware that this subjection is as threatening to their sense of independence and identity as is the wild, unknown world outside. In *The Rock Garden* this is particularly clear: the mother is seen as a monstrous castrator figure who mercilessly keeps both son and husband in positions of impotent, underwear-clad subservience. Indeed, the Man has been "civilized" to the point where he is a mere mockery of the stereotypical rugged American male: he plans a trip to the Arizona desert, but only to pick up stones for his rockery, and muses at length over which shade of "off-white" to paint his picket fence (that classic symbol of petit bourgeois respectability). The Man is viciously patronized by his wife ("He'll never learn. I don't think he wants to": 38), who also repeatedly ridicules her dead father ("He was a funny man") and belittles the Boy at every opportunity, requiring him to wait on her hand and foot. It is from this domineering figure which the Boy needs most urgently to escape, and he attempts to resist her by slowly dressing himself, building a defence against her scrutiny. When, for example, the Woman notes, "Your legs are a lot like Pop's . . . bony and – and kind of skinny" (37), he exits and returns wearing pants; when she starts examining his feet, he returns in shoes, and so forth. Yet, crucially, he never fully frees himself: after each exit he returns to his passive position in the rocking chair. He never actually leaves the Woman until, as the scene closes, his father arrives: his haste to leave at this point, and the Man's taking up of the place in the rocking chair, suggests a distinctly Oedipal twist to the play (the Boy occupies his father's place in his absence), one which also throws an entirely different light on the patricide hinted at in the final scene.

In the other plays, a similar frustrated awareness of the boys' continuing, unshakeable subjection to female influence is perhaps reflected in their irrational, misogynistic aggression toward the female characters, even those who pose no apparent threat. These attempts at intimidation – such as Howard's menacing attack on Pat in *Icarus*, and of course Jim's sustained assault on the Maid – are far nastier than any of the male-on-male confrontations, and tend to result in the women screaming for them to stop. The most notable example in this respect is Stu's occasionally brutal treatment of Joy in *Chicago*, since the entire dynamic of the play seems to spring from an anxiety over being so helplessly reliant on her (his rolling monologue is a prime example of Shepard's fear-expansion technique). Joy, he discovers, is about to leave him to go to a new job, and he is terrified at this prospect. (The plays' title, otherwise unexplained, reportedly derives from the fact that Shepard's own girlfriend, Joyce Aaron, had secured work in Chicago.) Yet he also becomes equally scared at the resulting realization that he has become too dependent on her, and the violent tension generated by these contradictory fears snowballs into ever wilder imagery. As Ralph Cook, director of *Chicago*'s Theatre Genesis premiere, noted in his commentary on it in Shepard's *Five Plays* collection: "The movement of the play is from Stu's minute particular subjective problem (i.e. Joy's leaving Stu and the threat of being chopped off if he follows) to the universal problem of Man's being civilized to the suffocating point of losing his balls."[25]

Chicago's shifting imagery finally arrives at two vivid, conflicting fantasies. In the first, the playful idea of sensual freedom, unmediated by any civilizing influence, descends into a vision of total, chaotic animalism. Stu's story about sailors and virgins screwing on the beach becomes a kind of bacchanalian nightmare in which the figures are lost in a chaotic orgy of flesh, hair, and juices. Turning away from this, Stu seeks an alternative: the people in the story suddenly stop screwing, build a house, and start a calm, domestic life weaving rugs. Yet this too becomes a nightmare, walling them in and suffocating them: "They start screaming all together because they can't breathe. On account of the rugs. The rugs are all sewn together and it's very warm. It's boiling hot inside" (57). The binary opposition of totally wild play and carefully controlled civilization thus dissolves, as both options prove equally deadly to the individual. Faced by this insoluble dichotomy, Stu resorts simply to swift oblivion in the engulfing wetness of the ocean: "They walk across the beach and right into the water. One behind the other. They just keep walking until you can't see them anymore" (57). Notably, *4-H Club* presents almost exactly the same pattern, establishing a contrast between images of the stifling neatness and order of small-town life, dominated by the smothering solicitations of old ladies, and the entirely unfeminized environment of the apartment, in which the boys live like savages. The kitchen becomes a garbage dump in which they smash full cups of coffee on the floor and roll around in the filth, and Joe is labeled a "fairy" for even attempting to clean up. Finally though, it seems that this anarchic extreme of the trickster mentality proves altogether too dangerous, and they begin to crave the watery oblivion of the womb. John's final words take them into a trancelike state, accompanied by a doom-laden beat on a saucepan: "I'm

going to do some swimming too. Floating on my back. You just float and
stare at the sky. You just float and stare at the sky. You just float and stare
at the sky" (100).

Yet another such image is apparent in *Red Cross*, when Jim speaks
ecstatically of swimming alone in the dark at night ("A constant wetness.
. . . You stay down there and there's nothing but water": 132). Indeed, the
preponderance of Oedipal imagery in these early plays begs the question
of whether or not Shepard was actually conscious of feeding such implications into his writing. Certainly he has long been familiar with the
basics of both Freudian and Jungian psychology, and a deliberate manipulation of this imagery would be consistent with the more overt development of mythic themes in some of his later work. On the other hand, it is
at least possible that Shepard's impulsive mining of underlying fears and
desires produced material which was to some extent out of his conscious
control: by his own account, the speed with which these plays were written produced "a certain spontaneous freaky thing."[26] Either way, the particular "freakiness" of these pieces lies in the way that the apocalyptic
overtones of so much of the imagery starkly contradicts the creative exuberance of the writing style. Musically, one might say that the plays present a kind of grotesque dissonance. Or, in Freudian terms, they perhaps
suggest an encapsulation of the basic conflict between Eros, the life
instinct, and Thanatos, the (ultimately stronger) instinct for self-erasure
in death.

The beat poet Allen Ginsberg has defended art of precisely this sort,
arguing that, while the embracing of the dark, subconscious urge for
oblivion may represent a defeat for the impulse for life and independence, "defeat like that is good for poetry . . . you go so far out that you
lose touch with what's been done before by anyone, you wind up creating
a poetry-universe."[27] Unlike Ginsberg's poetry, however, Shepard's plays
suggest a distinct unease with this sense of defeat. *Chicago*, for example,
follows up the grim conclusion of Stu's story with a somewhat forced gesture of faith in life: he finally emerges from his bath and exhorts the audience to "breathe the outstanding air" (59). Yet the hollowness of this
image is then pointed up by the menacing tap of a policeman's truncheon,
which continues into the final blackout: the play appears to be drawn in
two directions at once. This kind of ambiguity is perhaps more effectively
realized in some of the other plays, which pursue the apocalyptic imagery
to the point where it attains a paradoxical redemption of its own. In
Icarus's Mother, for instance, the plane crash is described with such awed
wonder by Frank ("You should have seen – this is something to behold

this is": 77) that it takes on a phoenix-like quality of life emerging from death. The pilot's fall is a final, self-defining blaze of glory which, Frank tells us, brings people for miles around out of their houses to watch in amazement, and which recalls Pat's earlier monologue, when she spoke of the anticipated fireworks display as a means to possible transcendence: "to see just that one beautiful flashing thing across the whole sky" (71).

Red Cross is even more intriguing. The Maid's final speech, in reducing Jim to mesmerized silence, provides the tantalizing glimpse of an alternative to his frantic masculine aggressiveness. Her imagery of drowning, and the slower, hypnotic, rhythms which she deploys seem to hint at a kind of *jouissance*, an ecstatic experience derived from willingly surrendering to the loss of self:

> . . . once it's over it isn't bad. Once you get over the shock of having water all around and dragonflies and water lilies floating by and little silver fish flashing round you. . . . You move through the water like you were born in that very same place and never knew what land was like. . . . And the family in town forgets where you went and the swimming coach forgets who you are and you forget all about lessons and just swim without knowing how. (136)

Yet the mysteriously uncertain potential of the "feminine" is an issue Shepard proved unwilling to confront further at this stage, and his next play, *Fourteen Hundred Thousand* (1966), heads in quite the opposite direction. Its imagery is essentially a reworking of the previously established dichotomy of deadly, chaotic freedom versus deadly, castrating civilization, but for the most part it lacks the kind of anarchic, creative child-masculinity which makes the trickster plays so exciting. Tom shows early flashes of verbal mischief, but these rapidly dissipate after the entrance of his wife, Donna, who proves to be a female influence even more monstrous than the Woman in *The Rock Garden*. Here the equation of woman with stifling civilization suggests a particularly repellent degree of misogyny, with all three male characters becoming Donna's helpless slaves as she keeps them in line with sarcasm, patronizing physical touches, and the manipulation of guilt. She has coerced them into the ceaseless task of building a gigantic bookcase, on which she plans to store fourteen hundred thousand books in whatever neat, ordered (civilized) patterns she cares to invent. "Libraries fascinate me to death," says her Mom, significantly (106). By the end of the play, Donna has verbally reduced Tom to a pathetic state of infancy ("Prone on your back forever and ever. You'll cry aloud to be read to. . . . You lie in pools of urine for days on end until the bed and you become one thing": 115), and taken control of him so completely that he surrenders all pretense at individual identity, and speaks in unison with her, consenting to stay where he is rather than go away with their friend Ed, to his cabin in the woods. Ed himself, meanwhile, enunciates the contradictory terrors of wild freedom, fearful of going to the isolated cabin since he will be totally alone there, as good as dead.

In the closing section, the play abruptly changes gear, and the actors begin systematically dismantling the bookcase and set until the stage is left totally bare. Meanwhile, Mom and Pop recite a science fiction story, in which America is built up into one huge city until every last piece of "open green space" has disappeared. This contradictory juxtaposition of action and dialogue underlines the play's conclusive erasure of binary opposites, implying that, ultimately, building up and tearing down, smothering and freeing, lead to the same state of nonexistence. There is no escape, and no chance of individual expression, as is demonstrated by the complete unison in which all the actors are speaking by the end of the play.

This seemingly unrelieved nihilism makes *Fourteen Hundred Thousand* something of an aberration in the general development of Shepard's work. So too do the mostly rather clumsy attempts at alienation devices it employs (possibly inspired by Shepard's contact with Brecht enthusiasts like Jacques Levy), such as the sudden shifts of lighting states when characters enter or exit, the loud hammering on walls occurring simultaneously with dialogue, and the establishment of a metatheatrical second frame (by having some characters sit down, their backs to the audience, watching other characters perform their tasks). The most entertainingly theatrical element of the play is the stylized paint fight between Tom and Donna, which Tom O'Horgan (who refers to this as "the paint play") took to extremes when staging it for National Educational Television's "Three from La Mama" in 1966. As a whole, though, the disparate effects do not gel well: the premiere production at the Firehouse Theatre in Minneapolis was particularly awkward, and led to a falling-out between Shepard and director Sydney Schubert Walter. For his next play, *La Turista*, Shepard returned fully to the elliptical, musical style he had been developing previously. This play represents both a decisive summarizing of, and a break from, the underlying themes of his early work. Rather than submitting to annihilation, it takes on the overtones of a rites-of-passage

play, an attempt to deliver the central male figure from fear and dependency.

La Turista

La Turista was Shepard's first attempt at expanding his writing beyond
the one-act form. It was originally written as a three-act piece, while he
and Joyce Aaron were on vacation in Mexico, staying in "a tiny sweltering
motel room in the Yucatan," suffering from "a semidelirious state of
severe dysentery." (*La turista* is both the Spanish word for tourist and the
local Mexican term for "Montezuma's revenge.") The result was a play
written out of an extreme state of inner turmoil, and for Shepard this
seemed like a guarantee of its authenticity: "In that state any writing I
could manage seemed valid, no matter how incoherent it might seem to
an outside eye."[28] Jacques Levy, the director of the play's first production
at the American Place Theatre, did not agree. Feeling that the original
second and third acts were altogether too incoherent for production, he
insisted they be rewritten. Shepard responded by scrapping the idea of a
third act altogether, and writing an entirely new second act. The resulting
play is an intriguing juxtaposition of two radically different halves. The
first, set in a surreal version of the Mexican motel room in which it was
written, is a kaleidoscopic assembly of shifting colors and bizarre stage
imagery, which is always on the verge of complete fragmentation: the
tourist characters Kent and Salem career through poses and speech patterns ranging from medical jargon to tour-guide-speak, and from market
hawking to autobiographical recollection. By comparison, the second act,
written (as it were) in the cold light of day, is inevitably less spontaneous,
and at times feels somewhat forced and repetitive in its use of imagery.
Yet Shepard makes this downshift in tone into an actual thematic concern
by moving the play's location to a "plastic American" motel room. Thus
the glaring, livid yellow-and-orange set of act 1, which reflects the sweltering heat and nausea of the Mexican environment, is supplanted by the
cooler, more sterile, tan and gray colors of act 2, just as the writing itself
becomes cooler. The contrast between the acts is further underlined by
complementary variations in costume, character-type (the silent Mexican
witch doctor of the first act, for example, is replaced in the second by a
verbose American country doctor, played by the same actor), and even
the facial complexions of the main characters. Taken together, the two
acts demonstrate a marked progression in Shepard's work, suggesting not
simply a single, sustained outpouring of creative energy, but a calculated

juxtaposition of contrasting elements. In effect, the play adds a new dimension to Shepard's concern with musical structures: the two acts represent two "movements," connected not by any chronological link in narrative, but by interrelated variations on the central theme of Kent's debilitating sickness.

As in the previous plays, Shepard's basic technique in act 1 is to develop a highly subjectivized sequence of speeches, images, and events from his starting point in autobiographical reality. In particular, he plays on the by now familiar method of exaggerating personal anxieties into paranoid terrors. In this case, the fear of incapacitation through sickness seems to be the key: Kent's and Salem's acute sunburns, for example, become the spur for a vivid speech on third-degree burns growing worse still, and reaching an unprecedented fourth degree. Similarly, the fear of being infected by their unhygienic surroundings leads to wild fantasies about Third World poverty and disease, and prompts the arrival of a local shoeshine boy, who sends Kent into hysterics when he spits his unhygienic phlegm at him. Mexico thus becomes another variation on Shepard's recurrent concern with the threatening dangers of the wild, and the terror it evokes is again contrasted with the emasculating influence of civilization. Kent describes America as "an isolated land of purification" where "they're breeding a bunch of lily-livered weaklings . . . simply by not having a little dirty water to toughen people up."[29] Caught between two equally deadly options, he too admits that what he really craves is oblivion. When Salem asks him why he wanted to come to Mexico, he replies: "to relax and disappear." And if he truly disappeared, what would he do with himself? "Nothing. I'd be gone" (257).

Thus far, there is little new thematically in the material. But the play's second act, while it cannot recapture the sheer craziness of the first, instead introduces a reflective distance on the established themes, and so takes them into new territory. Abandoning the Mexican dysentery, for example, Shepard gives Kent a disease more appropriate to the life-sapping sterility of the American environment: Doc diagnoses his ailment as Encephalitis Lethargica, or "sleepy sickness," a somnolence akin to living death. But he also labels it "von Economo's disease," thereby introducing for the first time in Shepard's work the notion of economic systems as constricting forces: "civilization" ceases to be merely an abstract concept. The idea is developed further when Shepard picks up on his curious decision to name his two main characters after cigarette brands: Kent delivers a parable about the helpless subjection of his and Salem's family to an infernal, all-powerful cigarette company, which dictated even the naming of the children (this apparently makes the pair brother and sister rather than lovers, further destabilizing the audience's tenuous grip on the play's situation). At the same time, the theme of somnolence is carefully woven back in, with the suggestion that cigarettes are another form of addictively deadly analgesic: Kent recalls "Pa dying for a smoke," at which point the fatherly Doc promptly yawns and falls asleep (283). Moreover, when Kent finishes his story, Sonny (Doc's son; the Boy from act 1) ties this together with his experience of impotent subjection to the earth mother figure, Old Lady Tuttle, who plays a violin which hypnotically lulls the listener into oblivion. The language here is highly reminiscent of the Maid's final speech in *Red Cross*: "we two . . . Just lookin' on. Growin' slowly. Rooted in one place. Lettin' seasons change us" (Doc, 285).

The theme of subjection to female influence is once again a recurrent element. Predictably enough, the play's only female character, Salem, rapidly moves from being Kent's fellow sufferer (as Joyce Aaron was with Shepard in the Yucatán), to being a castrating mother figure, calling him "boy" and treating him with patronizing indulgence. In the second act she is not sick at all, but nursemaids Kent throughout. The adolescent trickster persona also reappears in the first act, yet significantly it is not Kent, the central male figure, who is given this function. Instead, it is the Mexican Boy who appears vital, healthy, and animalistic: he is immune to the wild germs of Mexico, and is magically able to speak perfect English, to communicate on a disconnected telephone, and to make rude gestures at the audience.

The distancing of these trickster qualities from Kent enables a new perspective on the issue of the masculine will to maturity and independence. The Boy is a dynamic, playful figure who becomes a kind of nemesis for Kent, forcing him to confront his own unmanly feebleness. Kent is terrified of him: cowering behind his sheets in his underwear, he describes the Boy's primitive savagery in the manner of "an English safari hunter warning someone about a man-eating lion" (260). When Kent finally plucks up the courage to "act like a man" and confront the Boy, the latter simply spits in his face: his reaction – a panicked retreat to the bathroom, screaming about infection – confirms his complete impotence. A real man, says the Boy, remains calm under pressure. Kent does not. But a real man would also be justified in "blowing his cool" and seeking vengeance for being humiliated (264). Again, Kent does not. His inadequacy is most hilariously realized by the juxtaposition of the Boy's movie star fantasy of a cool, confident, and dangerously powerful ideal male, with Kent screaming from the bathroom about his diarrhea ("Salem! It's getting worse! It's very, very loose!": 264). When he does try, belatedly, to retrieve some credibility, reemerging from the bathroom dressed as the cowboy-hero that the Boy has just described, he still has no pants on. His attempt to play the role of a paragon of manhood is thus pathetically unconvincing, and he collapses in a dead faint when he sees that the Boy – in an Oedipal move reminiscent of *The Rock Garden* – has supplanted him in the bed next to Salem. Kent remains motionless for the rest of the act.

The fear suggested here, of an ineffectual male adulthood unable to face the demands of the world, is clearly something that haunted Shepard at this time. (A dream of his, recorded in a notebook as late as 1969, reproduced almost exactly Kent's crisis: he sees himself arriving at school, only to realize in horror that he is dressed only in underwear, T-shirt, cowboy boots, and an overcoat.)[30] Yet while in previous plays the creativity of the tricksters had seemed like a response of sorts to this lack of mature identity, in *La Turista* this is clearly inadequate. Although the Boy is certainly a more vital figure than Kent, replacing him completely as the focus of act 1, he is still only a child, who can fantasize about ideal manhood but does not actually grow up. Indeed, his supplanting of Kent also involves donning his clothes (which he himself has described as poisoned) and adopting Salem as a dominating mother figure (he repeatedly refers to her as "Mom"). She responds first by touting him around to the audience as the perfect example of willing servility, and then by taking on the role of buyer, trying to persuade him to return to America with her as a housepet. Tricksterism, as the earlier plays had implied and the Boy's subjection makes clear, cannot lead to independent identity.

Yet where Shepard's previous plays, and in particular *Fourteen Hundred Thousand*, had appeared to concede defeat to this inability to achieve a mature sense of self, in *La Turista* there is the sense of a newfound determination to resist and survive. The play is full of images of self-realization, such as Doc's account of shaking off the hypnotic influence of Old Lady Tuttle's violin ("my boy here realized and snapped us both out of it": 285), and the moment at the end of act 1 when the Boy refuses to capitulate to Salem's solicitations. A telephone call, apparently from his father, presents him with an alternative: the Boy describes the prospect of returning to his father, of being greeted as an equal, and then – his manhood apparently conferred on him by this encounter – of leaving again to find true freedom and independence. The act concludes with his liberating vision of riding in a beat-up truck, "the radio turned up loud as it goes and singing Spanish as we drive out into the Gulf of Mexico and float to the other side" (note that on this occasion the sea does not swallow the speaker). Salem reaches him as the lights fade, yelling for him to come back to mother, to think again: "You'll never make it alive!" (276).

The Boy's story of meeting his father is just one instance of the new possibility of being initiated into manhood that the play presents. Whereas the fathers in *The Rock Garden* and *Fourteen Hundred Thousand* were laughably ineffectual, in *La Turista* the older man takes on the potential to act as a mentor figure. This role, which is common in mythology, is seen in psychoanalytic interpretations as symbolizing the necessary guidance a boy must receive to be ushered into manhood. Just so, in both acts, the doctors (who are both father figures, by virtue of having sons tagging along with them) seek to counteract Kent's desire to "disappear," to "sleep," through the enactment of symbolic rites. In act 1, a complex ritual of exorcism is carried out by the Witchdoctor, and described in minute detail in the stage directions. Acting as an anthropological tour guide, the Boy adds a manic running commentary that pointedly equates this mysterious spectacle with other Mexican Indian traditions of male initiation rites: "By the time the penis has healed," he concludes of one such ceremony, "the boy has become a man" (270). The chickens whose blood is dripped over Kent, he further notes, are substitutes for the more primitive habit of sacrificing women, a point which is underlined when Salem screams in agony from the bathroom just as the chickens are decapitated. There is, perhaps, an allusion here to the purging of the maternal-feminine influence which is also a commonplace stage in initiation myths.

The second act follows a roughly parallel course to the first: Kent lies comatose in bed, and the arrival of Doc and Sonny initiates the rescue attempt. Here, though, the approach is less unhinged and more systematic, Shepard apparently forcing through the initiation/exorcism more deliberately. Doc sees his role as being to "get ya' out of what looked to me like suicide. Plain and simple" (290), and Kent is forced to his feet, pumped with benzedrine (a stimulant), and dragged around the room in circles in a bid to force him to wake up and stay awake. For a long time, he remains mentally absent, speaking "in a world unrelated to anything on stage," but finally the cure begins to work, and Kent starts to acquire a new vitality, as Doc appeals to him to follow in his fatherly footsteps: "Just watch me . . . let me show ya' the way" (296). Kent's rebirth is vividly described by both Doc and himself. He is suddenly capable of anything, and demonstrates this power, verbally and visually, with a mercurial (and very difficult to act) application of the Open Theatre's transformation exercise: "He becomes a mouse and changes into a cobra and then back to the floor." Finally, his lethargy fully cured, Kent transcends even the boundaries of the stage reality itself, and leaps cartoon-like through the back of the set. This much-praised image was actually devised in rehearsal by Jacques Levy, but it was, significantly, a response to Shepard's specification that Kent simply escape. In the previous one-act plays, the central male characters had been helplessly trapped in the stage space, terrified to venture into the unexplored territory beyond. Here, freedom seems finally to have been embraced.

Crucially, though, Kent's acquisition of this new vitality is treated with a considerable degree of ambiguity. The ostensibly benign mentor-doctor figures, for example, also have distinctly sinister dimensions: Doc's motives in particular seem highly dubious. While claiming that he is there to "transform the dying man into a thing of beauty" (291), Doc also appears to have a Frankenstein-like desire to control Kent's rebirth for his own ends. This is, perhaps, the first case of many in Shepard's plays of a father figure's seeking to indoctrinate his "son" into his own version of manhood. For the newly awakened Kent, Doc is a manipulative influence who must be resisted. Kent describes himself breaking loose of the operating table in a premature bid for freedom, and then confronts Doc in a Mexican standoff for the play's verbal showdown.

An even more acute danger, however, is suggested by the description of Kent's incomplete new body. Composed of natural elements and possessing magical powers, it is nevertheless a monstrosity which is disintegrating even as it revels in its liberation: "His arms rip from the shoulders and chest, and juices gush down his sides. . . . His hair tears and floats away, flapping in air like an owl at night" (297). This flawed new creation takes on the aspect of a primal, self-destructive force unleashed on the world. The rampant Kent-creature may have escaped the state of subjection felt by the characters in the earlier plays, but he also prefigures the "heroic" male characters in many of the plays that followed, in which adult masculinity is seen not only as violent and hubristic, but as completely out of control, divided against itself.

In extending and developing the "masculine identity crisis" dimension of the plays that had led up to it, *La Turista* highlights both the wildly unhinged creativity and the uncertain attitude toward masculinity and the adult world generally which typify Shepard's early work. The raw tension between playfulness and fear is again evident, but in extending the improvisatory approach over two acts, the play also sows the seeds for the

more sophisticated exploration of entrapment and bewilderment which
was to follow in later plays. *La Turista* also anticipates subsequent developments by presenting a markedly more diverse and jagged collection of
role playing and cultural quotations than previously. Less attempt seems
to have been made here to subsume these within a consistent authorial
style: in this piece and those that follow, the imagery and characters
become far more obviously the fragmentary debris of American popular
culture. Turning from the private tensions of the solipsistic nightmare
format, Shepard began to dramatize a more direct confrontation with the
constricting and disorientating pressures of postmodern society.

2

Kicking Out

Rock and Ruin, 1967–1971

SHEPARD'S PLAYS OF THE LATE 1960S demonstrate an
abrupt change in the tone and style of his writing, which suggests not
merely a continuation of the maturing process apparent in *La Turista*, but
a radical revision in his whole approach. He continued, in the main, to
write one-act pieces for Off-Off-Broadway venues, and further developed his concern with the individual self's crisis of survival and definition
in a frightening, unstable world. Yet the influence of jazz gave way to that
of rock music, while the influence of abstract expressionism was transplanted somewhat by that of pop art. Hollywood movies also became a
central source of inspiration. In these plays, stage action, character, and
language itself are dominated less by solipsistic fantasy than by a newfound interest in the external world, as Shepard began manipulating and
parodying the fragmented discourses of popular culture.

In effect, these changes indicate a significant shift beyond the self-
absorbed, primarily modernist sensibility of the early work. While pre-
serving the tendency toward stylization and self-reflexivity, there is simultaneously, and paradoxically, the introduction in these pieces of a more or
less explicit critique of the "real world" (a real world which remains
impossible to define or depict uncomplicatedly: there is no pretense here
at the illusion of naive realism). In particular, these plays explore the artifice and superficiality of contemporary life: the gnawing, indefinable fear
felt by the tricksters is replaced by a more overt sense of disillusionment
and oppression, as Shepard's characters lash out helplessly against their
environments. Crucially, though, there are still traces of a search for some
unifying vision, a source of hope beyond the deadly, all-pervading hol-

lowness. This tendency persists through these plays in direct contradiction to the much bleaker but equally prevalent suggestion that such redemption is impossible. There is, in short, a direct confrontation between modernist and postmodernist perspectives in several of these plays. The unresolved tension between the various elements opens up all kinds of provocative gaps and ambiguities: these pieces are among the most uneven of Shepard's work, but are characterized by a bewildering and highly abrasive kind of pop theatricality.

End of Innocence

One of the most obvious manifestations of Shepard's shift in concerns is the appearance in these plays of "hero" figures, usually cowboys and rock stars, who actively battle against forces of oppression in the outside world. In effect, Shepard's male characters have grown up: the mischievous narcissism of the tricksters is replaced by the ostensibly more serious struggles of these adult figures (dressed in more or less garish variations on Shepard's dreamed-of adult outfit: jeans, cowboy boots, T-shirt, overcoat) who confront the dangers of the world head-on. It might be tempting, following on from the preceding chapter, to ascribe this development to a natural psychological growth process, for this newfound interest in heroes is entirely consistent with the development of traditional myth cycles. Anthropologists have shown that the mythological figure which succeeds the trickster in such cycles, worldwide, is that of the classic hero-figure: Jungians argue that this represents the archetypal image of the next phase of masculine maturation.

However, it is vital to note that Shepard was at this stage becoming much less of a purist in his pursuit of subconscious impulses, and this raises question marks over any attempt at psychoanalytic readings of this sort. The experience of rewriting parts of *La Turista* had given him, he notes, a "first taste . . . of regarding theatre as an ongoing process," and subsequently, while continuing to rely heavily on an intuitive exploration of rhythm and emotional states, he also began taking more time to rework his initial ideas, sometimes submitting them to extensive revision. (*Back Bog Beast Bait*, for example, first appeared on stage in 1971, two years after he penned the initial version). As a result, the presentation of character and theme seems far more self-conscious here than in his previous pieces, an impression reinforced by Shepard's own account of his change in emphasis. In 1969, in his first *New York Times* interview, he told Mel Gussow that he now saw his earlier work as "kind of facile": "You get a certain spontaneous freaky thing if you write real fast. You don't get anything heavy unless you spend real time. . . . Now I'm dealing more with mythic characters, a combination of science fiction, Westerns and television."[1]

This comment suggests that for Shepard, the first pieces were simply a warm-up for this "heavier" material, and that his turn to more overt pop culture quotation in these plays was indicative of a more calculated attempt to achieve a mythic resonance in his work, by circumventing the intellect through the use of material with immediate emotional currency for a very wide audience. "Draw primitive visions and feelings into the open," he wrote in a 1969 notebook: "find areas of correspondence in people's submerged minds."[2] Shepard's application of the idea seems more than a little odd, however: his use of cowboys and spacemen is a far cry from the use of "primitive" mythological material mined in modernist classics like Eliot's *The Waste Land*, and much of the pop imagery mined is utterly superficial. If Shepard was indeed aiming for psychic depth, then perhaps he was also guilty of wrongly assuming that just because certain material is widely recognized, it must carry some such resonance with it. Such an attitude ignores the fact that it is precisely the lowest-common-denominator shallowness of much pop culture which makes it so immediately accessible to such a wide audience. If viewed only in terms of up-front profundity, these plays often appear far more "facile" than the ones preceding them.

Yet if, at the time, Shepard chose to justify the shift in his work through this somewhat unconvincing appeal to the notion of mythic depth, I would suggest that there were also other, far less romanticized reasons for the changes of direction. In continuing to pursue, as honestly as possible, the exploration of hidden fears, Shepard opened his work up to a growing sense of personal unease and dislocation. In particular, it is evident that he felt increasingly *trapped*, both by his cultural environment and by his own hitherto pleasurable role as experimental playwright. Under increasing pressure from the attentions of producers and critics, the uninhibited self-exploration of the early work was no longer possible. The very success of his previous plays meant that he was now constantly aware of writing material which would be scrutinized by others, and this inevitably resulted in a somewhat stifling degree of self-consciousness about his role as a writer. Shepard's notebooks from the late '60s indicate such anxieties clearly. He records, for instance, a dream in which he is being pursued by a critic who demands that he explain the meaning of his work. He tries to deny accountability, but the pursuit continues: "I feel like I'm still in handcuffs behind my back," he concludes.

For a time Shepard had sought to stave off such pressures: he attempted, for example, to ban the press from reviewing the premiere production of *La Turista*. This commercially suicidal gesture was apparently inspired by an awareness that, thanks to its status as his first "full-length" play and its appearance at the midtown, Off-Broadway American Place Theatre (a significant move up from Genesis and La Mama), *La Turista* was bound to attract an unprecedented degree of attention. Yet the attention came, despite his unease: Elizabeth Hardwick defied his ban and reviewed the play, very favorably, in the prestigious *New York Times Review of Books*. In the next few years, Shepard surrendered to the inevitable, and an increasing number of his plays began to make the move up from Off-Off's makeshift environs to the Off-Broadway theatres. (There was a growing trend for alternative fare in more mainstream theatres, demonstrated most spectacularly by the success of *Hair* on Broadway in 1968, as directed by La Mama's Tom O'Horgan, who also directed two Shepard premieres in 1967 and 1969). The temptations of this "promotion" were obvious: the modest financial rewards were compounded by the award of a succession of arts foundation grants (which, with supreme irony, he gained by peddling Hardwick's review as credentials). In 1969 Shepard even accepted a sizable advance from Robert Redford to write a screen treatment of his play *The Unseen Hand* (never completed). In 1970 he was finally embraced, albeit briefly, by the establishment when Lincoln Center mounted his parodic stab at "the great American play," *Operation Sidewinder*.

This mounting public exposure was further intensified as, during this period, Shepard's plays began to find print. The first such collection, *Five Plays*, appeared in 1967, and again this was something Shepard – in self-promotional mode – had actively sought: he even ensured that his photograph appeared on the front cover. Yet he was also uneasily aware that his work would now be "imprisoned" on the page, available to be minutely scrutinized as writing rather than simply experienced in the moment onstage. He clearly indicated his ambivalence toward this new exposure by including in the collection a then-unproduced piece, *Melodrama Play*. This is the story of a rock star, Duke Durgens, who glories in the fame and adulation his one global hit has brought him, but who is now suffering from an acute case of writer's block. His attempts to write an original song as a follow-up result only in "Shit. Garbage. Stuff I could have done in school," and his frustration is exacerbated by the decision of his manager, Floyd, to lock him up and force him to produce to order.[3] As Dan Damon (a gleeful parody of the academic critic) remarks at the end of an hour of agitation and violence: "I do hope we have given all of you somewhat of an indication of just exactly how the personal life of an artist is affected and/or altered by the reception of his work by the public at large" (143).

Duke's loss of spontaneity and "originality" clearly reflected Shepard's own frustrations. This is further underlined by the play's radical shift of tone in comparison with his previous style: it sets the agenda for much of the work in this period by being marked less by a sense of spontaneous creativity than by a frightening mood of artifice and contrivance. As the title implies, Shepard robs his characters of any pretense at authentic self-expression by constructing their language and behavior out of the corny melodrama of B-movies and comic books ("He's a desperate man. He needs a new song and he'll stop at nothing to get it": 139). Crucially though, Shepard succeeds once again in translating private anxiety into a more universal theme: behind the parodic jokes lies an acute sense that superficiality and insincerity are now cultural norms. This is voiced most clearly by another character, Peter, as he pleads feverishly for somebody to say something to him which is heartfelt and spontaneous:

> . . . say whatever just comes into your head in that split second. What-ever happens to be sitting there in your memory of the second before and it just spiels out trippingly off the tongue. It just gushes out in its most accurate way. Word for word, without a moment to calculate where it's going or how or why. It just falls out into the air and dis-appears as soon as its heard. That's what I want to hear. Right now, before it's too late! (141)

For Shepard himself, though, it was perhaps already too late. This speech is indicative of a growing skepticism toward the high modernist belief in the possibility of authentic self-expression, and in the plays that followed this one, his inability to recapture the simple impulsiveness of his earlier work is evident in a rather awkward fumbling for new direc-tion. The year 1967 also saw, for example, his first tentative excursion into treating theatre as a collaborative process: the somewhat ramshackle *Forensic and the Navigators* was written not as freewheeling improvisa-tion but as a result of workshop sessions with Theatre Genesis actors (including his wife-to-be O-Lan Johnson, written into the script as Oolan). Even more significant, however, was the appearance of *Cowboys* #2. In offering a not-at-all-disguised rewrite of his first play, this writer who had previously prided himself on never rewriting anything was per-haps openly acknowledging that – as even some of his more supportive

critics were suggesting – he had begun repeating himself, that his established style had become predictable. Moreover, *Cowboys #2* is different
from the original in one very important respect: here Shepard adds two
new characters, the anonymous Man #1 and Man #2, whose peripheral
presence robs Stu and Chet of their playful freedom. Functioning initially
as mysterious offstage voices, they prompt the play's opening by feeding
Chet the first line, and then, intermittently through the events that follow, they further punctuate and cajole the young men's repartee by
whistling across the stage "as if calling a dog."[4] At the end, they walk
onstage and begin reading the entire script again from the start, in a flat
monotone, as the lights fade and Stu dies. Clearly, Stu and Chet's
attempts to create a sense of spontaneity are nothing but a pretense, for
even as they are seen enacting a sequence of games and speeches on the
spot, the intermittent interruptions of the Men provide a constant
reminder that they are engaged in a rehearsed routine, which is all the
time conditioned from the outside. This metatheatrical device comments
directly on the actors' position in relation to the script itself: in a written
play, the performer's creativity is always trapped and channeled by the
script (this was being violently reacted against at the time by groups like
the Living Theatre, who had abandoned the use of playwrights, seeing it
as a constriction of performative freedom). Conversely, though, and more
importantly for Shepard, one sees that the writer's vision is also being filtered through the potentially distorting channel of the actors. The play
implicitly points up the conceptual flaws in the high modernist ideal of
drama's achieving a sense of immanent presence in the "Now," by openly
acknowledging that in performance it is a reproduction of a script written
in the past, a repetition of rehearsed actions performed many times
before.

A related sense of entrapment is suggested by another aspect of the
Men's entry: when they finally appear, they seem like deadened alter egos
of the defeated Stu and Chet, "the same age," but "dressed in suits" (193).
The pressures of societal conditioning and conformity hinted at here are
further developed in subsequent plays as Shepard begins to toy with elements of social critique. Again, this was partly a function of the period in
which they were written, when it became impossible not to take some
stance on what was happening in American society at large. Violence and
tension dominated events on a national scale: the assassinations in 1968 of
Robert Kennedy and Martin Luther King, the election in the same year of
a hard right-wing president in Richard Nixon, the growth of
the radical left in the form of student activism and the black power

movement, and, of course, the increasingly controversial involvement of America in the bloody conflict in Vietnam. "Everything," Shepard remarked later, "shifted to a very grim perspective," and in this fraught atmosphere his previous self-absorption no longer seemed like an adequate response.[5] Yet if Shepard, like many of his generation, felt an impulse for rebellion, it was also directly contradicted by the fear – visible in both *Cowboy #2* and *Melodrama Play* – that escape from societal pressures is an impossible fantasy. The resulting tension between pessimism and defiance is a distinguishing feature of his work during this period.

"Cut with a New Demon"

Another important factor in Shepard's shift of perspective was the change in the New York zeitgeist in the late '6os. The rapid rise of the hippie counterculture in America (signaled most notably by the 1967 "Summer of Love" in San Francisco) was celebrated by many, but for Shepard it destroyed any sense of the city as a source of freedom. From his point of view, both the carnivalesque creative atmosphere in which he had begun working, and the "incredible feeling of community" which had been so vital a stabilizing force for him, were "completely blown apart when acid hit the streets":

> When this sudden influx of essentially white middle-class kids hit the streets, the indigenous people – the Puerto Ricans, the blacks, the street junkies and all the people who were really a part of the scene – felt this great animosity toward these flip-outs running around the Lower East Side in beads and hair down to their asses. There was this upsurge in violence and weirdness, and everybody started carrying guns and knives . . . in New York it got very scary.[6]

Shepard's disillusionment with the city, and his desire to kick back against the various pressures on him, manifested themselves most obviously in his newfound fascination with rock and roll as a musical inspiration (first evident in *Melodrama Play*, a watershed piece in more than one respect). Jazz had represented "an urban thing," "a kind of sophistication" with which he could no longer identify: "I started reacting against that, the whole jazz influence. So I began to think rock and roll music represented another kind of back to a raw gut kind of American shitkicker thing."[7] The inelegant statement reflects the inelegance of the sentiment: the simpler but more violently impassioned rock idiom replaced the celebratory immanence of jazz with a pounding desire for transcendence.

In 1965, the potential of rock and roll as an artistic medium was belatedly brought to the attention of Greenwich Villagers (most of whom had previously tended to consider it as mere commercial bubblegum) when Bob Dylan first fused his folk-based protest music with the power of an electric guitar. Others quickly caught on, and for Shepard, his conversion to rock came as something of a salvation, providing a new lease of creative energy at a time when his writing had begun to lose its initial impetus. For a while it was all he cared about, as is evident from such delirious ramblings as "Rip It Up," from the prose collection written during this period, *Hawk Moon* (published 1973):

> Rock and roll made movies theatre books painting and art go out of the window none of it stands a chance against The Who The Stones and the old Yardbirds Credence Traffic The Velvet Underground Janis and Jimi and on and on the constant frustration of the other artists to keep up to the music of our time Rock and Roll will never die . . .[8]

This infatuation was serious enough that, from 1967 to 1970, he made a serious attempt to forge an alternative career for himself as the drummer with the cult "amphetamine rock band" The Holy Modal Rounders (a.k.a. The Moray Eels). It was another deliberate reinvention of his public identity: "First off let me tell you that I don't want to be a playwright," he stated provocatively in a 1971 program note: "I want to be a rock and roll star."[9] The comment was not altogether facetious. Recording and touring with the band meant long periods away from playwriting: that fact, combined with his abortive attempt at writing a screenplay for Antonioni's *Zabriskie Point*, led to an unprecedented stage silence of two years between the New York premieres of *Forensic and the Navigators* (December 1967) and *The Unseen Hand* (December 1969).

When he was not neglecting theatre altogether, Shepard appeared to be trying hard to merge his two careers. The original production of *Forensic and the Navigators* (a title which itself sounds more like a band than a play), despite the opposition of director and critics, concluded with the Holy Modal Rounders hammering out electric rock through the audience-engulfing smoke of the climax. In 1970, he went further by writing the band's music into the text of *Operation Sidewinder*: the Rounders' songs form an ironic, mock-Brechtian commentary which loosely links the twelve fragmentary scenes. Live rock performances were also written into *The Mad Dog Blues, Cowboy Mouth*, and *Back Bog Beast Bait* (all 1971), as well as *Melodrama Play* and Shepard's rock masterpiece, *The Tooth of Crime* (1972). Of the remaining texts of this period, *The Holy*

Ghostly (1969) and *Shaved Splits* (1970) contain lengthy speeches about the merits of rock, and *The Unseen Hand* (1969) calls for electric guitar backing to two of the speeches.

Needless to say, the playing of drums and amplified electric instruments, especially in the tiny theatres of Off-Off-Broadway, created an extremely abrasive impact on stage. This was further enhanced by Shepard's "rock 'n' roll" treatment of language. Dispensing almost completely with his elliptical, aria-like monologues, with their internal rhythmic dynamics and surreal imagery, he began to treat speeches with a more prosaic bluntness. Where they do acquire a musical quality, it is the driving, linear tempo of rock. Shepard retained his interest in providing a rhythmic context for the emotion implied in the words of speeches, but the emotion here, more often than not, is extreme excitement or agitation, rather than anything more subtly inflected. The Kid in *The Unseen Hand* and Dana in *Melodrama Play*, for example, have lengthy speeches which – like "Rip It Up" – are entirely lacking in punctuation, resulting in breathlessly overexcited performances on stage. More commonly, the speeches have regular periods and repetitive sounds or phrases which create the effect of a thumping, rocklike beat. Take, for instance, Emmett in *Forensic and the Navigators*:

> It's no good being disappointed, Forensic. We've been through that. We have to just lay low for a while. We need you a lot so don't go feeling left out of things. Right now we have to take care of certain business. We have to transfer the guns and equipment. We have to individually escape. We have to be quiet. (158)

The shorter the sentences and the heavier the repetition, the more violently abrupt is the sound, as in the frantic, claustrophobic rage of *Cowboy Mouth*:

> CAVALE: Fucking dark in here. Fucking old black dog. You fucking. Where's Raymond? Where's Raymond, goddammit? Shit. Raymond, Raymond, where's my crow, my old black tooth?
> SLIM: Your Raymond! My wife! Kidnapped in the twentieth century! Kidnapped off the street! Hot off the press! Don't make no sense! I ain't no star! Not me! Not me boy! Not me! Not yer old dad! Not yer old scalawag! This is me! Fucked! Fucked up! What a ratpile heap a dogshit situation! (147)

Shepard himself has neatly summed up the effect of such language in his description of *The Unseen Hand*: "They crash around in this space for a while making a certain kind of rough music. . . . Words are like hammers and nails."[10]

Rock is also a major influence on the characterization in these plays, almost all of which feature actual or would-be rock musicians as central figures. This factor is immediately apparent from their names, ostentatious titles like Kosmo, Duke, Geez, and Ice, which suggest something of the unusual, legendary texture of the names of the period's rock heroes (Jagger, Dylan, Hendrix, Joplin). And while there is always some degree of irony in Shepard's portrayal of these larger-than-life figures, these "handles" nevertheless seem to express a genuine sentiment, an urge toward extravagant individualism and defiant self-definition in the face of a hostile world. Where his earlier, more mundanely named characters had only dreamed of heroism, in the idealized figure of the cowboy (*Cowboys, La Turista*), rock stars could actually aspire to that legendary status: a true hero of our times would be – in Cavale's oft-quoted words – "a rock-and-roll Jesus with a cowboy mouth" (157).

The wild, anti-urban frontier life of the cowboy-individualist was a popular theme in the rock music and rock-inspired movies of this period (see, for example, Dennis Hopper's *Easy Rider*), and it is notable that in this group of Shepard's plays, those which do not boast a rock musician as hero instead feature his equivalent, the old-time cowboy – Blue, Cisco, and Sycamore in *The Unseen Hand*, Slim in *Back Bog Beast Bait*. (The one exception to this rule, *Operation Sidewinder*, has a central male figure who therefore remains literally anonymous, the "Young Man.") In either case, however, the impression created by the lead characters is much the same, suggesting a strength and machismo in keeping with rock music's aggressively masculine style and sound. Moreover, in keeping with both rock prejudice and conventional western narratives, female characters are all but expunged from these plays. Women, it seems, no longer constitute a threat to Shepard's male characters, who have effectively emerged from the womb into the outside world, which is now the principle source of danger. When present at all, female characters tend to be reduced to the level of domestic servants or sex objects. The notable exception to this rule is *Cowboy Mouth,* which Shepard co-wrote with the poet and singer Patti Smith, and the character of Cavale is clearly based on her – strong, magnetic, and at times overwhelming.

Cowboy Mouth is exceptional in other ways too. In writing it, Shepard and Smith reportedly pushed the typewriter back and forth, writing alternate lines as they went, and this account seems to be verified by the play's almost total lack of plot. This is essentially a rock-based variation on the raw improvisation of the trickster plays, full of unconnected role-playing, reality-inventing games, memory monologues, and so forth. (Shepard's character, Slim, even adopts the animal persona of Coyote, the trickster figure in Navajo and Hopi Indian mythology.) This was, however, an untypical throwback to the collage structure of Shepard's previous work: for the most part, he was now adopting a more linear approach, accommodating his heroic figures by placing them within narratives which pit them against forces with which they can struggle heroically. Unremittingly masculinist in approach as these pieces undoubtedly are, though, the ironic undermining of their basic premises is also an ever present factor.

Imprisonment by the System?

The adoption of story lines is another clear indication that Shepard was taking more time to think through the structuring of his work. Again, *La Turista* was a turning point in this respect: it is noticeable that Shepard's first real denouement-demanding plot premise (will Kent be successfully cured?) appears in the *rewritten* second act of that play. Some of the early experiments with narrative represent unwieldy transitions from his previous, more elliptical approach: *Forensic*, for example, opens with outlaws planning a jailbreak but disintegrates into a mishmash of unrelated songs, witticisms, and even a passage about how to eat Rice Krispies. Yet Shepard worked hard at refining the linear form, and in 1968 even attended a screenwriting course at Yale, as a result of which he began experimenting with applying filmic narrative techniques to the stage. The first example of this was *Operation Sidewinder*, an "epic" in which an episodic narrative is built around a chronologically ordered sequence of set piece scenes in various elaborate locations. This, however, resulted in cumbersome set changes between each scene: the "single-frame editing" approach, Shepard realized, "doesn't work on stage. It was very static."[11] Learning from his error, he produced *The Mad Dog Blues*, another two-act attempt at "A Staged Film" (this was the subtitle to an early, abandoned draft of the play, then called *Dog Meat*). This time he left the stage empty, thus making possible the creation of multiple exotic locations in the imagination. The action flows more freely, often cutting rapidly back and forth across the stage between groups of characters playing different scenes. This "switchback editing" technique also appears in subsequent Shepard plays in the 1970s, but for the most part he chose to refine his narrative approach while adhering to the more theatrical convention of the single set. By 1972, Shepard could, with some justification, describe one such fixed-location piece, *The Tooth of Crime*, as being "built like *High Noon*, like a machine western."[12]

The basic plotlines Shepard creates for these plays almost invariably pit his protagonist-heroes against forces of authority or government which are seeking to oppress or imprison them, stifling their individualistic impulses. The ostensible project for most of the characters is therefore to try to free themselves. Yet they rarely, if ever, succeed. In *Melodrama Play*, for example, Duke and friends try to break out of the room that Floyd, the record company boss, has locked them in: they are systematically battered into oblivion by Peter, a stereotypical thug dressed in a police-type uniform. In *Forensic and the Navigators*, Forensic and Emmett plan how to liberate the captives of a giant desert fortress (reminiscent of the all-controlling desert factory in *La Turista*), only to be foiled by the preemptive invasion of the Exterminators, dressed in highway patrol outfits with giant gas guns. The allusions to authority become even more obvious in *The Unseen Hand*, in which Willie the Space Freak seeks help in freeing the oppressed races of Nogoland – a land which, with its southern swamps and northeastern rulers in the Capitol, is a thinly veiled metaphor for the United States itself. The eponymous hand is a brand on the heads of the people of Nogoland, which limits their brain patterns and sends them into violent fits of pain if the prescribed limits are exceeded. This theme of the brutal suppression of nonconformity is made explicit in *Operation Sidewinder*, as the Young Man rails against an American society in which "you'll be arrested, accosted, molested, tested and retested. You'll be beaten, you'll be jailed . . . decapitated, dehumanized, defoliated, demented and damned" (226). Such speeches hint at a kind of Orwellian nightmare: the heroes' unorthodox individuality is not to be tolerated, and is hunted down and flushed out. The theme was a common one in the late '60s: in George Roy Hill's film *Butch Cassidy and the Sundance Kid* (1969), for example, two Wild West outlaws are tracked to their deaths by faceless lawmen.

It would be far too simplistic, however, to infer from all this that Shepard was simply embracing the emerging counterculture's agenda of unambiguous opposition to existing power structures. He resigned as screenwriter for *Zabriskie Point* in 1968 precisely because he did not share Antonioni's desire to "make a political statement about contemporary youth, write in a lot of Marxist jargon and Black Power speeches."[13] Indeed, in some respects, *Operation Sidewinder* (despite crediting Antonioni as a "keen inspiration") is a blatant mockery of that film's themes, focusing as it does around a ludicrous Yippie-style plot to put dope in an air force base's reservoir and thus liberate the minds of the benighted military. The play relentlessly ridicules the utopian dreams of both revolutionary radicals and hippie flower children as equally futile. If there is anything attractive for Shepard in the various counterculture figures he presents, it is simply their underlying insistence on personal freedom. There is, for example, a delightfully defiant quality about the rhetoric of the revolutionary, Geez, in *Shaved Splits*: "everywhere I walk, sit, stand or lie down," he announces casually, "is liberated territory."[14] Politics itself, however, is unable to solve anything. Blue's historical account in *The Unseen Hand*, for example, mixes the Kennedy assassination with futuristic whimsy to create an ironically resigned vision of political failure:

> Things change overnight now. One day there's a President, the next day he gets shot, the next day the guy who shot him gets shot. . . . Then they change the government from capitalism to socialism because the government's afraid of a full-blown insurrection. Then they have a revolution anyhow and things stay just like they was.   (16)

Shepard's rejection of political radicalism seems to have stemmed partly from a conviction that even those in supposed positions of power are themselves not so much exploiters as co-victims with the exploited. Far from presenting authority figures as evil geniuses, he tends to show the ostensibly powerful as being every bit as confused and bemused as the powerless: Floyd is desperate for a new record, Peter is a helpless child, and the Exterminators seem far more interested in groping Oolan than in capturing Forensic and Emmett. Even the more sinister scientists and military men in *Operation Sidewinder* are highly parodic (the wheelchair-bound Doctor Vector is a blatant reference to Stanley Kubrick's 1963 film *Dr. Strangelove*), and are made to appear ridiculous when their expensive sidewinder computer escapes its cage, and when the homely rambling of old Billy renders their pompous interrogation tactics useless.

Shepard's refusal to see the powerful as bogeymen is brought out most clearly in *Shaved Splits*, a savage satire on bourgeois complacency. Miss Cherry hides in her "fuzzy pink womb" of a bedroom, waited on by various bizarre servants, trying in vain to construct a safe, "comfy and warm" world for herself through the escape fantasy of pornographic novels (from which the play's title is derived). But the revolution is raging outside, and her world is invaded by Geez, a gun-toting rebel who takes her hostage. Returning home to violence and chaos, Cherry's husband, D.T. (the name suggests alcoholism and nervous tension), is forced to admit that his and

Cherry's rich lifestyle is "a losing battle against reality." He has wasted his life in an attempt to find a comfortable niche, and has been swallowed up by a faceless machine: "I could have had a life of my own. . . . You get caught up for no reason. I just found myself in a corporation. Incorporated. Nice operation" (197). This tale of lost innocence, of a promising life being stifled, is poignantly intercut with Geez's vivid description of a beautiful deer being slaughtered: "one blast that shatters the whole forest. Everything bolts and screams. The doe twists in a circle, the rear end sinking into the ground, the front hooves thrashing, the head points straight at the sky" (198).

The entrapment that Shepard portrays in these plays is not, on balance, the result of some calculated conspiracy from above, which one can fight directly. Rather, individuals find themselves conditioned by social structures which have developed their own insidious logic. The songs in *Melodrama Play* make this especially clear, by expanding the frame of reference from Duke's particular entrapment, and referring to a whole range of influences – from family and friends to hometown and employers – which inhibit any attempt to achieve self-realization, keeping the victim "in either Sing Sing or Alcatraz" (122). It is this subjection to "unseen hands," to "a certain terrorism in the air" of contemporary culture (as Sycamore Morphan has it), which represents the most recurrent theme at this stage of Shepard's work. As such, it also clearly indicates a movement toward the type of postmodernist perspective which views the mechanics of power not in the traditional binary terms of oppressor and victim, but as being altogether more complex and bewildering. "Everybody," he suggested in a 1973 article, "is caught up in a fractured world that they can't even see. What's happening to them is unfathomable but they have a suspicion. Something unseen is working on them. Using them. They have no power and all the time they believe they're controlling the situation."[15]

This more personalized vision of mysterious, self-perpetuating forces pushing the world toward fragmentation and the individual toward terminal insignificance (effectively a development of Shepard's earlier, less specific fear of the forces of civilization) becomes particularly prevalent in the plays written in 1971. By this time Shepard had lost interest in any pretense at political references, possibly because satirizing the idealism of late-'60s youth culture had lost its appeal in the new mood of numbed disillusionment which was setting in. This change of emphasis is evident in the development of *Back Bog Beast Bait*. Shepard's original 1969 notes, headed "Beast Play," refer to a beast (lurking somewhere outside the swamp shack which is the set, and which therefore becomes another kind of prison) that is somehow representative of the system, armed with technologically advanced weaponry, set to castrate mankind. But by the time *Beast Bait* emerged in 1971, after postponements and considerable rewriting, the beast had become more of a supernatural scourge, composed of elements from horror movies and comic books. Moreover, when it appears at the play's (anti)climax, the beast, too, seems lost and bewildered, unable to account for the chaos which has beset the house.

Similarly, in *The Mad Dog Blues*, Kosmo is haunted by dreams of global apocalypse ("I see the whole world going up in smoke. . . . Wild dogs circling": 277–8), but the play's plot makes no reference to power struggles, concentrating exclusively on the personal crises of the characters. The source of Kosmo and Yahoodi's anxiety lies in their immediate social circumstances: the shattered city is tearing them apart. Yahoodi, for example, has a speech describing the crowded New York subway full of people who "couldn't care less" about each other: "And how separate we were" (260). *Cowboy Mouth*, also written that year, takes this sense of urban fragmentation to a feverish extreme. Set in a version of the room which Shepard and Patti Smith temporarily shared in New York's Chelsea Hotel, the piece at times pushes its language and pacing to the verge of hysteria, as the protagonists strive to create a savior (in the form of a perfect rock hero) who will heal "all the broken, busted-up pieces of people's frustration" (156). But the struggle is in vain, a fact acknowledged by the bitter ironies of the play, and by Shepard's final exit from New York later the same year. "And far off," he noted in *Hawk Moon*, "you could hear the sound of America cracking open and crashing into the sea" (126).

Fragmentation

Shepard's sense of apocalyptic breakdown, of a hopelessly "fractured world," while often being explicitly stated in the plots, dialogue, and song lyrics of these plays, is communicated most powerfully and consistently through their fractured construction. For the ostensible linearity of these narratives is constantly in danger of breaking up into total incoherence, and although – especially in some of the earlier pieces – this sometimes appears to be simply the result of carelessness or awkwardness with the form, it seems clear that Shepard pursued such "indiscipline" as a deliberate policy. He seems to have allowed his conflicting impulses toward random spontaneity and conscious structure to play off against each other, thereby creating a dangerous tension between the underlying story line and the disjointed, moment-by-moment succession of events. These plays, far from retreating from modernist collage to a more stable, conservative narrative form, imply a postmodernist fear that the incoherent fragments of experience cannot be bound together, except in a string of events connected only by the most arbitrary and blatantly artificial premises.

Ironically enough, Shepard's interest in rock music may well have been an influence on this concern with fragmentation, as well as on the more direct, linear aspects of the plays' construction. This is indicated most clearly by the music he himself was playing with the Holy Modal Rounders. Where the influence of Charles Mingus had suggested the weaving together of diverse musical themes into a sophisticated collage effect, the Rounders simply took wild ideas and threw them together, without regard for coherence, to create a kind of comic-psychedelic chaos. The one album that they recorded on a major label while Shepard was with them, the bizarrely titled *The Moray Eels Eat the Holy Modal Rounders* (Elektra, 1968), contains not one conventional, formulaic rock song: instead it is composed of jarring fragments (including cartoon voices and a cappella ramblings) which run into each other without breaks or logical transitions. The lyrical content, too, often points to a sense of mental fragmentation, via both crazed ramblings ("If you wanna be a bird . . .") and bleakly ironic self-analysis ("Once upon a time / I had quite a time / Having all of my mind"). The record concludes with Shepard himself delivering a depraved version of the Pledge of Allegiance while backed by a caterwauling chorus of "America the Beautiful." Taken as a whole, the album is ample demonstration of a tendency which these self-proclaimed "subliminal motherfuckers" shared with other avant-garde bands, such as the Velvet Underground (a major influence on Shepard), toward wild oscillations between straightforward, driving rhythms and melodies, and disjointed, more or less atonal noise effects.

It is this kind of tension that Shepard was feeding into the construction of his plays in this period. Retaining his interest in the unpredictability of the theatrical moment, he used the linear narrative format as little more than a convenient peg on which to hang a succession of set pieces, and freely exercised his penchant for flying off at tangents. Characters tend to burst into sudden, performative fits of language or song with little or no provocation, and indeed in most cases the plays are composed more of tangents than of narrative. In *The Unseen Hand*, Blue Morphan's rambling opening speech to himself is followed firstly by a lengthy, apoplectic fit of sci-fi jargon performed by Willie the Space Freak, and then by the Kid's catalogue of revolutionary jargon and delirious listing of the virtues of American life, Willie's recitation of that same speech backward, and Sycamore's final, anticlimactic mutterings. Shepard, throughout all this, pushes his development of each separate performance to its limit, so that the thread of the narrative itself is constantly in danger of being lost. The audience has to struggle to keep hold of the through-line, only to find their desire for a satisfactory denouement frustrated by the abruptly aborted and wildly contrived conclusion. The overall effect is to create a kind of bizarre rock opera, a loosely grouped series of incongruous performances strung together on a narrative as tenuous as the links joining the fragments of the *Moray Eels* album. Arthur Sainer's *Village Voice* review of *Shaved Splits* neatly summarizes the crazily disorientating impact of this unorthodox approach: "Sam has a kind of B-movie mind. He cuts the plot to ribbons, zooms in for giant, bubble-gum close-ups, and stands cheering from the sidelines. . . . The plays cohere by virtue of an almost primeval enthusiasm."[16]

In some of these plays, the tension between narrative and random events is made particularly obvious. In *Melodrama Play* (another piece composed largely of individual turns), the entire storyline is hijacked from the rock star Duke by the unexpected intervention of Peter, who takes over the central focus and sends the events off in a totally new direction. In *The Mad Dog Blues*, narrative instability is raised to the level of explicit theme, as Kosmo and Yahoodi escape the city by disappearing into a hallucinatory odyssey, imagining a journey through jungles and across oceans. The proceedings gradually acquire their own deranged momentum and descend into chaos, driving Yahoodi to attempted suicide, and Kosmo to the desperate cry: "It's out of control. The whole thing's crashing in on me" (298). The narrative finally disintegrates completely, and the characters are left wandering hopelessly around the stage, calling out to each other but unable to reestablish any kind of contact or coherence.

In one sense, Kosmo and Yahoodi's entire crazy journey is a drug-induced mind-trip, and it must be acknowledged that one major cause of the sense of fragmentation Shepard himself felt in the late '60s was his own use of drugs, which had gone beyond speed to acid and other hallucinogens, and had escalated beyond his control. "My state of mind wasn't the best," he confessed years later: "In fact it was probably worse than it ever was in my entire life."[17] Shepard's drug experiences often fed directly into these plays. Some of Kosmo and Yahoodi's apocalyptic visions, for example, such as that of the eagle seizing the earth in its talons, are lifted almost verbatim from the "Notes on a Hallucination Meditation" which appear in one of Shepard's notebooks from this period. *Back Bog Beast Bait*, rather like a staged extract from Hunter Thompson's gonzo journalism, depicts characters eating magic mushrooms and transforming into various crazed animals. Most extreme of all is the *Hawk Moon* prose collection, which is full of hallucinatory material that sometimes seems to border on the psychotic. It is hardly surprising that Shepard decided he had to kick his habit: one of his stated intentions in fleeing New York for London in 1971 was to try to get off drugs.

It would be a mistake, however, to write off the instability inherent in these plays as resulting simply from the ramblings of a drug-addled mind. Throughout this period, Shepard's finger remained firmly on the cultural pulse: indeed, it could even be argued that his drug habit was a key reason for this. The prevalence of drug abuse at this time was regarded by many as a reflection and a symptom, rather than a cause, of America's social fragmentation. As Shepard himself put it, "Junk, heroin, and all that stuff is a social condition and it's also an emotional response to . . . society."[18] The Velvet Underground song "Heroin" (the nightmarish sound of which Shepard wrote into the opening of *The Tooth of Crime*) states this view even more bluntly: "I have made a big decision, to nullify my life," so as to get "away from the big city / where a man cannot be free." Similarly, in Thomas Pynchon's novel *The Crying of Lot 49* (1965), Oedipa Maas's husband, Mucho, dissipates his mind through LSD, so as to escape the responsibility of confronting an insane world. The fragmentation of Shepard's work represents an integral part of his growing concern with contemporary cultural conditions.

Pollock to Warhol

Shepard's loss of faith in the authenticity of automatic writing, his concern with the imprisoning effect of unseen hands, and his growing sense of cultural fragmentation, are all brought together in these plays through his exploitation of the chaotic languages and images of popular culture. This tendency, which first emerged strongly in *La Turista* (with its various references to magazines, cigarette brands, movie stereotypes, and other plastic Americana), was pushed to extremes in *Melodrama Play*, and thereafter became a staple of Shepard's writing. The inspiration for this new direction seems to have come from a somewhat belated recognition on Shepard's part of the impact of pop art, whose key practitioners (including Andy Warhol, Roy Lichtenstein, and James Rosenquist) had, beginning in the early '60s, transplanted the abstract expressionists as the dominant figures on the American art scene. Pop art took the familiar imagery of mass consumer culture – from soup cans to billboards – and transformed them into huge, colorful gallery displays which simultaneously celebrated and ironized their subject matter. In casually rejecting modernist notions of originality, depth, and texture, and in its obsession with surfaces and the repetition of familiar images, pop represented one of the earliest and most distinctive manifestations of the postmodern sensibility in the arts.

Shepard moved in the same direction by drawing on a hugely eclectic range of pop-cultural sources. The tenuous narratives of the rock plays relentlessly parody, and sometimes openly plagiarize, the formulaic plots of films, television serials, and popular novels. *The Mad Dog Blues*, for example, suggests a bizarre combination of elements from sources as diverse as *The Treasure of the Sierra Madre*, *The Wizard of Oz*, and *Huckleberry Finn*. The characterizations are also mostly built from pop stereotypes, including not only rock stars and cowboys but also Indians, spacemen, cartoon authority figures, and, in *Mad Dog Blues*, comic portrayals of the movie stars Mae West and Marlene Dietrich – a move reminiscent of Warhol's pop treatments of Marilyn Monroe, Liz Taylor, and so forth. Even the plays' settings tend to be composed of the debris of pop Americana literally so in some cases. (It is notable that where the domestic garbage required for the set for *4-H Club* had been nonspecific, generic garbage, the trash on the sets of *The Unseen Hand* and *Cowboy Mouth* is carefully detailed: Coke bottles, Nescafe, southern license plates, even a full-size 1951 Chevrolet convertible.) The hermetically sealed fantasy worlds of the earlier work are replaced with ostensible real-world locations in New York, Arizona, Mexico, Louisiana, but these are environments conjured up by a kind of pop-iconic shorthand rather than by any attempt at realism. Azusa, for example, the setting for *The Unseen Hand*, is the suburb of Los Angeles adjacent to Shepard's hometown of Duarte, but the name is used here simply as an evocation of the qualities of "junk magic" and "accidentalness" he associates with southern California. The play takes place in a garbage dump next to a highway, and Azusa becomes an American Everytown: "Everything from 'A' to 'Z' in the USA."

It should be noted that some of Shepard's specific cultural references are located very firmly in the 1960s, and at times make these plays, like

many of the key pop art pieces themselves, seem somewhat dated in ret-
rospect – more so, in fact, than the earlier plays. But along with pop's cultural specificity, Shepard also adopted the form's less immediately transient concern with brash colorfulness and extravagance (this also acts as a
complement to the aggressive loudness of the rock influence). The characters' outfits and bizarre personal props are carefully described so as to
ensure sufficient showiness, and (in the wake of Kent's cartoon leap
through the back of *La Turista's* set) Shepard also began to concoct
overtly theatrical special effects. Colleagues such as Tom O'Horgan had
assured him that he should feel free to write whatever stage directions he
wanted (as a director, O'Horgan has always thrived on finding ways to
stage the seemingly impossible), and Shepard responded by jettisoning
his previous care over economy and practicality. Hence the colored Ping-
Pong balls raining from the roof in *The Unseen Hand,* the colored gas
engulfing the audience in *Forensic,* and the welter of machine-gun fire
and torrents of stage blood in *Shaved Splits. Operation Sidewinder,* of
course, set in a series of locations from laboratories to deserts, takes this
self-conscious, cinematically inflected theatricality furthest: cars drive on,
and one is hoisted on a hydraulic lift; there are banks of computers, a pit
full of live snakes, elaborate lighting effects suggesting everything from
desert storms to UFOs, and even a six-foot-long self-propelling sidewinder snake. Though Shepard subsequently regretted going so far with
all this, since it made the play impossible to stage anywhere smaller than
Lincoln Center – where it was, he says, "a total disaster" – he clearly rel-
ished the chance to indulge himself to this extent.

There was, of course, nothing intrinsically new in Shepard's adoption
of pop art and pop culture influences in his playwriting. Indeed, so far as
New York audiences were concerned, he was somewhat behind the times:
the exploitation of pop iconography had been one of the distinguishing
features of Off-Off-Broadway ever since Joel Oppenheimer's play *The
Great American Desert* (built on the stereotypes and formal devices of the
western genre) had inaugurated the work of the Judson Poets' Theatre in
1961. Yet Shepard now pushed his combination of pop quotation and
chaotic theatrics further than almost any of his contemporaries. The
notable exceptions would be the playwrights of the Theatre of the Ridiculous, Charles Ludlam and Ronald Tavel, whose plays display a range of
random quotations surpassing even Shepard's. This comparison is a useful one in highlighting the distinctiveness of Shepard's work at this time.
The Ridiculous plays, like a great deal of other Off-Off-Broadway output,
were written and performed by members of New York's underground gay

community, and their emphasis was on the use of a kind of consciously decadent camp which rendered nonsensical the familiar, socially conditioned expectations about gender roles and "moral" (monogamous heterosexual) behavior.[19] Shepard's work reflects the spirit of the times with a certain tendency toward the jokey manipulation of camp incongruity: in *Mad Dog Blues*, for example, he rewrote the pirate, Captain Kidd, as "moral and self-righteous," and created a love affair between Marlene Dietrich and folk-legend Paul Bunyan. Yet Shepard's approach also suggests an element of serious critique, as opposed to pure ridicule: these plays create a sense of emotional distanciation and hollowness rather than of knowing decadence.

As Shepard's introductory note to *Melodrama Play* has it: "everything about the play should be abrupt and flashy." By marrying noise, energy, and excitement with a curiously alienated gaze, these plays capture something of "the supreme formal feature" of postmodernism: "a new kind of flatness or depthlessness, a new kind of superficiality in the most literal sense."[20] Unlike the camp effusiveness of many of his Off-Off-Broadway contemporaries, Shepard's work also recalls pop art's "cooler" qualities, as well as its coy celebrationism. To see Roy Lichtenstein's giant cartoon frames at full scale (benday dots no longer creating a general illusion of color but looking like huge blobs vainly attempting to fill the empty expanse of white canvas), or Warhol's multiple Marilyns side by side with his relentlessly repeated images of electric chairs and car crashes, can be acutely disturbing. There is a detached, affectless quality about these paintings that implicitly questions the very mass-production methods (photography, silk-screening, printing) by which they are produced. Shepard's rock plays achieve something similar to this, in that their visceral impact cannot disguise the fundamental lack of real emotional depth. Witness, for example, the extreme violence of the multiple shootings in *Sidewinder* and *Shaved Splits*. These fail to elicit horror because they are treated less as murders than as neutral, almost incidental occurrences – "I'm dying!" screams D.T.; "Knock yourself out!" Geez suggests helpfully (195). Yet the very casualness of such moments is likely to create a paradoxical tension in the audience, as does Warhol's series of "Death and Disaster" paintings, in which human agony is treated with cool disinterest, as if the artist were simply reflecting the passionlessness with which the television viewer absorbs horrific news every day. Reviewing an Off-Broadway double bill of *Forensic* and *The Unseen Hand* in 1970, *New York Times* critic Clive Barnes found himself forced to acknowledge that these plays, however seemingly disposable, "linger oddly in the imagination," leaving

Newspaper advertisement for the 1970 Off-Broadway production of *The Unseen Hand* and *Forensic and the Navigators*, illustrating the extent to which Shepard's work was being presented as theatrical pop art during this period.

a "disenchanting and disturbing" aftertaste precisely because they *are* so unremittingly superficial: "His themes of disaster are so vast, [yet] his off-hand methods so casual."[21]

The discomforting impact of this "casual" approach is exacerbated by the seemingly slapdash way in which Shepard juxtaposes his diverse pop references, thereby creating worlds almost completely lacking in stability or coherence. Having apparently conceded, with *Cowboys #2* and *Melodrama Play*, postmodernism's skepticism toward the idea of the writer's unique, homogenous presence being captured in his or her work, his writing here embraces heterogeneity with a vengeance. Whereas the early plays had displayed the modernist penchant for drawing diverse sources together through consistent stylization, so that each character speaks with a variation on a single voice (the author's own), the rock plays – contrarily – mix together incompatible materials in such a way as to *highlight* the tensions and gaps between them.

This *bricolage* approach is immediately evident in the jarring diversity of vocal styles Shepard employs in these plays: not only multiple forms of melodramatic movie-speak, but also parodic, rhythmic variations on numerous "real-world" American accents and idiolects. *Operation Sidewinder*, in attempting to paint a broad, cartoon canvas of America in the late '60s, takes this tendency furthest, with vocal styles ranging from the black jive-talk of Blood and Dude to the pompous authoritarianism of Captain Bovine, and from the Spanish babble of the Apache braves to the old-time homilies of Billy, the gold prospector. Yet this kind of linguistic fragmentation is ultimately less significant than Shepard's wild juxtapositions of incompatible plot elements. Settings, genres and time zones career into each other without logical cause, creating an impression akin to that of multiple television stations all competing for attention on the same wavelength. In *Back Bog Beast Bait*, two refugees from a Western arrive in a gothicized Southern swamp-shack, encountering monsters, voodoo rituals, and a deranged priest reciting lengthy quotations from the Book of Revelation. In *Shaved Splits* the revolution invades the boudoir of a porn queen. In *The Holy Ghostly* a would-be New York rock star meets Indian demons in the middle of the desert while his father totes a bazooka. In both *The Unseen Hand* and *Operation Sidewinder*, images of the past and future mingle into an incoherent present, as figures from the Old West of a century ago are found wandering around the contemporary Southwest, bumping into hippies, schoolchildren, and tourists, and becoming caught up in plots lifted out of science fiction.

Shepard shares this tendency for colliding incongruous fragments with postmodernist novelists as diverse as Kurt Vonnegut and Angela Carter, each of whom could be said to presenting visions of "heterotopia," Michel Foucault's term for "the disorder in which fragments of a large number of possible orders glitter separately in the dimension, without law or geometry."[22] This idea is exhibited in glorious microcosm in *Shaved Splits*, in which Chunky Puke's seemingly endless list of pulp fiction titles ranges from "Sheba Meets the Warlock" to "The Castrated Male in American Society" to "Cheeseburger Hard-On" (172–3). Clearly there is a degree of facetious humour involved here, but the joke suggests a serious point; namely that this jumbled confusion of contradictory discourses (fiction, history, science, trash, lies: which is which?) is representative of how the world is experienced in postmodern culture. As Mae West declares in the midst of the media-inspired confusion that is *The Mad Dog Blues*: "This is real life" (273).

Character as Void

If the depthlessness and fragmentation of these plays throws into question the nature of reality, Shepard's presentation of character throws into doubt the idea of humanity itself. Again, the link here is to pop art: whereas Pollock had sought to project his essence, his human presence, onto each canvas, the mechanistically produced superficiality of pop, ceaselessly repeating variations on the same tired images, was utterly soulless. Andy Warhol's cool resignation to antihumanism in both his art and his public persona (in which he played out his stated belief that people should behave like machines) epitomized a growing awareness that the very notion of originality or personal authenticity was becoming obsolete. Similarly, in Shepard's rock plays, characters are not even permitted the tenuous, blurred, but nevertheless creative characteristics given to the tricksters. Flesh-and-blood actors are reduced to the status of plastic cartoons: created from the assemblage of incoherent fragments, and lacking any sense of center or wholeness, these figures fight, fall in and out of love, even murder each other, with alarming speed, noise, and regularity, and with a minimum of emotional expenditure. The effect is typified by Cherry's ranting, which forms an insistent, highly volatile, and totally affectless cocktail of philosophical insight, political comment, obscenity, racist offense, and teenage jargon: "Neato jet. Super keen. Out a' sight. Far fuckin' out!" (168).

The plays thus question the idea that there is any essential basis to behavior. This point is enunciated explicitly in *Forensic and the Navigators*, in which Emmett advocates the adoption of artificial personae as a defensive maneuver vital to survival, stressing that this should be no mere act, but a wholesale adjustment of attitudes: "we have to switch our sensibilities so that we're not even pretending. So that we are transformed" (158). Such abrupt and inexplicable channel-hopping (a new and more serious variant on the "transformation" game visible in earlier plays) is commonplace among the figures in these plays – perhaps the most unnerving is the Kid's total about-face from sophisticated revolutionary jargon to reactionary hysteria in *The Unseen Hand*. Character is simply surface image: the outside eye cannot see behind the mask, a mask which perhaps hides nothing but another mask anyway. Visually, the idea is underlined most simply and effectively by Shepard's frequent insistence that his characters wear dark glasses (in *Melodrama Play* nobody is without them). This is not merely another exercise in fashion cool: an insuperable distance is forced between audience and actors, whose eyes – the windows to the soul? – are completely obscured.

It might be argued that such deliberate flattening and emptying out of character cheapens the entire theatrical event, and indeed some of Shepard's stereotyping seems just too easy. *Sidewinder*'s parodic depiction of radical black "dudes," for example, was (at the very least) insensitive to the genuine sense of outrage felt by many African Americans at their continued abuse and marginalization in a white-dominated society. (The play's intended premiere at Yale was abandoned after protests by black students. Lincoln Center appeased its conscience by appointing a black director, Michael Schultz.) Similarly, the depiction of female characters in both *Sidewinder* and *Shaved Splits* as sex-starved bimbos is nothing short of offensive. In the former play, Honey is raped twice (by the snake and the Young Man) and enjoys it, while in the latter (as with some of Tom Wesselman's pop paintings) the parody of dehumanizing pornography steers perilously close to becoming pornographic in itself, thanks to the lengthy voice-over extracts from pulp novels, and Cherry's seminaked writhing as she reads them. But if these plays are at times guilty of an incipient racism and sexism (and Shepard was hardly alone at this time in his unexamined prejudices), it should also be stressed that there is a quite deliberate cheapness about *all* the characterizations – white, black, male, female, alien. The effect is to depict contemporary life as a meaningless spiritual void.

The crucial paradox here is that many of Shepard's helplessly plastic people are also seen to be *seeking* a depth and a stable reality which the superficiality of the plays denies them. There is a humanistic desire to locate and affirm the existence of an essential self, an appeal to the ideal of rooted, centered, self-knowing identity, even within the savagely dehumanized environments depicted. And yet this impulse is portrayed as one which is as desperate and futile as the desire to escape entrapment. In *Melodrama Play*, the bodyguard Peter, who appears initially to be little more than two-dimensional set dressing, takes center stage to inquire urgently just who he is supposed to be: "I'd like to ask you what you think of me as a person . . . I want to know what I'm like, that's all. Not anything else" (136–9). Nobody is able to provide him with an adequate response, and his only means to provoke any reaction at all is to club the other characters into submission one by one. In doing so, he simply reinforces his inescapable status as a cartoon thug.

Such savage ironies litter these plays. The basic urge of the central cowboy and rock star figures toward self-assertion and independence is seen to be self-defeating, since they seek to realize this through the adoption of ostentatious names and costumes, and through noisy performances of songs and rants. These seem to be predicated on the assumption that, in this postmodern world, an individual can only gain personal attention through self-display so spectacular and obtrusive as to *demand* attention. And yet there is nothing in this kind of posturing to suggest any intrinsic personal identity: as Cavale damningly notes in her assessment of Mick Jagger in *Cowboy Mouth*, "he got too conscious . . . He's not whole" (156). These performances constitute a more extreme version of the tricksters' narcissistic attempts to attract an audience, but where the tricksters had at least been driven by some sense of underlying emotional need, the rock stars project only surface style. As I discovered directing *Melodrama Play*, the notion of playing "outside the character" is actualized here in that actors have to push outward, self-conscious display to extremes, to embody the cliché as fully as possible (as opposed to embodying, say, fear). Their crippling lack of personal depth is also evident in the characters' fates, as when Duke Durgens – though claiming to be an inspirational rock legend – turns out to be a fraud who stole the song that made him famous.

The characters' adopted "handles" are similarly problematic, since they have no firmly established signifier-signified relationship with their owners, and so tend to detach themselves and float freely. In *Forensic*, for example, the name Forensic itself is used at different times to address almost every character in the play, while in *Melodrama Play* Drake and Cisco's names are swapped so often that an audience could be forgiven for losing track of which is which. *The Holy Ghostly* makes this loss of rooted identity explicit as the old man, Pop, berates his son's foolishness in abandoning his given name, Stanley Hewitt Moss the seventh, and taking on the title "Ice." In cutting himself off from his roots in this way, and inventing an artificial persona, Ice has made himself homeless, and exposed himself to the destabilizing forces of the culture around him: his true instincts, Pop tells him, have "been shot to shit in that damn city" (180).

Clearly this exchange was of particular poignancy for the author himself, who feels, as one acquaintance notes, "some kind of uneasiness" about being Sam Shepard: "He'll let you know in a very short time that he's really Sam Shepard Rogers the seventh."[23] Indeed, *Holy Ghostly* reads partly as an attempted antidote to the fragmentation of personality: it has less in the way of pop bricolage than most plays of this period, and contains lengthy passages detailing a family history which matches Shepard's own almost word for word. In such personal material, perhaps, there is the assurance of something unique to oneself, which cannot be stripped away. And yet in going back to his roots, Ice also makes himself vulnerable to abuse and domination by his father, the very influence he had sought to escape by rejecting his name. This Catch-22 dilemma is a recurrent trap in these plays: those who cannot (artificially) define themselves are either anonymous or arbitrarily defined according to another's perspective. "Hey, what's your name anyway?" the Young Man in *Sidewinder* is asked by his equally directionless companion: "Do you have a name? My name's Honey. That's because my husband called me that" (224). With or without a name, it would seem, the characters in these plays are adrift, their lives as broken and confused as the worlds they inhabit.

The futile search for direction and identity is developed furthest in *The Mad Dog Blues*. Kosmo just wants to be unique, and to express his essential self in the form of "my own special music" (286). Yet he has no idea what this might sound like, and so resorts to self-invention, trying on different personae in search of "a different me" which will give him a sense of fulfillment (268). Abandoning his initial role as rock star, he flirts with images of himself as a son (he imagines hunting for his father, who tells him to "fuck off"), a husband and father (he arbitrarily invents a family for himself), and even as a flower child and political radical. Yet when he declares that the revolution is on, Mae West simply responds, "What channel?" (262). Kosmo's search for salvation seems doomed because the roles he tries are all simply secondhand ideas borrowed from a limited range of cultural sideshows. He cannot be sure that anything he thinks or feels is the product of authentic personal experience, rather than merely a figment of something he has seen on television: "I have an awful memory of places I never was!" (273). His entire imaginative odyssey is composed of the figments of popular culture, which have even colonized his dream life. Meanwhile, his companion Yahoodi, who feels that he is "so many different people at once" (273), is so lacking in individuality that he finds himself helplessly reenacting the murder scene from *Treasure of the Sierra Madre*. The duo share the same degree of depthless transience as all the other characters, who are mere products of their drug-induced hallucinations. The search for firm identity itself, *Mad Dog Blues* implies, is just another hallucination.

These plays, then, depict a contemporary America in which people are hollow shells, their perceptions swamped by the meaningless trivia of an illusory cultural environment which they themselves come to mirror. "Society is a ghost that everyone becomes the image of," Shepard wrote in his notes. Moreover, this unseen hand of the postmodern condition is inescapable. Ridiculing the utopian fantasizing of the flower children and Marxists, Shepard consigns his heroes to ignominious defeat in their struggle to overcome the more or less invisible forces that oppress them. How do you rebel against nothing-in-particular? Shepard's immediate response to the pressure he felt in New York was to run away, but on the broader scale, as Geez bluntly remarks at the end of *Shaved Splits*, "There's nowhere to go. This is it. Dead end city" (195).

Fantasy Escapes

Even given the bleakness of this perspective, however, the plays persist in trying to envisage a way out, a transcendent glimpse of a free life beyond the pressure of these conditioning forces. Despite his characters' failure to discover any firm sense of self on which to fall back, Shepard continued to maintain a paradoxical belief in a human essence which exists within the socially determined exterior. Even as he was dissolving the traditional oppressor/victim version of social relations, he was attempting to prop up another kind of binary split:

> You have this personality, and somehow you feel locked into it, jailed by all of your cultural influences and your psychological ones from your family, and all that. And somehow I feel that that isn't the whole of it,

that there's another possibility. . . . You can't escape, that's the whole thing, you can't, but there is always that impulse towards another kind of world, something that doesn't necessarily confine you in that way.[24]

This notion of an alienated division between the inner and outer self is manifested in various ways in the plays, perhaps the most explicit being some of the song lyrics written for pieces like *Melodrama Play* and *Operation Sidewinder*. The latter's "Alien Song" is a prime example:

Now I can see my whole body
Stranded way down by the creek
It looks so alone while it looks for its home
And it doesn't hear me while I shriek.   (229)

This image, reminiscent of Edvard Munch's high modernist painting "The Scream," indicates the limits of Shepard's initial move toward the postmodernist perspective – a position according to which the very idea of personal angst, deriving from a sense of authentic inner depth, is not only philosophically suspect but utterly meaningless in a culture founded on pure surface image. Shepard appears to have been unwilling to accept this view wholesale, and as a result there is in the rock plays a fundamentally unresolved contradiction between his bleak, fragmented view of plasticized character, and his underlying faith in "another possibility." This position was, in fact, characteristic of the period. In 1967, for example, R. D. Laing asked grimly, "are persons possible in our present situation? . . . Is love possible? Is freedom possible?" Yet he also insisted that cynical resignation was no answer, and that there was a transcendent, if neglected, dimension of human life: "We are bemused and crazed creatures, strangers to our true selves. . . . Humanity is estranged from its authentic possibilities."[25]

Shepard seems to have seen it as the function of his art, at least in part, to present the imaginative possibility of a liberation from cultural determinism. The plainest example of this exorcistic tendency is in *The Unseen Hand*, when the half-naked Kid delivers a maniacal speech exposing his junkie-like subjection to pop culture ephemera: "I love the foothills and the drive-in movies and the bowling alleys and the football games and the drag races and the girls and the donut shop . . ." (28). Willie follows this up by reciting the entire speech backward, as if to call it back from ever having been spoken. This act, he says, releases the people of Nogoland from the unseen hand. Of course, as Shepard was well aware, the notion of shedding one's cultural baggage like this is an impossible fantasy. But he seems to have felt that the very act of imagining such liberation might in some way inspire his audience to look at things from a fresh perspective.

Shepard's fantastic visions of liberation often take on a blatantly spiritual dimension. In this respect his plays bear a tangential connection to the work, during the same period, of ensemble companies like Julian Beck and Judith Malina's Living Theatre, or Richard Schechner's Performance Group, who were trying to restore to the theatre a sense of prelapsarian communality through their neo-Dionysian rites (or "group gropes," to the skeptics), and their appeals to shamanism or Eastern spirituality. Such groups claimed to be appealing to the unifying power of universal myth, but in practice were effectively setting up another binary opposition between the West (read "decadent materialism") and the supposed spiritual wisdom of the primitive. Shepard followed suit, embracing the same tendency to romanticize otherness. In *Shaved Splits*, for example, an explicit contrast is drawn between desacralized Occidentals and mystical Orientals, and at the play's conclusion Cherry's Chinese manservant, Wong, goes into a trance dance which magically exorcises Geez's anxieties: the chaos of the battle outside suddenly just stops and Geez becomes silent, poetic, at peace. Similarly, *Operation Sidewinder* presents the first and most explicit of Shepard's recurring references to the Hopi Indians of Arizona, another culture seen as being more in touch with the spiritual. In act 2 scene 2, the Spider Lady (an old shaman, according to the script, but also the name of the Hopi equivalent of Mother Nature) recounts a sci-fi version of the Hopi myth of the Fall, which concludes that humanity can only be saved, and the gods restored to the earth, by holistically reuniting the divided realms of material and spiritual need. Shepard's specifications for the mysterious atmosphere of the Spider Lady's scene makes it clear that – as with the initiation rite in *La Turista* – his intentions are serious: "You must see the truth of this myth I have told you" (235). The play then climaxes with an enactment of this longed-for redemption, as the sundered halves of the sidewinder are symbolically reunited in an intricate re-creation of the Hopi's Snake-Antelope ritual (the highlight of their ceremonial year), complete with transcribed trance-chants.[26] As the snake is restored, the Spider Lady's prophecy is fulfilled, and the protagonists are all transported to another dimension, safe from the government's invading stormtroopers.

Endings of this type make for vivid theatre, yet they also pose all kinds of questions, not only because of the dubious romanticization and appropriation of alien cultures, but because they tend, inevitably, toward self-deconstruction. *Sidewinder*'s Hopi ceremony may be intended as an image of humanity rediscovering its "authentic possibilities," but it is itself fundamentally inauthentic, a simulation stripped of context (and originally performed by white actors in redface). Moreover, such arbitrary, deus ex machina conclusions solve nothing, since they simply sidestep the cultural crises established elsewhere. The resulting contradiction forces a yawning disjuncture into the plays: the sense of horrific emptiness created by a play like *Sidewinder* cannot be expunged by the wishful thinking of its conclusion, and so hope and despair are left coexisting in a bizarre state of mutual antipathy.

Shepard was not, it seems, unaware of this agitated condition, and at times openly undermined his endings: Willie's celebrations at freeing Nogoland, for example, are abruptly soured by Cisco pointing out that their problem remains unresolved: "we're strangers too. We're lost, Willie" (30). The play concludes with Sycamore delivering a tired, resigned speech as he waits to die. In some of the later plays of this period, such ambiguity gives way to an outright skepticism which swamps the transcendent impulse completely: thus *Cowboy Mouth* ends with a grotesque parody of a fantasy salvation, as Slim and Cavale (a name literally meaning "escape") create not their dreamed-of rock hero but a Lobster Man. This character sheds his lobster skin, like a fairy-tale prince, and steps out a handsome hero, but he is armed only with an unloaded gun, which he puts to his own head without effect. Slim heads for the door, sickened by the futile fantasizing.

If there is a positive potential in the escape images, it lies in the fact that – however unfocused or unreal – they express the *desire* to overcome the fragmentation and achieve some new form of harmony. These images do imply a clear resistance to the disintegrative societal pressures that the plays present: as Kosmo bluntly remarks, "I'm getting fucking tired of apocalypses. . . . What about something with some hope?" (264). Moreover, this desiring impulse is one which periodically finds expression in a tentative form of *post*modernist resistance to deracination. Even as the plays frankly acknowledge that the prevailing cultural conditions cannot be escaped, they at times seek – paradoxically – to present sources of hope *within* those conditions: amid the pop culture debris which so traps his characters, there may yet be – as Shepard himself puts it – "images that shine in the middle of junk."[27] After all, popular art forms may be compromised and clichéd, but are they not popular precisely because they express underlying human desires in widely understood ways?

In his introduction to *Melodrama Play*, Shepard hints that if some sense of humanity is to be found in the piece, it must be by excavating it from within the all-pervasive banality: "a production of this play should . . . be aimed toward discovering how it changes from the mechanism of melodrama to something more sincere. This change does not just occur slowly from one thing into the other in the course of the play but rapidly as well and very frequently" (115). This paradox is central to the effect of the play, and is epitomized by Duke's twice-performed hit song, "Prisoners, Get Up Out of Your Home-Made Beds," which is *both* ridiculously corny *and* a kind of defiant call to existential self-realization. Moreover, Shepard's treatment of rock music throughout these plays balances on the same fence. The artificial posturing of rock, the fact that (as Pop says in *Holy Ghostly*) it has largely lost touch with its "good roots" in the blues and been turned into a manufactured and melodramatic form – all these drawbacks are openly acknowledged in the plays. And yet there is also the sneaking hope that even when compromised to such an extent, rock retains the potential – in Cavale's words – to "raise me higher than all of Revelations" (156). Thus, in a passage like Geez's concluding speech in *Shaved Splits*, cliché is inherent (the lines are delivered in the same consciously hackneyed voice-over format used for Cherry's porn novels), and yet the words describe a persuasive vision of rock's liberating power, in which Geez joins the ultimate band and knows instinctively how to play: "The music filled him up and poured out over the dusty tables and chairs. He was alive again" (200).

Much the same is true of Shepard's recurrent concern in these plays with the old-time cowboy. He is well aware that this idealized figure is based entirely on media fabrications, and has admitted that the nearest he ever came, as a child, to meeting a real cowboy was seeing the stars of *The Lone Ranger* and *Hopalong Cassidy* at the Pasadena Rose Parade. The play which most persistently manipulates the cowboy myth, *The Unseen Hand*, backhandedly acknowledges the Morphan Brothers' real roots as figments of 1950s pop culture by having them launch incongruously into a rendition of Bill Haley's "Rock Around the Clock." Shepard thus implicitly admits the historical nonexistence of the Golden Age of the West that he looks back to, and also stresses – via Sycamore Morphan's devastation at the prospect of there being no trains to rob anymore – that the whole cowboy-outlaw ethos is now an anachronistic irrelevance. Yet at the same time, he uses the cowboy's heroic status as a response of sorts to the American malaise. This is not naive nostalgia, but self-conscious, "postmodernist nostalgia."[28] The Morphans represent a different age, which is probably entirely fictive, but which nevertheless implies a critical perspective on the present: their discussion about cars, for example, presents a refreshingly healthy derision of modern flashiness and superficiality. Blue, by his own account, is "a simple man" ("I eat simple. I talk simple and I think simple"), and it is precisely this kind of naiveté which Willie says he needs to free the people of Nogoland from their slavery: "If you came into Nogoland blazing your six-guns they wouldn't have any idea how to deal with you. All their technology and magic would be at a loss. You would be too real for their experience" (8). Similarly, in *Operation Sidewinder* the gold prospector Billy (like Blue, an old man who belongs back in the last century and so is clearly not real in any conventional sense) proves "too real" for the combined might of the CIA and the military. He rebuffs his interrogators' attempts to have him isolate "the pertinent facts," and amiably drives them to distraction with his downhome homilies. Waco Texas, in *The Mad Dog Blues*, is yet another old westerner for whom the simple practicalities of life are a saving grace: "If ya' worried more about yer feet smellin' bad and less about things that don't exist you'd be a happier fella" (269).

Of all these plays, it is *The Mad Dog Blues* which explores this postmodernist version of compromised, ironized, but nevertheless possibly inspiring humanism most thoroughly. The images of transcendence here are drawn not from the realm of mysticism, but from the very pop detritus that pressurizes the characters. These include Waco's love of the music of Jimmie Rodgers ("He had heart"), Kosmo's vision of the voice of Janis Joplin leaving her dead body like a bird, Yahoodi riding "free from fear" in Crazy Horse's war party, and the dream of a band of musical heroes playing together in heaven. Throughout the play, the idealized touchstones are the notions of heart and home, both of which suggest the rhetoric of a million crassly sentimental movies (as indeed do remarks such as Marlene's "Never give up hope. Never say no to life": 282), and yet acquire a kind of ironically impassioned currency. The play concludes with a gleefully contrived happy ending which cannot disguise the sour taste of the hopeless fragmentation depicted just moments before, but which nevertheless suggests a provisional vision of hope. The acquisitive gold-digging which has driven the entire narrative is totally rejected when, with a comic variation on the end of *The Treasure of the Sierra Madre* (in which the gold dust blows away in the wind), the buried treasure turns out to be worthless bottle caps. The characters realize with gay abandon (as in the film) that real happiness is only to be found "in the heart." They then decide, with the sentimental delight of Dorothy at the end of *The Wizard of Oz*, that they want to return home, where the heart is (even though, as Shepard has remarked elsewhere, "home is really always an illusion").[29] Abruptly overcoming their separation, they join together to sing and dance their way out of the theatre: "Just follow your heart. . . . It'll lead you right out of this world and into the next" (282).

Rather than simply surrendering to dehumanization and unseen hands, these plays suggest that a value and a direction of sorts can be found in the characters' attempts to retrieve some kind of personally meaningful perspective from the clichéd artifice that makes up their existence. The contradiction is perhaps summed up best in the Young Man's key speech in *Sidewinder*, in which he first acknowledges himself to be a Frankenstein creature shaped by the surrounding culture ("I have American blood. I dream American dreams. I fuck American girls. I devour the planet"), but then screams out his profound need for independence and uniqueness: "But now I'm myself. Now I'm here. And it's all going to happen now. Right now" (228). In the context of the play's deadly plasticity, this kind of self-proclaiming defiance ("I", "I", "I", "I") smacks of hysterical desperation, and yet perhaps there is also a kind of hope here – humanism at the extreme; desire grounded in nothing but its own self-assertion.

Masculine Duality

Shepard's bewilderingly paradoxical concern with the establishment of individual identity is further complicated in these plays by a subtheme which, at this stage, remains largely distinct from the issue of cultural disintegration: the question of masculinity. On the one hand, his adoption of pop-cultural images of strong, defiant masculinity seems to represent – at least in part – an attempt to establish a sense of stable gender identity, which (unlike the playwrights of the Ridiculous) he was at pains to shore up rather than to erode. Yet on the other hand he also retains a persistent concern with exposing the self-destructive hubris and violence which seems to him to be an integral part of the masculine will to independence, to express the "I."

Shepard appears to have had deeply ambivalent feelings on this subject. To some extent, his work openly celebrates hard-nosed machismo, eulogizing the "Power in the man!" which Willie speaks of in *The Unseen Hand*: "Proud of his pride! Proud guy! Tall, lean and mean!" (18). The bizarre weaponry that his heroes tote, along with their strutting postures, often seem to serve no function other than to indulge a romantic fascination with violence (a tendency nakedly visible in prose pieces like "Letter from a Cold Killer" in *Hawk Moon*). His attraction to rock music was also in part because of its sheer aggression: "Rock and roll is violence manifest without hurting no-one except an occasional kick in the teeth or punch in the mouth" (*Hawk Moon*, 158). "The urge to violence," Shepard jotted in one of his notebooks for 1970, springs from "a certain desire to establish absolutely the difference between myself and whatever is not myself – the desire to be absolutely independent."

Conversely though, the same note makes it clear that this realization shocked him – "the myth of my personal divinity exploded" – and that he found his own attraction to violence repulsive, something he desired to purge himself of. In a country founded on the relentless pursuit of masculine endeavor, Shepard's bluntly honest exploration of such impulses stands in refreshing contrast to the more familiar American attitude of denial, as typified by Frederick Jackson Turner in his influential essay "The Significance of the Frontier in American History" (1893). Turner relentlessly eulogizes the qualities of heroic individualism which he believes characterized the days of frontier expansion ("coarseness and strength combined with inquisitiveness; that practical, inventive turn of mind") while reducing to a footnote "the lawless characteristics of the frontier . . . the gambler and the desperado . . . that line of scum that the waves of advancing civilization bore before them."[30] Turner is unwilling to acknowledge what Shepard sees as self-evident: that these positive and negative facets are two sides of the same, very American coin.

It is the notion of unresolved duality which provides Shepard's most persistent means of treating the issue of American masculinity in these plays, most often by depicting the hero and his sidekick as complementary opposites. In *Back Bog Beast Bait*, Slim is an old-fashioned, whiskey-drinking gentleman outlaw, armed with pearl-handled pistols, while his assistant Shadow is a much cruder, abusive young pill-popping mercenary, armed with a sawed-off shotgun. Conversely, in *Forensic*, it is the eponymous hero who is hotheaded, violent, and not a little stupid, while his shadow, Emmett, is calm, calculating, and devious. *Mad Dog Blues* develops this same contrast further, with Kosmo and Yahoodi introducing themselves in a prologue designed to emphasize their oppositions: the former is "tall, lean, angular, wolf-like. Leads with his cock," the latter, "short, dark, strikes like a serpent. . . . Loves how the brain works" (257–8).

The complementarity of these pairings is also emphasized by the fact that in each case a white cowboy-type is accompanied by a dark, Indian-type sidekick. Here again, Shepard centralizes the European and locates

the native figure as Other, but in this instance his inspiration seems to
come from similar light-dark pairings in popular American classics like
those of Cooper (Hawkeye and Chingachgook), Melville (Ishmael and
Queequeg), and Twain (Huck Finn and Jim). Such light-dark duos are also
common in mythology, and given Shepard's newfound interest in "heavy
and mythic" imagery, he may well have been consciously appealing to the
Jungian interpretation of such pairs as a means of portraying his own sense
of internal division. In this reading, the light hero and dark counterpart
represent the tension between the conscious ego and the mysterious,
unconscious "Shadow." The latter is supposedly composed of those contradictory characteristics which the conscious mind has had to suppress
in order to achieve a clear sense of self, but which must eventually be
accepted and reintegrated if psychic wholeness – or "individuation" – is
to be achieved. Yet Shepard's variation on the theme is significant, in that
it abandons the familiar notion of complementary camaraderie between
the partners (the two sides thus making up a single whole) in favor of presenting them in a state of permanent and crippling division. As Shepard
has remarked, "I think we're split in a much more devastating way than
psychology can ever reveal. It's not . . . some little thing we can get over."[31]
This is made most explicit in *The Mad Dog Blues*, in which Kosmo and
Yahoodi live in a state of impossible symbiosis: "We support each other's
inability to function. There's no friendship" (295). The two share a telepathic link, and together create the picaresque fantasy of the play, yet their
diametrically opposed attitudes lead to constant friction. Yahoodi is sick
of Kosmo's futile dreaming, Kosmo is sick of Yahoodi's cynicism – "You
turn everything to shit!" They grow further apart during the course of the
play, thereby exacerbating the prevalent sense of mental crack-up, and
their final confrontation provides a striking encapsulation of the conflicting feelings of resigned pessimism and hope-against-the-odds which
inform all of these plays: "I'm struggling with something in me that wants
to die!" Yahoodi yells. "And I'm struggling with something in me that wants
to live!" Kosmo responds. "I guess that sums it up"; "I guess so" (295).
Here the ego-shadow conflict seems to convert directly into the Freudian
battle of Eros versus Thanatos. There is no balance to be found here, only
a permanent state of crisis.

Unfortunately, having established these binary oppositions between
his central characters, Shepard does not develop them very far. Even *Mad
Dog Blues* finally opts to bury the character division under the artificially
engineered happy ending. It was not until *True West* in 1980 that he
achieved something of the complexity that the theme of mythic twins

demands. The issue of mental duality achieves a more sophisticated treatment in these plays only at the points where the tension of opposites is
felt within a single character. The first, heavily ironic example of this is
Melodrama Play, in which Duke is torn between his attraction to the violence of long-haired rock and his desire to croon romantic love songs. Yet
in plays like *The Holy Ghostly* and *Back Bog Beast Bait*, the crisis of conscience between brute machismo and thoughtful maturity is presented
far more seriously. For all their playfulness and bricolage effects, these
are stern, almost moralistic visions of men being consigned to a kind of
eternal damnation for failing to rein in their violent sides and find a
mature mental equilibrium. Originally intended as a double bill, both
pieces present supernatural scenarios in which an aging male is faced
with a stark choice: "You either die like a dog or you die like a man."[32]

In *The Holy Ghostly*, Pop is living by himself in the desert, like some
festering, worn-out parody of a lone macho hero, when the ghostly Chindi
and his "ole lady," the Witch, materialize out of the night to try to persuade him that his time is running out. He needs, they claim, to reassess
his life and balance out his divided instincts, for the sake of his immortal
soul: "Imagine hanging around for eternity in the state of mind you're in
now. Strung out between right and wrong, good and evil . . . the body and
the spirit. You're a fucking mess" (189). But Pop resists all suggestions that
he change or repent. Denying any responsibility for his violent life ("I was
only following orders"), he thus damns himself to be "strung out forever"
in the hellish state of un-death in which he is seen at the end of the play,
whirling around in the fire, screaming like a demon: "BURN! BURN!
BURN!" (196).[33] By contrast, *Back Bog Beast Bait* presents almost the
inverse of this same scheme, with the graying gunfighter Slim earnestly
wanting to reform his violent, lonely life. A fresh variant on the old western cliché, he dreams of getting out of the hired-gun business, and of finding domestic peace with a wife and children. (It is significant that this Slim,
his namesake in *Cowboy Mouth*, and Kosmo all crave the stability of "a
wife and a life of my own": these three pieces were all written in 1971,
shortly before Shepard and O-Lan finally quit New York together.) Yet
Slim finds himself marooned in a demon-infested swamp, a dark reflection of the state of his soul, in which his change of heart is exposed as too
little, too late. The demonic voodoo violinist Gris-Gris – performing an
opposite function to that of the Chindi – torments him into readopting
the attitude of a cold, emotionless killer for the sake of self-defense.[34]
Once again tasting this bloodlust, Slim realizes that it is this he still secretly
craves for: "That incredible power to kill and not be afraid!" (331). Like

Pop, he finally descends into rampaging insanity, transforming into precisely the kind of mad "coyote dog" he had feared becoming: "I howl! I chew on the carcass of a skunk! I am the beast! The beast is me!" (332–3).

Shepard's plays of this period do not hold out any real hope that the male characters will be able to mature gracefully. Rather, there is an underlying sense of terror which seems to spring from a suspicion that a perverse attraction to brute machismo has been drummed into the American male so deeply that it can never be expunged. As Slim observes at the last in *Beast Bait*: "I never chose my moves. Something moved in me like a silent hand. Every action. Every thought" (333). The Pop-Ice relationship in *Holy Ghostly* indicates a similar concern: it seems to represent, at least in part, an exploration of the extent to which the son has been infected by the attitudes of the father. As a character in *Hawk Moon* remarks, preempting the imagery of later family plays like *Buried Child*, "the old man [is] right there living inside me like a worm in wood" (130).

The "silent hand" of masculine conditioning is as persistent an element in the rock plays as is the "unseen hand" of cultural conditioning. Yet each play tends to concentrate on one or the other pressure: they remain largely unrelated, as do so many other elements of these chaotic and difficult pieces. However, with *The Tooth of Crime*, Shepard finally gained sufficient control of his material to draw an explicit connection between cultural and gender pressures. In doing so, he ushered in the beginning of a more mature phase of his writing. Yet if the work gains in control, it also hardens in vision: the result is every bit as disorientating and unsettling as anything that has gone before.

3

Sorting Out

An English Interlude, 1971–1974

SHEPARD, HIS WIFE, AND THEIR YOUNG SON lived in London for three years from 1971 to 1974, returning across the Atlantic only to spend summer vacations in Nova Scotia. England was chosen on the grounds that it was not America but that its inhabitants spoke English, and also because Shepard thought vaguely that he might be able to start a more serious rock career in London, home of the Who and the Rolling Stones. He quickly abandoned this latter idea, however. After the chaos of his last years in New York, he and O-Lan attempted to create a quieter, more domesticated life for themselves, settling in the London suburb of Hampstead. Director Nancy Meckler, who knew him well at this time, notes that the legends of Shepard as a drug-addled wild man of rock always seemed bizarre to her: she recalls him as a man who liked to cook, read, and look after his son. During this period, Shepard took the opportunity to sit back and take stock of where he was going, and wrote a variety of very different plays in the process of this reassessment. First among these was *The Tooth of Crime*, written in 1972 and still regarded by many as his most remarkable achievement. *Tooth* effectively represented the summation of the rock/pop phase of his writing (just as *La Turista* had both crystallized and moved on from the work of the earlier phase), and it clearly benefited from the new sense of perspective afforded by his distance from home: "It wasn't until I came to England that I found out what it means to be an American."[1] The play combines the various, diverse anxieties which had dominated his recent work – anxieties about New York's decline, the wider crisis of American cultural fragmentation, the corruption of rock music, the loss of rootedness, the brutal masculine will to power – in an unnerving portrayal of high-gloss violence.

Tooth also, however, seems to have purged something from Shepard's system, and shortly thereafter he decided to abandon his pursuit of movie-based, forward-progressing plots: "I'd like to try a different way of writing now," he announced in 1974, "which is very stark and not so flashy and not full of a lot of mythic figures and everything, and try to scrape it down to the bone as much as possible."[2] The most obvious manifestation of this new concern was *Action* (1974), a stark, plotless, even deliberately tedious depiction of an undefined family group enacting a series of unrelated domestic rituals. Stripped of all but a few specifically American references, and lacking any vestige of the kind of raw, spontaneous energy that had characterized most of his previous work, the piece was initially greeted with astonished disgust by many of Shepard's devotees, who were unprepared for the degree to which he had pared down his approach. And yet the rigorousness of the slower, more deliberate process adopted in writing *Action* also had its benefits, producing a density of thought which captures and crystallizes many of the themes which had floated in and out of his previous work. Along with *Tooth*, it is now generally recognized as being among Shepard's most important works.

This chapter focuses primarily on explorations of these two pieces, but it is also important to note that Shepard's time in London produced a number of other, lesser works: the journey between these two points was not an easy one. For if *Tooth* had benefited from a newfound distance from the States, the longer Shepard stayed in England, the more he lost touch with the American zeitgeist that had always been a key source of inspiration: in this alien environment he at first struggled awkwardly for new direction. Much of his writing at this time directly expressed this personal sense of crisis, of being a stranger in a strange land, but without a real home to return to. Yet in these pieces he largely failed to transform these private anxieties into anything of broader relevance. Both *Blue Bitch* (a short play produced by BBC Television in the spring of 1973) and *The Speedy Downfall of Spider Lee* (an unfinished manuscript) are slight pieces focusing on American men who, with their wives, have come to live in London "to get away from it all," and are feeling somewhat lost. *Geography of a Horse Dreamer* (1974) is more successful as a play, but again is a thinly disguised metaphor for Shepard's frustration.

Like *Melodrama Play* before it, *Geography* focuses on an "Artistic Cowboy" being held captive by gangsters and forced to create to order: Cody has the magical ability to predict horse race winners in his dreams, and so is mercilessly exploited for financial profit. Yet at the play's outset, Cody's winning streak has dried up, a plot point which reads as an obvious metaphor for writer's block: "At first it's all instinct. Now it's work."[3] Moreover, his immediate sense of frustration springs from the play's location in a seedy hotel room in London: his enforced disconnection from his American homeland has clouded and distorted his horse dreaming. During the play, he instead taps into the local psychic atmosphere and starts to dream of the winners at London's greyhound tracks. Thus the geographical location of the horse dreamer is seen to be of crucial significance in the activity of his imagination, and again the autobiographical connection is clear. Shepard has said of his writing that "the physical place I'm in at the time of sitting down to the machine" plays a very significant role in what he manages to create: "*Geography of a Horse Dreamer* was written in London, and there's only one truly American character in the play."[4] It must also be said, however, that the English voices in *Geography* – and especially that of the effete gang-leader, Fingers – are little more than crude caricatures, as heard by an outside ear. (*Blue Bitch* is still worse, reducing a Scots voice to incomprehensible growling and barking.) It was not until *Action* that Shepard found a way of turning his prolonged exposure to British speech patterns to his advantage: "the English tendency [to] overblow sentences" is accommodated here in a collection of nominally American figures who speak at a more controlled, deliberate pace than in any of his previous work.

If *Geography* works as more than simply a metaphor for the writer's situation, it is because Shepard here continues to work out the themes of desacralization and the death of the West which he had explored in some of the rock plays. These translate into a kind of modern Fall myth, a Fall from which (contrary to *Operation Sidewinder*) there is no redemption. Cody, we learn, was born into an Edenic paradise, growing up in Wyoming, a region to which even Fingers ascribes spiritual significance: "The prairie stretching out and out like a great ocean. I felt God was with me then" (301). Yet Cody was seduced away from home, "wined and dined" with the promise of fortune, and is now in hell – imprisoned in a claustrophobic room in the sinful Old World of Europe. The shift from horse dreaming to dog dreaming also implies a debasement of sorts, despite Shepard's obvious enthusiasm for his new English hobby of greyhound racing: this is evident, in particular, in the way Cody's speech patterns shift from a dreamy, romantic tone when envisioning horses, toward the hard-nosed commercialism of his captors when discussing dogs. Yet Shepard's indulgence, through Cody, of the jargon and technical details of dog races (also prevalent in *Blue Bitch*) also renders large parts of the play somewhat obscure for audiences unfamiliar with the sport. This is symptomatic of the fact that despite its attempts at broad relevance, *Geography* displays very little of the allusive richness of his best work. The relative straightforwardness and consistency of both its movie-parody narrative and its use of the Raymond Chandler/film noir "hard-boiled" dialogue style (chosen to evoke an appropriately murky, gangland atmosphere) means that the audience are never really thrown off balance: it becomes easy to defuse what stage impact the play possesses by tidily rationalizing it as a "dilemma-of-the-artist" piece. Shepard once remarked that *La Turista* seemed to him to be drowning in self-pity, but that accusation could be far better applied here. Particularly hard to stomach are the numerous references to Cody as a tortured "genius" put upon by dull brutes who drain him of his creativity because they are entirely lacking in imagination of their own (Santee does not even dream).

Shepard followed up *Geography* with *Little Ocean*, which was the first sign of his new concern with a simpler, stripped-down style. A short play specifically intended for club performance by his wife O-Lan and two of her friends, it was written by improvising loosely around themes of motherhood and childbirth (the title refers to the womb). With its plotless, playfully elliptical form, and central device of characters bringing up an idea and then reflecting on it via adopted voices (adolescent girls, prudish old ladies, comic mother-daughter exchanges, and so forth), it plainly resembles a female version of *Cowboys*. Yet this recourse to old methods, while perhaps helping to clear the decks after *Geography*, was not in itself a step forward. Nor was the gently "feminine" tone of the piece something Shepard wished to follow up at this stage: he clearly saw it as a gift for O-Lan (whose pet name, Lo, is both her character's name and an acronym of the play's title) rather than a part of his own development. He has since forbidden any subsequent performance or publication of the piece.

However, if this period saw a degree of fumbling uncertainty in Shepard's actual playwriting, the lessons he was learning about the nuts and bolts of the performance process were crucial to his future development. Through his close association with actors of the caliber of Stephen Rea, for whom he wrote the part of Cody in *Geography*, and who directed *Little Ocean* at the Hampstead Theatre Club, he gained much more respect for the creativity required at every stage of making a play. It was also Rea who encouraged him to experiment with directing his own work for the first time, and the Royal Court Theatre – following a successful production of *The Unseen Hand* in their tiny new Theatre Upstairs – agreed to give him complete freedom in directing *Geography*'s premiere, despite his lack of previous experience.

Shepard's decision to take this step was no doubt partly a result of his growing frustration with other directors, who seemed unable or unwilling to produce his work in ways which coincided with his original intentions. Having disowned Charles Marowitz's premiere production of *The Tooth of Crime* at London's Open Space (after falling out with Marowitz over his treatment of both text and actors), Shepard also discovered that Richard Schechner's American premiere in 1973 had openly contradicted many of the explicit directions of the text in its pursuit of an environmental staging approach. This was despite lengthy correspondence over permission to mount the play in the first place, and Shepard did not disguise his irritation: "The reason a play is written," he wrote Schechner, "is that a writer receives a vision which can't be can't be translated into any other way except a play. . . . It's a question you really should look into rather than sweep it aside as being old-fashioned or even unimportant."[5]

The irony is that Shepard's experience of directing *Geography* (with Rea and a cast which also included the now-renowned British actors Kenneth Cranham and Bob Hoskins) actually resulted in a considerable change of attitude on *his* part. His approach in the first rehearsals was simply to have them read through the entire script, before taking them off to play poker or to see his greyhound, Keywall Spectre, at local race meetings. Gradually, though, he realized there was more to it than simply running over the words and finding the feeling. As he told Kenneth Chubb, while still working on the production:

> I've learned that the rehearsal process is actually a process. The reason it takes three or four or five or six weeks is because it actually needs that amount of time to evolve . . . you begin to find out what it really means to write a play. That it isn't a piece of paper, it's something that is really happening in real life. And the more you find out about it the more you can grow as a writer.[6]

There is, perhaps, an unnecessary modesty in these remarks: Shepard's writing had always demonstrated an instinctive sense of theatrical dynamics. But he certainly seems to have gained a fresh awareness of the actual process of developing text into performance. Indeed, it was in working on this play that his early, Kerouacian "holy art" attitude (which had been softened considerably during the late '60s, with his increasing tendency to redevelop or rewrite sections of his plays) seems to have met its final demise. As his remarks to Chubb imply, the notion of the writer simply spewing his consciousness onto a page and then expecting this vision to be magically reproduced on stage was now seen as a fallacy. Shepard began to perceive theatre as a process whose results are determined as much by the input of actors, directors, and designers as by the writer, and in subsequent years he took an ever-increasing role in directing his own work, working collaboratively with casts and musicians to develop scripts through the rehearsal period.

The Killer Machine

Yet another feature of Shepard's maturing process while living in England was the voracious appetite for reading which he only now developed, having been (by his own account) "too cool" to read much in the 1960s. He became fascinated by writers as diverse as James Joyce (whom he has described in tellingly personal terms as "the Charlie Parker of language") and Bertolt Brecht, and this new erudition quickly began to make itself felt in his playwriting. His favorite Brecht play, for example, *In the Jungle of the Cities*, with its pulp-gangland setting and dualistic central conflict between old crimelord and young protégé, seems to have served as a key inspiration for *The Tooth of Crime*. *Tooth* also lifts its title from a phrase in a poem by French Symbolist Stephane Mallarmé, and is the first of Shepard's works to suggest the influence of Greek tragedy (a form which increasingly interested him during the 1970s): it owes much of its impact to the cruelly simple logic of a plot which seems to move inexorably toward the protagonist's doom. Hoss, a traditional, Elvis-style rock star in black leathers, is the established King in this science fiction future, but the rules of the bizarre battle game he dominates are crumbling on all sides during act 1, as violence escalates nationwide. Hoss begins to fear for his position, despite the reassurances of a string of fawning assistants, and when Crow, a lone "Gypsy" (a lawless killer working outside the rules of the Game), breaks through his security cordon, the stage is set for act 2's battle between the two, which Hoss inevitably loses. He is forced into the only gesture he can think of to salvage his honor: suicide. The almost Oedipal relationship between the old master and the young upstart who usurps his big black throne lends this otherwise bizarre play something of the familiarity of myth: to the *Time* critic T. E. Kalem, it seemed "as chillingly old as a tribal rite."[7]

Shepard no doubt appreciated such accolades. Yet it is vital to note that this underlying plot structure – in suggesting clear similarities with sources as diverse as Greek tragedy and the John Ford western *The Man*

Who Shot Liberty Valance (1962)[8] – is as much of a borrowing, a cultural quotation, as all the other elements of the play. Loosely structured around its basic trajectory toward an outcome which seems a foregone conclusion, the play's real emphasis is on following the disjointed events from moment to moment rather than tracing a gradually developing throughline. The plot seems almost a "ready-made" template, a simple skeleton on which to hang as strange a collection of songs, individual performances, and gratuitously theatrical imagery as any Shepard had yet devised. This, in fact, is Shepard's most sophisticated version of heterotopia, a polyglot world of colliding time and space, which appeals simultaneously to past (with its classical overtones and references to the Old West), future (the ostensible sci-fi setting), and the 1970s present (there are numerous references to the music and pop culture heroes of that period, and Hoss even describes a boyhood that could only have taken place in the bobby-sox and gang rumble era of the 1950s). The rationale behind this strategy is also stated more pointedly here than in any of the previous work: as Hoss warns in the opening song, the play reflects the (hyper)reality of an America in which competing media fictions have colonized the collective imagination to the point where cognitive distinctions between the authentic and the manufactured are impossible:

> You may think every picture you see is a true history of the way things
>   use to be or the way things are
> While you're ridin' in your radio or walkin' through the late late show
>   ain't it a drag to know you just don't know
> you just don't know
> So here's another illusion to add to your confusion
> Of the way things are . . . [9]

If *Tooth* is a nightmare vision of the state of American culture, Shepard's most immediate inspiration for writing it seems to have been his growing sense that rock music, specifically, had "committed suicide. [It's] been co-opted. Into fads, into style, and into fulfilling the needs of self-destruction."[10] There is not even a provisional appeal here to rock's saving simplicity: Hoss longs whimsically for the lost innocence of the 1950s, citing "Blue Suede Shoes" and "Yackety Yack," but in this environment such nostalgia simply suggests that he is "going soft" (218). Likewise, rock's association with impassioned rebellion is also seen as "Old time shuffle" (212). The fashion now is for Crow's "violent arrogance" and "true contempt" (227), a style-oriented attitude to the world which functions as an end in itself.

Part of the play's power lies in the fact that it acknowledges – and to some extent draws its audience in to enjoy – the perverse attractiveness of such posturing. Shepard's own ambivalence is visible in his specification that Crow "looks just like Keith Richard" (lead guitarist with the Rolling Stones), and in his remarks elsewhere that the part would ideally be played by Lou Reed of the Velvet Underground: both these men were personal heroes of Shepard's. Yet the latent violence they represented, and the "lurking evil" of much of their music (Reed's "Heroin" is described in these terms in the stage directions), are here extrapolated into a vision of the future in which rock stars have ceased merely to enact violence: they battle each other in souped-up cars, with glittering displays of sophisticated weaponry, in an ongoing battle for territorial supremacy over vast tracts of the American West. It is hardly surprising, in light of this depiction, that Shepard abandoned any further attempt to fuse playwriting and rock music after *Tooth*. This in itself, though, appears to have been a major factor in his temporary loss of direction: in *Geography*, Cody's dream blockage is attributed not only to the alien environment but also, crucially, to his loss of connection with music, which he insists is "the source of inspiration" (285). Despite his protests, the gangsters refuse to let Cody hear his favorite record, and when it is finally played, it comes too late to save him. By then, he has been rescued by his shotgun-wielding brothers, Jasper and Jason (who obliterate the bad guys in an orgy of flying ketchup-gore), but is clearly lost and broken, hopelessly out of touch with the sacred. Shepard's choice of Clifton Chenier's upbeat Cajun zydeco sound, heard over the groans of the dying as the lights fade, is surely bitterly ironic.

The "Sam Peckinpah sequence" which ends *Geography* (Shepard's own words for Jasper and Jason's turkey shoot) is that play's single most arresting theatrical image – a cataclysmic moment in which the death of the West, and the congenital violence of the American male, are alluded to as viscerally as they are in any Peckinpah film. *The Tooth of Crime*, however, treats those same themes with far greater depth and complexity. Building on his unease with rock star posturing, Shepard seized on the notion of depicting real killers as performers who "treat their situation like a rock musician – this whole macho thing, you know, the masculinity trip." This he saw as an apt representation of an ethos operating "in every aspect of American life, from pimps up to Nixon."[11] President Nixon and his Secretary of State Kissinger, still orchestrating the war in Vietnam, were notorious for their allusions to themselves as cowboys, pioneers, or sports competitors, and in response to this and many other factors, Shepard used *Tooth* to draw his most explicit connection yet between the masculine-individualist ethos of the frontier and the conditioning effects of contemporary American culture. There is no appeal here to even the most provisional notion of a positive side to the frontier dream: visions of "ranchers, cowboys [in] open space," putting down roots and "just livin' their life," are ridiculed as "old-time boogie" (219). Instead, the play implies that today's corrupt, self-perpetuating system of American hegemonic capitalism springs from, and still relies on, a self-serving "pursuit of happiness" which involves the brutal annihilation of anything or anyone who stands in one's way.

Hoss's America functions on a system of brutally Darwinian principles, which are enshrined in the Game of rock violence of which he is a part. Unlike a film such as *Rollerball* (1975), a comparable sci-fi vision of a deadly sport spinning out of control, *Tooth* does not present its Game as a social pressure valve, an Orwellian spectacle of sanctioned violence which acts as an outlet for the audience's animal passions. Rather, the Game is simply the highest, most polished form of a brutality which oils the wheels at every level of society: "The streets are controlled by the packs. They got it locked up. The packs are controlled by the gangs. The gangs and the Low Riders. They're controlled by cross syndicates. The next step is the Keepers" (219). The Keepers, the mysterious, unseen hands of total control, also run the Game, which enshrines this ubiquitous violence in a code that legitimizes and perpetuates it. The painful sense of upheaval in America at the time of writing is also reflected by the play in the suggestion that the Game itself is now disintegrating. But far from representing some positive, countercultural change, this shifting of ground simply drives the same violent principles to new extremes. The sanctioned "art" of individualistic brutality is now seen as too tame ("We ain't flyin' in the eye of contempt. We've become respectable and safe": 215), with the result that young people are now abandoning the Game and going underground, "flocking to the Gypsy Kills." A further, bitter twist to this vision lies in the suggestion that this change is simply a logical way for the culture to renew itself. Here the play seems almost prescient in anticipating the 1970s emergence of punk rock: the Gypsies' newer, still more ruthless form of ritualized murder, far from being a form of anarchic rebellion, will itself become legitimized when the possibilities for profit are realized – "It's a market opening up, Jack. I got a feeling. I know they're on their way in and we're going out" (211). Sure enough,

Crow, having defeated Hoss, takes his place as the new king of rock. The cycle of violence continues, but descends to a still lower circle of this American hell.

The nightmarish paradox in all this is that, in a system of commercial exploitation that is built on – and absorbs all new forms of – defiant individualism, that ethos simply becomes an insidious and inescapable form of social conformism. Any notion of unique self-expression becomes laughable: "I'm a fucking industry," Hoss realizes, "a trained slave." True individuality, he tells his assistant, Becky, "is something outside the game. The game can't contain a true genius" (207). But when Hoss toys with abandoning the game, the idea is regarded as both treasonous and idiotic by his staff, who point out that there is no "outside" to escape to, unless he joins the packs or gangs, who are equally subject to the authority of the Keepers. The play, in effect, presents a bleak metaphor for the postmodern condition: there is not even a tenuous hope of transcending or escaping the all-pervasive system. "Power. That's all there is," Becky insists: "The power of the machine. The killer machine. That's what you live and die for" (218).

". . . to add to your confusion . . ."

If this interpretation of the significance of *Tooth*'s fictional world suggests a deeply serious, even savage indictment of the assumptions underlying American society, it must also be stressed that the play refuses to submit itself entirely to this reading. The background details are never laid out in a coherent exposition, and so have to be inferred from dispersed references: many of these contradict each other (Hoss, for example, sees his own role variously as that of an animalistic killer and an honorable warrior), and all of them might be deceptions. As Hoss tells Crow: "I wanna find out what's goin' on. None of us knows" (229): isolated in his private domain, Hoss – like the audience – has no way of knowing whether anything he is told about the outside is actually true.

Moreover, the audience's search for significant meaning is repeatedly obstructed by the play's plethora of pop culture references and playful diversions. Speeches such as Doc's lengthy reminiscence about his namesake Doc Carter (sidekick of Buffalo Bill) operate to impede any attempt at a smooth reading of the play. Doc even apologizes for the apparent irrelevance of his meanderings: "Don't rightly know what made me think of that" (217). The use of blatant non sequiturs intensifies in the second

act, when the already gratuitous indulgence of stage spectacle is pushed
to extremes, becoming a kind of freak show variety performance. As Hoss
and Crow continue their confrontation, the other characters reappear
variously as pom-pom-wielding, bottom-exposing cheerleaders, a self-
abusing striptease artist dressed as a character from Jean-Luc Godard's
film *Alphaville*, and a group of tuxedo-clad a cappella crooners. Reviewing the play's premiere at the Open Space, critic Irving Wardle responded
to such elements by dismissing the play as "a camp piece, intended as
much to raise giggles as to repel."[12] His attitude is predicated on the conventional assumption that a play should have a unified tone and render up
a clear set of meanings: by this logic, a degree of throwaway cheapness
thereby reduces the whole play to that level. *Tooth*, however, presents not
a univocal critique of American culture, but an immediate sense of its
noise, spectacle, silliness, schlock, and brutality. As the Open Space's
American director Charles Marowitz suggested at the time, *Tooth* "looks
exotic and unreal in England. Only a public that has been conditioned by
the assault course that *is* contemporary American life can fully appreciate
its psychic implications. [It is] as telling and realistic as anything Chekhov
ever put on paper."[13]

The most remarkable feature of *The Tooth of Crime* is unquestionably
its use of language, which – even more so than its use of spectacle – simultaneously conveys the playfulness, the utter confusion, and the inherent
sadism of Hoss's world. This is by far Shepard's most sophisticated manipulation of rock language, combining slick, superficial brutality with a sizzling rhythmic energy, and a use of cliché which almost becomes an art
form in itself. This high-octane cocktail of pop culture speech patterns
borrows its dominant phrases and imagery from the cutthroat worlds of
boxing, motor racing, gambling, gangsterism, westerns, and, of course,
rock itself, to create a hybrid language comparable to that of Anthony
Burgess's novel *A Clockwork Orange* (1962) in its seductive violence. But
there is also a crucial difference between Burgess and Shepard. Whereas
the former narrates his novel through the eyes of a single anti-hero, Alex,
thus maintaining a consistent, unified (modernist) perspective, *Tooth* creates an immediate sense of (postmodern) cultural chaos by violently
clashing together diverse vocal styles. The characters all speak in radically
different pop dialects, ranging from the essentially comic jive-talk of
Galactic Jack (an open quotation of the style of disc jockey Wolfman Jack:
"Back flappin', side trackin', finger poppin', reelin' rockin' with the tips on
the picks in the great killer race": 209) to the gangland language of the
Markers, which is soaked in metaphors suggesting possession and rape:

"Root Force has probably got Vegas locked up. It's gonna be hard pene-tration" (214); "I can't seem to get it up like the other kills" (222). It is, significantly, on the battlefield of language (as opposed to guns, cars, or "shivs") that Hoss and Crow finally face each other. This life-and-death struggle thus becomes Shepard's most explicit expression of his ongoing concern with speech as power performance: each combatant seeks, liter-ally, to score points by commanding attention through verbal ingenuity and forcing the other into the passive, defeated position of recipient audi-ence. At the point where Crow produces such a blisteringly insistent piece of rhythmic derision that Hoss cannot recover sufficiently to get a word in edgeways, the referee declares a knockout (241).

Shepard makes use of a bewildering array of techniques to foreground the play's linguistic extravagance, from his usual rhythm and rhyme (taken to fresh extremes), through bizarre mixed metaphors ("the shit's gonna hit the fan before we can get to the bank"), to rolling successions of word association which completely lose track of the image where they began: "Come on dice! That's it. Roll 'em sweet. The sweet machine. Candy in the gas tank. Floor it. Now you got the wheel. Take it!" (212). Disparate slang phrases from the streets of white New York, Harlem, and London collide in single sentences. Verbs are replaced by nouns. Dis-armingly innocent terminology acquires lethal implications: "If the keep-ers whimsy it all they do is scratch 'em out" (211). Perhaps Shepard's most disorientating device, though, is his tendency to use words with several possible meanings. This slippage of signification applies to the most basic language of Hoss's world: the term "the charts," for example, is used to refer both to rock-star rankings and to maps marking territorial owner-ship (the implication is that in this world the two are linked, or even iden-tical). Astrological "charts" are thrown in as an added complication, and the word "star" also takes on both astrological and celebrity connotations. "Cold Killer" is used both literally, of the current, murderous rock musi-cians, and figuratively, of old-time rock heroes.

In most cases the listener is able to make some sense of such floating phraseology: "meet him in a singles match," for example, could refer to cutting records, or to sport, but the general implication is clear (216). Yet some remarks remain utterly confusing, and with Crow's entrance this opacity becomes rife, setting up a real obstacle to understanding. Crow's scarcely comprehensible snarl, representative of the next stage of lin-guistic bastardization, has even Hoss begging him to slow down and speak more clearly. The lightning-fast jumble of words speeds by like a foreign language, leaving only tantalizing hints of meaning: "Got the molar chomps. Eyes stitched. You can vision what's sittin'. Very razor to cop z's sussin' me to be on the far end of the spectrum. . . . No shrewd from this end either. We both bow to bigger fields" (227). *Tooth's* audience has no glossary which might explain this language, nor even the time to look at one (as one does with Burgess), and so must struggle to piece together a sketchy understanding from the fragments of jargon which they *can* follow. The effect of the play's language is to create a sense of plunging forward through time, by denying the audience a chance to get their bearings, while dragging them ever deeper into this chaotic verbal maze.

The relevance of this approach to the play's implicit cultural critique is immediate. The extreme bricolage effect suggests semantic overload, a sense of crisis brought on by the proliferation of pop-cultural language forms. So debased by usage in jargon, cliché, and overstatement that they can come to connote almost anything, words (and, by extension, speech, and even thought itself) seem in danger of losing any vestige of reliable meaning. Characters operate in worlds shut off from each other, comprehending their own speech patterns but growing further and further from those of others: consequently, words are used as weapons rather than as a means of communication. In such an environment, the very concept of truth becomes utterly irrelevant, as Hoss discovers to his cost when Crow wins the first round of their battle by inventing a humiliating past for him (describing him reduced to adolescent masturbation, and forced into fellating a prison warder). Hoss protests to the referee: "How can you give points to a liar?" The response is blunt: "I don't. I give 'em to the winner" (237). Crow knows what Hoss has not registered; that the past is not a set of concrete facts, but a conceptual history which can be rewritten at will by whomever has the power to do so. In this world of language games, reality itself is a reinventable fiction. Hoss sums up the instability in his final, desperate realization that "I'm pushed and pulled around from one image to another. Nothin' takes a solid form. Nothin's sure and final" (243).

Yet even as he depicts this postmodern linguistic chaos, Shepard appears to be fighting something of a rearguard battle in response, by paradoxically attempting to reintroduce a modernist conception of language's potential depth. While apparently accepting the hopelessly slippery status of signification itself, Shepard demonstrates a concern here (more so than in any of his other work) with the strangeness of individual words and phrases, playing with the actual texture of language sounds as an end in itself. In this respect, the influence of Stephane Mallarmé on this play extends far beyond simply providing its title. Mallarmé's over-riding con-

cern, as one of the central figures in the school of French Symbolist poetry
at the start of the century, was with placing words in unusual, poetic contexts which stripped them of their conventionally assigned meanings, so
as to highlight their sound or their shape on the page. In making familiar
words seem strange, he aimed to draw attention to the indefinable, evocative quality of language, to make words incantatory rather than commu-
nicative. Similarly, Shepard – who had been introduced to Mallarmé's
work, as well as that of Rimbaud and Baudelaire, by Patti Smith – turns
in this play to an exploration of "words as logos (in the sense of symbols,
like corporate logotypes)," so as to "see what kind of forms they can create in space. You don't want to look at the words themselves but at the
things behind them, inside them."[14] In particular, he exercises a penchant
for oddly polysyllabic, often foreign-sounding words, and makes extensive
use of Mallarmé's *pieuse majuscule*, or "holy" capital letters (obviously
these cannot actually be seen as such in performance, but the use of proper
names and logo-words implies them nonetheless). This interest was first
evident in Shepard's program notes for *Cowboy Mouth* in 1971, in which
he chose to describe himself to the audience simply by listing "a few of
my favorite words: Slipstream, Tahachapi, Wichita, Choctaw, Apache,
Switchblade, Bootleg, Fox, Vixen, Feather, Coyote . . ."[15] In *Tooth*, the
text is crammed with words of this sort: Maserati, Mojo Root Force, Scor-
pion, Cheyenne, El Caminos, Venus, Neptune, Baretta, "whiplash magic
and rattlesnake tongue" (209). In this context, perhaps even the play's
bizarre slang-rhyming ("Solo's the payolo!") is intended to have a symbolist quality to it, similar to Mallarmé's fascination with "rare rhymes" which
torture meaning to the limit. Notably, the name Crow itself has been
described by Shepard as an example of the vocabulary of Native American poetry, in which "a religious belief in the word itself" re-creates words
"as living incantations and not as symbols. Taken in this way, the organization of living, breathing words as they hit the air between the actor and
the audience actually possesses the power to change our chemistry."[16] And
it seems it was this aspect of the play which attracted Richard Schechner
to seek to direct the American premiere: he describes *Tooth* as using language as Hindus use chants, "to raise certain aspects of the subliminal to
consciousness."[17]

Surely, however, assertions of this sort need to be questioned. A play
like this is clearly a long way from being a religious ritual, and in this context such expressions of faith in the mystical, logopoeic essence of word
sounds seem dubious, at the very least. Would an audience be more likely
to read a transcendent dimension into the repetitive use of corporate

logos, or to see them simply as further proof of the glittering emptiness of mass-consumer pop language, another dimension of the irretrievably desacralized world the play presents? If there is a conflict in *Tooth* between modernist and postmodernist attitudes to the treatment of language, then the latter – perhaps somewhat against Shepard's will – surely comes out on top.

Hoss vs. Crow

Much the same is true of the central character battle between Hoss and Crow. There are all sorts of contradictions in the way the combatants present themselves, but in general it is possible to interpret their confrontation as a conflict which allows Shepard to lay out, with almost dialectical clarity, the opposing ideas of self which had been apparent but largely undeveloped in the previous rock plays. Here, Crow's sense that identity is no more than a fragmented composite of surface images is played off against Hoss's continuing insistence on the idea of an essential self existing beneath the unstable, pressurized social persona. The latter notion is, it seems, alluded to by the choice of title, drawn from Mallarmé's line "in your heart of stone there is dwelling / A heart that the tooth of no crime can wound."[18] But while this and other clues make it clear that Shepard's own sympathies lie with Hoss's more traditional perspective, the play leans toward the unsettling suspicion that Crow's position may be more "realistic."

Crow is the figure who best embodies Shepard's fascination with, and abhorrence of, both masculine brutality and the polished superficiality of contemporary culture. For him there is no such thing as depth or intrinsic identity: deriding Hoss's insistence on the "necessity" of finding one's own roots or essence, he subscribes instead to a nihilist postmodernist conviction that the self is plastic, in the sense both of being artificial, and of being unfixed and fluid, without any genuinely transcendent dimension: "there ain't no Gods or saviors who'll give you flesh and blood." For Crow, the only reality is that of self-inventing performance: "I believe in my mask – The man I made up is me" (232). As Hoss repeatedly points out, this means that Crow has "no heart," no center, no fundamental bottom line. He manipulates his surface persona to achieve maximum impact in any given situation, hopping channels to take on new masks at will and without scruple: "Switch to suit, Leathers, and mark to kill" (249). This fluidity makes him the perfect survivor for the contemporary world, a "master adapter" who cannot be attacked effectively because there is no soft inside to strike at. Hoss, by contrast, has cultivated a more stable, individual style, but this very rootedness makes him predictable ("Stuck in my image") and gives Crow a target. From his entrance, Crow seeks to strip away the pretense of uniqueness on which Hoss grounds himself, trying first to absorb and possess his walk, and then, in round one of the language battle, violently appropriating the rhythms and jargon of Hoss's home territory of '50s-style rock and roll, and turning them against him:

> Lonely in a bedroom. Dyin' for attention. Starts to hit the small time. Knockin' over payphones. Rollin' over Beethoven. Rockin' phenmonia. Beboppin' to the Fat Man. Drivin' to the small talk. Gotta make his big mark. . . . Losin' like a wino. Got losin' on the mind. Got losin' all the time. (236)

Crow's method is summed up in the contemptuous remark "we catch debris beams from your set. We scope it to our action then send it back to the garbage game" (229). The sheer coolness and perverse inventiveness of this approach is seductively fascinating to witness, and an audience – presented with no clear moral guidance in relation to what they see – must deal with the ambiguity of their own response to Crow's skills. Equally, though, it would be a mistake to see *Tooth* as lacking conscience or failing to provide a critical perspective on Crow. For a figure who recognizes no transcendent dimension to life, for whom surface is all, has no reason to adhere to any "outdated" notions of ethics or even humanity. Crow also seems aware, moreover, that such willful indifference to any imperative but self-aggrandizement requires a particular kind of denial to maintain: "If I'm a fool then keep me blind. . . . Keep me in my state of grace / Just keep me rollin' down" (251). The play thus explodes Cavale's (Patti Smith's?) concept of the rock-and-roll "savior" being a hero in his "highest state of grace," by suggesting that any such state is only maintained by willfully and foolishly ignoring the destructive and self-destructive results of one's own behavior. Seeing through Crow's posturing, Hoss's final judgment on him is damning: "I just hope you never see yourself from the outside. Just a flash of what you're really like. A pitiful flash" (248).

Hoss is distinguished from Crow in that, during act 1, he appears to be growing in maturity and self-awareness, and so rejects such blind anarchy in favor of a more rooted and considered attitude. He questions the purpose and morality of his violent life ("He's my brother and I gotta kill him?": 224), and, like Slim in *Beast Bait*, envisages himself ending up as a dead animal if he continues this way. Likewise, in the second act, Hoss

Richard O'Brien as Crow and Mike Pratt as Hoss in the Royal Court Theatre's production of *The Tooth of Crime*, London, 1974: "Re-program the tapes . . . Empty your head." (Photo: Mick Rock)

ultimately rejects Crow's tuition in the ways of the Gypsies. Having been
defeated in battle and lost everything, he realizes that to survive he must
learn these new rules. But the core of Crow's lesson is that he must dis-
pense with his personal, centered approach, and effectively murder his
own sense of self: "Start with a clean screen. Are you blank now?" (246).
Although he initially welcomes the release from human concern that this
method affords ("Laughs with his whole being. Passed beyond tears.
Beyond ache for the world. Pitiless. Indifferent and riding a state of
grace"), Hoss finally thrusts it away, insisting that it clashes with an intrinsic sense of self which he will not abandon: "IT AIN'T ME! IT AIN'T
ME! IT AIN'T ME!!" (247).

Hoss's insistence on such centeredness is exhibited most poignantly in
round two of the battle, in which Hoss has Crow "on the ropes" by adopting the aspect of a "menacing ancient spirit": he insists on the need for
rock musicians to acknowledge their roots, in Delta Blues, in New
Orleans jazz, in the defiance of oppressed blacks who expressed through
music the spirit of "somethin' inside that no boss-man could touch." By
reducing rock to surfaces, Hoss says, Crow has lost touch with everything
that really matters: "You miss the origins, milk-face . . . You doin' a pan-
tomime in the eye of a hurricane" (239). The referee, however, disallows
this attack on the grounds that "somethin's outta whack." That something,
it seems, is simply that Hoss's derision is hollow because he himself has
no more authentic roots than Crow: the cowboy and the Delta Blues
character are simply poses he has put on, as indeed is his supposedly
"ancient," "inborn" walk, which he could have copied as easily as Crow
copies it from him. Indeed, Shepard stresses that Crow "gets inside the
feeling" of that walk, "not just the outer form" (228). That is, Crow too
comes to appear "authentically" ancient, before finally pinpointing the
walk as yet another hybrid of preexisting styles: "Skip James via Ginger
Baker" (234). This is symptomatic of the play's subversion of any appeal
to the notion of real origins or depth: the distinction between the two
combatants is blurred and dissolved as both prove to be equally artificial,
equally violent, equally "heart"-less. Even Hoss's stories of his youth
recount a past which is no more than a reified jumble of clichés lifted
from 1950s pop nostalgia: "Vandals, juvies, West Side Story" (216). Significantly, it is by mercilessly ridiculing Hoss's claims to originality that
Crow finally achieves victory in the language battle: he accuses him of
simply collecting and imitating musical influences – from the blues to
Dylan and Jagger – in a desperate attempt to "get it together" (240–1).

Hoss's most brutally accurate self-observations come in the first act,
after which he falls for his own sales pitch (the inverse of the classical

hero's journey toward tragic insight). It is in these early moments of quiet reflection that he acknowledges the true extremity of his situation: "You'd be OK, Becky, if you had a self. So would I. Something to fall back on in a moment of doubt" (225). He clearly intends his ultimate suicide to resolve forever his sense of soullessness: this will be a final act of redemption, a defiant, unique, and self-defining moment, "a true gesture that won't never cheat on itself 'cause it's the last of its kind. It can't be taught or copied or stolen or sold. It's mine. An original" (249). He administers the gunshot in the mouth, implying a dismissive contempt for the language games which have destroyed him. Yet Hoss's suicide is far from being the unique, authentic, personal gesture he claims: this too is an imitation, a copycat version of Little Willard's recently reported suicide. His decision to die violently is as derivative as everything else about his character (his avowed heroes, James Dean and Jackson Pollock, also died violently), and as hollow as the Lobster Man's pathetic failure to blow his brains out in *Cowboy Mouth*. Despite evident admiration for the show-stopping performance value of Hoss's act ("A genius mark"), Crow finally dismisses the gesture as a pointless, anticlimactic irrelevance: "He was backed up by his own suction, man. Didn't answer to no name but loser" (250). Hoss's death, it seems, is just one more event in the play-world's accelerating cycle of futile violence. Shepard himself has suggested as much by describing *Tooth* as a bleak parable about "what happens when people get so carried away with death, to really craving that. Because death has become really hip in New York. The more self-destructive you can become, the hipper it is."[19]

No Meaning Yes

If *Tooth* was Shepard's most sophisticated critique yet of the chaos and violence at the heart of contemporary American culture, *Action* – which premiered at the Royal Court's Theatre Upstairs under Nancy Meckler's direction in 1974 – displayed an altogether different kind of maturity, and laid much of the groundwork for the writing that was to follow in the remainder of the 1970s. It clearly demonstrates the effects of Shepard's prolonged stay in Europe, in that it is almost entirely lacking in both overt American pop culture references and the American-style high modernist spontaneity of Pollock or Kerouac. Instead of being yet another fast-and-loose exercise in improvisatory creativity, *Action* is far more controlled and precise than any of his previous work, suggesting the much starker influence of late modernist writers like Samuel Beckett. Indeed, *Action* is closer in spirit to the European theatre of the absurd than anything else

Shepard has written, presenting a remarkably spare examination of a state of existential crisis, which makes no appeals to redemptiveness of any kind.

This move might seem surprising, given the urgent desire for some kind of positive hope which is visible in even the bleakest of Shepard's work up to this point. But it is clear that in his reading and rethinking during this period, he absorbed with new clarity the implications of Beckett's writing in particular. He was also perhaps helped in this regard by his acquaintance with the renowned director Peter Brook, whom he came to treat as a kind of guru. "It is the wish for optimism that many writers share which prevents them from finding hope," Brook notes in his book *The Empty Space*, stressing that, paradoxically, the sheer honesty of Beckett's drastically attenuated outlook creates a hope of sorts: "he forges his merciless 'no' out of a longing for 'yes' and so his despair is the negative form from which the contour of its opposite can be drawn."[20] Shepard, who repeatedly praised the dark rigor of Beckett's work in interviews in the early '70s, appears to have been seeking a similar impact, and for him *Action* represented a new move toward "the heart of what [I'm] after . . . the real meat and potatoes." Regardless of the largely negative response to the opening productions, it was "the first thing I've been happy about in a long time."[21]

The influence of Beckett on *Action* is immediately evident in its basic premise. The wall-less, weakly illuminated, and sparsely furnished stage, together with the various teasing references to conflagration and collapse, suggest that the play is set in a kind of postapocalyptic wasteland not dissimilar to those in *Waiting for Godot* and *Endgame*. This is an undefined "time of crisis" in which social structures have disintegrated along with any pretense at plot or narrative. Like Vladimir and Estragon, the four characters (two men and two women, whose relationships to one another are as uncertain as everything else) have nothing to do but idly search for games, topics of conversation, and domestic rituals with which to fill the yawning void of their existence. Indeed, certain actions and phrases are blindly repeated again and again: Shooter smashes three chairs at different points in the play; Lupe states, "we're lucky to have a turkey" four times in two minutes (176–7). *Action* shows Shepard confronting head-on, without the diversions of plot, escape fantasies, and so forth, the numbing fear that in an absurd, Godless universe, life has neither meaning nor purpose, and that the only thing to look forward to is death. Like Beckett, Shepard presents characters trapped in an immutable, existential moment, waiting for the end.

Yet there is also an important difference between Shepard and Beckett. In *Godot*, for example, the tramps at least have the pretext of "waiting" to explain their continued presence on stage. Their self-deceptive insistence that Godot will come provides a reason for their empty existence. In this respect, Beckett appears to critique the condition of modernity, in which the void is papered over with various grand explanations for existence. By contrast, Shepard's play appears to present the condition of postmodernity, with its "incredulity toward meta-narratives."[22] Wistful references are made to an American past in which the nation seemed to be have a direction or future ("Walt Whitman was a great man. . . . He expected something from America. He had this great expectation": 179), but such faith has now been decisively shattered. These four characters have, as Jeep says, "no references" by which to structure their lives: indeed, their lack of a sustaining narrative is repeatedly stressed as they take turns to hunt vainly through a large book for their place in the story. They never find it, and no other explanations for their condition suggest themselves: all sense of reason, continuity, or cause and effect is shattered, to the point where characters will leave the stage to collect something, and return having forgotten why they left. Everything, even the very coexistence of the characters in this space, seems simply accidental.

The result of this is that whereas Didi and Gogo manage, for the most part, to avoid acknowledging the extent of their desperation, Jeep and Shooter – lacking even the most tenuous structure for their lives – are all too aware of theirs. (This is true also of Liza and Lupe, but to a lesser extent: the women divert themselves more successfully – if no more hopefully – via absorption in repetitive domestic activities.) Every time a particular, time-filling thought or action expends itself, the result is an awkward and highly self-conscious search for something new to do. Time and again they admit how scared they are, and crave for the slightest shreds of meaning or motivation, so as to put the crisis off until later: "Shooter," Jeep pleads (a whining parody of the Method actor adrift), "could you create some reason for me to move? Some justification for me to find myself somewhere else?" (186).

It is worth noting that the acute self-consciousness with which these characters confront their dilemma is, at least in part, a result of the writing process itself. Working on it around the time that he directed *Geography* for the Royal Court, Shepard was driven by a fresh awareness that "the spoken word, no matter how you cut it, is different than the written word." With this in mind, he experimented with the idea of sounding every line out loud before setting it to paper. This technique, as he acknowledged, "necessarily sets up a slower tempo" than his more usual free-flowing approach.[23] But it also, crucially, results in each line's being scrutinized and problematized with a rigor never before seen in Shepard's work. This generates a hypersensitive atmosphere in the play itself: the very first line, for example, a general observation from Jeep to nobody in particular, is instantly placed under question by Shooter's demand to know "Who're you talking to?" (170). Similarly, Shooter repeatedly interrogates and ironizes his own choice of words, puzzling over metaphors and figures of speech: "I've never been afraid of baths," he remarks, before adding, "I've always plunged right in." He remembers a friend who would not take baths: "Stank to high heaven. 'High Heaven.' That's a good one" (182).

In short, the new self-consciousness with which Shepard set his words to paper seems to have resulted in a profound distrust of language itself: the characters, as Jeep notes, find it "hard to have a conversation" (174). Words become an obstacle, rather than an aid, to communication, and inchoate "um" and "uh" sounds litter the script as language fails. Yet it is noticeable that the superficial pop jargon of the rock plays is almost entirely absent: where *Tooth* had emphasized the debasement and destabilization of language in contemporary American culture, *Action* suggests that *all* processes of signification are merely provisional, dependent on the tenuously assigned meaning given to them by each individual. (In this respect the play is consistent with poststructuralist theory, which was also being developed during the 1970s.) This instability is seen most poignantly when the characters discover that they cannot define the word "community": they have a vague sense that they know what it means, but it no longer connects with their atomized frames of reference (183). On other occasions the peculiar arbitrariness of signification is stressed by the blunt collision of apparently incompatible words and actions. When Shooter hands a flask back to Liza, she insists, "You can keep it," even as she tucks it into her apron (172).

With language and any claims to meaning appearing increasingly untrustworthy, Shepard lends an unprecedented amount of detailed attention to movement and gesture. Indeed, at bottom, as the title implies, the play is simply a succession of physical actions in the stage space – leg scratching, arm gnawing, fish slicing, and so forth – which provide the characters with momentary diversions from their sense of emptiness. The willful contrivance of these actions is stressed by their strangeness: a soft-shoe shuffle, for example, is performed by two of the characters while seated at a table, palms upturned, staring blankly at each other. Seen in such distorted and unusual contexts, and stripped of any kind of (meta)narrative significance, the play's actions all become events unto

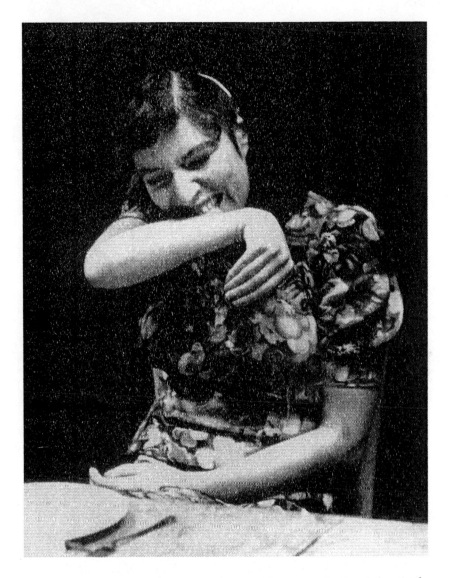

Jennie Stoller in the world premiere production of *Action*, at the Royal Court's Theatre Upstairs, London, 1974. (Photo: Willoughby Gullachsen)

themselves, a sequence of almost wholly unrelated present moments in time.

To some extent, this removal of any pretext of continuity suggests a return to Shepard's early concern with the immediacy of the theatrical event, and this is underlined particularly by actions such as carving up freshly cooked, steaming turkey, which – in a small theatre space – creates not only sight and sound but a direct sensory impact on the nose and saliva glands. But Shepard's interest in exploring the consciousness of the moment seems far more precise in this play than it had ever been in the early work. Effervescent playfulness gives way to ruthlessly detailed observation; in the absence of any kind of transcendent musicality, the repetitive, rhythmic qualities of many of the actions (water poured over and over into a bucket, clothes cranked along a pulley-driven washing line, the perpetual flipping through the book's pages) seem painfully monotonous. This is not, in other words, a celebration of immanent presence in the metaphysical, modernist sense of trying to capture something of the human essence in the artwork. Rather, the play explores presence in the postmodernist sense of blunt, three-dimensional, physical fact. The turkey and fish, for example, are incontrovertibly real, and not merely stage representations of life; the actors' actions of carving and slicing them are actual occurrences, not merely a mimetic fiction. Yet this is, paradoxically, a kind of presence which bespeaks *absence*; the absence of a unifying narrative, the absence of coherent meaning, of spirit, of motivation, and even the absence of theatrical illusion. These contrived and awkward stage events constantly point back to the fact that there is no rounded-out fiction or comprehensible characterization being presented here, just a set of arbitrary actions which bear the dull precision of scripted routine. (The characters' periodic tendency to scrutinize the audience further highlights this de-illusionistic strategy.)

This interest in using theatre as a forum for emphasizing the consciousness of perception, uncluttered by the urge for rationalization, was one Shepard chose to develop beyond *Action* into the ostensibly realistic plays of the later '70s and '80s. Intriguingly, it was also a concern he shared with a new wave of American avant-garde directors emerging in the early 1970s, such as Robert Wilson and Richard Foreman, whose abstract theatre creations were dominated by an emphasis on formalist imagery, and were conspicuous for the lack of logical rationale in their own construction. Although there is no evidence that Shepard was directly influenced by these practitioners, he does acknowledge a considerable debt to the Austrian dramatist Peter Handke, whom he has described as "the contemporary playwright I admire most"; "maybe the best in the world."[24] Handke's play *The Ride Across Lake Constance* (1971) appeared in London while Shepard was there in 1973, and, like *Action* after it, is littered with minutely detailed business and bizarre dialogue from which no clear significance can be intuited. Yet there is also a crucial difference between the plays which seems to point to a profound unease on Shepard's part toward the implications of this postmodern theatricality. Handke, by his own account, was seeking to replace the "often performed tragedy" of existence with a kind of "Utopian comedy." By ridiculing and dispensing with all tortured attempts at finding meaning, Handke's play advocates the idea that "the forms of everyday life. . . seem to operate without any pattern in a 'Free play of the Forces.' "[25] This is, perhaps, *post*absurdism: the fear of living in an absurd, Godless universe is succeeded by a willing acceptance, even celebration, of that emptiness.

Some critics have suggested that Shepard's apparent inability to embrace this position fully is the result of a retrograde craving for the modernist ideals of depth, consonance, and authenticity, which prevents him from seeing his way out of the existential dilemma he depicts, from turning crisis into celebration.[26] Yet Shepard's discomfort with the situation seems motivated less by nostalgia for old assumptions than by an instinctive awareness that postmodernism's simple acceptance of the absence of coherence or meaning will not necessarily liberate anything.[27] The characters' numb terror, as we have seen, springs not from any lingering adherence to old metanarratives, but from the total absence of such. Stripped of all coherent structure, whether social or dramaturgical, these characters are nevertheless *still onstage*, still required to perform, to live. The result is very far from being a utopian comedy.

One aspect of Shepard's discomfort with the emptiness of the situation springs from the same underlying moral vision which had seen Crow, a man without faith in anything but his own masks, as an affectless sociopath. In *Action*, the loss of continuity or coherence leads plainly to an atomized environment in which the most basic precepts of human coexistence – community, conversation – are problematic or meaningless. Helplessly unable to communicate, indifferent to others and turned in on themselves, the characters have sunk to the point where they react with Warholian detachment to violent events such as chairs being smashed, "as though seeing it as an event outside themselves" (175). Even the creative imagination has no power to evoke or inspire. The succession of pictures that Jeep attempts to describe at the play's outset are disjointed and incidental: the self-consciousness of his own attempts at creativity strips them of any connotative properties they might otherwise have. There is no beauty or joy here, only numbness.

The most serious consequence of the situation, however, is a severe crisis of identity. The characters are obliged to be onstage, but are provided with no motives or direction, since they are unable to draw any stabilizing connection between their present existence in the moment and their past or future lives. This results in a kind of schizophrenic condition in which the characters try out a succession of fragmentary roles, adopting new ones in relation to whatever events are currently occurring on stage. In a disturbing variant on Shepard's by now familiar concern with surface performance as a way of life, this shifting role-play becomes a perpetual search for a fleeting sense of structure in each given situation. This is especially evident in Shooter's behavior: whereas Jeep tends simply to talk about his perceived roles, projecting them forward as if at some future point he will fulfill himself ("I'm looking forward to uh – me. The way I picture me": 169), Shooter acts out each new option on the spot. He picks up, for example, on Jeep's image of a performing bear (despite the latter's protests), only to abandon this enactment abruptly, acutely aware of being scrutinized by the audience and by his fellow actors. Later he seizes on the arrival onstage of a big armchair to adopt the more reassuring role of "a father. Very much at home." He insists, "This is more in line with how I see myself," and swears never to leave the chair (181). Yet within minutes, the role has grown tedious, and Shooter regrets his decision, imagining instead the diametrically opposite role of a roving traveler. This fantasy too plays itself out, resulting in another desperate hiatus: "now I've ruined it. Now I've had my cake. Now neither [role] is any good. The chair doesn't get it on, and neither does the adventure. I'm nowhere" (184).

This last dichotomy is reminiscent of the tension between macho heroism and domesticity which is apparent in so many of the rock plays. Yet Shooter dissolves this binary distinction by rendering them two equally inadequate options. Similarly, the tension in the early plays between cozy, stifling civilization and loneliness in the wild is recalled and dissolved by Shooter's dissatisfaction with either the "Inside" or the "Outside." Existing alone, he says, is no good: "You get a cold feeling being outside. Separated. You have an idea that being inside it's cosier." And yet, he notes with terror, the alternative is no alternative. Going inside is

> a shock. It's not like how you expected. You lose what you had outside. You forget that there even is an outside. The inside is all you know. You

> hunt for a way of being with everyone. A way of finding how to behave.
> You find out what's expected of you. You act yourself out. (178)

This erasure of any meaningful distinction between Inside and Outside is also made visually evident when the border line between the dark, exterior upstage, and the lit, interior downstage eventually becomes a washing line on which clothes are hung – centralized as a hive of activity, its dividing function blurred and lost. It is Shooter's formulation, however, which points most disturbingly toward the implications of postmodernity. Existing alone outside, he suggests, is impossible because it entails self-annihilation: with no clear structure to their lives, the only way for these characters to define themselves at all is to find an audience to perform to. The Cartesian *cogito* has been redefined as "I am seen, therefore I exist."[28] Shooter therefore creates trouble for himself when he hides under the armchair, because he can no longer see if anybody is watching him, witnessing his behavior: "Is there anyone to verify? To check it out?" (188). A further problem, however, is that when "Inside," surrounded by this necessary audience, each character is constantly aware of watching and being watched: this too has frightening implications, since it creates a paranoid self-consciousness about one's appearance and performance ("hunting for a way of being with everyone"). If one is always performing oneself for others, how can there be any certainty that one's actions are not based purely on a shallow desire to please or impress? "If you were alone, would you have done that?" Jeep asks cuttingly when Shooter tips over in his chair: "You wouldn't call it showing off?" (187). According to Nancy Meckler, Shepard himself was haunted by precisely this anxiety at the time: he would often "stop talking because he would suddenly feel so false. He could feel himself acting himself out."[29]

The play's recurrent sense that the whole of life is, like it or not, a process of acting oneself out on a stage one did not select is summarized in Jeep's final speech, in which he implies that his entire life has been a process of performing a *prewritten* script over which he has no control (just as the actor playing the part has no option about the words he speaks). The fear of unseen hands manipulating one's every action (first apparent in *Cowboys #2* and recurring as a theme throughout the rock plays) here reaches its most paradigmatic expression. Jeep describes the sense of always having been thrown into prescribed roles, from birth ("Once I was in a family. I had no choice about it") to adulthood ("I was being taken away by something bigger. . . . A vast network. A chain of events"). He realizes, finally, that there is no transcendent outside which will provide an escape from these influences: he is helplessly entrapped, "FOREVER!" As he enacts the speech, Jeep moves around the stage space, the observed arena of his life, vainly hunting for a way out.

If Jeep's speech seems to allude to a lingering insistence on the notion of some inner soul trapped within the performing surface personality, it would nevertheless be a mistake to see this as some kind of last-ditch romanticism. The play's most chilling implication is that *regardless* of whether one's sense of identity is founded on an appeal to essentials ("Something inside") or on a more provisional proposition ("the way I picture me"; "how I see myself"), this self-conception will inevitably be rendered inadequate by the fact of living in an arbitrary world which resists even the most temporary kinds of rationale. As Shooter notes, foreshadowing Shepard's increasing emphasis during the 1970s on the schizophrenic instability of character,

> I get this feeling *I can't control the situation*. Something's getting out of control. Things won't work. And then I smash something. I punch something. I scream. Later I find out that my throat is torn. I've torn something loose. My voice is hoarse. I'm trembling. My breath is short. My heart's thumping. *I don't recognize myself*. (173: emphases added)

Written at a time when Shepard himself was reappraising the whole question of his role as playwright, it is perhaps not surprising that *Action* addresses so bluntly the highly tendentious nature of all attempts at self-definition. Yet the sheer rigor with which he stripped his vision down, to emphasize the idea of life's fundamental lack of stability or reliable meaning, also leaves the play at something of a dead end. Shepard had nowhere to go with this existentially based, (post)absurdist approach unless he were to follow the Beckettian lead in distilling the same basic ideas down to a point of almost complete self-erasure (Beckett eventually succeeded in summing up his art in his 1969 piece *Breath*, which lasts thirty-five seconds). *Killer's Head*, a monologue written as an afterpiece for *Action* in 1975, perhaps indicates a brief move in this direction, with its single image of a man desperately but unsuccessfully seeking to distract himself from the fact of his imminent death (the two periods of almost a minute's silence in the midst of his babbling seem pregnant with unspoken terror). But Shepard proved unwilling to pursue such minimalism further. Shaking off the European influence, he headed back to America to find fresh inspiration.

4

Nightmares of the Nation

Improvisations and Collaborations, 1976–1979

SHEPARD AND HIS FAMILY returned to the United States in 1974, "to find our roots," and set up their home in the first of a series of locations in the San Francisco Bay area. Inevitably, the move further disrupted his attempts to find his feet again as a writer, and there was more than one false start. *California Heart Attack* (1974) remained unfinished, an exercise in the same writer-and-wife-lost-in-hostile-environment vein as *Blue Bitch*, but transplanted across two continents. *Man Fly* (1975) was a somewhat uninspired adaptation of Marlowe's *Doctor Faustus* which was turned down by the theatre that commissioned it, the Mark Taper Forum in Los Angeles.[1] However, from 1976, having oriented himself in his new location, Shepard settled into one of the most prolific phases of his career, and over the next three years or so produced a remarkably diverse range of work, from essentially light-hearted projects like the satirical comic-operetta *The Sad Lament of Pecos Bill on the Eve of Killing His Wife* (written for America's bicentennial celebrations in 1976), to the Pulitzer prize–winning play *Buried Child* (1978).

Unquestionably the most important catalyst to Shepard's fresh output was his new association with the Magic Theatre. Founded by John Lion in 1967, this small, adventurous outfit had acquired a reputation for challenging audiences with plays by writers from Ionesco to Shepard himself (the Magic's 1969 production of *La Turista* was the first outside New York). Shepard's arrival in San Francisco coincided with Lion's decision to move his theatre into the city after years of working in temporary locations in Berkeley. The pair were introduced by a mutual friend, beat writer Michael McClure (also an associate of the Magic), and it was quickly realized that a collaboration would be to the advantage of both. Among the initial inspirations for Lion's theatre had been the Off-Off-Broadway model of intimate, informal atmosphere, the promotion of experiment, and (crucially) the right to fail, and as such it proved to be an ideal base for Shepard and became his artistic home until 1983. He was granted almost total freedom in shaping his own projects, and exploited this to the full. In particular, he took the opportunity to pursue, in a variety of ways, the exploration of the performance process he had begun with *Geography of a Horse Dreamer*. In the first instance, with the Magic based in the tiny upstairs room of the Rose and Thistle pub, he experimented further with directing his own scripts (*Action* and *Killer's Head* in 1975, *Angel City* in 1976). Then from 1976, with the theatre housed in its permanent waterfront home at Fort Mason, he initiated collaborative work on a major and minor scale, as well as working on projects instigated by colleagues like his wife, O-Lan, whose group Overtone Theatre was also founded during this period.

These experiments were no doubt partially inspired by Shepard's new environment. During the '70s, San Francisco had become recognized as a leading center for experimental performance, with pioneering work in everything from "life art" in galleries to site-specific installations. The Magic Theatre was itself actively involved in fostering the latter, and also served as home to some of the groundbreaking formalist experiments of Alan Finneran's group Soon 3. In addition, the Magic was at this time able to draw on a rich pool of young acting talent for its dramatic productions, including now-established names like Ed Harris, Amy Madigan, and Danny Glover. In short, Shepard had arrived in the middle of what Lion calls "an incredibly fecund period" for the arts in San Francisco, and proved "voracious" in his absorption of the new stimuli: "He was insatiable to be filled up with literature, with film, and he was very open to being taken places and shown things."[2]

Shepard's most ambitious collaborative project during this period was *Inacoma*, funded in 1977 by a $15,000 grant from the Rockefeller Foundation, which inaugurated the Magic's second space at Fort Mason, a 99-seat, three-quarter-round studio (the main space was a proscenium stage with an auditorium then housing 130). *Inacoma* made use of a company of fifteen actors and musicians, who worked together intensively for six weeks to devise a loosely structured work-in-progress presentation. Among the inspirations Shepard drew on for this project was his experience of watching the Open Theatre's workshops in the 1960s: he made particular use of their "Sound and Movement" exercise, in which actors respond with nonverbal sound and pronounced physical movements to each other's sponta-

neous inputs in order to generate material. It was perhaps fitting, therefore, that in 1978 and 1979 Shepard went on to co-create two performances, *Tongues* and *Savage/Love*, with the former director of the Open
Theatre, his friend and mentor Joseph Chaikin. These pieces, which developed from Chaikin's and Shepard's improvising either singly or together,
are collage-like in structure, loosely grouping together segments of text
which revolve around the same thematic concerns (reflections on life and
death in *Tongues*; love in *Savage/Love*). Spoken by a single voice
(Chaikin's), they rely heavily on the musical qualities of the language: certain verbal patterns are repeated with minor variations each time; certain
phrases or words recur within segments as rhythmic punctuation; in
Tongues different "voices" explore different rhythms of speech.

Shepard's return to such improvisatory collage structures was significant, in that it also marked a revival of his interest in jazz music. Indeed,
both *Inacoma* and *Savage/Love* made use of live jazz instrumentation. The
former's musicians styled themselves as "the San Francisco Theatre Jazz
Ensemble," and the piece as a whole was structured according to the classic jazz format, using a backbone of scored music and sections of written
text to hold together other, more free-form sections, which were improvised by actors and musicians alike on each night of performance. In its
original presentation, *Savage/Love*'s fragmentary tone poems were also
held together partly through the use of an underlying score of bluesy,
horn-based jazz performed by three musicians, as directed by Shepard
(one of these, percussionist J. A. Deane, became a long-term collabora-
tor, continuing to work with him into the 1990s). In *Tongues*, Shepard himself initially performed as the solo percussionist, seated behind Chaikin:
the patterns he developed (described in the published text) work either
to complement or counterpoint Chaikin's speech rhythms.

The revival of Shepard's interest in jazz was no doubt partly a result of
his once again feeling comfortable in an urban environment which
encouraged innovation (he immersed himself in San Francisco's thriving
musical scene, playing drums at various jazz clubs, and even conceiving
an experimental performance piece, *Drum War*, for a battery of nine
tympani). It also signaled his final loss of interest in rock music as a source
of inspiration. In 1975 he had accepted a dream invitation to join
Bob Dylan's Rolling Thunder Revue rock tour as scriptwriter for a pro-
jected film about its stars. The film was never completed, though, and the
whole experience – as described in Shepard's *Rolling Thunder Logbook*
(1977) – only confirmed his suspicions that the 1960s rock scene was dead
and buried, and its devotees merely wandering around blindly in search
of direction.

Playing Outside

By contrast, Shepard had found himself clear new directions by recon-
ceiving a more sophisticated notion of the relationship of music and
drama, which resulted in the writing of the five play texts which Shepard
produced between 1976 and 1979. Responding to the jazz terminology of
playing "outside" and "inside" preconceived structures, he simultaneously applied both approaches to his playwriting. As he explained in 1979,
"I've been following two streams. One is the outside play, more improvisatory, the kind of writing that writes itself. . . . The other is the inside
play, the family play, much more structured."[3] The "outside" plays of this
period – which are the focus of this chapter – were *Angel City* and *Suicide in B♭*, both of which were written in 1976 and feature live jazz instrumentation, and *Seduced* (1978). Each of these pieces, as Shepard's comments imply, was written more or less free-form, as he pushed himself to
rediscover the kind of raw spontaneity which had marked his earliest
work. He had decided, it seems, that the slowed-down writing technique
he had used in *Action* had limited creative potential, and here he swung
back to the other extreme in search of fresh inspiration.

Clearly written at considerable speed, these pieces revive something
of the "freakish," hermetically sealed nightmare quality of the early plays.
Yet they are also very different from those previous jazz-influenced works
in a number of respects. For one thing, there is no backtracking here to
the modernist view of spontaneity and personal style as a means to authentic self-expression. *Angel City* and *Suicide*, in particular, are characterized
by extreme forms of the bricolage effect introduced in the rock plays: a
particularly unsettling form of eclectic theft is employed here, with Shepard drawing on a kaleidoscopic range of seemingly incompatible fragments from both "high" and "mass" culture, and pushing the fragmentation of structure almost to the point of terminal breakdown. These pieces
are arguably the most radically decentered of all Shepard's work: the musical inspiration, it would seem, is derived from the fractured outer
extremes of free jazz (quite explicitly so in *Suicide*, which deals with the
supposed death of an experimental jazz composer). *Seduced* also relies on
loose improvisation and multiple sources, but is less unstable than its predecessors, by virtue of focusing largely on a single character, Henry Hackamore. For that reason it is also perhaps the least challenging of the three.

The abrasively disorientating effect of these pieces derives not from
any particularly new developments in Shepard's writing, but from the
abrupt juxtaposition – through a particularly raw kind of free association
– of stylistic elements drawn from the whole gamut of his previous exper-

iments. Linguistically, for example, he draws on both the loud, pounding extremes of the rock plays (a tendency to print language in hysterical capitals is indulged more freely than ever before) and the subtler, more elliptical approach of the earliest work: the jazz-solo technique of creating self-contained, aria-like monologues with their own internal rhythmic dynamics is resurrected and used to often hypnotic effect. Similarly, Shepard combines the jazz-collage construction methods of the early plays with the more linear, plot-pretext method developed in the rock plays. Each piece begins by establishing a loose narrative premise, thus leading audiences to expect some form of development and resolution. In each case, however, this expectation is thwarted as the improvisation process results not in story structures but in loose collections of images and speeches, riffing off the established motifs. This collage method, in turn, is undermined by Shepard's tendency to interpolate completely unrelated material into the proceedings, whenever a consistent pattern seems to be emerging. *Angel City*, for instance, in addition to its underlying reliance on the interplay of clashing elements from various film genres (film noir, schlock-horror, and disaster movies), periodically veers off on alarming tangents, incorporating everything from television channel-surfing to Hopi Indian lore and Japanese martial arts. Shepard's approach here invites parallels with that of contemporary performance innovators like Richard Foreman and the Wooster Group (whose first piece was devised in 1976), who have also utilized abrupt juxtapositions of apparently unrelated material to suggest a form of mediatized postmodern consciousness in which discontinuity is the predominant mode of experience.

Shepard's use of collage structures is also more sophisticated here in that his improvisations revolve not only around visual motifs (as in the early plays) but around identifiable themes. These pieces evolve into unstable, disjointed meditations on familiar cultural reference points: *Angel City* deals with a *Day of the Locust*–style apocalyptic vision of Hollywood; *Seduced*, with the paranoia and power mania of a tycoon recluse (clearly based on Howard Hughes); and *Suicide in B♭* with a detective story murder investigation. Moreover, as *Suicide* makes particularly clear, through numerous passing references to the "the nation," each piece is a reflection on the state of the post-Watergate, post-Vietnam America to which Shepard had returned. His use of jazz is itself a part of that concern, Shepard now seeing it not only as a model of free-flowing creativity, but also as an inherently American phenomenon: as he had noted in a jazz review written for *The Village Voice* while still living in London, "these guys give us the feeling of America, then and now."[4]

The other dominant motif linking these pieces is the notion of chaos itself, to which Shepard alludes not only through the disorientating (lack of) structure, but also as a self-conscious thematic thread. Combining *Action*'s European-influenced, postabsurdist sense of human existence as a structureless void with *The Tooth of Crime*'s more American vision of pop-cultural chaos fed by ruthless individualism, these plays suggest an increasingly sophisticated treatment of postmodern instability. Paradoxically, Shepard also continues to appeal somewhat desperately to the modernist notion of underlying essence, as an antidote of sorts to the chaos. Yet here, too, his method has become more sophisticated: the various mythic images of rebirth or wholeness to which he appeals are offered not as escape fantasies, as in the rock plays, but as implicit comments on the existential/cultural crises being presented. The writing here is constantly undercutting itself, pressing the plays' characters toward schizophrenic breakdown.

Without a Clue

The increasing sophistication and self-awareness of Shepard's exploration of postmodern incoherence is perhaps made most evident in the basic premise of *Suicide in B^b*. The desire to impose clear meanings and structures onto chaotic experiences is exposed and lampooned by this play's gleeful demolition of the generic conventions of the detective mystery. In this respect, it is intriguing to note Brian McHale's definitions of modernist literature as a primarily epistemological form, and of detective fiction as "the epistemological genre par excellence." That is, the genre is concerned with the question of how one knows things: the detective hunts down answers by piecing together clues; the modernist assembles fragments to create fresh structures of understanding. Just so, *Suicide* begins with a detective story, posing the question of who murdered the composer, Niles. Yet this question, and the desire to resolve it, are made to appear gradually more ridiculous as Shepard destabilizes the very reality of the stage world in which the detectives operate. He thus steers the play toward the kind of ontological questions – questions about the very nature of being – which, McHale argues, characterize *post*modernism: "Which world is this? What is to be done in it? Which of my selves is to do it?"[5] These questions, moreover, remain forever unanswerable.

Pablo and Louis's ability to solve the crime, it should be noted, is in doubt from the very outset: they are incompetents, a Chandleresque variation on Shepard's penchant for Laurel and Hardy duos. Yet they are not helped by the fact that they have no firm evidence ("no references") to go on at all: the body even lacks fingerprints and a face. Like the characters in *Action* hunting through the book for a foothold in the narrative, Pablo searches desperately through his briefcase for "our one piece of evidence," but his hunt is fruitless. He insists that his documents hold the answer, that they are "Super Confidential," but Louis ridicules him, claiming that they are "as valuable as yesterday's Daily News."[6] Blatant contradictions of this kind litter the play, as the detectives resort to wild speculation, spinning a series of incompatible, and completely unfounded, hypotheses: Niles committed suicide because he was a musical failure; Niles was so successful that fame got too much for him and he had to stage his death and disappear; Niles became involved with a cult which murdered him when he tried to escape. "We haven't tried a stabbing yet!" Pablo eventually remarks when all other ideas fail: "His face was blown off!" Louis points out, helpfully (199). In a sense, this succession of contradictory theories is itself an aspect of the play's chaotic musicality: abandoning linear plot development, Shepard provides statement and counterpoint, holding them in a state of tension and never providing resolution.

Among this proliferation of vain attempts to explain the death, are a succession of paranoid conspiracy theories: "some very big steam in some very high places" must be involved (196), or perhaps the Mafia, or political subversives "distorting the very foundations of our cherished values" (205). Here the play appears to be parodying the plethora of conspiracy theories that were appearing in the '70s, in the aftermath of Watergate and new revelations about the death of Kennedy. In *Suicide*, as in the postmodernist conspiracy novels of Thomas Pynchon, the theories grow increasingly ridiculous and all-embracing: "It got so I felt they were personally responsible for a bad count of smack" (206). Yet the need to imagine a world which makes some kind of sense remains acute: the attraction of conspiracy theories, as Pynchon writes, is that without them, "nothing is connected to anything, a condition not many of us can bear for long."[7]

It is precisely this sense of terrifying arbitrariness that Shepard dramatizes here. Despite the detectives' best intentions, there is nothing to make sense of: things simply happen. The play is full of strange, unconnected events similar to the "pure" theatrical gestures in *Action* (characters sitting on each other's laps, a silent saxophone, offstage screams, Petrone's surreal account of his bones sticking out of his elbows). Yet in the detective genre context, these moments acquire the connotation of mysterious clues (or perhaps red herrings), thereby exacerbating the audience's inability to attach meaning to them. The very idea of a hunt for answers, the play implies, is merely wishful thinking, a vain attempt to impose structure on chaos. As Petrone points out, even Raymond Chandler only succeeded in creating connections in his work by willful artifice: "He always started out knowing who the killer was first and spent the rest of the time covering it up" (212).

The confusion is further exacerbated when the very reality of the stage world Pablo and Louis inhabit is placed in doubt. The supposed victim of the murder/suicide, Niles, enters the stage action, apparently very much alive, but also invisible to the other characters, who remain frozen as he speaks. He and his companion, Paullette, occupy the same physical space but appear to be on some altogether different plane of being, delineated by lighting changes. It is unclear whether they are alive, ghosts, or merely figments of Petrone's imagination (they appear just after he has begun to tell "the story of Niles, from the top"). It is even hinted that the other characters may all be figments of Niles's imagination. Shepard thus destabilizes the ontological status of all the events and characters: by bifurcating the stage into two planes of existence, he subverts the "reality" of both. The original pretext of solving the death thus becomes utterly irrelevant.

When Paullette's invisible weapons begin to traverse the dimensional boundary, striking down the detectives, the status and relation of the stage worlds becomes even more problematic. And when, at the end of the play, Petrone and Niles somehow meet in a neutral street space, and Niles is led – dead, fictitious, or otherwise – back into the room where the detectives are, the confusion reaches the point of total overload: Pablo, for one, finds himself able to "subscribe to no system of thought. I'm on the verge of total madness" (228). Meanwhile, Niles ditches all pretense at sanity, and in a final, raving speech openly taunts the audience with the futility of their desire to find a coherent explanation for what has transpired:

> What's everybody waiting for?. . . Am I alive or dead? Is that it? In my own house? Is this me here, now? Are these questions or answers? Are you waiting for the truth to roll out and lap your faces like a bloodhound's tongue? Are you diving to the bottom of it? Getting to the core of the mystery? Getting closer? Moving in for the kill? Waiting for one wrong move when they're all wrong moves? (229)

Character as Collage

The destabilization of a familiar genre, and the concomitant descent into chaos, are the bases on which *Angel City*, too, is built. The play initially sets itself up as a stylized "Tale of Hollywood," opening with a Shepardian variation on the familiar scenario of the established writer being called on by the movie industry. Rabbit Brown, a kind of artist-shaman, arrives in a nightmare version of a Hollywood production office, which is replete with all the clichéd ingredients (dictatorial producers, would-be-starlet secretary, hack script needing rewrites). Rabbit, one initially assumes, is another version of the familiar artist-at-odds-with-the-system figure (already a feature of *Melodrama Play* and *Geography of a Horse Dreamer*). Representing "the old ways" (he is named for a famous jazz musician, wears cowboy boots, believes in prayer, and rides into town on a buckboard), he is expected to stand up against (or possibly be seduced by) the evil machinations of power. Moreover, he is expected to represent the audience's perspective within the play: his detective-style overcoat connotes his role as the character appointed to investigate and shed light on this environment. Three modernist hero roles are thus rolled into one: at the outset Rabbit seems, simultaneously, to be the detective searching for answers, the avant-garde artist defying the temptations of commerce, and the lone, Kafkaesque individual up against the monolithic system.

Yet it quickly becomes clear that Shepard is mocking his entire premise. The studio, for example, takes on the ludicrously exaggerated dimensions of an all-powerful hierarchy which even regulates the density of the Los Angeles smog for its own ends. This Pynchonian fantasy of a dominating "They-system," which knows exactly how to manipulate each of its subjects ("They'll swallow you whole and spit you out as a tax deduction . . . They'll feed off your hunger. They'll keep you jumping at carrots": 73), is another figment of paranoia, created by the need to fend off the even greater fear of the total lack of stable structures. It transpires that the producers are not in control at all: their nightmare system has acquired its own, self-destructive momentum and is crumbling into depraved chaos. As for Rabbit, he is far from being the longed-for hero (as Wheeler explicitly points out in act 2). Within minutes of the start of the play, and at the end of a speech establishing his credentials as an inspired loner, Rabbit abruptly undermines this stereotyped role by lapsing into pure greed: "I'm ravenous for power but I have to conceal it" (69). Thereafter Rabbit's behavior becomes every bit as opaque and inconsistent as that of his captors. The hero-villain and us-them binaries collapse, and the audience – as in *Suicide* – is left groping for footholds: it becomes increasingly clear that Rabbit is a figure of pastiche as he rattles off clichéd jargon which suggests everything from hard-boiled tough guy ("Listen, Mack, no matter how many greasy skinbags . . .": 73) through literary critic ("on the whole I think it showed a remarkable economy of language": 75) to military tactician ("I'm not sure if I can accurately assess the danger that we're in here": 76).

Rabbit's instability is symptomatic of *Angel City*'s entire approach: here Shepard takes to a logical extreme the suggestion of *Action* that, in a world deprived of structure, identity itself fragments beyond repair. Indeed, Rabbit is relatively stable in comparison with some of the other figures in the play. The producer, Lanx, in his opening interrogation of Rabbit is by turns ingratiating, dismissive, humorous, intimidating, and nervously terrified. Over the course of the play he then retreats ever further into a private fantasy world, casting himself as a heroic boxer figure, and switching manically between this role and that of producer. The drummer, Tympani, and the secretary, Miss Scoons, also envision themselves in reassuring roles drawn from the pop-cultural debris of moviedom, in which they seem to immerse themselves ever deeper. Watching over these maneuvers in bewildered disbelief is Wheeler, who is himself perhaps the *most* unstable figure in the play. Introduced at first as a "shy and intimidated" backroom nerd, he becomes a deranged prophet of apocalypse within the space of his first major speech, before inexplicably supplanting Lanx in the position of head producer and gradually turning into a lizard. His behavior shifts almost from line to line, a wheezing, screaming, calm, insane, professorial, megalomaniacal, dying genius.

Angel City represents a radical experiment on Shepard's part, in which the depthless superficiality of character implied by the rock plays is replaced by a vision of characters who are equally opaque but enormously complex. Their identities are made up of fragmentary collections of impulses, fantasies, and experiences, any of which could force its way to the surface at any given moment. One source of this instability appears to have been Shepard's own state of mind at the time: his papers from the mid-'70s include an entire collection of broken poetry, *Fractured*, which is prefaced by a note to the reader explaining that the pieces are "merely a reflection of my own inner condition."[8] Another influence may have been Peter Brook, who had persuaded him that he needed to explore the issue of character more deeply. Aware that his previous fascination with overall form, with "exteriors" (inspired by his concern with music and painting), had "sort of played itself out," Shepard took Brook's suggestion to heart.[9] Ironically, though, the presentation of such "schizoid" behavior enabled him to employ his fascination with music and painting in a new, directly character-oriented direction, by applying precisely the collage and improvisation techniques he had previously used to construct the overall shape of a piece. As he explained in *Angel City*'s "Note for Actors":

> The term "character" could be thought of in a different way when working on this play. Instead of the idea of a "whole character" with log-

ical motives behind his behavior which the actor submerges himself into, he should consider instead a fractured whole with bits and pieces of character flying off the central theme. In other words, more in terms of collage construction or jazz improvisation. [The actor is] mixing many underlying elements and connecting them through his intuition and senses to make a kind of music or painting in space. (62)

Shepard directed the opening production of the play himself, and put these ideas into practice by encouraging his actors, quite literally, to construct pictorial collages of their characters' psyches, using the assembly of images to represent their various contradictory desires, and to compare them to animals, objects, famous people, and so forth. This exercise was aimed at helping the actors to hold these disparate elements in tension, rather than iron them out into some synthesized coherence. Moreover, it is evident from Shepard's original, handwritten manuscript that the few revisions he made to the first draft were also intended to exacerbate, rather than ease, the sharply jarring shifts within the play and its characters' behavior.[10] My own experience of directing the piece reinforced the impression that it would *only* work on stage if the characters' mood swings were made as abrupt and obvious as possible. The actor playing Miss Scoons, for example, found it useful to think of her character as having three basic personality types, each of which was drawn from Hollywood stereotype (dumb blonde, ballbreaker, small-town-girl-trying-to-make-good). The transitions between these personae often had to be made without even a pause for breath.

The abrasive extremes to which *Angel City* pushes its fragmentation of character remain unmatched in Shepard's subsequent work, as he began to find subtler methods of pursuing this sense of identities in flux. Certainly the characters in *Suicide in B♭* are far less volatile, except perhaps for Niles himself, who appears to suffer from a kind of multiple schizophrenia: "THERE'S VOICES COMING AT ME! . . . THERE'S VOICES FROM ALL SIDES!" (210). One of the most disturbing ontological twists in the play is the suggestion that all the other characters may merely be his own subpersonae, facets of the chaos within his mind (his "house"), whom he has "invited in" so as to be able to cope with his life: "So I wouldn't have to feel that loneliness" (216). On the other hand, if the other characters in *Suicide* remain, for the most part, stubbornly two-dimensional, this may simply be another attempt to cope with the confusion surrounding them. The detectives have constructed tenuous and simplistic self-definitions for themselves (Louis sees himself as blunt and simple; Pablo repeatedly refers to his education as something that grants him status – "I've got a master's degree!"), and they become hysterical at the tiniest threat to the validity of these roles. When Louis feels his role and his sanity slipping away, he threatens to kill himself in a last-ditch bid for meaning or self-definition. But the gesture is even less convincing coming from him than it was from Hoss, and is viewed with bored contempt by the others, who accuse him of performing emptily for the benefit of an audience which is not even watching:

> LAUREEN: Just get up.
> LOUIS: Not until I get some guarantees!
> PETRONE: Let him kill himself. Who gives a fuck. (206)

Art as Structure?

The frantic search for "guarantees," for some glimpse of a coherent structure to life, is manifested in numerous different ways in these plays. *Suicide*, for example, alludes frequently to the idea that the nation should provide some lead, but that – in post-Nixonian America – it is "broken in half. . . . Aren't we leaderless? Jobless? Destitute? Forlorn?" (206). In the face of such confusion, Louis resorts to nostalgia, appealing to his experience as a soldier fighting for the nation during "The Real War in the Real World" (213): he seems to hope that this memory of life-and-death struggles will provide some bottom line to his disintegrating sense of self. Similarly, in *Angel City*, Wheeler hypothesizes that what is needed to save the day is a "big, major world war," which would bring "a focus to the people. They take sides. Us against them. Simple." Yet even this ironic appeal to tidy (and deadly) binary schemes is perceived as an outdated irrelevance: as Wheeler says, there are now only incoherent nightmare wars such as the one in Vietnam, "secret little creepy wars in the swamp. So. No war, no focus. No focus, no structure. No structure spells disaster" (95). A further irony is that Louis and Pablo, despite their claims to innocence, also appear to be implicated in such destabilization: they refer obliquely to secret intelligence operations and Cuba, as if they were with the CIA in the Bay of Pigs.

With the nation providing no firm structures, only deaths and conspiracies, the characters in both plays look to the arts as a means of possible salvation, new sources of structure which might draw together the fragments of experience. In *Suicide* the subject is music, and Shepard explores it extensively, beginning most notably with Louis's hypothetical speech about Niles's life. Niles, he suggests, experienced a terrifying sense of chaos from the moment of birth, in the form of random and oppressive noise: "Nuclear rushes of wind through his nose holes. Toenails rubbing blankets in the dark. Books falling on pianos. Electricity humming even when the lights are off. Internal combustion engines. Turbo jets." Thus, when he discovered music, it came as a saving revelation: "An organization. Another way of putting it. . . . An adventure. A way inside" (196–7). For the listener too, as Petrone observes, the consonance of music provides a kind of religious experience: "transforming me. Changing me. Filling me up. Taking away everything deadly. Taking away this awful, empty loneliness and making me whole again. Making me feel alive" (226).

Conversely, though, the play also sees music as a dangerously uncontrollable force which may only add to the sense of chaos: as Pablo suggests early on, Niles might have been the victim of "macabre overtones" which "spiraled toward his eventual downfall" (203). Particular reference is made to the disintegration of reassuringly familiar musical patterns, which have been undermined by the fragmentation of free jazz. Pablo, for example, rails at contemporary musicians for "breaking with tradition!" and "turning the classics to garbage before our very eyes! . . . rubbing up against the very grain of sanity and driving us all to complete and utter destruction!" (205). Of course, Shepard is a confirmed fan of free jazz, and there is clearly a satirical side to the detectives' complaints, a parody of the attitudes of traditionalist music fans. Nevertheless, the fears that the detectives express are realized forcefully in the play's onstage music. The three musicians (an anonymous, wordless pianist, the saxophonist Petrone, and the double bass player Laureen), frequently launch into runs of improvised music which is free of all moorings, working simultaneously with, but unrelated to, the dialogue. Shepard even remarks that it does not matter if the actress playing Laureen cannot really play: what is required, presumably, is a random scraping on the bass which need not be coordinated with the other instruments. As Robert Woodruff noted of his production of *Suicide* at the Magic Theatre in 1979, the entire play "turned into a jazz piece, one very long jam. The music was improvised every night, which creates an incredible risk factor."[11] But it seems that the greater the risk and instability, the better, so far as the play is concerned, since this exacerbates the detectives' sense that "Everything's crazy!"

By contrast, the live jazz in *Angel City* is more structured, harking back explicitly to bebop and "prebop" styles: the solo saxophonist, who operates outside events to provide occasional bursts of "lyrical loneliness," combines with Tympani's kettle-drumming to create various aural effects from high-speed hysteria to slow, mesmeric insistence, but in all instances these rhythms are carefully integrated with the mood of the dialogue. Instead of music, Shepard's main concern here is with the art of movie making, which offers another highly ambiguous source of consonance. Trying to diagnose what a movie needs to achieve, Tympani, Rabbit, and Miss Scoons decide that people are suffering from a "paralyzing fear" which "produces severe nausea and depression." This terror, they argue with comic frankness, springs from both "the expectation of a death unknown" and from a sense of life's meaninglessness: "We're only going around in circles. We're only going around and around" (86–7). They thus conclude that the movies must provide a larger-than-life experience which proposes a clear, binary structure for the world as an alternative to gray confusion:

> TYMPANI: It's either an Angel or a Devil. Which one's it going to be?
> RABBIT: There must be something in between.
> TYMPANI: But that's totally boring. . . . That's where we are right now.
>   IN BETWEEN! (84)

Movies, the play suggests, provide their viewers with a focus, an escape, gods in a godless world. The result of this dependence, however, as Miss Scoons makes clear in an appropriately hypnotic rhythmic monologue, is that "real life" becomes still more difficult to face, that the movies even come to seem *more real* than the viewer's everyday drudgery:

> I look at the screen and I am the screen. I'm not me. I don't know who I am. I look at the movie and I am the movie. I am the star. I am the star in the movie. For days I am the star and I'm not me. I'm me being the star. I look at my life when I come down. I look and I hate my life when I come down. I hate my life not being a movie. I hate my life not being a star. I hate being myself in my life which isn't a movie and never will be . . . (77)

The destabilizing potential of screen media is also made apparent in Shepard's use of formal devices, and most notably his recurrent use of the "jump cut" device. In plays like *The Mad Dog Blues*, he had utilized cinematic crosscutting to facilitate rapid plot progression between scenes, but here he creates not the illusion of seamlessness, but jarring juxtapositions. Like a sequence of film put together from waste oddments from a cutting room floor, the play frequently shifts gear into material completely unrelated to the preceding moment: the actors have to transform on the spot into entirely different roles. The most extreme example of this device is the television sequence in act 1, in which Rabbit and the drummer Tympani suddenly, inexplicably, become the voice of a television set and a child watching. The commentary moves rapidly from a news broad-cast, though continuity announcements, to a sports show (Lanx suddenly appears as a boxing champion), and back to the news, while the child (Tympani) goggles and becomes louder and louder, until he is screaming to be taken to the movies. He, in turn, is then interrupted by Miss Scoons' reentry, which prompts the action to cut back to the studio setting as sud-denly as it had departed.

The characters then make no reference to this episode, as if it had never happened; or as if it had taken place on another channel. And this in itself is symptomatic of the notion that as media illusions colonize and supplant the world of the real, any notion of ontological stability is stripped away. This becomes increasingly apparent over the course of the play as the characters descend ever further into their personal movie-fantasies, thereby gradually eroding any trace of a shared sense of reality. Even the relatively straightforward exchanges of the first act often display a bizarre, multiple-focus effect (see, for instance, the exchange on Dixie cups, good moods, and guinea pigs), and by the second act the situation has descended into utter chaos, with the characters lost in private uni-verses, helplessly unable to communicate with each other in any mean-ingful way. The effect onstage is rather like watching five television chan-nels playing simultaneously. Any remaining illusion of a coherent plot or focus is abandoned, and the audience can only sit and watch the confu-sion – even as Lanx insists, in flat contradiction of the visual evidence, that nothing has gone wrong, that "everything's exactly the same" (93).

Objective reality thus disappears out of the window; quite literally so, since the rectangular frame at the back of the set appears to function both as a movie screen and as a window on the outside world (which appears to be either a smog-covered city, or "sculptured hedges," or just "all yel-low," depending on the character's point of view). This frame-within-the-frame is used on numerous occasions by the actors, who act on either side of it at will, freely traversing the boundary and thereby erasing any notion of clear oppositions between fiction and reality, inside and outside, or even two- and three-dimensionality. The irrelevance of such distinctions in this environment is summed up by Wheeler's maniacal declaration, "Anything is possible here! We can recreate the world and make you swallow it whole!" Rabbit fights a desperate rearguard action for ontological clarity: "You can't mix the movies with real life!" "THE MOVIES!" Wheeler cries in derision: "THIS IS THE MOVIES!!" (103). Wheeler proves his own point when he then falls victim to the very instability he has celebrated, being swallowed up into his own cinematic illusion, and finding himself being watched from the far side of the frame by Lanx and Miss Scoons, who are suddenly teenagers at a drive-in, looking in on the stage world. The events of the entire play thus become those of a B movie: *Angel City* disappears inside itself in a kind of trompe l'oeil effect which brilliantly summarizes its implications. This is Shepard's most advanced vision of a world where all human experience is mediatized, filtered through and conditioned by the illusory fictions of postmodern hyper-reality.

Individualism Run Rampant

Yet Shepard's concern in these plays is not simply to examine the bewilderment of contemporary existence with ironic resignation. As ever, a resistant, even moralistic impulse is written deeply into them: there is a clear implication that the American ethos of macho individualism is a major catalyst in this downward spiral toward destruction. Combining the cultural critique of *The Tooth of Crime* with the existential concerns of *Action*, Shepard suggests that the rapacious egoism of his key characters springs directly from their attempts to deny their fear of the void. As Miss Scoons says with disconcerting clarity during one of her trances, the individualistic ambition "To kill. To win. To get on top" is a direct result of the need "To make things safe. To beat death. To be victorious in the face of absolute desolation" (88–9). This connection had been hinted at in the monologue *Killer's Head* (in which Mazon appears to be trying to ignore the fact of his imminent execution by talking incessantly about the details of his cowboy lifestyle) and made explicit in the operetta *Pecos Bill*: the eponymous cowboy folk-hero harps on and on about his mythical exploits ("Wasn't it me / Who dug the mighty Rio Grande / All by hand?"), so as to demonstrate his godlike power. But his boasts become increasingly pathetic, a vain attempt to deny the fact that – as Slue-Foot Sue tells him – "from death you can't never escape."[12]

In *Angel City*, this theme acquires much darker (and funnier) overtones, as the executives Wheeler and Lanx begin to dabble in the black magic of a new kind of disaster/horror movie in an attempt to gain a personal sense of control over the undifferentiated chaos threatening to engulf them, and so establish "SOME KIND OF ORDER! SOME KIND OF ARRANGEMENT!" (89). This apocalyptic vision of depraved American enterprise is a development of some of the ideas which had first surfaced in Shepard's unproduced rewrite of *Doctor Faustus*, *Man Fly* (1975), in which "Big Business" is equated with Lucifer. Rabbit is modeled directly from *Man Fly*'s Faust figure, the shaman-poet Doctor Skeetz (both use Indian lore, enjoy campfires, and so forth), and like Skeetz he too rapidly abandons any principles when tempted: as Miss Scoons remarks pithily, "Money equals power, equals protection, equals eternal life" (74). Moreover, she points out that Rabbit's corruption is hardly surprising since artists are really no holier than anyone else: "The urge to create works of art is essentially one of ambition. The ambition behind the urge to create is no different from any other ambition" (88). The play thus implicitly ridicules the idealized and somewhat elitist view of creativity expressed in *Geography of a Horse Dreamer*. In act 2, *Geography's* binary distinction between holy creator (Cody) and commercial exploiter (Fingers) is also undermined. Rabbit tries to insist on his moral superiority ("YOU'RE THE PRODUCER, AND I'M THE ARTIST!"), but Wheeler simply ridicules him: "WE'RE THE SAME," he insists, because "WHAT WE FEAR IS THE SAME.... We're dying here. Right now. In front of each other" (102). As if to illustrate the point, Rabbit too transforms into a fanged serpent.

In 1978, Shepard distilled this bizarre blend of Beckettian absurdism and Marlovian moralism into the bleakly direct form of *Seduced*, a play which took his new interest in developing character in another direction by providing a sustained study of a single figure. Henry Hackamore is both the ultimate Faustian-American individualist (a tycoon and ex-movie producer who has amassed a fortune in an attempt to assure himself of godlike power) and an obviously absurdist figure: the allusion to Hamm in Beckett's *Endgame* is blatant, as Hackamore sits (impossibly ancient and wizened) in his giant reclining chair, attended by the Clov-like Raul (whom he hates and mistrusts but depends on), interminably waiting for the end. Hackamore represents an extreme incarnation of the paranoid control mania displayed by Lanx and Wheeler. He seems determined by sheer force of will to defy even the grave, and there is a sense of his having succeeded in stopping time just before the point of his death. He is caught in a putrefied state of suspended animation, and – like the characters in *Action* – passes the time by working endlessly through the same meaningless, mechanical activities. At one point, for example, he scrupulously tears off and sets down paper towels, and lays manuscripts on top of them, as though going through a "private ritual which has lost its original purpose." As he does so he sings the same musical phrase to himself – "Hey ba ba re bop" – over and over, like a record with the needle stuck forever in one groove (241).

The compulsive precision of these rituals is just one example of Hackamore's obsession with order. The play takes place in a personal, hermetically sealed world in which every last detail is prescribed to Hackamore's specification. He fears infection from the slightest speck of dirt and, like some geriatric vampire, even refuses to allow daylight in from outside.

Nobody enters this sterile environment except those he has invited, and these characters are expected to "live inside the very rhythm of my needs" (234). They seem, moreover, to be further manifestations of his own control fantasies. When two women arrive dressed as Hollywood starlets from the 1930s, it is as if he has dreamed them up: they have "stepped directly out of Henry's past without ageing" (252). Yet Luna and Miami are also corporeally present to Raul, and have lives of their own even when Henry is unconscious: as in *Angel City*, the megalomaniac has created a hyper-reality in which the line between fact and fantasy is blurred to the point of nonexistence. Moreover, like Wheeler, Henry finally meets with a Faustian comeuppance as Raul pulls a gun on him and forces him to sign away his fortune on a contract written in blood. Raul, it transpires, has always been the one in real control, and Henry is nothing but the pitiful dupe of a gangster conspiracy, the They-system he has always feared. Unless, that is, this treachery itself is yet another manifestation of his paranoid fantasies: by this stage nothing can be taken at face value.

The rampaging egoism of both Hackamore and Wheeler thus exposed as pitifully inadequate and self-deceptive: like so many Shepard characters before them, these tycoon-individualists prove to be mere dupes, controlled by the unseen hand of the dominant American ethos. As Hackamore finally realizes, explaining the play's title: "I was taken by the dream and all the time I thought I was taking it. It was a sudden seduction . . . I'm the demon they invented. . . . The nightmare of the nation!" (274). Yet if there is a tragic side to these pieces, it lies less in such moments of pathetic self-awareness than in the Marlovian implication that these Faustian figures, through striving for immortality, have forever lost touch with "God." The notion of an underlying spiritual dimension to life, of an essential quality that has been lost sight of, is again a recurrent feature in these plays, sitting in an odd tension alongside the more nihilistic sense of an existential void. Yet this spiritual impulse also manifests itself in a less romanticized, more fatalistic form than in the rock plays: Shepard here exploits the imagery of myth as a means of providing fresh perspectives on the extremity of the situations depicted, but holds out very little in the way of hope. The rapacity of the American ego is seen as having forever polluted and corrupted the soul of the nation.

Shepard approaches this theme by developing the binary scheme first hinted at in *Geography of a Horse Dreamer*, in which the spiritual dimension of life is equated with the primordial wilderness of the American West ("God's country"), and the corrupt impulse of greed with the urban rat-race. Hackamore, for instance, perceives the Nevada desert as "holy ground . . . the only place that makes sense" (273). Yet he feels not the appropriate reverence toward it, only an unrequitable desire to own and dominate. In a long, rhythmic monologue, he describes the awesome vastness of this natural world as something which must be run from, since it provides an uncomfortable reminder, to the would-be immortal man, of his ultimate insignificance:

> Enormous country. Primitive. Screaming with hostility toward men. Toward me. . . . As though men were a joke in the face of it. I heard rat-tlesnakes laughing. Coyotes. Cactus stabbing the blue air. Miles of heat and wind and red rock. . . . And far off, invisible little men were hud-dled against it in cities. In tiny towns. . . . I saw the whole world of men as pathetic. Sad, demented little morons moving in circles. Always in the same circles. Always away from the truth. Getting smaller and smaller until finally they disappeared. (271)

Hackamore himself, having retreated to his sterile hideout, is one such "sad, demented little moron," moving endlessly in circles. But the speech also functions as a comment on the hellish urban environments of *Angel City* and *Suicide*, in which the circles have constricted to the point where people are devouring themselves. The Chandleresque language in both plays produces a murky, claustrophobic atmosphere far removed from the "dreams of the life of man free and unfettered . . . on the plains of Nebraska" which Miss Scoons describes: this is "the hard core cement" (74). Tympani suggests that in the city, some vital connection to the true values of life has been lost: "We've been locked out of time," he insists. "We're locked into the narrowest part of our dream machine" (97). Lust for power is the only logic of this "demented brain," and has created an insane, self-perpetuating system of dog-eat-dog competition. The city, says Petrone in *Suicide*, is the source of "A raw despair" (225).

The very spirit of the nation, Shepard suggests (perhaps with a degree of tongue-in-cheek irony, but also with distinct feeling), has been poi-soned by the ever-expanding tendrils of urbanization. Just as the Lucifer-ian plan in *Man Fly* is to cover God's country with concrete, so Hack-amore takes vengeful delight in the way the obscene spectacle of Las Vegas has been built on the very holiest part of the Nevada desert. The apocalyptic implications are underlined by the biblical image of a blood-red full moon which hangs over the set. A still more striking picture comes at the conclusion of *Angel City*: Wheeler opens one of Rabbit's Indian medicine bundles (designed for prayer, but being used to create the ultimate disaster movie), to let loose a stream of green slime which drips onto the floor as the lights fade. Virtually guaranteed to produce an audible gasp of revulsion from audiences, this cartoon-horrific image seems to summarize the sense of putrefaction and corruption which runs throughout the play. That impression is further reinforced if one notes that, in certain Native American cultures, the four points of the compass represent opposite, complementary qualities which it is the aim of life to hold in balance: thus, in the play, we are told that the medicine bundle for the North represents innocence and trust, in contrast to the South's sage-like Wisdom, while the East represents a place from which to look out on the world, in contrast with the West, the "Looks-Within Place" (this scheme is adapted from Hopi lore).[13] But in Rabbit's wheel all the bundles are fake except "The West," and it is this which drips green slime when opened: it seems that only the insatiable frontier dream of westward expansion, the desire to conquer further still, remains "true" in the American psyche. The nation is stagnating because it long ago reached the limit of its possible frontiers: as Wheeler says of his city of fallen angels, "We can't get any further West than this" (101).

Rebirth of a Nation?

Suicide in B♭ offers an alternative take on the nation's stagnation, by presenting – among all the red herrings – a tentative vision of deliverance from this self-destructive egoism. The ostensibly dead musician Niles, whose situation is repeatedly equated with "the nature of a nation" (212), at times appears to be a kind of American Everyman who is being led through a ritual of rebirth by his mysterious assistant Paullette. She insists that the various life roles he has played are no longer helpful to him: they have taken him to the point where "you can't get to anything new. You're repeating yourself" (216). In keeping with the Jungian notion of individuation, the maturing process in which old ego drives are sacrificed in order to seek a deeper personal wholeness, Paullette begins dressing Niles up in the costumes of the different personae he needs to kill off in order to move on. Intriguingly, these roles appear to represent different stages of America's development as a nation. Niles first dons the costume of a frontier cowboy, named explicitly as Pecos Bill, and adopts the persona of the death-denying egomaniac already familiar from the operetta: "Pecos Bill, Pecos Bill, never died and never will" (214). He recalls the days when this role was vital and healthy, envisioning "the nation being built in every small activity" (218). But Paullette insists that this old attitude is now merely "a parasite. He's sucking your blood" (215), and even goes so far as to demythologize the figure's past ("He's no hero. He's a punk psychopath

built into a big deal by crummy New England rags": 217). She shoots him
with an arrow to purge the character from Niles's psyche. Next, Niles
dresses up as a cigar-chomping capitalist type in full evening dress. Again,
Paullette exposes the flaws in this figure's ego drives for wealth and power.
He has "the kind of face that looks overfed. . . . Too much rich food and
not enough exercise." As with Wheeler and Hackamore, material success
has not satisfied this figure: "He was miserable. He was surrounded by
everything he ever wanted" (222). She shoots him dead.

Paullette's activities are meanwhile complemented in Pablo and
Louis's "reality" by Laureen's equally unsettling meditation on the necessity of facing up to the inevitability of death, in order to move into "a new
dimension." Again consistent with the notion of individuation, her comments even tie in with Jung's observation that this maturing stage usually
takes place during the proverbial midlife crisis (is Shepard depicting
America's midlife crisis?). If one tries to avoid it, Laureen observes, it simply "comes at the end of your life instead of in the middle" (220). In a
long, aria-like speech, accompanied by dissonant jazz, she paints a chilling portrait of the realization in old age, in hospital, that the conscious ego
on which "you" have always relied is only a fraction of your full, true self,
and that it is too late to do anything about this:

> You can still hear your life going on. Somewhere outside. . . . You strug-
> gle to the window. You hold yourself up by both elbows and stare
> down at the street, looking for your life. But all you see is yourself
> looking back up at you. . . . He's pointing to his head, to his own head,
> then pointing back to you. He keeps repeating this over and over as
> though . . . it's something you should have understood a long, long time
> ago but never did. . . . "If only I don't die before I find out what he
> means!" you say. . . . Then you see him more clearly than before. You
> see for sure that he is you. That he's not pretending. He yells up to you
> in a voice you can't mistake. He yells at you so the whole street can hear
> him. "YOU'RE IN MY HEAD! YOU'RE ONLY IN MY HEAD!" Then
> he turns and walks away. (220–1)

If cultural and personal fragmentation is to be overcome, the play seems
to suggest, this must be achieved not through seeking yet more frontiers
to dominate, but through a growth process which might lead to the relin-
quishing of masculine egoism and the discovery of other, neglected dimensions of experience. The fact that it is female characters who voice these
warnings is particularly significant: in Shepard's plays of the mid- to late
'70s there is a growing but as yet unexplored sense of some potentially positive alternative in what he has described as "the female side." Several

Linda Hoy, Ebbe Roe Smith, and Mark Petrakis in the Magic Theatre's production of *Suicide in B♭*, San Francisco, 1979. (Photo: Ron Blanchette, courtesy of the Magic Theatre).

strangely prophetic female characters (Paullette and Laureen; Miss Scoons in *Angel City*, when in her trance states; to some extent Shelly in *Buried Child*) seem at times to operate halfway outside the frames of their respective plays, as sources of comment or new perspective. Paullette, in particular, is able to function as a voice explicitly critical of masculine ego drives, and while her role remains cryptic, it is notably consistent with the Jungian notion of the *anima*, the female figure in dreams and myths who represents the hidden, feminine side of the male psyche, which must be assimilated into the conscious mind as a central part of the individuation process. Shepard seems to be manipulating this idea in a manner akin to his use of Jungian ego-shadow imagery in some of the rock plays: the anima supposedly often manifests itself just as Paullette does here, in the image of a small, mysterious female figure, drawing a much larger male figure forward into unexplored territory. Moreover, Paullette's discomfortingly contradictory treatment of Niles, alternating between ruthless manipulation and comforting reassurance, is also said to be typical.[14] (Or is it perhaps simply typical of the male suspicion of women?) Her behavior is reminiscent of Doc's similarly ambiguous father-mentor role in *La Turista*, initiating Kent's entry into an earlier phase of masculine maturation.

The idea of a dualistic complementarity between male and female, developed openly here, had been a feature of Shepard's work ever since *Operation Sidewinder*, with Honey and the Young Man's "mystic marriage" during the concluding Hopi ritual. This intricately described ceremony (their hair is melded together in an act of soul union) is another "authentic" piece of Hopi ceremonial, but it is used out of context as part of the Snake dance: Shepard clearly chose to combine the two elements because the imagery seemed significant to him.[15] More negatively, Becky's self-assault scene in *The Tooth of Crime* can perhaps be seen as an externalization of Hoss's attempt to achieve the ultimate in undiluted masculine brutality, by "raping" his own anima (Becky functions throughout the play as a female extension of Hoss's needs, and this episode occurs just as Crow has instructed Hoss to wipe his mind clear and become "indifferent"). In *Action* the theme of union is reintroduced: the moment which offers the play's one flickering vision of hope is Shooter's tale of a (masculine) moth which unites with the source of his longing, a (feminine) burning candle: "With his forelegs he took hold of the flame and united with her joyously. He embraced her completely, and his whole body became red as fire. . . the flame and the moth appeared to be one" (185). This kind of sexual-spiritual imagery is developed still further in the climactic movie-footage section of *Angel City*, which is strongly reminiscent of the apocalyptic-orgasm-as-rebirth scenario observed by Jung in numerous mythic sources.[16] As Lanx and Miss Scoons ferociously act out a Japanese kendo bout, Wheeler tells the story of a cosmic battle through time and space between two great generals:

> The planets howled in space. Their primitive weapons performed a conversation in empty space. Finally, after days of constant combat, one of the generals revealed himself as a woman. In that moment, the opposing general was caught off guard and the female plunged her weapon home. At last the generals saw their situation. They were one being with two opposing parts. Everything was clear to them. At last they were connected. In that split second they gained and lost their entire lives. (107–8)

Yet if visions of rebirth are glimpsed in these plays, they remain tantalizing but unfulfilled fantasies, because Shepard's characters seem unwilling or unable to embrace them. Niles, for example, is eventually enticed back into the house where the detectives are waiting to arrest him, despite Paullette's prophetic cries that "THEY'LL TEAR YOU APART!" (228). Similarly, Henry Hackamore is intent on maintaining absolute ego control, despite his recognition that the dark Luna and blonde Miami (moon and sunshine; a blatant reference to the twin, dark and light poles of idealized femininity) are in a sense his own internal anima figures: "This is between me and myself," he tells Raul when Luna arrives (245). The women's presence, he says, has the potential "to fill me up. To ease me into the other world. To see me across. To bring me ecstasy and salvation." Yet he remains stubbornly unwilling to learn from them, treating them simply as slaves to be controlled, "the ultimate acquisition" (251). It is this continuing need to dominate which dooms him.

Still more seriously, the plays betray a suspicion that rebirth imagery such as this, however inspiring, is nothing but another form of wishful thinking. Such ideas are rendered almost meaningless if one doubts the existence of an essential self. Moreover, the Freudian reading of the male-female bonding imagery would simply be that they indicate further manifestations of the perpetually unsatisfiable yearning for the lost state of primal union with the mother. Shepard displays his own doubts about these images by relentlessly undercutting them with mockery or contradiction. The fable in *Action* is undermined by the other moths' inability to comprehend what their leader has found, and by the fact that as Shooter conclude his tale, Jeep abruptly pulls a fish out of a bucket in an act of calculated absurdity. Likewise, Rabbit dismisses Wheeler's movie scenario as laughable kitsch: "Corniest stuff I ever saw. . . . Hanky panky love stories romantically depicting the end of the world" (108).

In short, these pieces are marked by an intense anguish: an urgent desire for a way forward (personally and nationally) butts up against an implacable fear that there is none, and all glimpses of hope are pressurized to the point where they appear to be little more than incidental whimsy amid the chaos. The dilemma is epitomized by Shepard's use of the saxophonist in *Angel City*, which provides an achingly emotive, human presence which is never quite swamped by the insanity of the play, since he is able to remain "aloof and above the chaos for the most part" (61). Yet this aloofness could signal either resistance or irrelevance: his contribution may simply be an outdated form of romanticism with no bearing on the present crisis. "Continually trying to reverberate us into the past with that solo crap!" mutters Lanx: "When will these guys wake up?" (69).

Ultimately, these plays must number among the bleakest, most fractured of all Shepard's work. The tortured paradox presented in all three is that although fear of chaos and death drives people to seek the protection of godlike power, they succeed only in creating insane structures which produce chaos and death. Shepard does not attempt to make clear whether this vicious downward spiral originated from some innate, absurd human condition (an ultimate lack of meaningful narratives, which has only been confronted in the postmodern age), or from the rampant greed of America's frontier ethos, which has reached apotheosis in late capitalism's urbanized hell. Instead, he renders the whole question of such origins irrelevant: life is simply an insoluble and painful mystery. As Pablo screams:

IN THE END WE WERE NOT CERTAIN! WE COULD MAKE NEITHER HEAD NOR TAIL OF THE PREDICAMENT! WHETHER OR NOT WE WERE DESTROYED FROM WITHIN OR WITHOUT! NOW IT MAKES NO DIFFERENCE! THERE IS ONLY THE REALITY OF MY DYING! (223)

The fact that, finally, the only certainty is the inevitable process of decay and ultimate erasure, is made chillingly apparent by the very end of *Angel City*. After Wheeler has vanished into his own film, after the green slime, the final blow is a simple, five-word line as the bickering teenagers relapse into silence: "Just shut up will ya'?" (111).

The Soul in Limbo

If the desire for spirituality and transcendence is reduced, by sheer weight of skepticism, to a minor key in the playwriting of this period, it should be pointed out – by way of postscript – that this theme, and the related question of the search for essential self, simultaneously dominated much of

Shepard's collaborative work. *Inacoma*, for example, focused around the question of whether or not Amy, a vegetative coma victim, is in any sense still alive, despite the apparent death of her ego-consciousness. Though drawing heavily on the details of the recent Karen Ann Quinlan case, which had raised legal questions about whose right it was to say when or if one could "pull the plug" on coma patients, the project largely evaded the social and ethical issues involved, in favor of concentrating on the spiritual angle. Amy was portrayed hanging in a kind of disembodied limbo, watching family, doctors, and lawyers gather around her bed, arguing over her fate. In the view of William Kleb, who saw the production, even this idea was not adequately developed: he judged that, as often happens with devised group work, collaboration had also meant compromise, and that no real substance was achieved. Kleb concluded that there was a dire need for Shepard's own distinctive vision to have been expressed more.[17] Yet as Shepard stressed in his program notes, the reason for the collaboration in the first place was that, although he had tried for three years to write a play on this subject, he had found it impossible to "fit into a fluid written structure." Like Pablo and Louis, all he could come up with was "supposes," a series of aching questions without answers which served as a starting point for the project, and which he listed in lyrical form in one of its fixed text segments, "Demon Chant": "Who is the person / Who is the person when the person's gone / When the body's left alone . . . Who was the person all along . . . Did the person name the person who the person thought she was / Was that all the person was . . ."[18]

Similar territory had been covered in Shepard's fragments of script contributed to the Open Theatre collaboration *Nightwalk*, in 1972, and when Shepard worked with Joe Chaikin on *Tongues*, the questions of self and soul again resurfaced. The piece was more successful than *Inacoma*, however, probably thanks to the more focused process of a collaboration between only two men, and to the simple, distilled approach of having a single actor speaking into the void. Chaikin, moreover, seems to have a calming influence on Shepard's tendency toward the agonized second-guessing of his every impulse. *Tongues* is a carefully modulated piece whose shifting segments present many different voices but never suggest the threat of chaos. Certainly there are moments of skepticism and confusion within the piece, as when a living voice asks a "Voice from Dead" whether in fact he is not just making "making you up? Conjuring up the shape of you?" or when another voice hunts frantically for a secure sense of self: "I - There - I. Me. Me saying 'I' to myself. That was me. Just then. That was it. Me. I speak. Me. No one else. That was me just then. Must've been. Who else? Why should I doubt it?"[19] Yet overall, the cumulative effect of *Tongues'* strange combination of everyday voices, dream voices, spirit voices, and so forth is to conjure up a remarkably poetic sense of human possibility, a sense that there are many different dimensions of being besides the waking ego. In particular, the concluding segment points clearly to the persistent sense of something beyond, and the last line finally confesses what the whole piece has implied, the complete inadequacy of words or concepts to express the life of the spirit: "Tonight the tree bloomed without a word / Tonight I'm learning its language" (318).

Shepard's second collaboration with Chaikin, *Savage/Love* (1979), deals with less esoteric questions (see Chapter 6), but in their third piece, the radio monologue *The War in Heaven* (1984), the notion of some spiritual dimension to experience is again placed at the fore as an angel gives voice to his experiences. The dilemma here, though, is that the angel has inexplicably fallen to earth, and has lost touch with the transcendent reality and purpose he once knew: his resulting sense of brokenness is realized vividly in the intermittent passages of stuttering, painfully broken language which resulted directly from Chaikin's attempts at communication following a sudden stroke he suffered during the collaboration process, which left him with an aphasic speech impediment. These disconnected word patterns perfectly complement Shepard's narrative passages, in which the angel describes his acute sense of lost direction. He tells, for example, of his old duties of liberating souls from their graves after burial, and of the alarming experience of finding that some men no longer had souls to be saved. Now he is stranded on earth, without a clear role or identity, forever cut off from heaven. The words which open and close the piece sum up its mood, and typify the sense of personal dislocation prevalent in so much of Shepard's work:

I died
the day I was born
and became an Angel
on that day

since then
there are no days
there is no time
I am here
by mistake [20]

5

Strychnine in the Gut

Curse of the Starving Class (1977)
and Buried Child (1978)

In the middle of this diverse, experimental period of the mid- to late 1970s, Shepard took his writing in an unexpected new direction. When *Curse of the Starving Class* premiered in London in 1977, it was seen by many as marking a shift away from avant-garde pyrotechnics toward more a conventional dramatic form. Built around a conventional three-act structure and set in a recognizable domestic location (a farmhouse kitchen), it dealt with a family made up of familiar types (absent father, world-weary mother, anguished son, rebellious daughter) enacting a series of personal conflicts. When *Buried Child*, which featured very similar basic components, appeared the following year at the Magic Theatre, it was seen as confirming the notion that Shepard was finally moving toward the mainstream of "serious" American drama, adding to the roll of family plays by O'Neill, Odets, Miller, Williams, and so forth. In 1979 *Buried Child* was rewarded with that ultimate accolade of the established theatre, the Pulitzer prize. Certainly these pieces have many elements in common with their famous predecessors. Yet even as the subject of family is embraced in an apparent search for a sense of rooted, stable identity, these are distinctly postmodern dramas, characterized by discontinuity, pastiche, and a sense of insoluble tension in both family structure and dramatic form. Shepard, far from making some belated bid for mainstream respectability, was bringing his sense of experiential crisis home to roost.

That these two plays bear only the most cursory resemblance to the stabilized dramaturgy of domestic naturalism was evident from some of the confused, even angry responses which initially greeted them. "Sam

Shepard: What's the Message?" demanded *New York Times* critic Walter Kerr in the headline to a scathing attack on *Buried Child*, a play he saw as merely pretending at dramatic substance, "a posture that has not yet grown into a cohesive play."[1] Yet to dismiss these plays, as Kerr and others have, simply because they do not present a cohesive "message," is akin to writing off *Suicide in B♭* for not resolving who done it. Certainly they defy attempts to view them as either psychological case studies or social commentaries (the classic functions of domestic naturalism, from Ibsen and Chekhov onward), but this is precisely because Shepard, by his own account, had no interest in exploring here either the dynamics of interpersonal "squabbles" between family characters, or the family's relation to "the American social scene" (which "really bores me").[2] While both of these elements inevitably play a part in these plays, his real preoccupation seems to be with the tortured question of why the family is a family at all, with what a family actually *is* and how it holds together (if indeed it does) in a world stripped of old consonances and certainties. Such questions, of course, have no simple answers, and these plays are marked by a sense of profound mystery about the families' underlying dynamics, mixed with acute dysfunctionality in the immediate present, resulting from the characters' apparent inability to agree on the most tentative of common reference points or unifying narratives. Shepard creates a form of realism which refuses to render itself up to neatly rational explanation, by adapting various of his more abrasive formal techniques and blending them with more familiar elements of domestic drama. In these plays, as in their predecessors, the cumulative impact of the diverse impressions and images creates in audiences a sense of emotional disorientation which mirrors that felt by the characters.

None of this, it should be noted, makes these plays especially unusual in the context of the 1970s: as William Demastes has argued persuasively in his book *Beyond Naturalism* (1988), the aftermath of 1960s experimentalism in American theatre saw many young playwrights turning back to realistic settings for their work, but in ways which absorbed the previous decade's lessons of chance and contingency. In plays by writers as diverse as David Mamet and Marsha Norman, the assumptions of traditional naturalism (internally consistent illusion, cause-and-effect logic, psychologically explicable character motivations) were being subverted in a variety of ways. Shepard mirrored that trend in continuing to pursue his intuitive, "halfway in the dark" writing style, the results of which tend to highlight, rather than iron out, the tensions and uncertainties that drive it. As Shepard's previously cited comments about "playing inside a structure" suggest, these pieces are not as raw in their improvisatory approach as plays like *Angel City* and *Suicide in B♭*. Yet he was still seeking to allow his writing to move fairly freely within the three-act outlines he had set for himself. That open-ended, "musical" approach is particularly evident in the continuing tendency toward long, rhythmic speeches and jarring juxtapositions of mood, and in the fact that the first draft versions of both *Curse* and *Buried Child* are substantially the same as the published versions, although act 3 of the latter was overhauled somewhat during rehearsals for the premiere. *Buried Child* was further revised by Shepard for Steppenwolf Theatre Company's 1995 production, and I discuss the effect of these small but significant changes in Chapter 8. It is, however, the original I focus on here, as an integral part of Shepard's development in the 1970s.

The Search for Roots

However distantly removed from consistently modulated naturalism these "family" plays may be, it should also be stressed that Shepard was not attempting gratuitously to destabilize established convention. Indeed, given the desperately fragmented worlds envisaged in his recent work, his turn toward the family seems to have been motivated at least in part by a desire for a firmer sense of rootedness and depth which might act as an antidote to contemporary cultural confusion. His previous treatments of family themes – *The Rock Garden* and *The Holy Ghostly* – had both presented a son attempting (ambivalently) to shake off the influence of parents. Yet as correspondence from the mid-'70s demonstrates, Shepard now felt it was necessary to confront and embrace his origins, rather than avoid them: "I've been trying to escape myself ever since I left home," he wrote in a draft of a letter to his mother, "and I realize now that I have to face things, I can't run forever." Evidently his various attempts to reinvent himself – as "Sam Shepard," as a playwright, as a rock musician, as an American abroad – had not solved his crisis of identity: "I'm at war with myself. I'm more confused now than I've ever been."[3] He decided that facing one's roots, however painful that might be, might be the real key to finding oneself: "If you could really understand [your family]," he noted in 1977, as *Curse* was about to open, "understand the chemistry and the reactions that are going on there, I've had the feeling that you'd understand a lot."[4]

Shepard's move back to California had been a clear sign of his new desire to find a firm grounding for himself and his family, and to rediscover his past. He was now within long-distance-driving range of both his parents (his mother still lived near Los Angeles, his father further afield in New

Mexico), and he set up home not only with his wife and son but also with
O-Lan's mother, Scarlett Johnson, and her husband, Johnny Dark. The
move also coincided with Shepard's first, unfinished attempt at a major
family play, *The Last American Gas Station*, which he wrote in Nova Scotia in 1974, en route from London to San Francisco.[5] That piece included
many thinly disguised autobiographical details, and foreshadowed the
more sustained exploration of personal experience in these subsequent
plays. *Curse of the Starving Class* is set on a southern Californian avocado
ranch akin to the one where Shepard spent his adolescence, and he locates
himself in the play in the shape of the teenage son, Wesley. In *Buried Child*,
the visit of a young man, Vince, to his grandparents' home in the Illinois
corn belt, appears to have been loosely based on a trip Shepard himself
made as a nineteen-year-old, and which is recounted as autobiography in
his prose collection *Motel Chronicles*. Both Wesley and Vince dress in the
Shepard "uniform" of jeans and cowboy boots, and Vince also comes armed
with a saxophone (a prop which remains purely decorative, a shorthand
allusion to Shepard's view of himself as a musician, which he had also used
in the unfinished *Spider Lee*).[6] The other characters also draw on autobiography. The wizened, patriarchal grandfather, Dodge, in *Buried Child*,
plays exactly the kind of hardened "Plain Dirt Farmer" role which Shepard's grandfather had reportedly reveled in, and the name Dodge itself is
borrowed from the Rogers family genealogy. Similarly, the figure of Shepard's crippled uncle appears in *Buried Child* as Uncle Bradley. (Both had
appeared in similar guises in *The Last American Gas Station*.)

It should be added, though, that Shepard channeled and adapted such
personal material in different directions according to the needs of each
play. Wesley's and Vince's fathers, for example, are far from being identi-
cal depictions of Shepard's father, Sam: though both are based on elements drawn from that source, two more different characters would be
hard to imagine. Weston is described as a "very big man" (a kind of Big
Daddy) and a wild, violent drunkard; Tilden is a desolate, quiet figure,
"profoundly burned out and displaced." Such varied choices of emphasis
are plainly not accidental. The fact that Shepard's family is, as he admits,
"so idiosyncratic it verges on the bizarre," is not, in other words, the only
reason for their strangeness.[7] Nevertheless, on one level at least, both
plays represent a need on the author's part to reconnect with his own past.
As Shelly says of the Shepard figure in *Buried Child*: "Vince has this thing
about his family now. I guess it's a new thing with him . . . he feels it's
important. You know. I mean he feels he wants to get to know you all
again. After all this time."[8]

In terms of the hunt for roots it is also significant that both *Curse* and *Buried Child* are set in agricultural areas. After the "raw despair" of the urban environments in *Angel City* and *Suicide*, such back-to-the-land locations might also seem to hold out the promise of natural stability and permanence. Certainly a side of Shepard still cherished an idealized view of Americans as a people "essentially geared toward a rural civilization. . . . To me, one of the biggest tragedies was moving from an agricultural to an urban-industrial society at the turn of the century."[9] Yet such nostalgic, even Luddite, sentiments do not begin to reflect the complexity or grimly bleak tone of these first two family plays, which are very far from advocating a return to some lost "Garden of the World" ideal. In both these pieces, land and family offer not succor but poison: the farmers are drunks; the fields are barren or untilled; the only items of farm produce seen are Weston's useless sackful of artichokes in *Curse*, and Tilden's corn and carrots in *Buried Child*, which are lent a spectral, unearthly quality by Dodge and Halie's denial that they could even exist. In these desolate environments, the families systematically tear each other apart with a primal savagery which rivals even *The Tooth of Crime*.

The starkness of Shepard's perspective alarmed even him. The notebook he kept during rehearsals of *Buried Child*, for example, contains anguished self-interrogations over the nature of its impact: "This play comes close to a vision. A vision of something lost. Is negativity a legitimate vision? Is darkness negative?"[10] Yet, as ever in his work, the plays' bleakness constitutes not self-indulgent nihilism, but an attempt to come to terms with a sense of helplessness: their "no" is forged out of an urgent desire for a "yes" (to borrow Brook's description of Beckett again). Hunting for a way to understand the family, and thereby his own identity, Shepard is once again forced to confront the fear that there is no understanding to be had. Always concerned with exploring the forces which entrap and manipulate the individual sensibility, he seems to arrive here at the conclusion that the unseen hand of home and blood bonds is the most insidious and mysterious influence of all, that "you're somehow ensnared beyond yourself."[11] Jeep's contention in *Action* that the vast, entangled "network" of societal influences is "Bigger than family" is supplanted by Ella's paranoid reverie in *Curse*, in which she suggests that family

> goes back. Deep. It goes back and back to tiny little cells and genes. To atoms. To tiny little swimming things making up their minds without us. Plotting in the womb. Before that even. In the air. We're surrounded with it. It's bigger than government even. It goes forward too.

We spread it. We pass it on. We inherit it and pass it down, and then pass it down again. It goes on and on like that without us. (174)

This kind of biological determinism was a characteristic concern of the modernist movement. In the wake of Darwin and Freud, many writers sought to explore the idea that, regardless of the whims of the conscious ego, the results of genetic and psychological conditioning will eventually manifest themselves no matter what. Eugene O'Neill, for example, in plays such as *Desire Under the Elms* (1924) and *Mourning Becomes Electra* (1931), presented stories of darkly destructive family traits repeating themselves down the generations. The latter, in particular, draws on the model of Greek tragedy (explicitly echoing the outline of Aeschylus's *Oresteia*) to create a sense of inevitable doom as the younger generation simply turn into carbon copies of their parents. Shepard, an admirer of both O'Neill and the Greeks, followed suit to some extent in these plays. Both *Curse* and *Buried Child* present younger generations replicating the mistakes of their elders in a cycle of self-destruction. To differing degrees, both plays are reminiscent of Shepard's own description of Sophocles' *Oedipus Rex*: "This devastating *harm* coming down from the heavens. No Jung, no Freud, any of that. No 'language' or trappings at all. Now that's a story."[12]

The paradox here is that the means by which Shepard creates this sense of doom in both these plays owe far more to postmodernist strategies of pastiche and destabilization than to modernist or Greek models. As he himself has argued, the power of traditional story forms has largely been neutralized by overfamiliarity in the media-saturated environment of the late twentieth century, and ancient myth patterns have to some extent been "explained away" by widely understood interpretative theories (see his comments quoted in the Introduction). In order to create an immediate emotional impact, a sense of approaching doom which is not defused by the instinct for rationalization, it is therefore necessary to find ways to throw the audience off balance. It seems to me that this is precisely what Shepard achieves through his depiction of confusing or unresolved incidents, his sudden shifts of pace, and the kind of self-demonstrative "language trappings" he admires Sophocles for avoiding.

The Postmodern Family

As in his pop culture plays, one of Shepard's most important destabilizing techniques is the self-conscious quotation of familiar imagery and plot elements. There is no illusion of uncomplicated realism here, no pretense

at the creation of an "original" crisis situation for the family. Rather, Shepard draws on material from numerous, already familiar discourses: the
plays' uncertainty over the nature of the nuclear family is thus fore-
grounded by stressing the derivative and conditioned status of all ideas
relating to such bonds. The technique also strips away the traditionally
privileged position of autobiographical detail within the artwork: details
from the writer's personal experience, mixed together with secondhand
material to the point where the two are indistinguishable, lose their aura
of "uniqueness," becoming simply another ingredient in an unstable
cocktail.

This approach is at its most obvious in *The Last American Gas Station*,
which locates its characters within a somewhat clumsy parody of John
Steinbeck's novel *The Grapes of Wrath*. The play presents a large, destitute family traveling along a desert road, against a sky backdrop specified
as looking like an Edward Hopper painting. They are dressed in 1930s
"Okie" outfits (openly clashing with other details which set the play in the
1970s), and their relational crises are heavily underlined by the immediate, physical problem of their vain search for food and work in the midst
of a kind of postapocalyptic Depression era. *Curse of the Starving Class*,
though less blatant, also seems unashamedly derivative in its plot pretext,
reading as a grotesque variation on Chekhov's *The Cherry Orchard*. The
family's home is invaded by a collection of marvelously plastic property
speculators and gangsters, bidding to turn their avocado orchard into low-
rent housing (or perhaps a miniature golf course) as part of the inexorable
march of progress. Ironically enough, the plot similarities have led to
unfavorable critical comparisons between the two plays. Michael Billington, for example, notes that "where Chekhov makes a perfectly reason-
able case for Lopakhin's wish to turn a rambling estate into summer vil-
las, Shepard turns his land-purchaser, Taylor, into a zombie-villain acting
as a front for anonymous organisations. . . . That, to me, is why the play is
romantic melodrama."[13] Billington's disparaging tone ignores the possibility that the confusion of classic plot device and B-movie melodrama
might in fact be quite deliberate, a formal device which requires emphasis rather than apology. Yet this was something about which Robert
Woodruff, director of *Curse*'s American premiere (and of *Buried Child*'s
world premiere), was in no doubt:

> The form of it is, of course, The Great American Melodrama. I got the
> deed! No you don't! I got the money! Here come the cops! And the guy
> with the black moustache comes on at the end twirling it. The problem

was basically seeing how far you could stretch the distance between these people and the audience and still have the play work.[14]

If *Curse* plays with elements of melodrama, *Buried Child* presents a veritable patchwork of allusions to well-known family plays. (As Shepard has remarked slyly, "it's sort of a typical Pulitzer prize-winning play.")[15] Tilden's position as a former "All-American" high school football star who failed to live up to expectations, ran away to the West, and then returned home in despair, is clearly reminiscent of Biff Loman in Miller's *Death of a Salesman*. His mother, Halie, endlessly dreaming about the young men in her golden youth, and obsessively dissatisfied with how her family has turned out, suggests echoes of Tennessee Williams's Amanda Wingfield in *The Glass Menagerie*, among others. The unexpected arrival of Vince, with girlfriend Shelly in tow, six years since he last saw the family, recalls Harold Pinter's *The Homecoming*, in which Teddy, with new wife, Ruth, in tow, returns to the nest after six years: in both plays the arrivals disrupt the hostile equilibrium existing among the family members at the plays' outsets. Most insistent of all, however, is *Buried Child's* echoing of O'Neill's *Desire Under the Elms*, a connection backhandedly signaled in the opening stage directions' reference to "the shapes of dark elm trees," visible beyond the house (63). Shepard's Dodge, an old farmer whose heart is as barren as his land, seems modeled after O'Neill's Cabot, while the intimations of incest between his wife and his son recalls the union of Abbie and Eben in *Desire*. The violent murder of the resulting baby is also common to both plays, and the darkly gothic atmosphere of *Buried Child* – further evidence of Shepard's continuing practice of generic smash-and-grab – suggests the probable influence not only of O'Neill but of rural-gothic novelists such as Carson McCullers, Truman Capote, and Flannery O'Connor. The play is characterized by precisely the kind of rustic creepiness typical of this genre: a mood of death and decay haunts the remotely situated farmhouse; some unspoken damnation hangs over the family, like a Damoclean sword, blighting their land and relationships alike. Also as in gothic tradition, the play is populated by grotesques. Dodge is a wheezing, hacking invalid, marooned on his sofa/deathbed, who even refers to himself as "the corpse"; Halie is still dressed in mourning for a son who died years ago; the vacant, half-mute Tilden desperately tries to avoid contact with others; the one-legged Bradley creaks ominously as he walks and removes his prosthetic limb when he goes to sleep. On one level, the entire play reads as an ironic pastiche of the gothic genre: indeed one critic's list of classic gothic themes could equally well be a catalogue of *Buried Child*'s devices: "order often breaks down: chronology is confused, identity is blurred, sex is twisted, the buried life erupts."[16]

Significantly, the choice of such openly derivative plot pretexts for these plays also enabled Shepard to sidestep complex exposition, which had initially proved a problem for him in trying to approach the family play. *Gas Station* fails largely through becoming bogged down in long-winded explanations of the events that drove the family out onto the road, and in the constant bickering necessitated by the simultaneous presence onstage of a dozen or so characters. That is, Shepard found himself writing against his real strengths – namely, his ability to locate a play in an ongoing but perpetually disorientating present.[17] Conversely, the melodrama of *Curse*, which relies on immediate sensationalism rather than background depth, and the gothic of *Buried Child*, which casts a veil of mystery over a supposedly significant past, both allow Shepard to transfer his sense of moment-by-moment temporal fragmentation to the family play. The former piece provides only the sketchiest details of the Tate family's history, and delights in its abrupt, gratuitous plot turnabouts, while in the latter the loss of any coherent connection with the past becomes an explicit issue, with the family's willful attempts to deny and distort memory through pacts of silence and blurred fantasizing.

Deprived of either stable temporal structures or clear frames of reference for their experience, the characters in these plays adopt the same tactic as their precursors in *Action*, blindly filling in time by immersing themselves in mundane domestic activities. These range from cooking to ironing, from shucking corn in *Buried Child* to the opening and closing of the refrigerator in *Curse*, a gesture so futile and repetitive that it becomes a kind of rhythmic punctuation for the emptiness of the Tates' existence. The very identities of these characters seem tenuous, demonstrating a direct descent from the schizoid collage-figures of *Angel City*, rather than obeying the naturalist convention of gradually modulated shifts of mood and rationally motivated action. In *Buried Child*, for example, Halie moves with jarring abruptness between romantic dreams of the past, hopeless despair (when she recalls the failure or loss of her sons), nagging complaints, and prim bourgeois religiosity. She acts like a harridan with Dodge, an irate citizen with Shelly, a flirty little girl with Father Dewis. She is also capable of contradicting herself inside a few lines (she tells Dodge to take pills, and then announces that pills are bad because they always make him crazy), or of simultaneously saying one thing and doing another (as when she kicks the corn husks all over the floor while complaining about the disorder of the house). At another extreme from this kind of blind inconsistency is Weston's frighteningly self-conscious awareness, in *Curse*, that he can channel-switch into a frame of mind in which murder will be a contemplatable option: "It's no big deal," he explains. "You make an adjustment" (170). The phrase is a verbatim echo of Rabbit's abrupt conversion to power mania in *Angel City*, and Rabbit is also recalled, still more unsettlingly, in the character of Shelly in *Buried Child*. As an outsider to the family, she too seems at first to offer the audience a way into the action. Yet she too proves to be highly unstable, moving from childish giggling, through abject fear, to quietly performing domestic chores, within minutes of her first appearance.

The crucial difference between these plays and *Angel City*, however, is that the characters' bizarre behavior is based largely on Shepard's subjectivized impressions of his own family, as opposed to accumulations of roles drawn from pop cultural debris. In a further evolution of the character explorations initially inspired by Peter Brook, Shepard was delving deeper into his "inner library" and so confronting his feelings about actual flesh-and-blood people: "I started with character, in all its complexities," he notes: "As I got more and more into it, it led me to the family."[18] Consequently, while there is still a distinct whiff of flattened stereotype about these figures, as though to emphasize their emotionally attenuated condition, their erratic and volatile behavior can nevertheless be seen as psychologically motivated. This is not to say that it can be accounted for according to the Stanislavskian notion of a "through-line" of cause-and-effect motivation. But just as Shepard had developed his production of *Angel City* by working with his actors to develop the characters as if they were musical collages of contradictory motifs, so here the family members' behavior is linked by certain consistencies in their inconsistency. For example, during rehearsals for my own 1994 production of the play, the actor playing Tilden eventually found that by focusing on the idea of the character being a child lost in a man's body, he was able fluidly to make the necessary shifts between Elmer Fudd-style redneck ignorance, wide-eyed innocence, patricidal malice, and silent terror (all of which are glimpsed within moments at the end of act 2). The triggers for these shifts are to be found musically, by riding the changes in rhythm and emphasis in the dialogue, without necessarily having to rationalize them.[19] As Robert Woodruff notes, in both these plays the finger-snap character shifts of *Angel City* have "evolved into a need for an actor to be very prismatic, able to play a side or a color of a character very strongly at one moment, and the next play another color or another side of that character." He adds that, as ever with Shepard, playing the moment, rather than looking for a through-line, is the key requirement: "the actor just has to commit and then he's fine."[20]

One apparent motivation for the strange behavior of many of these characters is a perpetual need to belittle and control other inhabitants of the stage space by whatever are the most immediately convenient methods, so as to establish or reinforce a position in the family pecking order. Little or no love exists between characters, and yet the struggle to dominate seems to be less a function of willful malice than of the characters' need to impose some kind of order on chaotic, nonsensical lives. There is, then, a link with the motives of the power mongers Wheeler, Lanx, and Hackamore, but in the family plays the portraits are less monstrous and more sympathetic. The unpredictable actions can be seen as desperately improvised responses to pressurized circumstances over which they have no control. In the words of Nancy Meckler (who directed the British premieres of both *Curse* and *Buried Child*), "Sam isn't writing about people who are crazy; he's writing about people under stress. They're doing what they're doing for real reasons, usually avoidance."[21] Weston's extraordinary character transformation in act 3 of *Curse* (when he suddenly cures his drunkenness and becomes a model, domesticated father) is a prime example of a character willfully ignoring the extremity of his situation, and making a last-ditch attempt to reimpose some order on a life that has spun out of control. Similarly, in *Buried Child*, Shelly explains her own odd behavior as a means of mentally blocking out the nightmarish situation in which she finds herself: "I'll stay and I'll cut the carrots. And I'll cook the carrots. I'll do whatever I have to do to survive. Just to get through this" (94).

Notably, this survivalism also extends to the characters' avoidance of relations with each other: often they seem to be striving to minimize any kind of contact. This too manifests itself at times in their immersion in chores, as when Tilden uses his corn shucking to ignore his father's presence, an attitude Dodge is quite willing to reciprocate: "Long pause. TILDEN husks corn, stares at pail. DODGE lights a cigarette, stares at TV" (77). At other times, the suspicion and fear of the intentions of other characters is depicted as a kind of primitive, animal instinct: Wesley and Tilden both repeatedly display the frightened, wide-eyed alertness of the hunted, often remaining tense and silent in company, or bolting offstage at the first sound of danger. Yet such self-preservation tactics only contribute further to the dominant atmosphere of hostility. There appears to be a self-perpetuating spiral of relational disintegration at work in both these plays, fed by both overt distrust and numbed isolationism.

This separation is perhaps most vividly seen in the bizarre lines of battle demarcation, which seem to have been drawn up by unspoken agreement. In *Buried Child*, the rift between Halie and Dodge is evident from the start, as Halie yells incessantly at her husband from her offstage, upstairs room, while Dodge remains alone on set. Notably, he insists that she need not come downstairs to see to him: he has his territory, she has hers. Similarly, in *Curse*, if the children wish to scream at their mother, it seems to be accepted convention that they go outside to do it, and this results in crazy yelling matches conducted from a distance (a striking theatrical device, with voices bellowing from the wings), so that inside the house the general mood of detached, emotionless interaction can be maintained. The ruling factor here is Ella, who shows no kind of affection for her children, and simply carries on with her own activities, ignoring the others as far as possible. When Emma threatens to ride off on the horse, Ella yells at her that it is too dangerous and tells Wesley to stop her ("That horse is a killer"). Yet when Wesley refuses, she will not inconvenience herself to lift a finger to save her daughter ("Well, maybe she'll be alright": 144). Such attitudes produce wild comedy on the surface, but a bitter mood of desolation underneath.

If the women seem to have the upper hand in these domestic environments, it is because the home is still assumed – in these families – to be their domain and responsibility. They maintain a semblance of control by reinforcing these desperately hollow but workable states of familial cold war. When men confront men, however, the rules change, apparently because their task is to "make it" in the outside world, a task at which they have, without exception, failed. Looking for targets on which to vent his frustration, the humiliated, debt-ridden Weston returns home in act 2 of *Curse* (drunk as always), and immediately begins ridiculing Wesley for acting "like a worm," not a man (164). Likewise, Dodge, who has been festering helplessly for years, rails contemptuously against the failures of his sons, announcing that Bradley belongs "in a hog wallow," and that Tilden has "lost his marbles" and might as well be dead (76–8). This kind of brutality often threatens to swamp the plays altogether, but it is counterbalanced by occasional poignant glimpses of a real concern for each other. Even Dodge shows a glimmer of concern for Tilden's well-being ("Are you in some kind of trouble?": 70), only to become instantly hostile again when Tilden, clearly not trusting him, denies there is a problem. For fear of appearing vulnerable, affection is retracted (the same is true of, say, Ella's concern for Weston). Such moments emphasize the tragic depths to which the families have sunk: with all traces of connectedness being immediately stifled, these families exist in a permanent state

of atomization. They are not nuclear units so much as collections of isolated individuals thrown together by accidents of birth. "You think just
because people propagate they have to love their offspring?" Dodge asks
Shelly: "You never seen a bitch eat her puppies?" (111–2).

Given the frighteningly solitary nature of these characters' lives, it perhaps seems remarkable that they stay together as families at all. Yet none
of them seems capable of making a complete break: even Weston, who is
apparently given to disappearing for weeks at a time, always comes crawl-
ing back home. His family, it would appear, for all his inability to live with
them, at least represents a constant element in his perpetually disap-
pointing life. Similarly, in *Buried Child*, Tilden has returned to the home
he loathes, and where he is himself loathed, simply for the sake of some
form of human contact. His acute dislocation seems to stem from having
escaped home once, only to find nothing but despair beyond it. He used
to dream of living free, as a Kerouac-style drifter ("Nothing I dreamed of
was better than driving"), but outside on the road he realized that there
was nowhere to run to. "I was alone," he tells Dodge: "I thought I was
dead" (102). The parallel with Shooter's Outside/Inside dilemma in *Action*
is self-evident. Tilden's need to return "inside" to the family, in spite of
their negative reactions to him, once again demonstrates the postmodernist *cogito*: I am seen, therefore I exist.

These families, then, hang together in a kind of sadomasochistic vacuum: the characters need each other's presence (witness Dodge's panic
every time he is in danger of being left alone), but only use that interre-
lationship as a forum for expressing their contempt for each other. Family life is viewed as a form of harshly competitive theatre, the characters
acting themselves out in conversations which tend inevitably to turn into
running battles for recognition. Performance becomes the sole law of
these environments, a fact Shelly and Vince rapidly realize in *Buried
Child*: totally ignored by Dodge and Tilden, they resort to overtly theatrical tactics to assert their presence and gain an audience. Vince tries to
impress with party tricks and fancy wordplay, but the most he can gain is
a blunt put-down from Dodge: "Do you know what you're talking about?
Are you just . . . lubricating your gums?" (89). Shelly, on the other hand,
reacts more directly to the lack of recognition by smashing crockery and
screaming: "I don't like being ignored. I don't like being treated like I'm
not here" (119).

The failure of such demonstrations also points to Shepard's continuing
concern, in the family context, with another problem enunciated most
clearly in *Action*: namely, that although performance is necessary to exis-

tence, the presence of a potentially hostile audience can also endanger whatever sense of self the performance creates. This too adds to the tense atmosphere: the characters are reticent to say anything, but also need to speak simply to avoid lapsing into the vacuum of silence. The result is a preponderance of oddly disjointed, desultory conversations. Weston tries to solve this problem by performing *Curse*'s longest speech not to another person, but to the lamb: provided with a silent, uncritical, and literally captive audience, he happily rambles away to himself. He refuses to continue, however, when he realizes that Wesley is listening to him: "Everything was all right until you came in. I was talking to myself and everything was all right" (158). Wesley himself displays a similar form of self-absorption at the outset of *Curse*, creating a huge, rhythmic, personalized reverie of a speech he seems to know his mother will blithely ignore. Such moments suggest another variation on Descartes: I talk, therefore I am. In these plays, this kind of quietly desperate attempt to confirm existence by listening for the sound of one's own voice, performing for *oneself*, is as prevalent as the more abrasive audience-grabbing approach familiar from earlier plays. As Tilden remarks with frightening simplicity: "you gotta talk or you'll die" (78).

And yet if the desire, indeed the need, to "act yourself out" creates difficulties and tensions for the individual, the crisis is no less acute for his or her audience, both onstage and beyond the proscenium. For if a character's actions are established as facets of a self-defensive (and therefore potentially evasive or deceptive) performance, this strips away one of the central assumptions of naturalistic dramaturgy: namely, that by closely observing that character's behavior, one can gradually come to understand the truth of their situation. This point is made explicit by Weston, who derides Wesley's urgent need to comprehend this man in whose image he is made: "You can watch me all you want to. You won't find out a thing" (169). At every turn these plays create bewildering ambiguities, refusing to concede any degree of certainty as to the root causes of the families' conditions. The sketchy accounts of the past represent a minefield of possible distortions, and in neither play is there any clear, unified causal chain for the onstage events. Thus the loss of reference points, which so threatens the identities of Shepard's characters, is transplanted with new impetus into the actual experience of the spectator, who (in accordance with the formal expectations associated with the family play) will tend to *expect* more of a resolution than when watching a more obviously "avant-garde" work. Both these plays, via different methods, "ensnare" audiences in a disorientating struggle for understanding. As Don Shewey remarks succinctly of *Buried Child*, "it becomes the things it is about – emotional violence and the mystery of the family bond."[22]

Starving Hysterical Naked

The very title of *Curse of the Starving Class* is a prime example of Shepard's refusal to permit unambiguous interpretation. It implies that a curse, some specific malaise which has led to the atomized state of the family, will be exposed by the play (just as, say, Ibsen's *Enemy of the People* explores how Dr. Stockmann becomes shunned by his community). Yet no such clarification is ever offered. Instead, Shepard openly teases his audience with the significance of the term "curse," using it to refer to anything from Emma's menstruation to the genetic heredity described in Ella's paranoid monologue. The term "starving class," too, remains confusing: one assumes it applies to the family, but while they are not rich, they are not on the breadline either, as they frequently remind each other. (The economic status of the family is perhaps better indicated by a draft title of the play, *Curse of the Middle Class*, which Shepard revised to render less specific.)[23] There is also the possibility that the family members are "starving" in a spiritual rather than a physical manner (there are even some blatantly biblical images, the "blood of the lamb" being the most obvious). Yet Shepard, gleefully exploiting the convention of the "meaningful" symbol within the realistic frame, undermines all such crudely ominous metaphors with an ongoing recourse to simple facetiousness: "I'm hungry," Ella quips at one point, "and that's starving enough for me" (142).

The games Shepard plays with his title are symptomatic of his approach to the entire play: the progression of the piece is dominated by internal self-contradiction. This is a kind of *grotesque* realism, in the sense that it mixes together clashing elements, particularly the comic and the horrific, so as to unsettle the audience by provoking conflicting emotional responses. And though, in these terms, much of Shepard's work can be described as grotesque, the approach acquires a particular potency in relation to realism, the conventions of which normally presuppose that a play should not draw attention to its own form, that a smooth surface illusion should be created so that the audience may suspend disbelief and focus on the significance of the events enacted. The action of *Curse*, conversely, veers wildly between a range of clashing generic styles, from kitchen sink banality to exaggerated melodrama, and from broad comedy to ritualized symbolism, thwarting any attempt to read into it a stable or unified depiction of a stable or unified real world.

By Shepard's own admission, this bizarre cocktail of effects was partly a result of the play's being written "off the cuff," as a wild experiment in drawing on feelings about, and memories of, his family: "That play just exploded in front of me, I just got so agreeably turned on to this stuff that was coming out."[24] It would be a mistake, however, to view the instability of the results as simple clumsiness. The impact is not dissimilar to that of the "jump cuts" in *Angel City*, and likewise relies on the accentuation of those shifts in production rather than on any attempt to play them down. *Curse*'s real strengths onstage lie in highlighting the violence of its construction, in bombarding the audience with this disparate material.

A glance at the opening pages of the play provides ample evidence of the kind of volatile discontinuity any production needs to stress. Wesley and Ella begin the play with a restrained, almost monosyllabic discussion about the violent events of the previous night, as Wesley picks up the pieces of the broken door. Then, out of the blue, Wesley launches into an enormous monologue about the same events. Full of descriptive detail which is entirely superfluous to the thrust of story, and even referring to Ella's part in events in the third person, the speech is a highly conspicuous obtrusion into the simple flow of the initial exchange. When Wesley finally concludes, Ella makes no response, and he simply walks offstage. Ella, in turn, then launches into a totally unconnected disquisition about (it gradually emerges) menstruation and tampons. This is directed at her daughter Emma, who has not even set foot onstage yet. The abruptness with which Ella's overtly comic speech (a parody of maternal homily-wisdom) erases the mesmeric effect created by Wesley's poetry is typical of Shepard's tendency, throughout the play, to undercut moments of poignancy with gleeful silliness. This creates a confused mix of impressions, sabotaging the audience's attempts to achieve a simple emotional identification with the characters' situations.

A closer look at Wesley's speech further illustrates how Shepard builds overt tensions into *Curse*'s construction. It represents one of the play's few descriptions of the past, yet it takes the form of a highly subjectivized sense-memory: recalling how he overheard his father arriving home drunk, Wesley describes the events down to the most minute aural details. He even switches into the present tense halfway through: he is living these events again. The speech, which builds up relentlessly to a fraught climax, is akin to the paranoid arias of the early plays, and needs to be exploited to the full for its use of alternately melancholic and violent rhythmic moods. Yet in this context the aria device seems particularly bewildering. Is one to see this extravagant linguistic display as a real event, with Wesley actually saying all this aloud to his mother? That would seem odd, not least because she appears not to notice him. Is it, then, some form of subjective expressionism, an insight into Wesley's mind, as one fragment of recalled time is distorted and exaggerated into a recurring mental nightmare? This would seem more plausible, but in this case, why do all the other indicators continue to suggest mundane realism? The speech is not delineated as, say, a spotlit "flashback" aside, outside of the play's "real time." Wesley simply goes on talking as Ella ignores him and cooks food, and he himself continues dismantling the door. He even punctuates the rhythms of the speech with his hammer blows. The speech thus seems to query the adequacy of any one performance style to express the "reality" of any given situation. Is one to see the truth of Wesley's experience in his mundane, surface activity, or in the chaotic, agitated state of his emotions?

A similar sense of the problematic status of "realism" is apparent in the confusion of signals built into the visual appearance of the play. On the one hand, the contrived, provisional status of the stage illusion is emphasized by the fact that only the bare skeleton of a set is sketched in: there is a total absence of walls, doors, or windows. Only a pair of little red curtains, comically suspended in midair, upstage, indicates the parameters of the "kitchen." Yet, on the other hand, this blatantly insubstantial set is crammed with the minutiae of actual domestic activity. There is, for example, a working stove on which real food is cooked in sizzling fat, producing real sounds and smells: as with the carving of the steaming turkey in *Action*, actors engage in behavior which draws attention to its actuality, rather than serving a mimetic illusion. Likewise, when Wesley pisses on his sister's charts on the floor, he is – explicitly – facing forward: the audience is confronted with the actual penis of the actual actor producing actual urine (either that or an obviously fake prosthesis, which creates another, somewhat sillier kind of de-illusionistic effect). Still more bluntly real is the extended presence onstage of a live lamb: this is the play's most extreme disruptive gesture, since the lamb inevitably behaves so "naturally" that the artifice of the human actors' scripted behavior becomes inescapably obvious. (If it *mis*behaves, though, as is likely, the obtrusive becomes the downright distracting: this is not one of Shepard's wiser ideas.)

Placed in stark and incongruous contrast to such awkward reality are the play's two-dimensional villains, drawn straight from cheap melodrama and comic books. These land-hungry speculators represent, in Wesley's phrase, a "zombie invasion," and are depicted as rampant embodiments of greed. Taylor, for example, lays out his brave new world of low-cost housing with a maniacal fervor reminiscent of Wheeler's: "There's nothing you can do to turn it back. The only thing you can do is cooperate. To play ball. To become part of us. To invest in the future of this great land. Because if you don't, you'll all be left behind" (179). The stark juxtaposition of these cartoon invaders with the relatively three-dimensional family members emphasizes the play's sense of insanity and imminent collapse. These figures unhinge the proceedings every time they enter: the arrival of the "bull-calf" bar owner Ellis, for example, shatters the atmosphere created by Ella's curse speech, ushering in Ortonesque farce as the dominant tone for the remainder of act 2. Still more jarring is Emerson and Slater's entrance at the end of the play: as Ella and Wesley attempt to comprehend the extremity of their situation (Weston and Emma having just deserted them), the two gangsters enter from nowhere, swinging the slaughtered corpse of the lamb and howling with laughter at having blown up Weston's car (apparently with Emma in it). These cackling hyenas, far from being some deus ex machina device introduced to tie up loose ends, are entirely extraneous to the plot: their arrival is a gruesomely hilarious intervention which assaults the audience with contradictory emotions: their giggling is highly entertaining, but should we laugh or weep? Is Emma dead? Where did they come from anyway? Look at that bloody lamb! This moment, flung seemingly at random into the play's climactic stages, epitomizes the grotesque thrust of the whole.

Besides creating an immediate sense of an insane and unstable world, the play's jarring stylistic approach also functions to complement the blunt contradictions which exist at the level of thematic construction. Shepard presents two entirely different possibilities as to the underlying cause of the Tate family's implosion, and then leaves both hanging unresolved, as impossible to iron out as the play's stylistic ruptures. As with *Angel City* and *Suicide*, it is not clear whether the violence and confusion spring from the "outside" or "inside," from the corrupting effect of exterior cultural conditions, or from some inherent existential or genetic crisis in the family.

The notion of a threat to the family unit from outside is a recurrent motif in the play: images of invasion appear in references as diverse as Ella's speech about tampons (which shares Hackamore's paranoid fear of an attack by germs) and Wesley's monologue, in which his father's drunk arrival is foreshadowed by a meditation on the idea that "any second something could invade me. Some foreigner. Something undescribable" [*sic*] (137). Of course, the foreign bodies which present the most obvious threat are the various speculators, who always walk into the kitchen set uninvited and unannounced. But the threat they represent also has a more insidious dimension than mere physical intrusiveness. As Wesley remarks, "They've moved in on us like a creeping disease. We didn't even notice" (193), and the family's behavior often suggests that they have been infected at a gut level by the greed and superficiality of the late capitalist culture which the invaders represent. When Ella broaches the subject of land, for example, she speaks in terms which echo the rhetoric Taylor has sold her. "People are building," she notes. "Everyone wants a piece of land. It's the only sure investment" (146).

The degree to which these characters have bought into the get-rich-quick ethos of their environment is made painfully apparent as both Weston and Ella draw down farcical confusion on themselves by plotting separately to sell off the farm for personal profit. Moreover, the financial crisis which drives them to sell in the first place apparently has been caused by Weston's profligate spending, which is also a direct result of his gullible, Willy Loman–like belief in the American myth of success: "I figured that's why everyone wants you to buy things. Buy refrigerators. Buy cars, houses, lots, invest. They wouldn't be so generous if they didn't figure you had it coming in" (193–4). Nor is Weston the only dupe. Each member of the family, like the drunks in O'Neill's *The Iceman Cometh*, survives by entertaining some impossible pipedream of a future in which the current circumstances are transcended. But in the Tates' postmodern environment, these dreams are all based on some bankrupt American pop fiction: the genuinely felt desire for change has been invaded and distorted by the endless promises of the culture they live in. Ella, inspired by travel brochures, wants to sell the land and with the proceeds take the children off to Europe, where they will encounter art and enlightenment. Emma, inspired by pulp adventure fiction, dreams of escaping alone to Mexico to disappear. Wesley, though more attached to the farm than the women are, still believes in the frontier myth, and thinks he might find fulfillment in the undiscovered wilds of Alaska. All these notions of escape are foolishly impractical, and the characters take sadistic delight in ridiculing each other's dreams ("Who wants to discover a bunch of ice?" Emma asks Wesley of Alaska). To give up those dreams, however – as in O'Neill – is to give in to despair: Emma is last seen as a curt, hardened, too-young adult who embraces crime (the ultimate pure-profit enterprise) as the only way to survive, and who cynically ridicules her previous fantasy of escaping to Mexico as "stupid."

In falling for the illusory, the Tates have allowed any sense of familial relatedness to wither away completely. Weston finally realizes this in act 3: "I kept looking for it out there," he says of his vain search for fulfillment. "And all the time it was right inside this house" (194). Abandoning his scheming, and becoming the model of a sober, industrious father, Weston explains his newfound hope in rootedness to a bemused Wesley:

> I felt like I knew every single one of you. Every one. Like I knew you through flesh and blood. Like our bodies were connected and we could never escape that. But I didn't feel like escaping. I felt like it was a good thing. It was good to be connected by blood like that. . . . It was an animal thing. It was a reason of nature we were all together under the same roof. . . . And I started feeling glad about it. I started feeling full of hope. (186)

This passage enunciates an idealized view of family in which Shepard himself would probably like to believe. Yet as with the romanticized leanings in *Angel City*, *Suicide*, and so forth, more hopeful sentiments of this sort are comprehensively overwhelmed by skepticism and fragmentation. Indeed, given the brutal facts that his "rebirth" ignores, Weston's rhetoric comes across as little more than a lamentable joke, yet another illusory attempt at a new beginning, a willful denial of the family's patent inability to function. Devoid of unambiguously optimistic images of the family, the play constantly feeds the suspicion that, far from being merely the result of exterior pressure, the characters' emotional separation from each other may be due to an internal hemorrhaging as inevitable as Emma's menstruation.

The internal crisis of the family is most vividly illustrated by the play's recurrent insistence on the inescapable influence of heredity. Ella's speech on genes "plotting in the womb" epitomizes the suspicion that there is perhaps a built-in self-destructiveness in family relations, as children end up helplessly replaying the mistakes of the parents whose genes and psychological influence have shaped them. The play's sense of generational similarity is obvious in the names themselves: Wesley is Weston's son, Emma is Ella's daughter. It is also repeatedly stressed that Wesley looks like Weston physically (Ella even mistakes her son for her husband at one point, an intriguing Oedipal twist) and has inherited the same psychic poison of masculine violence, or "nitro-glycerine" in the blood, as Emma puts it. At first, such references appear odd, with Emma herself seeeming more fiery and violent than the generally quiet and defensive Wesley. Yet in act

3, after being beaten up by Ellis, the still-dazed Wesley suddenly under-
goes a ritualized inheritance of his father's legacy. After taking the bath
which Weston has recommended (a kind of baptismal rebirth), Wesley
exits from the stage, naked and dripping, taking the lamb with him. He
returns, having donned his father's filthy clothes (which he found in the
trash) and having slaughtered the lamb. This blatantly nonrealistic
sequence of events, though theatrically striking, suggests an unusually
crude use of symbolism on Shepard's part: innocence is sacrificed; the
father's mantle is accepted. Nevertheless, there is a real poignancy to Wesley's realization that he is the helpless victim of a deterministic conditioning which has shaped every aspect of his identity. "I didn't do a thing,"
he tells Emma in bemusement at his transformation: "I just grew up here"
(196). Notably, Weston claims that the same thing happened to him, and
in act 2 he even takes a perverse satisfaction in prophesying Wesley's fate:
the males of each generation, he informs him, are like the lambs' corpses
which farmers lay out to poison predatory coyotes; they have strychnine
in the gut.

It is tempting to try to extend the significance of this image: are the
coyotes the speculators? But if they are, that simply begs the question of
how they relate, if at all, to the heredity theme. In practice, the two issues
remain helplessly confused: cultural pressure and familial determinism
coexist in the same situation, complicating each other but refusing to be
disentangled. The family can trace no single source for its predicament,
nor any way to escape it. That dilemma, in turn, is reflected by the audience's ongoing inability to resolve the oil-and-water stylistic incompatibility between the moustache-twirling melodramatic plot and the long
interludes of simple domestic activity. Weston's description of his disjointed life experience could equally well be taken to describe the
viewer's experience of the play: "I kept trying to piece it together. The
jumps. I couldn't figure out the jumps" (194).

As in Shepard's other recent work, the only certainty here seems to be
the inevitability of doom, and the hostility which springs from its antici-
pation. This bemused, confused fatalism is realized paradigmatically in
the tale of the eagle and the tomcat, with which Weston opens the third
act, and which Ella and Wesley conclude in the play's last moments. Like
the dripping medicine bundles at the end of *Angel City*, this story, in which
the two animals fight in midair over the castrated testicles of a lamb, suggests both the ominousness of myth and a certain coy, comic strip irony.
It allows for no direct, symbolic parallels with the plot, and yet the sense
of primal violence it evokes seems to bring together all the threads of the

play. The story could allude to the "animal thing" of inherited masculine brutality, to the struggle of the animalistic predators for the farm deeds, or even to the helpless victimization of the lamb's (and by extension Wesley's) "manhood" at the claws of disparate forces. However it is viewed, though, the concluding image suggests a horrific symbiotic unity, of simultaneous interdependence and self-destruction: "they come crashing down to earth. Both of them come crashing down. Like one whole thing" (200). This seems to mirror not only the condition of the men, the family, even the culture at large, but also the inextricable tangle of the play itself.

Subterranean Murmurs

Buried Child, like *Curse*, is distinctly unsettling in form, often displaying a mix of features every bit as jarring as that of its predecessor. This is especially true of act 3, which eventually erupts into savage farce, as glass bottles are hurled and smashed live onstage, Bradley crawls around helplessly in pursuit of his wooden leg, characters run in and out of doors, and Father Dewis (less an American-style Bible-thumper than that staple of English farce, the inept vicar) tries pathetically to make his excuses and leave: "I just came in for some tea" (131). The fact that act 3 is the most clearly disjointed section of the play, however, also indicates how much more controlled *Buried Child* is than *Curse*. Rather than bombarding the audience from the outset with "jumps" which refuse to be pieced together, the play achieves a kind of disorientation-by-stealth. Establishing the idea of a gothic-style mystery surrounding the family's past, it lures the audience in with the implicit promise that the truth will eventually be revealed. But a sense of pressurized unease gradually builds up over the course of the first two acts (just as the number of people onstage gradually increases), and this finally explodes into chaos in the third. At this stage the audience is made painfully aware that conclusive answers will not be forthcoming.

   Buried Child is also tighter and more unified than *Curse* in its thematic concerns, dispensing almost entirely with the issue of external cultural pressures, so as to make the question of the family's internal dynamics the play's central, uncontested subject. This is unsurprising: careering wildly across different surfaces, *Curse* never settles down sufficiently to develop its ideas about blood and heredity very far, and although that very sketchiness acts to complement the overall tone of disjuncture, it was logical for Shepard to try to dig deeper in his next piece. One significant difference between the two plays is therefore the change in location. *Curse*'s evoca-

tion of the plastic impermanence of southern California is replaced in
Buried Child by a sense of isolation and backwardness, set as it is in the
vast farm regions of the Midwest. The play suggests that the family's life
has gone on virtually unchanged for decades, and indeed that it is somehow bound to the land itself, tied in with the natural cycle of death and
rebirth in the fields.

Buried Child's subtler sense of unease is built into its visual appearance
from the start. Developing the tensions between the solid and insubstantial in the staging of *Curse*, Shepard again makes use of a skeletal set, the
living room being composed simply of a sofa, a television set, and a lamp.
Behind this is a back wall which is nothing more than a gauze screen,
through which the porch and the area beyond can be glimpsed. Yet this
simplicity is not used merely to reproduce the kind of overt contradictions
between the ultra-real and the obviously fake seen in *Curse*. Rather, there
is a more eerie sense of strangeness, of perceptions being oddly distorted.
The television, for example, flickers light onto the dim stage, but produces
"no image, no sound." Rain is heard falling relentlessly through the first
two acts, but cannot be seen through the gauze. The bottom of a flight of
stairs, unconnected to any wall, juts obtrusively into the downstage area
of the stage, leading offstage into apparent nothingness: there is, Shepard
specifies, "no landing." The stage illusion is thus made to feel like exactly
that, an illusory, almost ghostly environment which complements the mysterious quality of the play. The use of the screen wall is particularly effective in this respect, as is evident from photographs of the Magic Theatre
production, in which figures on the porch, beyond the screen, appear
shadowy and spectral, almost as though they are entering from a different dimension.[25] The presence of a "solid interior door" set into this insubstantial border further underlines the oddness.

Shepard's use of stage action and dramatic imagery also contributes to
the sense of strangeness and uncertainty. The play is full of vivid, often
provocative gestures, which an audience is bound to try to interpret as
elusive but significant clues, which might fit together to provide an
understanding of the family's situation. Moments such as Tilden carefully
covering his sleeping father's entire body with corn husks, Bradley shav-
ing Dodge's head (also while he is asleep), Bradley's sudden insertion of
his fingers into Shelly's mouth, and Shelly's theft of Bradley's prosthetic
leg, to name but a few, seem to cry out with a kind of symbolic resonance.
There are many possible connotations to some of these images: the act of
a man forcing his fingers into a woman's mouth, for example, has obvious
overtones of rape and domination about it. And yet, as Robert Woodruff

points out, there is also something ultimately inexplicable about this moment, which remains unconnected to the other elements of the mystery: "Why'd he stick his fingers in her mouth? I don't know. It's just something he does. There's something about the need to motivate an action that weakens it, not letting it be what it is."[26] Moreover, as in *Suicide in B♭*, many of the "clues" might simply be red herrings. "What's the meaning of this corn, Tilden?" Halie demands at one point, enunciating the very question the audience have (in all probability) been asking themselves about the husks he has strewn around the floor. Similarly, when the final act opens with sunshine and birdsong, and Halie dressed in bright yellow instead of mourning, Dodge openly mocks Shelly's (and by extension the audience's) attempts to read the conventional connotation of "hope" or "new beginnings" into these signs: "You think everything's gonna be different just because the sun's come out" (110). None of this, of course, rules out the possibility, or even the likelihood, that audience members will ascribe certain meanings to the events witnessed. Yet the play repeatedly seems to warn that whatever significance they choose to assign to these incidents is their own reading, not the result of decoding some fixed set of meanings or symbols. The experience of watching the play is a subjective one, and if the spectator arrives at the conclusion, as does Shelly, that "I can't find a reason for anything" (121), then this is at least as legitimate a response as any other. In a moment reminiscent of Niles's speech at the end of *Suicide*, Dodge ridicules the very idea of her attempting to solve the mystery: "She thinks she's going to uncover the truth of the matter. Like a detective or something" (122).

Yet if *Buried Child* echoes previous work in its implicit expulsion of the detective, the play also treats this theme with a fresh depth, which springs from its interest in the emotional complexity of its characters. Shepard himself became aware of this during rehearsals for the premiere: "One thing starts to become clear," he wrote in his production notebook. "The situation of the play evolved out of who the characters are. What the audience sees is a vision of the world seen thru the characters' eyes. *What if* each character saw the world only one way and each way was different?" The spectator, in other words, is obliged by the play to piece together an understanding of the family's predicament from the evidence provided by a range of mutually contradictory subjective perceptions.

The various individual perspectives of the family members suggest two key, underlying needs common to them all: first, the need to maintain the illusion of their own innocence by denying the reality of whatever it was that happened in the past; second, the need to insulate themselves against the threat of chaos which seems to lurk in every corner. Halie, for example, subscribes to Dewis's religion as a desperate buffer against the void – "We can't shake certain basic things. We might end up crazy" (118) – and takes refuge in rose-tinted memories of the past. These she has clearly invented for her own comfort: she lives upstairs in a room full of old photographs, and reminisces incessantly about a bygone golden age in which "Everything was dancing with life!" (66). She has even found a mythicized scapegoat for the family's collapse: "Catholic women are the Devil incarnate," she explains of the "Italian" who allegedly married her (fictitious?) son Ansel: "I knew she'd cursed him. Taken his soul" (74). Ansel's (alleged) murder, for Halie, was the turning point at which everything went wrong: she thus maintains her own "innocence" by rewriting herself as the tragic mother, weeping for her cruelly murdered son.

Dodge's method of reconstructing reality is somewhat different. He appeals to neither past nor future, instead choosing to live in a perpetual present, in which memory is instantly shut out: "You just forge ahead," he declares, echoing numerous other Shepardian males (78). This attitude appears to account for (insofar as anything is accounted for) his blunt refusal to recognize or even acknowledge the existence of his grandson, Vince. Dodge simply treats Vince's arrival as the given state of affairs in the present moment, to be turned to his own advantage by demanding that Vince go and buy whiskey for him. After Vince has left, Shelly asks "You really don't recognize him?" and Dodge demonstrates his extraordinary propensity for forgetfulness with the response, "Recognize who?" (100). The past holds dangers that must always be shut out.

Halie and Dodge's denial of the shadows of the past occasionally creates a sense that the play is dealing metaphorically with America's collective tendency to bury the intolerable memories of its bloody history of slavery and genocide, and so forth. Indeed, Shepard here echoes a commonplace theme in American family drama: the issue of denial is, for example, central to much of Arthur Miller's work. Yet *Buried Child* is distinctive in that it never provides the reassurance of a discoverable, objective truth that might finally explain the situation. The only truths available are the ones the various family members believe in, and since they all see things differently, resolution is impossible. Hopelessly bewildered by the conflicting information, Shelly is finally reduced to begging them to stop talking: "Don't anyone come near me. I don't need any words from you" (121).

These confusions become most evident whenever the buried child of the title is mentioned. Gothic convention would suggest that the alleged

murder of this baby, at some point in the past, is the crime which has
brought the present state of barren damnation to the family. And yet (at
least in Shepard's original text) it is impossible to assemble the various
references to the child into any coherent narrative that might explain
what "actually" happened. The first mention of the subject sees Dodge
bitterly raging, "My flesh and blood's buried in the back yard!" (77): this
and a later outburst ("They'll murder your children!": 93) seem to imply
that he was the father of the child and the rest of the family was responsible for the murder. Yet, in act 2, Tilden asserts his claim to paternity ("I
had a son once but we buried him"), prompting Dodge to refute this by
insisting that Tilden had not even been born at the time the baby was
killed (92). The issue is convoluted even further by the veiled inference
that Vince himself may, in some way, be the buried child come back to
haunt them: the confusion over the child's paternity is again recalled
when Vince refers to himself, in relation to both Dodge and Tilden, as
"their son!" (97). Halie's idealized vision of Vince as an angelic baby (128)
also suggests that he was the child in question, but her references to her
ideal-yet-murdered son Ansel might equally represent some kind of sub-
limation of the baby's murder.

   In act 3, Dodge claims to explain the mystery by implying to Shelly that
the baby was Tilden and Halie's, and that he, Dodge, therefore killed it to
bury the memory of the incest. This horror would certainly account for
his and the family's constant denial of past sins, and it is notable that even
in admitting the crime, Dodge refuses to take the blame for it, insisting it
was necessary in order to save the family's sense of identity from total
destruction: "We couldn't allow that to grow up right in the middle of our
lives. It made everything we'd accomplished look like it was nothing"
(124). Yet Dodge's revelation is also problematic, not only because it does
not tally with all the previous references, but because there is the unmis-
takable air of a self-conscious performance about his story. Following
directly from his mockery of Shelly's desire for a clear explanation of the
situation, it might well simply be a tale spun to cruelly exploit that need.
The other family members' reactions to Dodge's account only add to the
uncertainty. Immediately after Dodge confesses to drowning the baby,
Halie appears to corroborate the story by blurting out that "Ansel would
have stopped him!" And yet the next instant she repeats the statement
with an entirely different inference: "Ansel would have stopped him from
telling these lies!" (124).

   Of course, the spectator may well choose to accepts Dodge's account
at face value (and the chances of this are dramatically increased by Shep-

ard's 1995 revisions to the play, which function to resolve several of the contradictions outlined above). Even so, a great deal else is still left ambiguous: in particular, the play's richest vein of mystery lies in its positing of directly contradictory possibilities as to the underlying significance of the baby's death and ultimate disinterment. For *Buried Child*, more so than any other Shepard play, carries with it the suggestion of various overtones borrowed from myth: broadly speaking, the play can be seen to be quoting and manipulating two familiar but incompatible myth schemes, which are laid over the basic narrative premise in a kind of unresolved double exposure. The first of these schemes could be described as a Judeo-Christian pattern of fall and redemption. The impression is created, throughout the play, that the family has been cast into some supernaturally blighted limbo: the land has produced no crops since 1935, we are told, and the family has had no contact with neighbors for fifty-seven years. An eerie sense of numbed misery is maintained throughout the first two acts by the relentless sound of falling rain, rain which, Dodge claims, is *only* falling on them. In his third act performance for Shelly, he makes the fall allusions still clearer by describing life in the old days as a kind of American Eden: "The farm was producing enough milk to fill Lake Michigan twice over." The family then fell from grace, he suggests, because of the incest and murder: "Everything was cancelled out by this one mistake. This one weakness" (123–4).

This scheme is reinforced by complementary allusions to the Arthurian legend of the Fisher King (also the source of T. S. Eliot's *The Waste Land*). Dodge is the dried-up monarch "festering away! Decomposing!" on his thronelike sofa, and the lack of fertility in the land is thus related to the loss of vitality in the family, an impression reinforced by the fact that Dodge's sons are clearly not fit to relieve him of the crown and so bring new life to the farm. There are suggestions that both sons wish to usurp this throne: this might "explain" Bradley's act of supplanting him on his sofa, just as Tilden, allegedly, supplanted him in his marriage bed. Their gestures of covering (burying?) Dodge's sleeping body – with overcoat and corn husks, respectively – might also be seen as images of ritualized patricide. And yet both are as impotent as their father, damaged children who cannot save the situation. Some new source of hope must be found, it seems, and from the outset of the play there are hints that such a salvation is imminent. Tilden's apparent discovery of fresh crops in the dead fields seems to suggest that something is about to change: Shepard himself describes it as an instance of the kind of moment "when everything seems miraculous" and so opens up new possibilities.[27] Perhaps the family, tied into the natural cycle of life, has been through the winter of death, and spring's rebirth is about to arrive. And certainly Vince's unexpected arrival means that a vital new heir has been restored to the family: eventually realizing this, Dodge ritualistically recites his will, handing over the farm and everything on it to Vince, before simply lying down to die, knowing finally that the future is in safe hands. Vince covers up Dodge's corpse (burying him more successfully than either of his sons had), and takes his place on the sofa/throne. As he does so, the land comes back to life. Halie is heard calling from her upstairs window, announcing that Eden has been restored, that the fields have been mysteriously rejuvenated: "It's like a paradise out there" (131). Pursuing this pattern of fall and redemption, one could argue that it is completed by Tilden's climactic disinterment of the baby's corpse, which perhaps suggests that a kind of painful atonement is being enacted. In the play's closing moments, he is seen carrying a muddy bundle of bones up the stairs into Halie's room: is the family finally being made to confront its past sins, for so long denied and buried? Can the psychic wounds now finally begin to heal?

And yet if this Judeo-Christian scheme of interpretation lends the play a hopeful outlook, it is directly contradicted by other elements, which suggest a much more insidious, pagan sense of inescapable doom. For if the family is tied to the cyclical life of the land, they are also trapped, subject to the changing seasons without any control over their own fates. The natural world, so often a source of idealized hope for Shepard, is seen here – as in the work of American writers like Melville and Hawthorne – as a mysterious, even malevolent force, thwarting any feeble attempts of man to establish his own identity. Just as Oedipus could do nothing about "this devastating harm coming down from the heavens," so these characters find themselves playing out roles prescribed by powers beyond their understanding. If, for instance, Tilden's relationship with Halie *was* Oedipal and incestuous, then it seems simply to represent yet another case in Shepard's work of the inescapably natural (and in this case horrifically misdirected) desire of the alienated child for a return to primal union with his mother. And when Vince returns in act 3, reborn like some midwestern Osiris as an embodiment of masculine vitality, he has clearly had no choice about this transformation. Although, on one level, his rampaging entrance can be explained by a change in temperament wrought by alcohol (he slashes his way into the room through the screen door,

viciously drives Bradley out of the house, and proceeds to announce that
the entire family is as good as dead), it is also apparent that he has been
taken over by the unseen hand of his ancestry. The family's blood curse of
violent masculinity has been revived along with the fertility of the fields,
and in this light the other rebirth imagery also reads less as redemption
than as catastrophe: the disinterment of the buried child complements
the resurrection of Vince's latent genetic and psychological conditioning.
For Vince as for Wesley, this inheritance summarily puts paid to any
attempt at independent will. And yet there is also perhaps the hint, in
Vince's monologic reverie on his fate, of a certain wonder and awe in the
realization that while he has lost himself, he also – paradoxically – finally
knows who he is:

> I studied my face. Studied everything about it. As though I was looking
> at another man. As though I could see his whole race behind him. . . .
> And then his face changed. His face became his father's face. Same
> bones. Same eyes. Same nose. Same breath. And his father's face
> changed to his Grandfather's face. And it went on like that. Changing.
> Clear on back to faces I'd never seen before but still recognized. Still
> recognized the bones underneath. (130)

Buried Child succeeds, finally, in interweaving a range of mythic resonances in a manner which will allow them neither to be separated nor
clearly interpreted. No conclusive causes or explanations can be attributed – "Maybe it was the rain"; "Maybe it's the sun" (Halie: 132). There
are tantalizing allusions to death, decay, rootedness, resurrection, family
violence, the denial of guilt, confrontation with the past, murdered innocence, and so forth. Yet all that can ultimately be said is that the myster-
ies and contradictions of *Buried Child* seem to accumulate to form a
unnerving (if heavily ironized) sense of doom. Both this play and its predecessor capture something of the ancient spirit of tragedy for the postmodern world, *Curse* by bombarding its audience with uncertainties,
Buried Child by dripping them into the viewer's consciousness with the
relentlessness of the rain that continues throughout the first two acts (and
which may be the source of new life in the fields, or "Catastrophic", or
just "Plain old rain").

One major question looms over both these pieces, however. For in
tying together the cyclical repetition of nature with the inheritance of
masculine savagery, both seem to suggest that Shepard has here capitu-
lated to the idea of male violence as a permanent, natural given of Amer-

ican existence. Indeed, both seem markedly less "resistant" in tone than much of his previous work (even given *Curse*'s evident horror of exterior cultural pressures). Shepard's next plays further underline the bleak suggestion that disaster is inherited with one's genes, but simultaneously begin to sow the seeds of a new, more hopeful perspective.

6

The Real Thing

True West (1980)
and Fool for Love (1983)

"THE EVOLUTION OF AN ARTIST is a movement towards clarity."
This quote from the abstract expressionist painter Mark Rothko appears
in Shepard's notes for August 1979, and in many ways epitomizes the shift
of emphasis in his work which began with the play he was then preparing
to write, *True West*, which premiered at the Magic Theatre in 1980. In
that piece and the one that followed, *Fool for Love* (Magic Theatre,
1983), the grotesque collision of realism with cartoon characters, gothic
weirdness, and extravagant theatricality which had marked his previous
family plays all but disappeared. Such deliberately jarring effects made
way for what, on the surface at least, appears to be a consistently maintained use of realistic illusion. Both these plays, for example, eschew their
predecessors' bizarre, minimalistic staging in favor of detailed box sets,
reproductions of recognizable real-world environments. Shepard even
specified in the stage directions for *True West* that "no attempt should be
made to distort dimensions, shapes, objects or colors," or otherwise graft
on a "stylistic concept."[1] The only overtly nonrealistic device in either
play is the presence of the Old Man in *Fool for Love*, observing the action
from a platform outside the proscenium frame. Even this, however, was
a late addition to that play's development, and all other characterizations
in these pieces adhere – at least on the surface – to more orthodox conventions. Stripping his usual sprawling casts down to only four characters
in each play, and concentrating a tight focus on central, dualistic pairings
(the brothers Lee and Austin in *True West*, and the lovers May and Eddie
in *Fool for Love*), Shepard presents a more sustained and consistent
exploration of character than ever before.

Shepard's move away from overt internal contradiction made these plays more immediately accessible to a wider audience. Inevitably, something was lost of the disorientating, agitating power of the best of the previous work: Nancy Meckler, for one, finds these pieces "less interesting because in a funny way he's made himself less obscure."[2] Yet it must be stressed that Shepard's "movement towards clarity" did not simply mean an unquestioning acceptance of the realistic facade, any more than Rothko's mature work sought to abandon abstraction. Rather, the phrase indicates a desire to pin down and concentrate on the real concerns of the artist's work, "to simplify, to refine and distil", as Shepard has put it.[3] These two plays do precisely that, homing in with fresh emphasis on Shepard's recurrent theme of the tenuous status of personal identity. His continuing sense of instability and fragmentation is here transferred from the outward style and construction of his work onto the portrayal of individual characters who initially appear consistent and complete, but who on closer examination prove to be fragile figures reliant for self-definition on their assumed difference from each other. These plays also extend *Buried Child*'s concern with the unbridgeable gaps between different characters' perceptions of their situation and memories of the past, creating more subtly shaped interrogations of the subjective nature of truth, and even of reality itself.

Rhythm, Character, Performance

Perhaps the first thing to note about the construction of these plays is that their pared-down style seems to have resulted from a conscious effort on Shepard's part to "refine and distil" his use of improvisatory writing and rhythmic language, in an attempt to serve his development of more consistent characterization. He had begun to see his practice of juxtaposing sharply contrasting verbal rhythms, and his use of self-demonstrative monologic performances (as derived from his absorption of jazz and rock influences) as inhibiting further developments, and sought to weed these out. *Curse of the Starving Class* and *Buried Child*, he now decided, were "verbose and overblown," relying too much on a tendency toward indulging his wilder impulses, and so turning the characters into mere pawns of authorial whim.[4]

For Shepard, the solution to this problem was not to abandon his musical approach, but simply to find a way to harness it to the more consistent portrayal of character. Both these pieces were written as intuitively as much of his other work, the difference being that he threw material out whenever he felt he was not being faithful to his idea of the characters being presented, and began again, all the time refining his approach. "I was determined", he said of *True West*, "no matter what, to ride the characters out."[5] That piece, he claims, was completely rewritten thirteen times, while *Fool for Love* went through "about sixteen versions . . . and every time I came back to the first five pages. I'd write like seventy, eighty pages, and then bring it all the way back to the first five pages and start again. . . . They weren't just drafts. Every time I think this is the play."[6] The plays finally came right for him when he discovered "voices" and speech patterns for the characters which he could "listen to" through the whole course of the writing, following where they led rather than feeling that he was imposing behavior on them arbitrarily.

This more careful use of his intuitive, "musical" writing approach is evident in the texts of the plays. For while they avoid the trademark linguistic extravagance of his previous work, there is nevertheless a remarkably subtle rhythmic quality to much of the dialogue. Take, for, example, the opening of *Fool for Love*, in which Eddie finds himself obliged to keep talking, so as to cover May's frightening silence. In any of Shepard's earlier work, this might have been a cue for an aria-like monologue, but here Eddie just uselessly repeats the same information: "I'm not gonna leave. Don't worry. I'm not gonna leave. I'm stayin' right here. I already told ya' that. May? Let go, okay? Honey? I'll put you back in bed. Okay?"[7] However, having established this rather dull, repetitive vocabulary, Shepard uses it to build a kind of pulsating insistence into many of Eddie's subsequent comments, which insinuates itself into the listener's mind without necessarily drawing explicit attention to itself:

> I'm not leavin'. I don't care what you think anymore. I don't care what you feel. None a' that matters. I'm not leavin'. I'm stayin' right here. I don't care if a hundred "dates" walk through that door – I'll take every one of 'em on. I don't care if you hate my guts. I don't care if you can't stand the sight of me or the sound of me or the smell of me. I'm never leavin'. You'll never get rid of me. You'll never escape me either. I'll track you down no matter where you go. (40)

The overall structure of these pieces also reflects Shepard's concern for a more sustained, character-related "musicality." Rather than creating overt confusion and instability through the juxtaposition of disparate fragments, they evoke a sense of crisis at an interpersonal level through the creation of tense, one-on-one confrontations between the central character pairings, which persist over the whole course of the play. Shepard's handling of the constantly modulated ebb and flow of these relational tensions suggests a conscious attempt to transfer musical structures to the stage. In *True West*, the opposing brothers effectively act as statement and counterpoint, to be played off against each other with differing degrees of intensity in the play's nine scenes, which thus become akin to nine movements. Indeed, the brothers' "themes," which start off at diametrically opposed extremes, are eventually blended and blurred to the point where they cross over completely, in a role reversal which is as much musical device as it is character development. *Fool for Love*, by contrast, "is to be performed relentlessly without a break" (19): it forms a single, ongoing movement, rhythmically punctuated by the slamming of doors as the characters come and go. My own experience of directing the piece confirmed this sense of its debt to musical structures: in production it becomes clear that *Fool*'s overall dynamic (as opposed to *Buried Child*'s irregular, jerky rhythmic patterns) is a sustained pattern of two-way confrontations, which build, crescendo-like, to peaks of violent intensity before giving way to quieter, more reflective passages, which then in turn begin to become confrontational.

This newly concentrated emphasis on the characters' moment-to-moment interaction is also an important factor in relation to Shepard's concern with pursuing a greater consistency of motivation for his characters. For he realizes this not by creating conventional, "well-rounded" psychological portraits with clearly detailed histories, but by focusing instead on maintaining a consistent overtone of tension in the characters' immediate confrontations. The dominating factor in the central characters' behavior is always the immediate need for them either to forcibly command the attention of, or to survive the assaults of, their opponents. When Eddie, for example, fails to pound May into submission with a brutal display of rodeo tricks (culminating in roping a chair and flinging it across the room), he desperately changes tack: "Tell ya' what. I'll back off. I'll be real nice. I will. I promise" (35). The action veers off at a new tangent, the violent intimidation giving way to a quieter level of exchange, while the degree of underlying intensity remains undiminished. This moment is typical of Eddie's unstable behavior throughout the play, which follows an erratic pattern of coming and going, violence and calm. Such portraits suggest a further refinement of the "prismatic" behavior of the family characters in *Curse* and *Buried Child*. The Magic Theatre's John Lion has summed up the effect of Shepard's approach here: "we see

that the 'characters' he writes, while appearing whole, are actually fragmented, a series of masks, and, omigod, they are us."[8]

Both of these plays are effectively duels, in which the actors fence
around each other, occasionally lashing out violently, and in performance
this approach necessitates the development of a more vibrantly physical-
ized acting style than any of his previous work had required. This new
emphasis on the clash of actors' bodies within the stage space was again a
quite deliberate development on Shepard's part. As he explained in a pro-
jected article for *TDR* in 1980, he now saw the three-dimensional "confrontation of human beings" as the theatre's most distinctive feature, its
"true purpose." His task as a playwright was therefore to foreground the
importance of the "actor-performer," and to play down his own tendency
toward writerly excess. Such remarks make clear just how much Shepard's attitudes had changed over the course of the 1970s. As a result of his
hands-on experience of the production process, he now saw the actual
writing of a play as only a preliminary phase, one which facilitates the creation of a performance in rehearsal. His comments also indicate a further
stage in the development of his concern – seen in *Action* and subsequent
plays – with emphasizing the perceptual experience of the performance
as an end in itself. Picking up on the 1970s developments in physical theatre and "body art," with their emphasis on the three-dimensional fact of
the corporeal body in space, he noted: "I think the future promises the
migration of playwrights into the territory which performance artists have
begun to open up."[9]

The suitability of Shepard's new writing for a very physical performance approach took some time to be widely appreciated, since *True
West*'s New York opening in 1980 (which opened subsequently to the
Magic Theatre production but, of course, took most of the press attention) was dogged by controversy and never properly rehearsed.[10] However, when in 1982 an early revival was mounted by Chicago's Steppenwolf Theatre – a young company renowned for its raw, undisciplined, but
ruthlessly physical approach to its material – they took New York by
storm, and made a star of John Malkovich (who played Lee). The next
year, Shepard himself directed the premiere production of *Fool for Love*,
willingly giving his actors free rein to develop the physical dimension of
the play as far as they could. As he remarked later, Ed Harris and Kathy
Baker (who played Eddie and May) "were so hot, so intense, for the
whole period, that I took the production in that direction." Harris in particular "went right over a cliff for this role."[11] Shepard adjusted the script
to accommodate this, with the result that whereas the physicality of *True*

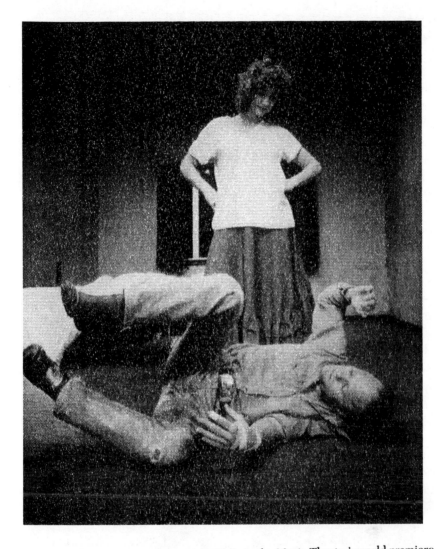

Kathy Baker as May and Ed Harris as Eddie in the Magic Theatre's world premiere production of *Fool for Love*, San Francisco, 1983. (Photo: R. Valentine Atkinson)

West had been largely implicit in the text, the finished version of *Fool for Love* has this element in the foreground. The opening pages stress an extraordinary, animalistic physical tension between the two lovers as they stalk the set, sizing each other up ("MAY begins slowly to move down stage right as EDDIE simultaneously moves upstage left. Both of them press the walls as they move": 23), and as the play develops they are required to slam against walls, physically assault each other, and fling furniture around. The play has become somewhat notorious for the toll it takes on the bodies of actors, and needs to be rehearsed to inch-perfect precision in order to avoid serious injury. The effect of all this is not dissimilar to that of the combined impact of the visceral sensory effects and alarmingly depthless characterization in some of the rock plays: the audience is obliged to view the stage events from a certain uneasy distance. While there is clearly more emotional substance to the characters in these later pieces, their motivations often remain somewhat opaque, and as the actors' bodies are hurled around the stage space, one is inevitably aware of watching a carefully constructed artifice.

Dirty Realism

Another aspect of the oddly distanced quality of these plays becomes particularly apparent if one notes their parallels with the school of American short-story writers and novelists who in the early 1980s were credited with having created a new literary subgenre; "dirty realism."[12] These writers, including Richard Ford (whom Shepard has repeatedly expressed his admiration for), Raymond Carver, Tobias Wolff, Elizabeth Tallent, and others, never made up an intentional "movement" but were grouped together owing to certain marked, if coincidental, similarities in their writing styles. These include a tendency to describe trivial and mundane details with minute precision, and to focus on apparently inconsequential narratives, tales of minor, often rather grubby incidents in the lives of ordinary Americans. These writers also, crucially, share a very sparse, unadorned approach to plot and dialogue, which creates a curiously unsettling experience for the reader: the stories seem flat, emotionally uninvolved, and are conspicuously devoid of strong or heroic characters, being peopled instead by figures about whom little is known beyond their involvement in the immediate events described. This is, in short, a realism for the postmodern age, which seems uncannily in tune with the sense of bewilderment and disquiet displayed in more overt fashion by the wildly fragmented, stylized work of the previous "wave" of American fiction writers like Thomas Pynchon and Donald Barthelme.

Likewise, Shepard's more "realistic" approach here represents a refinement of his earlier concerns. His affinity with the stripped-down tone of Carver and Ford is immediately evident in his own prose writing of this period: the pieces which appear in the *Motel Chronicles* collection (1982), unlike the drug-crazed weirdness of *Hawk Moon*, are very simple, often autobiographical fragments of narrative related from a coolly observant distance. Several similar tales are also inserted into the plays as story monologues. Shepard has acknowledged that both Austin's description of his father losing his dentures in Mexico, and the Old Man's tale of a late night road trip (*Fool for Love*), are derived from his own family history. Their place within the plays seems oddly incidental, seemingly unrelated to the flow of the action, but this in itself contributes to the vague unease they seem to generate: both these stories are faintly comic, but also involve menacing undertones. There is a distinct, nagging sense that more is being alluded to in these rather cryptic accounts than is actually being stated.

Much the same is true of the plays' dialogue, particularly thanks to Shepard's unprecedentedly extensive use of pauses and lengthy silences. In one respect, this was another facet of his more subtle use of speech rhythms: as he explained to an interviewer, he saw *True West* as more truly "a musical" than any of his previous work, because "rhythm is the delineation of space in time, but it only makes sense with silences on either side of it."[13] Yet the pauses also function, crucially, to underline the pronounced lack of real communication between the characters, creating undercurrents of tension which are almost palpable but remain unexplained to the audience. A prime example of this is the very first scene of *True West*. The brothers say very little of any substance to each other: the dialogue is quiet, desultory, and coyly amusing, and both are at times reduced to guttural grunts of "uh" when communication escapes them. A subject is raised, then dies, then a new one is introduced. Yet as Austin attempts to ignore Lee (with the excuse of trying to work), Lee calmly, insistently goads him with hostile sarcasm. Battle lines are all the time being etched out, and Austin's distractedness is visible in the tiny details of behavior Shepard specifies (running his fingers through his hair; rubbing his eyes). Conversely, *Fool for Love* begins at a kind of quiet fever pitch: in the extended silence which opens the play, the extreme tension is immediately evident from May's silent, despairing crouching position, and Eddie's stalking movements. He carves a sense of threat into the air even before speaking, with the prolonged waxing of his bucking strap creating a grating, repetitive screech of leather. The atmosphere of pressure and unease created by such details speaks volumes.

In the work of the dirty realists, this kind of emotional attenuation is accompanied by a related sense of cultural drift: their stories are almost invariably set in the contemporary West or Northwest, and conjure up a

world of used cars, trailer parks, down-at-heel drifters, modern-day cowboys, and disintegrating families. Shepard's fascination with the West had
long been dominated by a similar sense of its "accidentalness" and "junk
magic," and in these plays his attempt to evoke something of this atmosphere is more precise and refined than in any of his previous work. The
locations of both pieces are pinpointed exactly. *True West*, which Shepard
wrote during or after a stay at his mother's home in Pasadena in August
1979, is set in "a kitchen and adjoining alcove of an older home in a Southern California suburb, about 40 miles east of Los Angeles" (3). In *Fool for
Love*, plastic suburbia is replaced by the ramshackle, low-life setting of a
"stark, low rent motel room on the edge of the Mojave desert" (19). Both
sets are described in minute detail and are dominated by modern, artificial materials, with furniture made of plastic, Formica, and bare metal.
Similarly, there is intricate attention to costume details: Shepard even
specifies that Eddie, as a rodeo drifter who has seen better days, should
have cowboy boots held together with silver gaffer tape, and that his jeans
should "smell like horse sweat" (20).

Shepard's prosaic dialogue also reinforces the plays' sense of place, littered as it is with references to the everyday debris of the region – trucks,
horses, small-town trivia – "past the donut shop, past the miniature golf
course, past the Chevron station" (*Fool*, 50). Moreover, this descriptive-
ness at times creates a strangely lyrical effect, as, for example, when
Eddie lets his imagination wander: his memory of a "little white house
with a red awning" seems more reminiscent of Tennessee Williams than
Shepard's usual, supercharged extravagance: "I'll never forget the red
awning, because it flapped in the night breeze and the porch light made
it glow. It was a hot, desert breeze and the air smelled like new-cut alfalfa"
(50). The difference is that where the lyricism in a Williams play is sustained as a stylistic feature throughout, Shepard's (like that of the dirty
realists) feels broken and accidental, appearing in incidental moments
like the traces of some half-remembered dream.

Shepard's use of western locations to evoke both lostness and occasional
flashes of melancholy beauty was also no doubt influenced by his growing
passion for country-and-western music. In 1983 Shepard admitted that he
was now more interested in this form than in either jazz or rock, and *Fool
for Love* in particular demonstrates this influence, even acknowledging it
explicitly via the use of Merle Haggard songs to bracket either end of
the action. Each of the play's central threads seems drawn directly from
the recurrent obsessions of country music; storytelling, alcohol, the land,

small-town seediness, and, of course, the failings of heterosexual love. As Shepard has said (with a certain obvious irony): "more than any other art form I know of in America, country music speaks of the true relationship between the American male and the American female. . . . Terrible and impossible."[14]

Duality and the Other

This last comment brings us to the most obvious theme of these plays. In both cases, the immediate source of the violent tensions enacted is the "terrible and impossible" nature of the relationship at the play's center. Austin and Lee, May and Eddie, are bound together in dualistic, complementary pairs: each character appears to represent one side of a double-headed coin. Yet, as ever in Shepard's work, duality leads not to a healthy balance, but to perpetual division. Like the eagle and the cat in *Curse*, these pairings are both interdependent and self-destructive, caught in an impossible bind of mutual incompatibility. In *True West*, especially, this much is made crystal clear. Temperamentally, the brothers are polar opposites, and yet in some sense they are two halves of one unit. "I wanted to write a play about double nature," Shepard has noted with uncharacteristic bluntness. "I just wanted to give a taste of what it feels like to be two-sided. . . . If you could see it cinematically, you'd have one person playing both characters."[15] As such comments imply, there is an openly autobiographical dimension to the contrast of Austin as the comfortable, bourgeois family man, making his living as a writer and assimilated into suburban life, and Lee as the violent, macho loner, with his old-fashioned, if twisted, sense of honor. Yet the theme of duality also has a far wider application than the purely personal: the motif of hostile but symbiotic brothers is commonplace in legends and myths from all over the world, and is closely related to the kind of ego-shadow division previously evoked by the complementary cowboy-Indian duos of the rock plays.[16] Shepard, moreover, is well aware of the familiarity of this scheme, and there is a pronounced degree of irony in his treatment of the pairing. The play begins with an unashamedly stereotypical pair of opposites (Austin the artist at his typewriter, neatly dressed, working into the night with coffee and cigarettes; Lee the violent boor in his filthy outfit, drunkenly toting a six-pack), and goes on to add biographical details so blatant in their connotations of gentility and savagery as to appear self-parodic. Austin, for instance, was educated at an Ivy League school, whereas Lee arranges and gambles on illegal dogfights. Touches such as these, though modified by numerous subtler manifestations of this antithetical contrast, add further to the underlying sense of wry distanciation.

The pairing of May and Eddie in *Fool for Love* demonstrates a similar blend of archetype and irony. They are a pair of gender opposites, linked together (Eddie claims) by their blood-bond as half siblings, and (they both claim) by a kind of supranormal, telepathic understanding: "You know we're connected, May. We'll always be connected" (31). Such lines seem to wink askance at the clichés of romantic fiction, but simultaneously suggest that this play is building on the kind of anima-animus complementarity hinted at in the plays of the mid-'70s. As is evident from various interviews he gave during the '80s, Shepard was becoming increasingly interested in exploring his own sense of gender duality: "I'm beginning to realize that the female side knows so much more than the male side. About childbirth. About death. About where it's at."[17] Thus, in *Fool for Love*, May is clearly presented as the more sympathetic of the two lovers, displaying a practicality, an inventiveness, and a clear-eyed assessment of their situation which the violent, immature, self-deceiving Eddie completely lacks. There is a clear impression here of the writer playing his sense of internal masculine and feminine off against each other, exploring the idea that, as the Angel in *The War in Heaven* (1984) puts it, "I have a partner / the partner / is me / the partner / has a partner / in me."[18]

Yet psychic division is only one dimension of *Fool for Love*. It also deals very directly with an actual love relationship, and again a key source for the play seems to be autobiography: Shepard's newfound interest in presenting cross-gender conflict must have been influenced by his estrangement from his wife O-Lan (whom he left in 1982), and his burgeoning love affair with the actress Jessica Lange, whom he had met in 1981 while filming *Frances* (his fourth outing as a movie actor). Lange's description of their torrid relationship ("the jealousy, the passion, the insanity"), and Shepard's professed amazement at "suddenly becoming connected with someone in a way you never knew was possible," both read like lines lifted from *Fool*.[19] His involvement with Lange seems to have been the catalyst he needed to be able to write his first sustained dramatization of a strong female character, and to realize in dialogue form an interest in romantic love which had recently surfaced in two monologue pieces. Both *Jacaranda*, a solo dance piece choreographed and performed by Daniel Nagrin in 1979, from a libretto written by Shepard (who chose the subject), and *Savage/Love*, Shepard's performance-poetry collaboration with Joe Chaikin (also 1979), had a single, male voice exploring questions of involvement in a love relationship. With *Fool for Love*, both sides of the coin become visible, in a confrontation of the sexes which acted as precursor to several subsequent pieces on similar themes.

A question inevitably exists as to why, in these two plays, Shepard returned to a concern with clearly defined binary opposites in characterization. Since *Angel City* he had been presenting images of selves fragmented into any number of multiple personae, so was it not a retrograde step to create character pairings so clearly suggestive of neatly duplex identity models? One response to this suggestion is simply to note that at no time had Shepard in fact lost interest in dualistic splits. Indeed, *True West* was the culmination of an attempt to present a male pairing which dated almost all the way back to his last attempt at the theme, *The Tooth of Crime*. The seeds of the play are all evident in the unfinished *California Heart Attack* (1974), which is also set in bourgeois suburbia, and features the pairing of a frustrated writer, Frankie, and his potentially violent brother, Mitchell.[20] Those names, along with those of Lee, Austin, and Grebe, recur in a seemingly endless series of permutations in unfinished "two guys" manuscripts dating throughout the 1970s.

Yet if Shepard was still pursuing a long-term concern, his treatment of the theme is markedly more sophisticated than it had been previously. The dualities presented in these plays are not rigidly fixed, and tend to blur and oscillate in a manner which emphasizes the fundamental instability of all concepts of self. Even while appealing to archetypal images of binary opposition, Shepard implicitly undermines the idea that these pairings represent universal or biological givens. Rather, the brothers' and lovers' differences are treated (at least in part) as surface role play, as somewhat arbitrary polarizations of behavioral characteristics, which demand the repression of any number of other free-floating possibilities. The identities of Austin and Lee, May and Eddie, in other words, are to a large extent dependent on a kind of mutual repulsion: they have each shaped themselves in diametric opposition to their conception of the other. Indeed, it can be argued that the characters' gradual realization of this fact provides the key dynamic for each play's progress: the pretense at firm ego identity is compromised and undermined as the characters' confrontations expose the fragility of the roles they have chosen to inhabit. In both plays the destruction of stable identity is mirrored directly by the destruction of the stage spaces, which seem representative of the state of their occupants' psyches (in much the same way that Niles's "house" in *Suicide in B♭*, filled up with uninvited characters, in some way represents his mind's schizoid confusion). Austin's and May's control over their houses (significantly both are only temporary homes) is demolished by the uninvited invasion of their partners, bringing havoc with them.

This pattern is most immediately evident in *True West*. Austin believes himself to be a well-balanced, self-made man, entirely at home in the plastic, bourgeois environment of his mother's home. Yet Lee comes to function as a kind of nemesis figure, arriving from nowhere and gradually making him aware of the painful truth that he is who he is because he has actively suppressed other, undesirable characteristics. Chief among these are the crudely "masculine" qualities which were drummed into him during his upbringing, an inheritance he has sought to deny by cutting himself off emotionally from his father (a violent, unstable, lonely alcoholic). Austin repeatedly insists that he is nothing like "the old man," and owes him nothing, but Lee's presence inevitably brings the buried past back to the surface: in the first scene especially, speaking from the dark of the kitchen alcove, Lee seems almost like some nagging voice from the shadows of Austin's psyche.

Austin's initial response to Lee's disruption of his complacent lifestyle is barely disguised fear. Yet neither money nor flattery nor dismissal will drive Lee away (he does not even sleep, and so cannot be escaped for a moment – another lightly ironic touch). Consequently, Austin begins to attempt to reinforce his own position, seeking to gain a sense of control over the situation by adopting a kind of patronizing concern for Lee. He even takes it on himself to try to save Lee from himself by civilizing him: "You could really turn your life around, you know. Change things" (24). This approach is aided to some extent by the fact that Lee, far from being merely an implacable shadow voice, is a character in his own right who is obviously unsatisfied with his own, drifting lifestyle. His return to the city has been prompted by the fact that, like Tilden, he cannot survive indefinitely in the wild, and needs to find human company and some sense of stability. Austin has things he wants: a car, a job, money. But if Austin sees this as an opportunity to change Lee, and so neutralize the threat he represents, he is not prepared for the fact that he too begins to change, becoming increasingly attracted to the positive side of Lee's earthy characteristics (self-contained individualism, frankness, a sense of rootedness in the land). Thus, as the two men steadily grow more tolerant of each other's company, each also grows more aware of what the other has which he does not. By the end of act 1, the initial hostility and denial has been replaced by an apparent admission that each one has always been jealous of the other:

> LEE: I used to picture you walkin' round some campus with your arms fulla' books. Blondes chasin' after ya'.
> AUSTIN: Blondes? That's funny. . . . Because I always used to picture you somewhere. . . . You were always on some adventure. . . . I used to say to myself, "Lee's got the right idea. He's out there in the world and here I am. What am I doing?"
> LEE: You were settin' yourself up for somethin'. (26)

Just as Shooter, in *Action*, finds himself dissatisfied with both the roles of civilized domesticity and wild adventuring, so each brother now realizes that his own chosen role "doesn't get it on" for him anymore, and the initially rigid distinctions between them become increasingly blurred as each tries, in effect, to adopt the traits of the other. Having resorted to drunkenness and petty theft, Austin finally announces that his life is an inadequate sham, and submits himself to Lee, begging to be taken away to the desert. But Lee has become equally frustrated at his abject inability to take over Austin's role: abruptly abandoning his attempt to write a screenplay, he destroys the typewriter with a golf club, tears the telephone off the wall, and trashes the kitchen. The descent of both men from controlled, ordered ego opposition into undifferentiated chaos is completed in the final scene when – after Lee decides he will not take Austin to the desert after all – Austin erupts in a fit of frantic rage, and tries to kill Lee by wrapping the telephone cord around his neck.

Both men's personae thus prove to be highly unstable compositions of shifting, conflicting desires, devoid of any reliable sense of self and thus capable of extreme volatility. Paradoxically, though, a more essentialist reading of the situation exists alongside this contingent one: there are clear traces of the concern with biological heredity which had dominated the previous family plays, and to some extent Austin's climactic violence reads as another image of the resurfacing of an inherited blood curse. Yet his transformation is both less abrupt and less schematic than those of Wesley and Vince, and the savagery of both brothers at the end of the play seems to owe at least as much to agonized confusion as to any blood curse. After the demise of their arbitrarily opposed role playing, the only structure in their lives which remains intact is their mutual sense of relatedness and a-rational antipathy, which spirals into savage absurdity: "I can't stop choking him. He'll kill me if I stop choking him" (58).

The dynamic of *Fool for Love* is in many ways similar to *True West's*. Here, though, Shepard finally turns away from the vicious circle of male-on-male violence in search of an alternative. As he said at the time, *Fool* "is really more about a woman than any play I've ever written, and it's from her point of view pretty much."[21] The motel room is May's space, and it is her composure that is disrupted by the uninvited invasion of Eddie, who obliges her to confront ghosts of the past that she would rather forget. Yet where Austin attempts to suppress and deny the memories revived by Lee, May frankly confronts her terror that Eddie's presence will destroy her fragile sense of self: "You're gonna erase me," she insists at the outset (22).

The threat Eddie presents for May is twofold. First, she is aware that her unconquerable, almost masochistic desire for him ("You're like a disease to me": 30) may drive her back into a dependency on him which will simply end in further agony: she knows from bitter experience that he will walk out on her at some stage, and she will long to follow. She has forcibly broken her way out of this cycle of repetitions, and has sought to establish an independent, self-sufficient life for herself as "a regular citizen." Consequently, Eddie's unexpected arrival has precipitated an acute identity crisis, as she tries to hold onto her new, solo role while simultaneously being attracted back to her self-destructive partnership with Eddie. Her contradictory impulses are summed up by her very first movements: breaking from the frozen pose of silent desperation she has held since the lights went up, she clings to his body to prevent him from leaving, but then beats him violently with her fists. "I don't need you!" she screams, only to scream even louder with her very next line: "Don't go!" (22). The same pattern of contradictory behavior recurs, motif-like, at intervals throughout the play, the most vivid example being the moment when May breaks a passionate kiss by kneeing Eddie viciously in the crotch. In performance, there is a fine line to tread to ensure that May appears agonizingly torn rather than simply hysterical, but certainly the actor who played her in my own production was in no doubt that May's dilemma of being simultaneously drawn to and repulsed by her male partner was all too painfully "realistic."

Eddie too is split. Repeatedly wondering why he puts up with May's resentment of him, he seeks to regain his macho independence by walking out on her in a recurrent pattern of sudden exits (and so adding one more revolution to a vicious cycle). He does both within the microcosm of the play itself, and on the broader scale of years, in what is effectively an extrapolation of the key concern of Shepard's previous love monologues. *Jacaranda* centers on a man waking up in his lover's bed to find her gone, and his pain at her absence disconcerts him, making him realize that – in loving her – he has become more dependent on her than he intended.[22] Similarly, *Savage/Love*, with that abrupt slash through the title, explores the sense of disjuncture which results from feeling both the need for attachment to another and the (potentially savage) desire to remain independent. Numerous sections of the piece ("Acting," "How I Look To You," "Tangled Up") are concerned with an awareness that one is always playing out a role, perhaps several roles, for the loved one, and that this may swamp one's established sense of self. This realization, in turn, repeatedly prompts the impulse to "murder" the love (a transition seen at its most alarmingly abrupt in "Beggar"). It is this kind of simultaneous attraction and repulsion which drives the intensity and violence of *Fool for Love*, and which seamlessly welds together the play's archetypal and romantic elements: May and Eddie experience both a transcendent sense of shared identity and a numbing fear of losing themselves in this all-consuming bond: in each other they have (as Wheeler says of the gendered generals in *Angel City*) "gained and lost their entire lives."

But there is another, very significant dimension to May's fear of Eddie, which involves a clashing concept of gender roles. Eddie's fascination with her is bound up with a crass, patriarchal attitude to their relationship, in which he expects to "wear the pants" and dictate the course of both their lives. His passion for her is built around a fetishistic objectification of her body ("I kept crying about your neck": 24), rather than any understanding of her as a person in her own right. His language is littered with phrases illustrating his complete inability to conceive of her as anything other than a personal appendage to him ("I'm takin' you back, May"; "I'm not lettin' go of you this time"), and he has "everything worked out" for their future together, in a trailer home she has no intention of returning to. May's desire for independence, conversely, seems driven in part by a wish to defy this gender typecasting and prove that she can cope alone. The "tough drabness" of her initial costume connotes a practical, almost androgynous self-sufficiency. Yet Eddie's presence begins to entice her back into a more traditionally "feminine" role, a shift illustrated by her onstage costume change, which turns her into "a very sexy woman" (27).

Eddie's notion of May as his "girl" provides him with a reference point against which to reinforce his sense of his own masculinity. Expecting her to act as an admiring female audience for his butch cowboy antics, he even admits that his "love" for her is defined by the extent to which he can perform for her: "if I stopped trying to impress you, that'd mean it was all over, wouldn't it?" (35). Yet when May refuses to play the prescribed part as awestruck girlfriend, seeing Eddie's behavior as a thoroughly juvenile recourse to boy-girl dating games ("this is the same crap you laid on me in High School": 34), his "performances" turn into increasingly violent attempts to force her into the role of passive female. In what amounts to an extended process of rape, he steadily increases his control over her space, bringing in a shotgun (ostensibly to clean it, but the threat is clear), a bottle of tequila (which he begins drinking at speed, getting "real mean and sloppy"), a pair of spurs (another potential source of violence: in the film version, playing Eddie himself, Shepard uses them to dig holes in the walls and floor), and finally a lasso rope, which he swings around the tiny space, snagging bedposts and a chair and dragging them across the floor. May's state of mind deteriorates with the state of her room: "You're driving me crazy! You're driving me totally crazy!" (31).

As with *True West*, this pattern of mounting tension has several possible implications. In one sense, the play seems to present an image of the perpetually unsatisfiable nature of desire. The protagonists use the idea of their union simply as a cipher for some unattainable urge for transcendence, and when that idea fails to "get it on," they move on again in search of a fresh challenge, a fresh target for that desire. It is notable, in this respect, that Eddie and May want each other most at precisely the moments when the other is turning away: they can only desire what they do not have. This scenario also provides yet another variation on the theme of inherited doom: the lovers are seen to be simply reenacting the disastrous, eternally unsettled desires of their parents. Eddie, in reportedly pursuing relationships with both May and the unseen "Countess," duplicates the bigamous behavior of his father, the Old Man, whom he claims was married to both his and May's mothers. Meanwhile, May finds herself perpetually reenacting her mother's behavior, obsessed with her partner to the point of "hunting him from town to town" (53). Her description of her mother's reaction whenever the Old Man deserted her ("She'd pull herself up into a ball and stare at the floor. . . . Her eyes looked like a funeral": 53–4) directly recalls her own semicatatonic condition at the outset of the play, following Eddie's *arrival*: whether the men are coming or going, the women seem powerless to stop them from destroying their lives.

An awkward question raises itself here. Like *True West*, this play blends together a sense of the characters' roles being to some extent fluid, with a sense of cyclical, even biological entrapment. For Lee and Austin, both sides of this contradictory perspective simply contribute to the onset

of self-destruction: Shepard sees no hope for them. Yet in *Fool*, by suggesting that this "terrible and impossible" gender division simply perpetuates itself down the generations, he would appear, concomitantly, to be
denying the possibility that women can remake their roles and live independent of these doomed men (as May tries, and fails, to do), and so con-
signing them to an eternity of abuse and desertion. Yet Shepard has made
it clear that he has never quite been happy with the conclusion of *Fool*,
and this dissatisfaction perhaps springs from an awareness that in this
new context of gender conflict, simply resorting to further images of
impossible entrapment is not necessarily helpful or even truthful to his
own vision. As he remarked to Carol Rosen in 1992, his introduction of
stronger female characters into his work was partly an attempt to help the
men, too, to find their way out of the "fucked up" conditions they are
trapped in in *Curse*, *Buried Child*, and *True West*. In those pieces, he
noted, "you spent the whole play trying to figure out what these men were
about, who had no idea themselves. But then, when the women characters began to emerge, then something began to make more sense for the
men too."[23]

Despite the bleak conclusion of *Fool for Love*, the seeds of this new
vision can be seen emerging in the play. Not only does May's initial self-
sufficiency provide an image of escape from the inherited bind (if only
Eddie could grow up and leave her be): Eddie himself shows tantalizing
hints of his own potential to change the existing gender dynamics. This is
most obvious when he openly rebels against the Old Man's demands that
he tell the "male side a' this thing" and appears to endorse May's "female"
version of the story. Eddie's brutal and juvenile machismo is also frequently tempered by a softer, somewhat vulnerable side which in itself
represents a marked progression from the Old Man's coarseness. Yet this
very combination of machismo and sensitivity can also make Eddie seem
oddly endearing ("an adorable asshole," in the words of one female spectator at my own production), and though this helps make May's attraction
to him plausible, there is perhaps a problem when even his posturing and
strutting at times seems perversely enjoyable. The part embodies a fundamentally unresolved ambiguity in Shepard's depiction of gender roles,
and is so finely balanced that the particular inflection given to it in performance can radically alter the perceived meaning of the play. As Don
Shewey noted of the 1983 New York production:

> Ed Harris so dominated the stage as Eddie that *Fool for Love* seemed
> to be saying that sex roles are fixed, the woman is always the helpless

victim. . . . When Will Patton took over the role, he made it less macho and more androgynous, and Kathy Baker became more of an equal partner in the battle of the sexes, suggesting that their roles were more fluid.[24]

Utopia Undermined

As such comments suggest, the implications of the identity questions explored in both *True West* and *Fool for Love* go far beyond the purely personal. Shepard's tightly executed destabilization of each character's sense of self is concomitant with a destabilization of the illusory world-views on which those selves are founded. In various ways, these pieces undermine and problematize the very "reality" of the worlds they present, and in so doing, imply a broader critique of the "reality" of life in postmodern America.

The title of *True West* itself makes clear that Shepard has a wider agenda than a purely familial one. In one respect, it can be seen as indicating that the dichotomy between Austin and Lee represents another variant on the playwright's recurrent concern with the dichotomy between civilization and wildness: which brother's perspective, one might ask, is to be seen as representative of today's "true West"? Yet there is also a self-conscious irony at work here: the title is borrowed from a (now defunct) pulp nonfiction magazine of the same name, whose policy slogan "All True – All Fact – Stories of the Real West" unintentionally trumpeted the sensationalized artifice of its contents. Similarly, the play makes ingenious nonsense of its title by blurring and collapsing the binary contrast between the brothers' perspectives, and exposing both as equally artificial (just as the brothers' identities are equally unstable). The truth, it suggests, is that the American West – whether urbanized or wild – is an undifferentiated landscape of frustrated desire.

Although the mercenary and rather insipid Austin is for the most part presented as the less sympathetic of the two brothers, the play also stresses the attraction of his comfortable bourgeois lifestyle, typifying as it does the lives of so many Americans. The residential suburbs of Los Angeles – ironically described by Jean Baudrillard as "Utopia Achieved"[25] – are even eulogized by Lee. Having "cased" numerous houses for burglary potential, he offers a meditation on the media-inspired hyper-reality of these Ideal Homes: "Warm yellow lights. Mexican tile all around. Copper pots hangin' over the stove. Ya' know like they got in the magazines." Such comfort is, he notes, both seductive and deadening: "Like a paradise. Kinda' place that sorta' kills ya' inside" (12).

Saul Kimmer, Austin's producer, seems to embody the hollow artifice
of this environment. Unlike the monstrous, cartoon power-mania of his
earlier counterparts, Wheeler and Taylor, Saul is disturbing precisely
because he is so believable. His happily smiling insincerity (he uses the
same phrase, "You've really managed to capture something," to describe
both Austin and Lee's script ideas) and his plastic bonhomie ("That's ter-
rific!"), make him bluntly two-dimensional as a character, but he is nevertheless a type recognizable to anyone who has sat in a business meeting
or ordered fast food. The smile is the mask which has become real, and
the play traces Austin's gradual realization that he too is being "killed
inside" by this environment. Moreover, his sense of shocked recognition
allows for one of Shepard's clearest statements on the insubstantiality of
American culture. Looking afresh at the way immediate gratification is
mass-produced, Austin sees a world in which nothing is permanent or
unique unto itself, and which – most frighteningly – he himself has
become a reflection of:

> I keep finding myself getting off the freeway at familiar landmarks that
> turn out to be unfamiliar. On the way to appointments. Wandering
> down streets that I thought I recognized that turn out to be replicas of
> streets I remember. Streets I misremember. Streets I can't tell if I lived
> on or if I saw in a postcard. Fields that don't even exist anymore. . . .
> There's nothing real down here, Lee! Least of all me! (49)

Lee, of course, cannot help him. As he pointedly remarks, Austin will
never be able to step outside the culture of which he is a part. Yet this is
no mere callous condemnation: Lee, too, steadily realizes that he is as
much a dupe as his brother. His dream of living out the traditional western ideal of frontier freedom, and of finding a sense of connectedness (to
family, to the land) is shown to be futile. For his notion of getting back to
grips with the earth – as did "the forefathers" with their "cabins in the
wilderness" (6) – is as much an internalization of empty media myths
(like those promulgated by *True West* magazine) as Austin's more contemporary desires. His need for "something authentic. Something to
keep me in touch" (56) leads him to insist, for example, on "Real coffee:
From the bean" (6), and on bone china plates rather than plastic ones.
But the comic self-consciousness of such specifications demonstrates that
he is seeking after a hand-me-down notion of authenticity which is, by
definition, inauthentic. The painful truth is that, as Austin remarks,
"There's no such thing as the West anymore. It's a dead issue!" (35). The
frontier America which Lee dreams of no longer exists, if indeed it ever

did, and he can only live like a scavenger on the desert. Moreover, he is
eventually forced to admit that his entire wild-man persona is simply a
posture, a fake, and that he was driven out to the desert not through
choice but through failure: "I'm livin' out there because I can't make it
here" (49).

It is significant that Lee's violence seems to heighten and accelerate
with his growing awareness of the futility of his position. This is a more
sustained exploration of the kind of resentment and frustration displayed
by the male characters in *Curse* and *Buried Child*: Lee's malicious lashing out results from the stifling of his most basic personal desires for freedom and fulfilment. And it is in this light that Shepard's often misquoted
comments about "American violence" seeming "very touching" must be
viewed: "In full force it's very ugly," he notes, in a comment that could
refer to much of Lee's behavior,

> but there's also something very moving about it, because it has to do
> with humiliation. . . . This sense of failure runs very deep – maybe it
> has to do with the frontier being systematically taken away. . . . I can't
> put my finger on it, [but] you don't have to look very far to see that the
> American male is on a very bad trip.[26]

In short, neither brother can offer a way forward: Lee and Austin are
trapped between equally deadening options. The same crisis is seen in
microcosm in *True West*'s final scene, when Mom returns home from
Alaska. Up there alone on America's final frontier she had "never felt so
desperate before," so she has returned to L.A. in search of the security of
home, only to find that this too is a fragile dream. "This is worse than
being homeless," she says, surveying the wrecked house: "I don't recognize it at all" (58–9). This last line is especially pertinent because the real
strengths of this play lie less in its explicit statements of the theme of cultural bankruptcy than in the way it forces the audience to experience
something of Mom's sense of awkward nonrecognition. As has been mentioned, a variety of distancing devices function to highlight and problematize the artifice of the play itself and, by extension, that of the culture
it depicts. Pursuing this argument, it is useful to highlight another cross-
disciplinary parallel, this time with the school of painting known as super-
realism (or photo-realism), which emerged in America during the 1970s
as a kind of reaction to, and development from, pop art.[27] Artists such as
Ralph Goings, Richard Estes, and Harold Gregor – like Shepard and the
dirty realists – proved to be obsessed with the junk culture of the American West, but their method of representing it was controversial. Their

large canvases depict everyday sights like storefronts, motor vehicles, and diners, painted not from life but from photographs. And in seeking to reproduce such images with the same verisimilitudinal clarity as a photo, the artists implicitly query the process of painting, the process of the viewer's perception, and the "nature" of the objects presented. These canvases treat their subjects with a hardness of line and focus, and a vividness of color, which estrange them from the viewer, who is unused to viewing paintings executed with quite that degree of ice-cold precision.

Shepard's affinity with the superrealists was most clearly highlighted by Wim Wenders, whose 1984 film *Paris, Texas* – inspired by *Motel Chronicles* and scripted by Shepard himself – overtly reproduces the feel of some of those paintings. The camera tends to linger insistently on images of hardware stores and motels, old vehicles and expanses of wasteland, viewing this western iconography with an unusual crispness of focus and intensity of color. Wenders also picks out, and scrutinizes, numerous peculiarities of the postmodern landscape, from drive-in banks to spaghetti-like mazes of highway overpasses, and even goes out of his way to capture certain images from *Motel Chronicles* for the film, such as the giant plaster dinosaur outside a highway diner. Shepard fully endorsed Wenders's approach, suggesting that the director's "Europeanness" had enabled him to highlight "an obsessive quality about . . . American culture that certain American directors would totally overlook."[28]

Clearly a stage play cannot capture photographic landscapes in the way that film is able to, but Shepard's insistence on a rigorously detailed realism in the construction of *True West*'s set creates something of the same sense of perceptual estrangement. Without ever overtly breaking the illusionistic facade, he suggests the "obsessive" qualities of Californian culture, the plastic artificiality of this suburban home being gleefully highlighted – for example – in the specification that the floor of the alcove "is composed of green synthetic grass" (3). Similarly, many of the props which would "naturally" belong in such an environment come to appear strangely incongruous through the play's skewed gaze, as when Lee uses a golf club to smash up the typewriter. Most spectacularly of all, Austin produces a whole battery of stolen electric toasters, and proceeds to make round after round of "fluffy golden toast," thereby filling the theatre with the smell of "salvation" (to use Austin's curiously resonant word choice). The realistically conceived action of Austin's theft is followed through, realistically, to the point where realism transmutes into vaudeville routine, and the toaster becomes a kind of ironized icon of consumer culture. As Shepard himself says, the gesture "takes the impulse that was behind it to its absolute extreme, further than you would expect."[29]

Jim Haynie as Lee in the Magic Theatre's world premiere production of *True West*, San Francisco, 1980. (Photo: Ron Blanchette, courtesy of the Magic Theatre)

This kind of playful puncturing of the stage illusion is pursued throughout the play, as detail after realistic detail is queried or toyed with (and as Lee says, "all these details are important": 20). The clichés inherent in the simplest utterances are highlighted: "You git paid fer dreamin' up a line like that?" (8). Lee even remarks, "Those are the most monotonous fuckin' crickets I ever heard in my life" (9): this is hardly surprising, given that the sound is being produced by a self-repeating tape loop. Yet the most effective device of all, in subverting the stage illusion from within, is Shepard's manipulation of *True West*'s plot development, which appears logical on the surface and yet becomes naggingly disorientating. (Again, there is a parallel here with the superrealists, whose work, like some postmodernist pointillism, often reveals the use of unexpectedly abstract brushwork when examined in close detail.) Lee's encounters with Saul in the first act illustrate well this disturbance of the play's ostensible cause-and-effect realism. When they meet in scene 3, Lee badgers Saul with an idea for a screenplay, but it seems clear that Saul's consenting to an early morning game of golf is an insincere attempt to humor a pest: he has forgotten it twice even before the end of the scene. Thus, when Lee enters in scene 5 with a complete set of golf clubs, claiming that he won them from Saul, Austin treats this with disbelief, assuming that Lee (hardly the golf-playing type) has stolen the clubs from somewhere. The audience is likely to assume the same, but Saul then enters to confirm Lee's version of events. "It doesn't make any sense," Austin protests (31). The scenario becomes still more bewildering as Saul announces he has decided to buy Lee's ludicrously contrived idea for a screenplay, and claims, "We've got three different studios all trying to cut each other's throats to get this material" (34). Is he lying? Why should he? Has Hollywood begun to believe its own hype? Something simply does not add up, and yet who is to say Saul's behavior is not "realistic"?

Even more bemusing is the reversal of roles which Lee and Austin undergo. By scene 7, they have completed a total inversion of scene 1: using the same props and lighting effects, Shepard places Lee at the typewriter, and Austin in the kitchen providing the irritating, drunken commentary. It is now Lee who claims to be the artist ("I'm a screenwriter now. I'm legitimate!"), and threatens to throw his brother out of their mother's house. "Now I'm the intruder!" Austin notes gleefully of the role reversal, even as he adopts Lee's aggressive, mocking tone ("The pressure's on, boy!"), and Lee, conversely, becomes the weaker of the two, begging for advice and assistance. Described like this, the reversal seems blatantly contrived, which on one level it is. ("Those aren't characters," Austin pertinently announces of Lee's movie scenario in the middle of the same scene, "Those are illusions of characters": 40). And yet, at the same time, the apparent motivations of each brother have been laid out according to naturalistic convention: they have, as Shepard rightly claims, each followed a logical evolution. Lee has turned to screenwriting in an attempt to make some money and to feel as though he is doing something positive; Austin resorts to crime and the bottle partly in disbelief at his rejection by Saul, and partly in a vain attempt to prove his masculinity to Lee, who has so relentlessly maligned it. The unsettling impact of this (subverted) narrative lies in the fact that while all the actions appear to be motivated, one feels oddly tricked when the neatness with which the reversal has been accomplished becomes clear.

In effect, the play's machinations undermine the very idea of presenting a stable or unproblematic depiction of "reality" on stage. Moreover, that Lee and Austin spend a sizable chunk of the play attempting to write a script implicitly reflects the contrivance of the script they themselves are enacting. Lee's western scenario, as Austin insists, seems wildly implausible: "two lamebrains chasing each other across Texas!" (30). And yet as Lee points out, its component parts – just like the component parts of this play – are quite mundanely realistic (a truck running out of gas, a

man sleeping with another man's wife, western men owning horse trail-
ers). The paradox is compounded when Austin tells *his* version of a true
story, recounting how their father lost his teeth, bled all the way to Mexico to get fixed up, and then lost his new dentures in a doggie bag in a bar.
This story has the "ring of truth" precisely because it seems so bizarre that
nobody would dare to make it up. What, then, constitutes "truth"?

These questions are further complicated by the fact that Lee's story
implicitly mirrors the brother's own situation: "each one of 'em is afraid,
see. Each one separately thinks that he's the only one that's afraid" (27).
This self-deconstructing device is still clearer in one of the unpublished
preparatory pieces for *True West*, a neatly written radio play called *Pictures* (1979), in which "two guys" discuss a prospective script scenario
about "two guys" in a diner. At the end, it transpires that the speakers
themselves are in a diner, and the play thus disappears inside itself.[30] In
presenting a subtler version of this idea, *True West* is Shepard's most ingenious variant on the recurrent theme of characters being trapped within
textuality itself (also seen, for example, in *Cowboys #2* and *Action*), so
that the illusion of their existence as self-present beings is undermined.
The theme of the characters' conditioning by the artificial discourses of
their culture thus becomes quite literal; they are exposed as products of
the discourse of the script.

Fantasy as Reality

If *True West* is, in a sense, a continuation of the concerns of *Angel City*
and *Curse of the Starving Class* (southern Californian "impermanence"),
then *Fool for Love* takes up the baton from *Suicide* and *Buried Child* by
inviting the viewer to act as detective and solve the mystery of the true
nature of the lovers' relationship. Once again the fragmentary pieces of
the story which are provided never quite add up, and the search for objective truth is again exposed as futile, but this time in the context of a play
that initially seems much more "real."

To some extent, *Fool* pursues the superrealist techniques of *True West*
to draw subtle attention to its own facade, again using minute attention to
detail in set and costume, and the violently incongruous use of props such
as the cowboy's lasso roping motel furniture. Yet the focus here is less on
the question of cultural artifice than the collisions of the characters' subjective fantasy worlds, and the relation of those fantasies to reality. If
romantic relationships are "terrible and impossible," the play suggests
that this is in large part due to the subjective projections tangled up with
the whole question of love. As Shepard has remarked, "there's an imagi-

nary partner and an imaginary life that's always superseding the real one."[31] May's feelings about Eddie's desertions, for example, are clouded by a paranoid jealousy which has blown up to the point where she is fixated on a fantasy rival, "the Countess," whom she dreams of torturing and killing. A part of her is well aware that she is being irrational, but that does not help her shake the jealousy, and this contradiction only adds to her mounting sense of mental schism:

> I can't even see you now. All I see is a picture of you. You and her. I don't even know if the picture's real anymore. I don't even care. It's a made-up picture. It invades my head. The two of you. And this picture stings me even more than if I'd actually seen you with her. . . . And I can't get rid of this picture either. It just comes. Uninvited. Kinda' like a little torture. And I blame you more for this little torture than I do for what you did. (28)

Eddie, for his part, has created an idea of May as his perfect companion which bears no relation at all to the person she believes herself to be: "You got me confused with somebody else" (25). The lovers are trapped by fantastic notions of each other which have grown to such proportions that they cannot escape them even when they try to. Indeed, they seem far more concerned about the conflicts created by their own obsessions than they are about understanding the needs of the other: it is almost as if the mundane drudgery of their everyday lives fuels an urge to create crises of passion simply for the sake of excitement. But the lovers' delusions also hopelessly confuse the "reality" of their situation, since these condition their very real behavior toward each other. Fantasy supplants, indeed becomes, the truth of their relationship. "It's no fantasy," Eddie insists at one point of his plans for him and May. The reply is unambiguous: "It's all a fantasy" (25). The play, accordingly, presents an irremediable confusion between the actual and the imagined. This approach is signposted early on with the first interruption of the Old Man (himself apparently an actualized fantasy), who scorns Eddie for being a "fantasist" – contrasting this with his own relationship, which is 'Somethin' real, okay? Somethin' actual." Gesturing at a nonexistent picture of his beloved, he declares, "That's realism. I am actually married to Barbara Mandrell in my mind" (27). The sheer illogic of such distinctions undermines any idea of objectivity.

Concomitantly, the status of the stage reality itself is made to seem blurred and uncertain, bound up with the characters' subjective experiences. One of the methods deployed in this respect is to take realistic details and exaggerate their impact beyond the assumed norm for realistic drama. The doors and walls of the set, for example, are wired up to bass drums and microphones so as to make all the slamming and crashing much louder: the audience thus feels the wrenching impact of every entrance and exit with something of the heightened intensity felt by the characters. (In the original Magic Theatre production, Shepard placed loudspeakers underneath the seating, to make the audience literally feel the vibrations.) Similarly, the oppressive predominance of yellow in the composition of the set (in accordance with the tasteless motel environment) and the yellow-tinted lighting (ostensibly deriving from the street-light glimpsed through the window) lend a luridly pressurized atmosphere to the entire play. These details, in blurring the line between realism and subjective expressionism, are somewhat reminiscent of the use of sound and light in familiar American dramas such as Williams's *A Streetcar Named Desire* or O'Neill's *Long Day's Journey into Night*. (This technique is also used to some extent in *True West*, as with the intensifying of the sound of coyotes howling just at the point when Lee and Austin's conflict is reaching boiling point.) Yet the difference here is that Shepard actively draws attention to some of his effects: in doing so he highlights the collision of the conventions he is exploiting. May's reentrance at the end of Eddie's story, for example, is timed perfectly to fit his tale: she appears framed in the door of the bathroom just as he is describing how he first saw her framed in a doorway. But she then shatters the illusion that she is an extension of his fantasy with her next line, deriding the entire story as lies. In much the same way, at the very end of the play, Eddie and May's climactic kiss prompts a spate of apocalyptic sound and lighting effects. Yet Martin then reduces the sublime to the banal by explaining that someone has just driven a car into Eddie's horse trailer: the explosion, flames, and sound of screaming horses is reclaimed as "realistic." By ironizing its own construction in this way, the play mirrors formally the uncertainties generated by the characters' warped perspectives.

The supposed creator of the mayhem outside, "the Countess," is herself the most bizarre case of subverted realism in the play. When she is initially mentioned by May, it seems she is simply a figment of May's jealous fantasies, a delusion of a stereotypically dark and sexy European rival, probably inspired by a model on the front of one of "those fashion magazines" Eddie gave her, "those French kind" (26). Eddie fervently denies the Countess's existence, except for one moment in which he claims, "I took her out to dinner once, okay?" Yet this could equally well be simply an attempt to pacify May as an admission of infidelity. The Countess's subsequent arrival as a very real, exterior threat (shooting out windows, blaring her car horn, and screeching tires), comes as something of a shock. A sense of her unreality is nevertheless maintained by the fact that she remains unseen, and is still described more as a nightmare figure than an actual person. May reports that she is driving a "big, huge, extra-long, black, Mercedes Benz," which is – significantly – "the kind of car I always pictured her in" (37–8). May's fantasies seem to have become so real that they *are* "real life."

It is in the stories of their lives which Eddie and May tell Martin that the play's confusion of fantasy and reality is brought to a head. Eddie's version of events, implied at various points during the play and then stated clearly in his story, insists that May is his half-sister as well as his lover, and that for this reason they have an unbreakable bond. May's repeated attempts to deny this (she tells Eddie, "You made all that up," and Martin, "None of it's true": 31, 51) could simply be seen as a desperate denial of the facts ("Innocent to the last drop," Eddie mocks: 31). Indeed, her relatedness to the Old Man seems to be confirmed when she is seen listening to his road-trip monologue, as though remembering a story he told her as a child. Yet the lingering possibility that Eddie really has made the whole thing up persists right up until May appears to concur with him by finishing his story of their first meeting. And even then, it is possible that *she* is simply making *this* up in a last-ditch attempt to gain some purchase on a situation slipping beyond her control. She also directly challenges Eddie for repeatedly changing his own version, prompting his happy admission that "I never repeat myself" (51). What truth is there in all this? Martin, tempted to believe both May and Eddie, is taunted for his uncertainty:

> EDDIE: Did you think that was a story, Martin? Did you think I made that whole thing up?
>
> MARTIN: No, I mean, at the time you were telling it, it seemed real.
>
> EDDIE: But now you're doubting it because she says it's a lie? . . . She suggests it's a lie to you and all of a sudden you change your mind? Is that it? You go from true to false like that, in a second?
>
> MARTIN: I don't know. (51)

The audience, too, does not know: a stable grasp on the reality of the situation eludes them, as it does the characters. As with *Buried Child*, all perception is seen as fundamentally subjective, and with such competing views of the truth (perhaps further muddied by the telling of outright lies), nothing can be relied on for certain. The importance of personal per-

spective in the way the world is perceived is underlined most evocatively
by Eddie's incidental description, in his story, of the way "square patches
of color shifting" on a movie screen acquired the illusion of a familiar form
("It was Spencer Tracy") simply because he drew closer to it (49).

In the play's context of gender conflict, this theme of subjectivity also
acquires intriguing new connotations. It becomes clear that the women
referred to in the play (May, May's mother, Eddie's mother) are all abused
and damaged precisely because the men – who possess nothing of May's
self-aware scrutiny of her own potential for subjective distortion – are so
blindly insistent that their (masculine) perspective contains the innate
truth of the situation. In effect, the play presents an image of both the
dominating power, and the utter bankruptcy, of the patriarchal worldview. Even more appalling than Eddie's immature insistence on polarized
gender roles is the Old Man's justification of bigamy, on the grounds that
both women embodied his desire for the perfect partner: "it was the same
love. Just got split in two, that's all" (48). With his women, he insists, he
was and is "completely whole," yet he shows not a shred of concern for
their needs as individual entities. His fantasy of continuing bliss is so nar-
cissistically one-sided that he remains unaware of the (alleged) fact of
Eddie's mother's grisly suicide.

The extent to which the play's events are dictated by masculine delusions is perhaps made most apparent by the Old Man's perpetual presence on a downstage platform, beyond the frame of the stage, viewing
Eddie and May almost as if he himself were a member of the audience.
In the printed version of the play, Shepard glosses this by noting that the
Old Man exists "only in the minds of MAY and EDDIE," yet he also
makes clear that the Old Man has an independent perspective of his own
and "treats them as though they all existed in the same time and place"
(20). In production, the Old Man's position is still more ambiguous, and
indeed there are several hints that *he* could be the one who is imagining
them, from a position of godlike omnipotence. One of his speeches, for
example, appears to pause May and Eddie in midflow, as though he were
running a playback in his memory (40). Then, in the closing section of the
play, he moves onto the main part of the stage and begins interacting with
the lovers as an autonomous entity: his previous lines could all have simply been May's or Eddie's memories of things he said in the past, but here
he almost takes over the action completely. Moreover, while he is still not
an actual character in the "realistic" frame of the play (Martin remains
completely oblivious him), he remains onstage even after May and Eddie
exit (rather than disappearing in a puff of memory), and supplies the final

lines to round the play off. This is a trompe l'oeil effect not dissimilar to that which ends *Angel City*, which suggests the possibility that everything preceding it has been a fantasy of the Old Man's.

Intentionally or not, the play's structure implicitly exposes and queries men's traditional objectification and domination of women's lives and spaces, by presenting a scheme of masculine control much like that outlined by various feminist critiques of the domination of the male gaze in theatre and film. According to this scheme, the Old Man would represent the typical masculine observer in the audience, watching May from the outside as a feminine object whose own perspective he has no concept of (it is notable that the only time in the play when he addresses her, he speaks *at* her as if she were a child: he never communicates *with* her). Eddie, meanwhile, is the male hero within the narrative, who acts as a surrogate for the male viewer ("You gotta' represent me now," the Old Man tells him: 54), and who "is free to command the stage, a stage . . . in which he articulates the look and creates the action."[32] In so closely adhering to this model of objectification, the play also makes it seem highly unsettling. For Eddie's ability to "command the stage" results, throughout, in a shocking degree of intimidation and violence. And if the Old Man does articulate the audience's perspective, he makes it impossible for them to be comfortable with that fact. (Playing the part in my own production, I was made acutely aware of the disturbing effect this strange figure's proximity created in those sitting closest.) In particular, his reassertion of control in the final lines of the play seems to summarize the odious, destructive possessiveness of the male which has precipitated the play's crisis from the outset: "That's the woman of my dreams. That's who that is. And she's mine. She's all mine. Forever" (57).

May is shown, then, to be the victim of male assumptions and delusions. Yet, crucially, she is presented not only as a victim but as a character who is also very much a desiring subject in her own right (even if those desires are, in typically Shepardian fashion, confused and contradictory). Her strength is such that she succeeds on several occasions in subverting the dominant male gaze: indeed, the reason the Old Man enters the stage space is that her version of Eddie's story disturbs him to such an extent that he is drawn out of his powerful position as all-seeing observer and into the stage action itself. This loss of status is compounded by the increasingly panicked tone of the Old Man's speech, as he fears that May's hold on Eddie may prove more powerful than the loyalties demanded by the father-son bond: "You two can't come together! You gotta hold up my end a' this deal. . . . You're my son!" (55).

Though masculine control is subsequently reasserted, May has succeeded in highlighting the intolerable and untenable nature of this patriarchal status quo. Shepard offers no tidy solutions, and appears to wonder if one is possible at all. Nevertheless, in her moments of resistance
May's perspective represents a fresh, and potentially liberating, element
in his writing. After so many depictions of male-oriented American doom,
climaxing in Lee and Austin's impossible double bind, this flickering
glimpse of hope proved an inspiration to Shepard. In his next play he
went further, seeking to develop his female characters to the point of
imaginatively depicting the overthrow of America's dominant but self-
defeating masculine ethos.

7

Fire in the Snow

Two Movies and A Lie of the Mind, *1984–1988*

FOOL FOR LOVE WAS THE LAST PLAY Shepard wrote for the Magic
Theatre. Their long-standing and highly productive association ended
shortly afterward, with Shepard moving away from the San Francisco
area and eventually setting up home with Jessica Lange on a ranch near
Scottsville, Virginia (where they stayed until a further move in 1995, this
time to Lange's home state of Minnesota). All of this was a natural process
of moving on, but it had marked effects on his writing output, which
slowed dramatically from the mid-'80s. The day-to-day demands of running the ranch, and of bringing up a family with Lange, have meant that
Shepard has inevitably had less time to devote to his writing. Perhaps
more important still, the fact that he is no longer affiliated to a specific
theatre has meant less immediate motivation to write, since the effort
required in mounting new work has become far greater. The three new
stage plays that Shepard has written since he left the Magic – A *Lie of the
Mind* (1985), *States of Shock* (1991), and *Simpatico* (1994) – have all premiered in New York, but not without difficulty. *Simpatico*, for example,
eventually appeared at the Joseph Papp Public Theatre after it proved
impossible to find commercial backers to mount the play either on or off
Broadway. Financial difficulties have been even more pronounced with
Shepard's attempts to move into the expensive craft of filmmaking. Subsequent to the award-winning success of his first produced screenplay,
Paris, Texas (directed by Wim Wenders and released in 1984), Shepard
has written and directed two independent films, *Far North* (1988) and
Silent Tongue (1992), and the extended processes of finding backing and

mounting production for these inevitably consumed a great deal of time and energy.

If Shepard's interests have become more diversified and diffuse since he left the sharply focused creative environment of San Francisco, the tone of his work has also become generally more expansive than it was in the plays he wrote there. Since the taut economy of *True West* and *Fool for Love*, he has tended to throw his net out to encompass a broader dramatic landscape, concentrating less on the presentation of immediate, confrontational crises than on the ongoing exploration of characters and their situations over time, from a variety of different angles. He has continued to emphasize a profound sense of uncertainty and brokenness with regard to both interpersonal relations and personal identities, but at the same time Shepard seems – for the most part – to have acquired a greater sense of perspective on his material, a more philosophical distance from the crises he presents. His writing has become more controlled, perhaps more "mature," but at the same time it has lost something of the volatility and intensity – the sheer theatrical dynamism – of his previous work. This shift of tone also perhaps hints at another reason for Shepard's reduction in productivity: as a family man in middle age he seems to have found a greater sense of personal balance, and his work, consequently, is less tortured, less driven. Yet judged on their own terms, these pieces are still remarkably rewarding. In this chapter I focus on his remaining work of the 1980s, with its continued emphasis on the dynamics of family and love, and in Chapter 8 on his more diverse concerns in the 1990s.

Shepard and Film

Before moving on to this more detailed analysis, however, it is necessary to look in overview at the practical developments in Shepard's work over this period. In particular, his move into filmmaking needs careful consideration, for while I propose to consider his screenplays as extensions of the concerns evident in his stage work, film and theatre are very different media, and the differences have implications for his approach to writing. Shepard's stage work, after all, has always succeeded through its very theatricality – its use of the physical immediacy of the stage, its rhythmic, self-demonstrative language patterns, and the fragmented, agitative impact of its moment to moment progression. Yet that which is theatrical tends to look "stagy" in the cinema. Film, which by its very nature is an assembly of short fragments, lacking the cohering factor lent by the constant presence of actors in a stage space, usually needs more of an overall structure, or at least a provocative plot "hook," than Shepard's writing provides. Plotting has never been his strong suit, and his difficulty in translating the distinct strengths of his playwriting to screenwriting is evident from the fact that the several attempts he made at writing films between the late 1960s and early 1980s were all either abandoned by Shepard himself or rejected by producers (several such scripts are held in Boston University's Shepard archive). It seems that even his more ostensibly realistic playwriting style of the 1980s is unsuitable for translation to the screen, if one is to judge by Robert Altman's 1985 version of *Fool for Love*. Certainly that film might have been better had Altman taken more care over it: Shepard himself, who played Eddie, has bitterly criticized him for his offhand approach, which is evident in the inadequate direction of the actors, and the way in which key moments of dialogue are lost underneath irrelevant visual business. Yet this latter failure is partly because much of the dialogue feels awkwardly unreal on film anyway, and indeed several speeches were cut because of this. Still more problematic is that the claustrophobic intensity and violent physicality of *Fool for Love* simply does not translate to the screen (let alone the ambiguous presence of the Old Man, halfway outside the frame of the stage). In Altman's version, the confined stage location is "opened out" (using the whole motel compound instead of just one small room), and the intense dialogue is broken up with interminably tedious shots of the protagonists wandering around outside. Shepard himself pinned down the problem, in another context, by observing astutely that while "a play takes place in the flesh and blood," depending on the physical confrontation of the actors within an enclosed space, cinema "takes place in the mind."[1]

From *Paris, Texas* onward, Shepard has sought to put this realization into practice in his original screenplays, emphasizing not physicality or language (the extraordinary monologues which conclude *Paris, Texas* are the glaring exception to this rule) but visual composition. No doubt the insights gained from his occasional career as a movie actor helped him with this shift of tack, for while his acceptance of offered roles has been based more often on financial need than on creative interest (the films have often been less than impressive), a few of these experiences have been important to his own development as an artist. Perhaps most significant was his first part: in 1977, writer-director Terrence Malick cast him in *Days of Heaven* on the grounds that he thought he looked right, and no doubt Shepard agreed to take on the role of the sickly farm-owner partly out of an affinity with the subject matter (the film deals with a love triangle scenario in the isolated rural Midwest which moves toward disaster with the inevitability of Greek tragedy). Yet in Malick he had happened upon a teacher from whom he could learn much. Malick's sense of landscape imagery and visual collage through editing lends his work a texture which permits him to give narrative momentum a secondary role. For *Days of Heaven* he shot huge amounts of footage, and then discarded most of it (including most of Shepard's early, inept dialogue scenes, which became affectionately known in the cutting room as "Sammies"), selecting and arranging what was left into an almost dreamlike sequence of episodes and images.

Paris, Texas, which won the Palme d'Or at the Cannes Film Festival in 1984, could be described in very similar terms, and its success hinges on director Wim Wenders's ability successfully to translate the thematic concerns and uniquely American resonance of Shepard's writing into a distinctively cinematic form. (The project sprang from Wenders's desire somehow to transfer a piece from Shepard's *Motel Chronicles* prose collection to the screen.) The film uses the picaresque conventions of the road movie genre, together with a tantalizing mystery "hook" (what exactly happened to the hero, Travis, in his past, to reduce him to the mute desolation seen at the film's outset?), in order to lend coherence to a loosely constructed sequence of episodes. The mystery, like those in *Buried Child* and *Fool for Love*, is never adequately resolved, but that is one of the film's strengths. Like Shepard, Wenders is awkward with intricate plotting, and is far more interested in facilitating a gradual accumulation of imagery and emotional impressions. Indeed, *Paris, Texas* never had a preconceived outcome, and was developed by both men, scene by scene, over several months. Principal photography began with the script still incomplete, and the story was filmed chronologically, with the final monologues eventually being telephoned in by Shepard, who by then was filming *Country* with Jessica Lange, in another state.[2]

Paris, Texas, then, developed by the kind of improvisatory method with which Shepard felt most at home, allowing breathing space to his instinctive sense of character and image. It was the kind of release he needed, to go on to write realizable screenplays independently. If *Far North* and *Silent Tongue* are ultimately less satisfying than *Paris, Texas*, it is because they fail to find such engaging narrative hooks: both pieces are hung on rather tenuous plot threads which simply demand the resolution of yes/no questions (will she shoot the horse? will he burn the body?), and this inadequacy was sufficient to kill them with most critics. Yet for those willing to subordinate the demand for plot intricacy to an appreciation of the films' moment-to-moment development, the experience is quite different. Clearly drawing on the lessons learned from both Malick and Wenders, Shepard succeeds with both pieces in finding a cinematic equivalent for the painterly and musical concerns which dominate so much of his playwriting.

The "painterly" is particularly evident in Shepard's shot compositions, which strikingly utilize the textures of natural light and colors in capturing exterior landscapes. Often the camera will linger motionlessly on such pictures for unusually long periods of time, while characters move across or through them until they are out of shot. Overall, Shepard succeeds in conjuring a haunting sense of place in his use of both Minnesotan birch forests in *Far North* and the New Mexican prairie in *Silent Tongue*. His choice of more localized imagery is often equally evocative: Michael Almereyda, himself a noted independent filmmaker, has gone so far as to connect the latter film to "Noh drama, the way Shepard somehow charges single images – a fire, a tree, a man on a horse – with meanings that leap beyond themselves."[3] (Much the same applies in *Far North*: a horse galloping at full tilt; a bird soaring over a lake; eerily deserted railroad tracks; figures wandering lost in a moonlit forest.) Moreover, Shepard often knits these images together, collage-like, using patterns of cross-editing which acquire a rhythmic momentum in themselves. Significantly, these segments were conceived before shooting, and written carefully into the screenplays, rather than concocted in post-production editing as with most films. Shepard, in other words, has learned to adapt his writing process for this new medium, stripping the shifting, rhythmic dynamics of his dialogue down to a minimum palatable for film, but substituting the shifting, rhythmic composition of filmic sounds and images (the *Silent Tongue* screenplay, in particular, displays a remarkable attention to detail in the use of the tiniest sound effects). Even given his shortcomings in narrative construction, Shepard has developed into a cinematic craftsman of some skill.

Flesh and Blood

Shepard's films, however, still lack the density and allusive richness of his best stage work, and he himself acknowledged as much in an interview before the opening of *Simpatico* in 1994. "Theatre combines everything for me," he noted: "it allows you to explore language, which film doesn't, [and] the other thing is the relationship between actor and audience: that moment by moment hanging in the balance, that terror of the

moment. . . . It's like you pick up a saxophone and play."[4] Clearly, for
Shepard, the theatre affords a degree of creative freedom and a scope for
spontaneous risk-taking which is simply not lent by the kind of meticulous
planning required by movies. Moreover, his stress here on the physical
immediacy of the theatre event is particularly significant: his interest in
directing films has in no way diminished his desire to continue exploring
the very different process of stage production. Although the one-act
piece States of Shock was first directed for the American Place by his old
Theatre Genesis colleague Bill Hart, Shepard himself directed the premieres of both A Lie of the Mind and Simpatico, building on the collaborative dynamics first explored fully when working on Fool for Love.
Indeed, A Lie of the Mind began rehearsals with only a provisional script,
and Shepard worked cooperatively with a large cast, with an assistant
director (his sister, Roxanne Rogers), and with a live roots band (the Red
Clay Ramblers, whom he had discovered in North Carolina) to develop
the final version of the play, as performed and published. His emphasis as
director was on facilitating the development of the play *as a performance*,
rather than seeking to realize onstage a preconceived authorial vision. As
Shepard explained in an interview: "Many, many of the things that I
would have put in the script before – now, knowing that I'm going to
direct it, I leave open until the production's complete."[5]

The actors in these productions have commented repeatedly on the
fluid, improvisatory approach which Shepard fosters in rehearsal. "I've
never worked with a director who gave actors as much freedom as Sam,"
notes James Gammon, who appeared in both pieces: "He does not even
like to block a play."[6] This degree of openness proved unsettling for some:
Aidan Quinn, as Frankie in Lie, initially complained of feeling lost
onstage, but Shepard – while dealing with each actor according to individual temperament – was intent on encouraging them to solve the problems for themselves. "If an actor has any kind of chops at all, he's going to
find his own way round the stage and find the impulses," Shepard noted
during Simpatico rehearsals.[7] The term "chops" is borrowed from jazz
terminology, and it is tempting to see in Shepard's approach to directing
a theatrical equivalent to Charles Mingus's jazz workshop techniques, in
which musicians were encouraged to develop their parts personally, and
improvise off them. "They add themselves, they add how they feel, while
we're playing," Mingus once insisted of his work, an assessment con-
curred with by his musicians: "He doesn't impose his own ideas on you
but wants individual interpretations."[8] Similarly Ed Harris, returning to
work on Simpatico eleven years after the Fool for Love premiere, spoke

of Shepard's actively resisting invitations to tell him where to go with his new character, Carter: "I was asking Sam, isn't there some place where he admits all that [guilt] and gets close to it? He said, 'Sorry Ed, I can't let you off the hook.'"[9]

For Shepard, the director's job is not to prescribe, but to shape into a workable whole the discoveries made by his actors (the influence of Joseph Chaikin, who has always worked in this way, also suggests itself here). Here again Shepard's musical instincts are central to his approach: observers in rehearsals for both pieces have referred to his almost obsessive concern with the overall tone and cadence of the performance, and have noted that the only occasions when he imposes guidance on his actors come when the action needs to be drawn together for particular moments of rhythmic climax. Journalist Ross Wetzsteon, watching *Lie* in its final stages of development, spoke of Shepard's behavior in terms which clearly suggest the approach of a conductor rather than a director:

> The run-through resumes, one of his trademark scenes – the second held, held, held, its imminence nearly unendurable. "Yeah, yeah," he says quietly, almost to himself. "Now here's where you come on real strong," he calls down to the stage, lifting his right foot, cocking his right elbow, forming a fist with his right hand. Beat, beat, "here." He abruptly stomps his foot and drives his fist towards the floor like a piston. "Oh yeah," he says with a grin. "That's the place. Real strong. Yeah."[10]

Complementary to Shepard's emphasis on the musical immediacy of the stage moment is his continued development of a vibrantly physical, "flesh and blood" performance style. Although the texts of these longer plays are less obviously suggestive of physical confrontation than the tense duets which preceded them, he has encouraged actors to focus less on Method-type questions of psychological motivation than on exploring more basic, physical questions of what characters eat and drink, and how they express themselves bodily. The results have often been remarkable: Matthew Goulish, of Chicago's groundbreaking performance group Goat Island, was so struck – when watching *Simpatico* – by Ed Harris's gesture of thumping his fist violently into his own back to punctuate Carter's repeated line "they'll stab you in the back," that he chose to appropriate it as a kind of homage. The gesture subsequently mutated into one of the key motifs in Goat Island's piece *How Dear to Me the Hour When Daylight Dies* (1996): Shepard's debt to performance art, it seems, is being repaid.

It is also important to stress that Shepard's attempts to draw out individual creative contributions have not been limited to his work with actors. His work with the Red Clay Ramblers on *Lie* was aimed at developing an ongoing score for the play, which would be integrated with the stage action more organically than in any of his previous work. (He has subsequently worked with the Ramblers on both his films, and with another musician, Patrick O'Hearn, on scoring original music for *Silent Tongue* and *Simpatico*.) Similarly, the intricate description of lighting patterns in the finalized stage directions for *Lie* – suggesting the creation of pools, shafts, or whole areas of light, with notes for fading them in and out, and expanding or contracting the focus and intensity – is testimony to the degree of freedom to experiment given to the lighting designer for the original production.

In drawing on the various, diverse inputs of designers, actors, and musicians to develop these new works, Shepard has effected a dialogic relationship between text and performance: each is informed by the other; neither is treated as being of predominant importance. His role as director has functioned to dethrone the script, which he may rewrite at will if the performance demands it, but at the same time his script provides the starting point and inspiration for developments in performance. In his book *Performing Drama/Dramatizing Performance*, Michael Vanden Heuvel has described such approaches as representing a distinctly postmodernist theatre practice, moving beyond both the traditional prejudice toward simply "realizing" the literary text on stage, and the various modernist doctrines which gave precedence either to the notional purity of authorial vision or the holy presence of the performer. In Shepard's approach – as in that of many of his contemporaries in the '80s and '90s – plurality is celebrated, and authority is not ceded to any one source. Another vital point is that this open-ended approach to production, like Shepard's open-ended approach to writing, results in the potential range of meanings generated by the performance remaining very open, rather than being delimited along a certain line of interpretation (although for some this has been perceived as a problem: his production of *Simpatico*, in particular, was felt by many critics to be lacking in dramatic focus).

Dream Realism

Relaxed openness of form is central to the impact of the pieces focused on in the remainder of this chapter. In their use of spare yet resonant colloquial language, and their closely observed attention to detail, *Paris, Texas, A Lie of the Mind*, and *Far North* all build on the offbeat realism of plays like *True West* and *Fool for Love*. Yet the sheer length of *Paris, Texas* (at two and a half hours) and *Lie* (which can run between three and four hours) means that these pieces – in comparison, say, to *Fool*, which runs eighty minutes from start to finish – necessitate a more relaxed mode of watching. Confronted with these long, loose conglomerations of scenes and events, the audience members will respond to different scenes with varying degrees of concentration, to some extent picking and choosing those moments they wish to focus on with particular intensity, and those they will allow, in effect, to drift by.

The pieces themselves mirror this form of response. The loose narratives are presented in a flowing, seductive fashion, full of strange events and images which suggest something of the resonance of dream (as opposed to the jarring, nightmare quality of so much of Shepard's earlier work). There is in these pieces a bleak, bittersweet romanticism and a sense of simple humanity, or even optimism (albeit highly ambiguous), which stands in marked contrast to the viciously deterministic entrapment envisioned previously. It may well be that this shift of gear in formal terms is directly related to Shepard's growing thematic concern with exploring "the female side" of the situations he depicts. In a fascinating interview in 1988, he clearly implied that – for him – the difference between a "female" and "male" approach to art is "the difference between being touched by something and being assaulted by it."[11]

The mysterious, haunting atmosphere of *Paris, Texas* is, of course, partly a result of the typically slow-paced direction of Wim Wenders, but it is also a direct result of the film's basic premise, which is typically Shepardian. The protagonist, Travis, is found wandering mute and desolate in the Texan desert (these scenes owe much to an unforgettable performance by Harry Dean Stanton), and from here on there is an implicit promise that the cause of his Tilden-like estrangement from civilization will eventually be revealed and confronted. As in *Buried Child*, characters within the narrative explicitly voice the audience's curiosity ("Goddamn it! You tell me what happened Travis! I'm sick of this fuckin' mystery!"),[12] but again, the past remains indefinable. All that is clear is that some violent rift occurred between Travis and his wife, Jane, and when the pair finally meet again at the end of the film, the sense of mystery surrounding their relationship is only deepened further. As Travis brings himself to recount their story, his monologue moves into increasingly surreal, dreamlike territory, making unanswered questions about the specific details of their breakup seem mundanely irrelevant. The effect here seems to be less to draw the audience into agitated uncertainty (as in so many previous pieces), than to evoke a poetic sense of lament for a life which is forever unfathomable. If memory is deceptive, this is a source of pain for Travis himself ("I can't even hardly remember what happened. It's like a gap": 86), and the sense of profound human disconnection and loss he projects is perfectly complemented by the film's picaresque story development: its many loose ends (partly a result of the make-it-up-as-you-go approach to developing the screenplay) result in an elegiac sense of drifting consciousness.

Like *Paris, Texas*, *A Lie of the Mind* seeks to evoke something of the vast distances between people and places in contemporary America, but it does so through more abstract, theatrical techniques, which together create a still more dreamlike atmosphere. The play's action concerns two families linked by marriage, and the crises brought on when that marriage breaks down through violence. Again, this slenderest of plot threads serves as little more than a pretext for the play's real concern with depicting the moment-by-moment coexistence of these dysfunctional families, living hundreds of miles apart in Montana and California. Shepard places both families' homes onstage, using twin platforms located opposite each other in downstage corners of the stage area, and suggesting something of the vast expanse of land between them by backing and separating these areas with an engulfing darkness. This should create "the impression," Shepard says, "of infinite space, going off to nowhere."[13] Yet it is also a far cry from the blistering sunlight and landscapes of *Paris, Texas*: the ominous impenetrability of this void suggests irredeemable separation, and perhaps looming danger. The cluttered, claustrophobic quality of the sets for *Fool* and *True West* is thus replaced by a kind of agoraphobic emptiness.

Shepard also replaces his earlier attention to superrealist set detail with what he describes as a "simple and stark" use of the set rostra, which contain a minimum of furniture and freestanding wall-flats. Obviously this is partly a demand of logistics: before becoming the families' homes, these rostra are used for an almost cinematic sequence of varied scene locations, and more extensive set-building would be impractical. But Shepard is also clearly less interested here in obsessive precision than in evocation: the settings, he says, should suggest "a sense of realism," without resorting to a lot of minute details (42). Rather than interrogating the realistic facade to the point of implicitly subverting it, here the provisional, illusory status of the real seems simply to be taken as read. The insistently dreamlike use of stage lighting underlines this, and the constant presence of a glowing moon high in the enshrouding darkness adds greatly to the sense that this is, in effect, a "Long Night's Journey into Day" (to borrow Shepard's draft title for *Cowboy Mouth* some fifteen years previously).

The specification that *Lie* have an ongoing, almost filmic musical score also militates against the conventions of stage naturalism, while enhancing the play's atmospheric qualities. Just as Ry Cooder's haunting, shimmering use of bluesy slide-guitar adds so much to the texture of *Paris, Texas*, so roots-style accompaniment was integral to Shepard's conception of the *Lie*: "This play needs music," he insists in the notes to the published edition: "Live music. Music with an American backbone" (viii). In the Red Clay Ramblers he found ideal collaborators for the play's premiere, their music representing an unusually eclectic blending of diverse roots styles, from folk guitar to madcap bluegrass fiddle and even gospel-tinged a cappella. The Ramblers played underneath many of the scenes, and also provided tailor-made mood joins between them to lend the play the impression of almost seamless continuity.

The progression of the action itself functions similarly. For while the text presents as bizarre a mix of elements as in any of his previous plays – oddball interjections, incidental stories, cartoon-style humor, and moments of heightened emotional confrontation – these are not used to generate the kind of abrupt juxtapositions typical of so much of his earlier work, but are mixed together to create a more consistent form of slightly unhinged realism, underlain by moody, dreamlike imagery. Most important to the creation of atmosphere is the way Shepard blurs together "real world" events with subjective fantasy images to the point where the two are virtually indistinguishable. At the end of act 1, for example, Jake's idealized vision of his estranged wife, Beth (whom he glimpses across a vast expanse of night), is immediately followed by the equally evocative but notionally "actual" moment in which he blows his father's ashes into a shaft of moonlight. When, toward the end of the play, the "real" events become increasingly fantastic (Jake, for example, crosses four states dressed only in a flag), the already confused border between illusion and reality seems blurred to the point of nonexistence, stressing afresh the fundamentally subjective nature of all experience.

The film *Far North* is essentially a kind of whimsical coda to *A Lie of the Mind*, and echoes many of its techniques and themes. Again using the Ramblers to provide the music, and the magical moon as a central motif, Shepard presents another oddball northern family (this time in Minnesota rather than Montana), and recycles several of the character relationships and basic situations. At the same time, though, the underlying tone here is essentially much lighter and gentler. Written for his first attempt at film direction, and as an affectionate gift for its star, Jessica Lange (whose Minnesotan home and family were its inspiration), the film's relative lack of adventure and ambition is understandable. It is entertaining and at times moving, but Shepard is clearly playing for lower stakes than in either *Paris, Texas* or *A Lie of the Mind*, both of which allude to the state of a dysfunctional nation.

Shattered

Shepard had, of course, been preoccupied with familial dysfunction since *Curse of the Starving Class*, and there is an element of truth in the charges of certain critics that both *Paris,Texas* and *A Lie of the Mind* are themselves simply reworkings of old material. Indeed, the most cursory glance at *Paris, Texas* reveals a three-act triptych of relationships, each part of which builds on previous work. First, the pairing of brothers in *True West* is recalled as bourgeois suburbanite Walt rescues desert drifter Travis from his mute wandering in the Texan badlands, and brings him home to Los Angeles. Travis is thus reunited with his seven-year-old son, Hunter, and this creates yet another variant on the awkwardness of the father-son relationship, as they seek to bridge the gulf of time and culture that lies between them. Finally, Travis and Hunter set off to find Jane in Houston: we discover that the lovers were very similar to those in *Fool for Love*, shacked up in a trailer home and driven by obsession and jealous fantasies to violence and separation.

The action of *A Lie of the Mind* is triggered by the most horrendously violent of all Shepard's love relationships, with Jake having beaten his wife Beth near to death, in a rage apparently brought on by paranoid delusions. The pair are then both taken in by their families, which closely resemble those in *Curse of the Starving Class* and *Buried Child*. Jake's family, in California, is effectively Wesley's family a few years down the line. His mother, Lorraine, and tomboy sister, Sally, are close kin to Ella and Emma, while the memory of the now deceased old man continues to haunt them and condition their behavior as much as Weston ever had in *Curse*. (Shepard's own father had died in 1984, and this was clearly a major influence on the writing of the play.) *Lie's* similarities to *Curse* extend even to the repetition of such details as the model airplanes in Wesley's/Jake's room, and the old man's brand of whiskey (Tiger Rose), while the overall mood of suspicion and utter brokenness also remains:

battle lines are drawn ("I need an ally"); distrust rules. "Everything is kinda – shattered now," Sally remarks: "When wasn't it shattered?" Jake responds (60). Meanwhile, the Montana family – like their counterparts in *Buried Child* – are rural oddities living alone in a remote, inhospitable region, dominated by a festering, crotchety old dirt farmer, Baylor, and a slightly dotty mother, Meg. Each member of this family exists in his or her own world, driven by private obsessions and completely uncomprehended by the others. They are even snowed in by a blizzard whose existence seems to be in some dispute, and argue as to whether it is day or night outside (it is black). Like Shelly, Jake's brother Frankie finds himself marooned in this alien house, after having come up to find out whether Beth is still alive: "it's hard to tell anymore if anybody knows anything about anybody else around here," he notes: "Nobody seems to have the slightest idea what's going on" (109–10).

But if Shepard is here, to a certain extent, going back over familiar, often autobiographical territory, there are also crucial differences from the earlier work. One is that, in both *Paris, Texas* and *A Lie of the Mind*, the multiple permutations of broken family relationships, seen across large geographic spaces, accumulate to create the impression that a state of dysfunction exists on a national scale in America, as a kind of deracinated norm. Yet it is also significant that the divisions are presented less brutally here than in his previous work, with many of the characters actively involved in trying to bridge and heal the yawning gaps between the family members. Walt, for example, in *Paris, Texas*, is a good-hearted and brusquely practical man (well played by Dean Stockwell), far more admirable than his counterpart Austin, whose intervention saves Travis from self-annihilation. And this more compassionate presentation of the endemic problem of relational separation makes it seem – if anything – even more tragic: one of the bitterest ironies of *Paris, Texas* is that Walt and Anne's concern to reunite Travis and Hunter abruptly robs them of a dearly loved surrogate son, as Hunter runs away with Travis to Houston. In scene after scene, Shepard reinforces this sense that somebody will inevitably end up hurt and alone, that a terrible, cyclical brokenness persists despite all attempts to overcome it. *Paris, Texas* is filled with haunting images of America as a culture of numb separation: in one short, incidental scene, for example, Travis crosses a highway overpass, encountering a crazy man screaming out a deranged, prophetic condemnation of Californian superficiality ("they will snap you up from your hot tubs, they will pluck you right out of your fancy sports cars": 55). The speech – vintage Shepard, a bizarre mix of sci-fi and folklore – is both comic and oddly poignant, but its context speaks loudest: the man is screaming to nobody, an impassioned and futile performance to a world driving by without regard for him. Travis appears to want to make contact, but there is nothing to say. Later he experiences an even more helpless divide between himself and Jane. He finally finds her working as a stripper in a peep show, and they remain separated by an implacable two-way mirror which prevents them both seeing each other at the same time. The outside wall of the building which houses the peep show is painted with a giant mural of the Statue of Liberty: America, the film suggests, has become a place where isolated individuals stare at each other from an unbridgeable distance. And the peep show booth, where discretion is guaranteed, is a postmodern alternative to the Catholic confessional: Jane, before learning Travis's identity, finds nothing unusual in the idea that a client just wants to talk to her: "Is there something you want to tell me?" she asks the invisible observer: "I don't mind listening . . . I do it all the time" (80–2).

A *Lie of the Mind* pursues a similarly allusive sense of national breakdown, most notably through its recurrent use of the American flag. This does not operate as a simple symbol, since it appears in a variety of different contexts, defying any attempt to assign a coherent pattern of significance to it. Yet its presence is inevitably provocative, and its appearances accumulate into a kind of resonant collage. It appears first as the flag used to cover Jake's father's coffin, and is subsequently used as a cape for Jake's madcap cross-country journey, as an enslaving rein when Mike drives Jake along on all fours, as a rag for wiping the grease from a shotgun, and so forth. Loss, agonized memory, horrific violence, blind wandering: here is Shepard's America in microcosm.

Lie's most powerful images of emotional separation, however, are marked less by specific cultural allusions than by a constant sense of the yawning void between all its characters, represented powerfully by that black gulf between the separated stage areas. Indeed the very first scene epitomizes this connection of visual and personal division, showing Frankie and Jake stranded in small, separate, distant pools of light, speaking on a telephone link which could be cut off at any moment:

> FRANKIE: (*In dark*) Jake. Jake? Now, look – Jake? Listen. Just listen
> to me a second. (*Sound of JAKE smashing receiver down on pay-
> phone.*) Jake! Don't do that! You're gonna disconnect us again. (1)

Throughout the play, communication seems inherently problematic and distorted, a fact also underlined by Beth's broken speech patterns, the result of aphasia caused by the brain damage inflicted by Jake. (Beth's speech is much like that of the Angel in *The War in Heaven*, and Shepard was doubtless drawing again on his recent experience of working with Joe Chaikin after the latter's stroke.) Visually, verbally, and relationally, the play is dominated by a sense of profound brokenness.

Masculine Desire

These pieces also build on and develop the concern with frustrated desire evident in previous work. But if Lee's thwarted desire was for rootedness and authenticity, and Eddie's for a perfect, fantasy partner, Shepard here seems to *combine* these longings. In *Paris, Texas* in particular, Travis's desire for Jane becomes virtually indistinguishable from his longing for the land. As the inaccessible object at the end of his quest, Jane functions for much of the film not as a person but as an *idea* – the image of some eternal feminine essence, which is connected with nature in a way that the male can never be. (This was illustrated with alarming clarity by some of the film's publicity images, in which Jane's face was superimposed like a spectre over the Texan landscape.) This blurring of Travis's desires is summed up by the fact that his ultimate goal would be to go back to basics by taking Jane and Hunter to live on a plot of land he has bought in Paris, Texas, and on which he wishes to build them a home from the ground up. *Fool for Love* had touched briefly on a similar fulfillment package, in Eddie's insistence that he will take May to live with him in Wyoming, but here the fantasy is further entangled by Travis's admission that he has chosen Paris as his ideal home because he believes it to be the site of his own conception, the place where he "started out" in his mother's womb. In Travis's mind, frontier dream, romantic dream, and Oedipal craving are all inextricably fused together into a desperate desire for rootedness.

Various psychoanalytic readings suggest themselves here. In Jungian thought, for instance, the male tendencies to idealize both women and areas of land are viewed as examples of "anima projection." That is, a man's need to confront and explore his suppressed internal feminine (and so achieve psychic individuation) is misdirected as he invests external objects with romantic or numinous significance. Travis's mistake, according to this reading, is in looking "out there" (as had Weston, another buyer of site-unseen land lots) for the solutions to a personal identity crisis, rather than discovering them within. Yet the film is also consistent with the darker implications of Freudian/Lacanian thought, which suggests there might not be any solutions, since such yearnings are simply subli-mations of the unrealizable desire for a return to primal union with the mother. All other objects of desire will ultimately prove unsatisfying, and the individual is therefore inevitably driven by a perpetually frustrated searching. Travis's entire picaresque odyssey can be seen as an image of this state of restless desire, as he transfers his focus of longing from one object to another. And if desire, ultimately, can only be satisfied in the oblivion of death, Travis periodically displays a wish for just such un-being, which is inextricably confused with his aching love of the land. At the film's outset, he is found wandering mutely in the wilderness, an image of walking death: "All he wanted to do was sleep," he explains later, speaking in the third person: "And for the first time he wished he were far away. Lost in a deep, vast country where nobody knew him. Somewhere without language or streets" (92).

In a sense, then, *Paris, Texas* brings Shepard's work full circle from his earliest plays: here though, his treatment of Oedipal craving and the dream of oblivion seems far more mature, and impinges poignantly on another recurrent issue, the perpetual lostness of the American male. Moreover, in drawing together the various misguided masculine fantasies explored in Shepard's previous family plays, the film also queries the ide-alization of the feminine which Travis and his counterparts indulge in, and which seems only to add further to the all-pervasive brokenness. Indeed, Shepard and Wenders go some way to critique Travis's objectifi-cation of Jane, both explicitly in the dialogue ("He didn't see her. He saw this idea," Travis says of his father and mother, and by extension of him-self and Jane: 85), and implicitly through a partial deconstruction of the male gaze akin to that effected in *Fool for Love*. It is significant that in the film, Travis only ever sees Jane objectified within a frame. As Hunter per-ceptively points out, the paradisical image of her in an old Super-8 film is "not her. That's only her in a movie" (45). Similarly, Travis's view of Jane in the frame of the strip booth window is a deceptive one: the solid two-way mirror which separates them represents a gulf of perception between them as much as it does an emotional rift. From Travis's point of view, Jane appears to be smiling happily, a vision of wholesome kindliness unbowed by the degrading environment of the strip booth: here is "nat-ural woman" still smiling under the strain. Yet this image is cleverly jux-taposed with shots from the other side of the divide, which show Jane being obliged to smile stupidly at her own mirror image, assailed by a hos-tile, disembodied voice which accuses her of prostitution. Obliged to put up with such abuse in order to pay the rent, Jane has been reduced to a state of weary brokenness, as is clear whenever she is glimpsed outside these frames of the male gaze (passing in her car; across a crowded room).

Jane is now, as she was with Travis, the victim of destructive male fantasies.

If *Paris, Texas* remains partially ambivalent in its treatment of the female, it is because the narrative concentrates so heavily and sympathetically on Travis, and so precludes any deeper exploration of Jane's situation. Yet in *A Lie of the Mind,* though the depiction of male characters is still broadly sympathetic, Shepard is far less indulgent of, and at times scathingly critical of, their delusory desires. And at the same time, the horrific degree to which women are victimized by men is made one of the central threads of the play. From the outset, *Lie* appears to set out to demystify the dual American fantasizing of frontier and female. As the twin epigraphs to the published text imply, such dreams of ideal union are hollow: the first, from Latin American poet Cesar Vallejo, stresses the unbridgeable divide between even the closest of lovers; the latter, from historian and critic H. L. Mencken, brings home the distinctly nonidyllic nature of the journeyings of the American frontier pioneers: "When they halted, it was simply that they had become exhausted." The play itself makes clear that both fulfillment myths have devastating results when blindly acted out. Jake's idealized fantasy of Beth is the root cause of the brutal violence which has wrecked their marriage, and this is drummed home with more clarity and savage irony than in the cases of either Travis or Eddie. It becomes apparent that Jake's ludicrous paranoid belief that Beth has been sleeping around during her lunch break is based on not a shred of evidence. Her wish to have a career of her own as an actress has simply proved incompatible with Jake's preconceived ideas of their relationship, with disastrous results.

The frontier dream proves to be an equally destructive "lie of the mind" (the phrase first appeared in Shepard's work in relation to this latter theme, in *The Sad Lament of Pecos Bill*). Jake, like his father before him, is all too ready to just get up and abandon his home on a vague whim: "Is there any good reason in this Christless world why men leave women?" Lorraine asks in despair after Jake's departure, as though questioning an immutable law of nature (86). This contemporary wanderlust is shown to be a pale shadow of the old ideal. The promise of the West, after all, meant nothing if not the promise of finding a new place of one's own in which to settle down and define a life, free of outside pressures. Yet, as Sally remarks, the days when a man could just hang his hat "on a mesquite stump" and watch a town grow up are long gone, if they ever existed at all: "That was a whole other time" (67). Driven, like Travis, by impossible-to-satisfy desires, Jake will never be able to settle anywhere, and so has no concept of what a real home might be. He is, in Lorraine's damning words, a "stray dog": "Let him stagger around, lost and wild-eyed if he wants to. Let him bang his head up and down the alleyways moanin' like a baby about some mystery he doesn't even have a clue to. You can't save the doomed" (89). The significance of this bleak view to the broader American context is all too evident: "As long as we continue to define America as a frontier," note the historians Peter Carroll and David Noble, "we will not be people who live in America."[14]

Not all the men in the play are driven by fantasies of love and the frontier. Beth's brother Mike, for example, is more concerned with holding the family together. Yet even this laudable goal (yet another variation on the desire for rootedness?) is twisted by masculine arrogance. Mike is driven by an almost feudal sense of the honor of the clan, which must be upheld at all costs – or if impugned, avenged. This too proves counter-productive, as he grows increasingly abusive toward the women when they fail to subscribe to his wish to condemn and humiliate Jake's entire family in retribution for what he did to Beth. This violent pride, Beth says, is just another insane invention of the male ego-urge to conquer and sub-due that which is different: "You make a war. You make an enemy. . . . You have a big idea" (45).

The cumulative effect of all the men's "big ideas" is painfully evident, as Beth is far from being the only brain-damaged female in the play. Devel-oping the implications of May's story in *Fool for Love*, Shepard sets along-side the familiar cycle of male violence a profound sense of the damage done, cyclically, to women. Meg, for example, seems almost as broken and lost as Beth, and her defective memory is often unable to distinguish between her own experience and that of her mother, who was once "locked up" by the men in the family. Meanwhile, Beth claims that Grandma was forced by Baylor to undergo a lobotomy. These details are confused and uncertain, recounted as they are by damaged people, but what emerges is a clear sense of how generation after generation of women has been sys-tematically broken on the wheel of male delusion: "Like my old Mom. Old. Grand Mom. They cut her. Out. Disappeared. . . . My father sent her someplace" (74).

The Female Alternative

Yet it is not simply the women's status as victims which Shepard highlights in *A Lie of the Mind*. As the play develops, it suggests an increasing exas-peration with the foolishness of the doomed male, and the female char-

acters begin to take over the center of attention: for the first time, Shepard offers a clear and positive alternative to masculine failure in the shape
of the more resilient, and more genuinely rooted, female characters.
Rather than constantly looking "out there" for the answers to a mystery
that they "don't have a clue to," the women are more self-contained, seeking simply to cope with what they have rather than craving after elusive
fantasies. Intriguingly, this difference was even apparent in the physical
performance styles in Shepard's production: Sheila Rabillard noted that
"when the women hold the stage, the spectators at this play are not victims of a violent commandeering of attention, but sharers in the women's
self-regarding gaze."[15] Again, then, there is a sense that the "female"
approach entails "touching" the audience, rather than "assaulting" them.

The play sets up its most explicit contrast of gender traits in act 3,
scene 2, in the depiction of the gulf between Meg and her husband, Baylor. The latter embodies the festering, self-obsessed delusions of masculinity: he is hardened, shut off from his family, blaming them for his
own failures, and morbidly preoccupied with his body's loss of vitality and
the absurd inevitability of his approaching death. By diametric contrast,
Meg is open and self-giving, afraid not about her own well-being or death
("I don't care about any a' that") but for the needs of her family: "I'm
afraid for my daughter" (99). Beth sums up the difference between her
parents by gauging them against a single word: love. Baylor, she says, has
"given up love. Love is dead for him. My mother is dead for him. Things
live for him to be killed. Only death counts for him" (57). Meg, on the
other hand, is a perfect example: "You – you a love. You – you are only
that. . . . Only love. Good. You. Mother. You. Always love. Always" (46).

There is then, clearly a sense here that masculine and feminine characteristics are very different, even diametrically so. There is also a fear,
apparently grounded in the same sense of genetic or psychic determinism which has doomed so many of Shepard's male characters, that the
sexes may consequently be forever divided. As Meg says to Baylor:
"Maybe it really is true that we're so different that we'll never be able to
get certain things across to each other. Like mother used to say. 'Two
opposite animals'" (103). This theme is still more obvious in the *Far
North*, which recycles the Baylor-Meg marriage as Bertrum and Amy (the
latter played by Ann Wedgeworth, who also created the Meg role in
1985). Here the gender split is so extreme that the men and women
hardly ever appear in the same frame. In this case the men are reduced
to the status of a couple of comically pathetic old drunks, Bertrum and his
brother, Dane. Played by Charles Durning and Donald Moffat, they look

and sound like a geriatric Laurel and Hardy pairing (thereby bringing Shepard's males full circle from the adolescent double act of *Cowboys*), lost and bewildered in a modern world which has left them behind. By contrast, the women display a rootedness and adaptability which allows them to continue functioning. There are four generations of women here (Amy; her mother, "Gramma," who is just turning one hundred; her daughters Kate and Rita; and Rita's teenage daughter, Jilly), and while they all have their problems and petty arguments, their basic solidarity is clear. As Shepard notes of the Minnesotan women whom he says inspired the film, they are "very strong and clannish and family-oriented to the extent that, even if they have not exactly turned away from the men, they sure don't need them any more."[16] Bertrum is clearly terrified by this, and by his resulting obsolescence, railing against the women whose strength is beyond his comprehension: "It's in the blood, that's what it is, bad blood. . . . They've all got it. They keep passing it on like some disease. BARBARIAN WOMEN!!!"[17]

Far North thus states what *Lie* implies, the idea of a positive female equivalent to the biological "curse" of male heredity. There is, of course, a danger that such essentialist oppositions simply invite further blind idealization of women, this time not as objects of beauty and desire but as examples of a loving goodness which men can thus berate themselves for lacking. Such polarization also condemns men to the status of savage "animals . . . picking at each other's weakness" (Sally on Jake and his father: 93). Crucially, though, Shepard's fear of insurmountable male-female difference is counterbalanced in both *Lie* and *Far North* by the contradictory and more positive sense that gender traits might in fact be more variable than such biological essentialism suggests. Thus, while Meg and Baylor (or Amy and Bertrum), as the older generation, appear to represent the binary-opposite extremes of traditionally conceived "masculine" and "feminine" qualities, a range of other characters is also presented, who blend different degrees of masculinity and femininity, thereby suggesting not polarization but a certain fluidity in gender roles. If Meg, for example (like her own description of her mother), is "pure female," it is also the case that "Beth's got male in her" (104). In practice, this means that whereas Meg displays a "feminine" emotional vulnerability, and feels she needs the support of the harder Baylor ("the female – the female one needs – the other": 105), Beth, like May in *Fool*, has a "masculine" streak of independence. Indeed it is her wish to have her own career which so antagonizes the more "traditional" Jake. A similar pattern is seen in *Far North*, in which both Rita and Kate combine masculine and feminine qualities in well-balanced ways. Neither, it seems, needs a man to act as father for her child, a fact which further bemuses Bertrum: "Where in the hell is the goddamn man?" (71).

If *Far North* lacks dramatic dynamic, it is because these capable women face no real challenge or opposition from the enfeebled menfolk. Bertrum's most coherent response to his bewilderment is to try to guilt Kate into shooting his horse, and this is as close to a plot conflict as the film comes. As a result, the most persistent impression communicated is whimsical nostalgia, a bewildered elegy for the loss of old ways of life with which Bertrum, Dane, Amy, and Gramma felt more secure. In *Lie*, conversely, the damage done by the old ways, and the emotional costs involved in the need to move forward, are depicted much more provocatively. Sally, for example, seems to be caught between warring impulses: instinctively a tomboy who displays a "masculine" independence and practicality (she dresses in the Shepardian male uniform of jeans and cowboy boots), she finds herself increasingly uncomfortable with the wanderlust she has inherited from her father, which strikes her now as a drug addiction she cannot shake: "Every time I pack, I tremble now. . . . My whole body shakes from the memory of all this leaving" (66). Returning home, she tries to rebuild bridges with her family and effectively rediscover the neglected, "feminine" side of her heritage, in particular by appealing to the kind of emotional sensitivity which Beth admires in Meg. For Sally, love is something vital, and to resist it as her brother has done is to invite self-destruction. Yet she discovers that her own mother, whose potential for nurturing love has been so exploited and abused by her menfolk, has come to the opposite conclusion, and retreated to a very defensive, "masculine" self-absorption. She now sees love as "a crock a' shit" (92) which made her vulnerable to being bled of everything. Her attempts now to reduce Jake to infancy are clearly not made with his best interests at heart, but to fulfill her own need for smothering control over him (apparently a form of revenge for the humiliation Jake's father subjected her to).

Among the play's men, Sally's older brother, Frankie, stands out as the most gender-balanced. Entirely lacking in the violent delusions and selfishness so typical of Jake, Baylor, and Mike, he seems to represent a kind of ideal male, and demonstrates a genuine tenderness toward many of the other characters. The end of act 1, scene 3, for example, is especially touching, as he quietly assures the bewildered Jake that he will stay with him (15). It is also a gesture of pure, good-willed concern that takes him up to Montana to inquire after Beth. Again, though, self-sacrifice has its price, as he becomes trapped in a situation he has no control over. Mike sees Frankie as less than a real man, labeling him "pathetic" and "sniveling" (46), and treats him as a prisoner in the house, while Beth begins to make uninvited advances on him. In her strangely perceptive, brain-damaged state, Beth sees Frankie as a possible salvation for her, since he looks just like her fantasy male, Jake, but lacks his brutality:

> Your other one. You have his same voice. Maybe you could be like him. Pretend. Maybe. Just him. Just like him. But soft. With me. Gentle. Like a woman-man. You could be better. Better man. Maybe. Without hate. You could be my sweet man. You could. Pretend to be. (76)

The play seems, in short, to be appealing for a movement toward a kind of androgyny, cherishing the idea of a "woman-man" who might combine the best qualities of the traditionally distinct masculine and feminine gender roles. Where *Fool for Love* had presented the tantalizing hint of a softening in Eddie's inherited, masculine behavior (before his reverting to type), *A Lie of the Mind* represents Shepard's first distinct move away from his previous obsession with deterministic entrapment, toward a real faith in the potential for personal change. In this respect, the play mirrored his own concerted attempts to develop and temper his own sense of identity, as is clear from an interview given in 1988:

> You get to the point where you say, "But there's this whole other territory I'm leaving out." And that territory becomes more important as you grow older. You begin to realize that you leave so much out when you go into battle with the shield and all the rest of it. . . . You can't grow that way. . . . There just comes a point where you have to relinquish some of that and risk becoming more open to the vulnerable side, which I think is the female side. . . . It's much more courageous than the male side.[18]

The statement is reminiscent of Jungian discussions of the male "midlife" individuation process, in which a man comes to terms with his inner anima. Yet in *A Lie of the Mind* there is no suggestion – as there is in those pieces of the mid-'70s – of some natural maturing process, through which one reins in the battling ego so as to discover some deeper sense of essential self. The impression created in *Lie* is both less metaphysical and more ironic: human life is seen as an absurd void, and if change is possible, it is precisely because of this (frightening) fact. For if one's life is a construction designed to fend off the abyss, then gender attributes are not essential but socially inculcated or personally chosen: perhaps it is possible to construct an identity out of the preferable ones.

Life as Improvisation

In one sense, the notion of inventing oneself out of the void provides the underlying dynamic of *Paris, Texas*. The initially mute and desolate Travis gradually builds on his *tabula rasa* condition, reacquiring language, relationships, and motivation. In one memorable scene, the role-building process is made quite explicit as Travis hunts in magazines for an image of "*the* father" which he can adopt for Hunter's benefit. Carmelita, the maid, becomes his director and designer, providing him with a costume and with instructions on how to act: "You must always look to the sky. . . . You must walk stiff, Señor Travis" (46–7). *A Lie of the Mind* makes this theatrical analogy still clearer by making Beth an actress, who openly admits that her career and her life are indistinguishable. It is not simply that the role she had been rehearsing for – as an abused but resilient lover – mirrors her own life, much as Lee and Austin's script had mirrored theirs. All her behavior, she explains, is an attempt to create a dramatic narrative for herself, since the only alternative is to live a dull, meaningless routine of nonidentity: "Pretend is more better. . . . Because it fills me. Pretending fills. Not empty. Other. Ordinary. Is no good. Empty. Ordinary is empty" (75).

More so than any of Shepard's other family plays, *Lie* seems dominated by a sense of the structureless emptiness of existence, similar to that which is prevalent in *Action, Suicide in B♭*, or *Angel City*. Indeed, the characters' search for meaning and identity, by improvising roles for themselves, can be seen as yet another, entirely necessary kind of "lie of the mind." Their lack of stable grounding might be less immediately obvious than in earlier pieces, since Shepard's previous technique of using shifting successions of masks and attitudes has here settled itself to a point where most figures appear fairly consistent in behavior. Yet this consistency, though more ostensibly "realistic," is only possible because characters have constructed their identities around self-defining obsessions – love, motherhood, machismo, revenge, family honor – which provide them with a focal point in the emptiness. Just as Sally describes how her father had constructed a bizarre collection of photographs of film stars and relatives to keep him company in his solitary life ("Trying to make a family out of us all": 90), so the play itself implies that each person must construct, out of the incoherent fragments of existence, a liveable narrative for him/herself. This process is demonstrated with vivid immediacy by the fact that these characters are surrounded by a black void on all sides: in effect, the entire course of the play presents a process of building up a performance and so fencing off that darkness. Act 1 begins with pure, empty blackness, which is first encroached on by the sound of Jake's and Frankie's voices, and then by the appearance of the tiny patches of light they are standing in. Over the next several scenes, the darkness is gradually pushed back as more stage space is lit and acted in: in scene 3, for example, Jake and Frankie are confined to a dimly lit area around a standard lamp, but in scene 5 more of the same room becomes visible, enabling greater movement. Act 2 opens with wall-flats having been flown in.

Even as this gradual fencing off of the void develops visually, Shepard neatly counterpoints it with Jake's disgusted attempts to reject Beth's sense of performative contingency, and to reinforce a commonsense distinction between the constructed and the essential: "she tells me this is the real world. This acting shit is more real than the real world to her" (10). The irony, though, is that Jake is blindly unaware that his version of the real world is every bit as self-invented as Beth's. His fervent insistence on Beth's infidelity, for example, grounded on the most tenuous of assumptions, comes across as a drastic attempt to introduce a melodramatic twist to their dull daily routine. Just like his father, Lorraine says, Jake is always "play-acting," and "Tryin' to make a big drama outa' things" (24; 36). Shepard extends this idea to imply that *all* the stereotypically "masculine" behavior in the play – be it in the role of jealous lover, Hemingwayesque hunter, defender of the family honor, or wandering loner – might simply represent the mindless repetition of preconceived notions ("big ideas") of how "real men" should "act." Baylor, for example, goes out shooting deer not because he likes or needs the meat, but simply because "It's deer season. You hunt in deer season. That's what you do" (103). Such posturing is explicitly mocked by Beth when she dons her father's shirt: "Just feel like the man," she laughs as she struts about the room, puffing out her chest in a cartoon parody of a male swagger. Beth's aphasic confusion of the words "costume" and "custom" ingeniously underlines the notion that, far from being biologically determined, masculine posturing is the result of convention, of habit, and can be put on or taken off like the shirt itself: "Shirt brings me a man. I am a shirt man. Can you see? Like father. . . . Like brother" (75). Beth even takes on the role of aggressor, attempting to force herself on the hapless Frankie, and so putting him in the supposedly "feminine" position of passive victim.

This notion that all human behavior is simply a form of role-play is not, of course, treated lightly by Shepard. Indeed, a large part of the overwhelming sense of brokenness in both *Lie* and *Paris, Texas* stems from the fact that so many of the characters have their senses of self so comprehensively erased by the shattering effect of unanticipated events. The lovers in both pieces (unlike Eddie and May, who are still bouncing back and forth between conflicting self-images) have had the fragile strings that hold them together – and so provide them with a mutual sense of identity – decisively cut by Travis's and Jake's violence. Each has thus been reduced to a kind of living death: Jane, for example, describes how she "just gave it up" after Travis left: "Everything stopped" (95). Jake uses exactly the same phrase to explain the consequences of his beating Beth, while she declares that he has "killed us both" (19). A further twist to this destructive cycle is added when Jake, having attempted to embrace death by immuring himself in his mother's home (over two acts he grows increasingly corpselike in appearance), abruptly gets up and leaves: having staked her own identity on the idea of being able to mother him forever, Lorraine herself now shuts herself up in his room, refuses food, and consigns *herself* to die. Similarly, in *Paris, Texas*, when Hunter leaves with Travis, Anne is reduced to mindlessly singing herself to sleep on Hunter's bed.

In *Lie*, the notion of identity as role-play is further problematized by the recurring theme of subjective perceptions – and especially those conditioned by denial – distorting the reality of a situation. Jake, for example, in order to sustain his self-image of himself as a basically good man, tends blindly to reinvent the past for his own convenience. He not only attempts to blame Beth for what he did to her, but simply cannot remember his own previous acts of violence. Frankie, for example, reminds him of how he "kicked the shit" out of a goat as a child, but Jake insists that he could not have done so: "I loved that goat" (13). Similarly, he cannot recall the "other times when you said you'd killed [Beth]" which Sally refers to (60), or – astonishingly – the night when his father was killed by a truck, despite the fact that he was present, and perhaps even responsible. The selectivity of memory and the passing of blame are themes which recur throughout the play, often to highly comic effect, but the cumulative results are far from funny: the play presents yet another bewildering array of subjective accounts and denials which function to destabilize each other.

Nevertheless, for all these now familiar problems, Shepard seems in *Lie* to be prepared to contemplate a positive potential in the fundamental instability of identity, and of "reality" itself. The notion that the self might simply be a collection of surface roles, which had hitherto haunted Shepard's work as a nightmarish prospect, seems here to be invested with positive, if tenuous, potential, particularly if one can become *aware* of this performativity, instead of unwittingly playing out predetermined roles. This is seen particularly in the recurrent idea that the characters might learn to act out *love* for each other (and indeed for themselves), rather than capitulate to the numbed indifference which seems to be the given moral state of the contemporary environment. Beth, for instance, pleads with Frankie to try acting the part of her lover, and so facilitate possible salvation for them both: "You could pretend so much that you start thinking this is me. You could really fall in love with me" (77). Similarly, in *Paris, Texas*, Anne admits having taken to heart, with positive results for Hunter, her self-appointed role as his mother: "I was never 'pretending'. I love him just like he was my own flesh and blood" (52).

There is perhaps a danger that this newfound faith in love becomes simply a form of pious sentimentality, yet Shepard manages to avoid this, not least because the term "love" itself, though appealed to on many occasions in these texts, remains undefined and ambiguous. As a word simultaneously one of the most abused and yet one of the most resonant in the English language, it is itself a prime example of the slippage of signification which affects all contemporary attempts at communication, and Shepard acknowledges as much by placing it in the mouths of his most selfishly deluded characters, as well as his most idealistic. "Love" thus remains a term which may inspire without ever being stable or reducible to platitudinous simplicity. Moreover, even those lines which tread perilously close to the border of cliché – such as Travis's parting shot to his son ("I love you Hunter. I love you more than my life": 87), or Jake's to Beth ("I love you more than this life": 129) – are prevented from becoming trite by the tragic-ironic contexts in which they occur. In Travis's case, the words are spoken on a tape recording (he still does not know how to communicate such emotions face-to-face) which he makes before leaving Hunter and Jane forever. Unable to find a path toward reconciliation, Travis drives off alone into the proverbial sunset, leaving Jane, quite literally, holding the baby. Her reunion with Hunter is a joyous one, but will she be any more able to cope with him now than previously? Has anything really changed? Wim Wenders has aptly described the film as "the image of a circle."[19] Yet it is this very lack of closure which makes the conclusion so powerful: without resorting to a hackneyed happy ending, it leaves open the possibility that a healing, a transformation, has begun to take place. Travis, though he is moving on yet again, is apparently no longer seeking to blind himself, but to confront his inner demons. As he tells Hunter on the farewell tape: "Right now, I'm afraid. I'm afraid of walking away again. I'm afraid of what I might find. But I'm even more afraid of not facing this fear" (87).

The end of *A Lie of the Mind* is an equally moving blend of profound sadness and faint, strangely uplifting optimism. Moreover, it goes still further in presenting an ambiguous vision of change because, rather than simply seeking to heal wounds, many of the characters actually revolutionize their behavior. The term "love" is still less cozy here because enacting compassion for the saving benefit of both others and oneself appears to entail the need for a certain ruthlessness of action, a purging of the emotional baggage of the past. The increasingly bizarre final act presents a radical shake-up of received roles, which destabilizes the supposed realism of the play, as Shepard wrenches domination of the narrative away from the male characters, so indifferent to the needs of others, and moves the focus of attention to the women, and their greater solidarity. The result is a utopian re-visioning of the families' situations which provides a heavily ironized sense of hope for the future.

The first clear hint in the play that "the female side" is taking control comes at the end of act 3, scene 1, in which, after a "long pause," Lorraine suddenly snaps out of her deathly mourning for Jake. Apparently brought to a moment of revelation by Sally's passionate attempts to force her back into life ("What're we doin' in this room now? What're we supposed to be hiding from?": 96), she decides to reinvent herself from scratch, by casting out all her embittered memories of the men who have wrecked her life. Craving "one a' them fierce, hot, dry winds . . . that wipe everything clean and leave the sky without a cloud" (97), she builds a fire in which to burn everything which reminds her of her husband and sons (including – finally and most extraordinarily – the house itself). In the next scene, on the other side of the stage, Baylor's patriarchal command of *his* house is suddenly thrown into question when Meg's quiet patience with his insensitivity and selfishness finally gives way and she tells him to "just go. Why don't you just go off and live the way you want to live. We'll take care of ourselves. We always have" (106). Dumbstruck, Baylor finds his control is further subverted when Beth enters to ask his permission to marry Frankie. She too has wiped clean the slate of her past, having forged an entirely new identity for herself, as represented by the new costume in which she appears. This bizarre ensemble of grotesquely clashing styles, colors, and materials is another example of found fragments being thrown together to create a new reality. As Jake had feared, she has become "a whole other person who doesn't see me any more. Who doesn't even remember that we were together once" (85). She does not recognize him at all when he enters, focused as she is on the idea of marrying Frankie: "Once we're together, the whole world will change" (114).

Meanwhile, Jake too has abruptly changed. Having set out to prevent Frankie from stealing Beth, he is intercepted by Mike, who beats him up (offstage) and forces him into the position of a servile dog, bringing him in to make an abject apology to Beth. Significantly, though, this abuse turns the tables on Jake, making him the victim of masculine violence, and damaging him as Beth has been damaged. His broken speech patterns now resemble hers, and something has been rearranged in his mind. He still cannot demystify his idealized vision of her ("You stay. You are true"), but he finally sees how much he has hurt her through his deluded treatment of her: "These things – in my head – lie to me. . . . Everything in me lies." His jealously proprietorial obsession with Beth is now replaced by a more genuinely loving, self-sacrificial concern for her welfare. Withdrawing his claim on her, he accepts her desire to settle with the gentler, less volatile Frankie: "You stay. You stay with him. He's my brother" (129).

Notably, Jake's entire speech entails defying Mike's instructions on what he is to say to her: he has rewritten the script dictated to him. For his part, Mike realizes that he no longer has any power here, that the family has no interest in his masculine notions of honor and revenge, and disgustedly quits the house forever. Baylor, on the other hand, does not leave, but changes. When he sees Mike using the American flag as a gun rag, he is horrified, and his reverence for the flag brings him out of his festering self-absorption and prompts an oddly endearing attempt to make amends for Mike's abuse by folding it up properly. Even love of country, it seems, can bring about a saving epiphany: Baylor succeeds in folding the flag with Meg's help, and this little triumph prompts him to kiss her, reportedly for the first time in twenty years. As they go off up to bed together, after this bizarre reconciliation, Meg somehow glimpses the fire Lorraine has lit across the miles that separate them. She sees it as a miracle, a sign of the impossible coming to pass: "Looks like a fire in the snow. How could that be?" (131).

Of course, each of these little endings is deeply ambiguous, as is evident if one tries projecting the characters' stories into the future. Where will Jake go now? What will Beth and Frankie do given that she is brain-damaged and that he has no desire to marry her? What will happen when the Ireland to which Lorraine plans to return (in a direct reversal of the journey made by the pioneer fathers) turns out not to be the idyllic picture postcard that she imagines it to be? And, most bizarre of all, is faith in the American flag anything to rebuild a marriage on? Yet in a way these

questions are beside the point: what Shepard presents is a group of people who are willing to try to move on from their situations of breakdown,
to imagine and perhaps create a provisional salvation for themselves.
Indeed, if the play alludes to national dysfunction, this conclusion also
seems to capture something of the spirit of contemporary America, a
nation whose peoples, despite the crushing weight of corruption, deracination, injustice, have not yet given in to cynical despair. Inspired by the
even the most implausible forms of idealism (the flag itself?), Americans
continue to pursue hopes and dreams which, however naive, nevertheless
create a resistant energy that provides the faint possibility of changing
things for the better.

Such undirected passion might, of course, lead nowhere, or indeed
might lead as easily to fascism as to utopia, but in Shepard's newly hopeful vision of the future, this lack of grounding is a possible blessing as
much as it is a curse. The new outlook is perhaps epitomized by Beth,
whose jumbled, broken speech patterns in a sense represent the antithe-
sis of *The Tooth of Crime*'s brutally masculine language constructions.
Her words often make no rational sense at all, and are devoid of the
duplicitous machinations of power, yet they also carry a resonance, compassion and implicit wisdom greater than those of any other character. Is
she insane or in some way supra-sane? The indefinable sense of potential
which Beth's speech, or lack of it, seems to represent is summarized
by the final position in which she is seen. Following Jake's exit, Beth
embraces Frankie, lapsing into ecstatic silence and simultaneously silenc-
ing him. They hold this frozen pose throughout Meg and Baylor's final
exchange, and through the final slow fade of the lights. The image is both
beautiful and oddly troubling, suggesting a power in the "female side"
which goes well beyond any cozy ideas of loving goodness. Has Frankie
somehow been absorbed by Beth, drowned in her passion or perhaps
returned to the womb? Or is he forcibly silenced, unable to find a voice
to respond to her overpowering, a-verbal will? The image defies explanation, offering no sense of neat resolution, nor even any clear motives for
the characters' behavior. Instead, Shepard offers an overpowering silence
which bespeaks more about Beth, her past and her future, than any words
could seek to. It is a strategy that has also been adopted by feminist
dramatists from Susan Glaspell to Maria Irene Fornes: patriarchally controlled language is either inadequate or untrustworthy in expressing the
as-yet-unrealized desires of the female; silence or elision functions to suggest the potential for literally unspeakable new possibilities.

Claiming Shepard as a feminist per se would obviously be a highly dubious project, and it is, of course, up to individual spectators to interpret what they will from this broad canvas of emotions, with its dreamlike allusiveness, its connotations spilling in a multiplicity of directions at once. Nevertheless, it is through that very expansiveness that this play succeeds in blowing wide-open the questions of gender roles, gender identity, sexual power, and the possibility of positive change. It is only unfortunate that Shepard himself seems to have been unable to find a way to develop these concerns further, either in *Far North* or in subsequent work.

8

Victory and Loss

The Nation in the Nineties

S HEPARD HAD REMARKED as early as 1980, "You can't keep writing about the family for the rest of your life," and by the mid-'80s it seemed that particular furrow had been plowed as far as it could go.[1] Just as *La Turista* and *The Tooth of Crime* had rounded off earlier periods of Shepard's work, so *A Lie of the Mind* effectively summarized his phase of family plays, concluding almost ten years of thematic and stylistic development since *Curse of the Starving Class*. Although *Far North* briefly reprised the chorus in filmic form, it felt like an epilogue rather than a new beginning, and seemed to beg the question of where Shepard was to go next. Moreover, whatever pressure he was placing on himself to find new directions must have been greatly exacerbated by the weight of expectation being loaded on him by an arts press which had in the mid-'80s hailed this multi-award-winning writer-director-movie-star as a "Renaissance Man" and "New American Hero." Shepard responded by virtually dropping out of sight for several years, and his new work since then has been greeted, inevitably enough, by the kind of critical backlash all too frequently aimed at those who have failed to live up to the hype.

It took a full-scale Broadway revival of *Buried Child* in 1996 to get him back in the good books: any real American dramatist, it seems, should naturally be aspiring to put family dramas on Broadway (this was the first time a Shepard play had ever appeared in this arena). The idea of continuing to be a writer who experiments with both form and content in search of new directions seems to carry less credibility. Yet that is precisely what Shepard has been doing in the 1990s, redeploying previous techniques and branching out in different directions in a visible attempt

243

to challenge both himself and his audiences. *States of Shock*, a new one-act play which appeared in 1991 in the wake of United States involvement in the Persian Gulf War, utilizes the kind of wild, grotesque theatricality not seen in his work since the 1970s to convey a vividly immediate sense of disgust with American military hubris. *Silent Tongue*, filmed in 1992, is an extraordinary hybrid piece, a kind of magic-realist western set on the frontier in 1873, which draws on everything from the themes of polarized gender conflict explored in *Lie* and *Far North*, to the kind of supernatural horror elements last seen in *The Holy Ghostly* and *Back Bog Beast Bait*. *Simpatico*, which finally appeared at the Public Theatre in 1994, goes to another extreme: even given its film noirish undertones, it is in many ways his most restrained, most straightforwardly realistic play to date, display-ing the kind of studied precision more usually associated with the mature Pinter and Albee.

Of course, not all of the negative criticism has been unjustified. Exper-iments demand the right to fail, and there is, for example, an awkward-ness about *States of Shock* that is never quite disguised by its theatrical or linguistic ingenuity. Shepard clearly wrote it at speed, trying to recapture something of his old free-form wildness, but in aiming simultaneously for stylistic fragmentation and thematic focus, he does not quite achieve either. The play lacks the sheer, unhinged madness of pieces like *Angel City*, and tends in places toward rambling repetition. *Silent Tongue* like-wise is somehow lacking in overall coherence, largely because of the shortcomings of its narrative-based plot. And yet as a piece it gains momentum after an uneasy start, and conjures some truly memorable images. *Simpatico*, meanwhile, is as good a play as any Shepard has writ-ten, even if it also one of his least "user-friendly": structured as a long suc-cession of duologues, it demands of its audience an unprecedented degree of close concentration on the nuances of the dialogue between each pairing. Perhaps this helps explain the predominantly unfavorable reviews which greeted its American premiere. These, however, were thrown into relief by the raves the play received in Britain (where Shep-ard does not carry the same burden of expectation as at home) when it opened at the Royal Court in 1995. "*Simpatico* is long and hard to follow," noted Michael Coveney in *The Observer*, "but it's easily the best play in London," revealing "this wonderful playwright's . . . maturity and staying power."[2]

If there is an element which unites these three diverse pieces of work, it is their common concern with exploring the roots of America's con-temporary bewilderment. The end of the Cold War, heralded by the collapse of the communist bloc in 1989, should have left America as undisputed global leader, at the head of the "New World Order" proclaimed by President Bush. Yet the early '90s saw only increasing national tensions: widening racial schisms, escalating urban violence and drug problems, and acrimonious political gridlock. "How could we be so victorious," asks the Colonel in *States of Shock*, "and still suffer this terrible loss? How could that be?"[3] That question seems to hang over these pieces like a spectre, and Shepard's judgment is uncompromising. He seems here to be returning to a thread of his work which had been left hanging when he became obsessed with the family in the late '70s: while these pieces all feature elements of familial dysfunction, gender conflict, and so on, the predominant concern - as it was in *Angel City* or *Seduced* - is with depicting a Faustian nation mired in depravity and corruption.

Vaudeville Apocalypse

When *States of Shock* opened in April 1991, less than three months after the cessation of hostilities in the Persian Gulf, it was difficult not to interpret it as an immediate and angry response to the gung-ho patriotic fervor generated by Operation Desert Storm and its comprehensive demolition of the Iraqi armed forces. As American-based British journalist W. J. Wetherby pointed out at the time, Shepard was daring to fly in the face of national euphoria when even "professional controversialists like Norman Mailer and Gore Vidal have been largely silent," and this may in part explain the negative reaction the production received (despite the weighty presence of John Malkovich in the lead role).[4] Certainly there are elements of the play which directly recall the Gulf War: the recent memory of the blanket TV coverage of the night strafing of Baghdad was conjured up by the play's use of a cyclorama at the back of the set, periodically lit up with projections of tracer fire and explosions. The set itself is a sketched-in version of a plastic-American "family restaurant"; simultaneously the epitome of both the "family values" and the consumerism so relentlessly championed during the Reagan/Bush era. To the rear of the stage, two stereotypical bourgeois characters, White Man and White Woman (whited sepulchres in both skin and dress), sit complaining in a comically stuck-up manner about the poor quality of customer service (the waitress, says the Woman, "ought to be shot"), and blithely ignoring the eruptions of deafening drumming and the screened images of warfare. As an immediate depiction of middle America's complacent acceptance of the violence being enacted on its behalf, the premise is striking.

Yet if the play did indeed rankle post–Gulf War sensibilities, it was more openly criticized for *failing* to allude more directly to the particularities of the recent conflict, and for displaying a rather outdated, post-*Vietnam* perspective. This is understandable given Shepard's central character pairing. In the foreground of the stage are seated the Colonel and Stubbs. The former is dressed in a mix-and-match assortment of costumes from America's military history (Civil War sabre, World War II pilot's hat, and so forth), and so takes on the aspect of a kind of immortal, demonic Uncle Sam figure. With him is a young man, Stubbs, whose depiction as a maimed, wheelchair-bound war veteran immediately suggests the pop culture memory of Vietnam: like the crippled hero of Oliver Stone's film *Born on the Fourth of July* (1989), he is an inconvenient reminder of national folly, railing at the nation that has tried to ignore him. Yet where Stone embraced melodrama, Shepard creates grotesque comedy, more akin to David Rabe's Vietnam play *Sticks and Bones* (1971), by surrounding the victim with cartoon characters. Stubbs is treated with astonished distaste by the White Man and White Woman, who remain unmoved by his frantic attempts to confront them with his suffering. His shrill, disorientating blasts on a whistle, and his rhythmically insistent chorus of lines beginning "When I was hit . . . ," create a spectacle which is simultaneously comic and discomforting. Stubbs's sense of desertion by his country is indeed more immediately applicable to Vietnam than to the Gulf War, after which the troops were welcomed back as conquering heroes. But it is also significant that Shepard borrows satirically from the Newspeak rhetoric of Gulf War coverage to explain Stubbs's injuries: he was hit, he claims, by "friendly fire. It smiled in my face. I could see its teeth when it hit us" (31). It is not simply that Stubbs's wounds have been ignored by a nation uncomfortable with the memory of a foreign war: as far as he is concerned, it was his nation that shot him down, and in this memory there is a sense of all-encompassing disillusionment and disaffection: "Your face, lying. Smiling and lying. Your bald face of denial. Peering down from a distance. Bombing me" (43).

Shepard's target, it seems, lies beyond simply attacking military arrogance: the war scenario is symptomatic of an American blindness that is poisoning its people. If the Colonel, as Stubbs implies, is really his father and is now denying this blood link, placing him at a remove, it is less because he is ashamed of Stubbs's failure than it is because he cannot *explain* it: such loss simply does not tally with his view of the way the world operates, and that view must be upheld at all costs. "DON'T LET YOURSELF SLIP INTO DOUBT!" screams Stubbs, mocking the

Colonel's attempts to shore up his sliding perspective: "Lock onto an image or you'll be blown to KINGDOM COME!" (38). In effect, Shepard is here connecting a sense of national crisis to the kind of loss of stable reference points his work has frequently alluded to in respect to crises of personal identity. Specifically, he offers an intriguing variation on the theme - familiar from pieces such as *True West* - of defining one's own identity in dualistic opposition to some supposed "other." *States of Shock* clearly implies that the nation's self-perception depends on having an opponent to demonize: "LONG LIVE THE ENEMY!" the Colonel declares repeatedly: "WITHOUT THE ENEMY WE'RE NOTHING!" (15). It is here that the play's relevance to the '90s becomes most apparent: Wheeler, in *Angel City*, had remarked offhandedly that wars provide "a focus," and in the aftermath of the demise of the Soviet Union that idea acquires fresh currency. "I missed the Cold War with all my heart," remarks Glory Bee, epitomizing the bemusement felt in the absence of an "evil empire" against which to define America's righteousness (41). According to this view, Saddam Hussein's Iraq was in 1991 unwittingly stepping into a prewritten role in the nation's psychodrama, and so pulling down a wrath of Old Testament proportions. "I could not believe the systematic kind of insensitivity of it," Shepard told Carol Rosen in *The Village Voice*:

> there was this punitive attitude - we're just going to knock these people off the face of the earth. . . . Not only that, but they've convinced the American public that this was a good deed, that this was in fact a heroic fucking war, and welcome the heroes back. What fucking heroes, man? I mean, they bombed the shit out of those people.[5]

This sense of outrage translates in *States of Shock* into a merciless parody of the nation's obsession with reinforcing ideas of masculine heroism as some kind of answer to the sense of lost direction. "Even in the midst of the most horrible devastation," declares the Colonel, "we can't forget that we were generated from the bravest stock. The Pioneer. The Mountain Man. The Texas Ranger. The Lone Ranger" (24). Military power, he suggests, is America's manifest right because it is the logical extension of these frontier traditions. The play thus presents a savage, cartoon version of a theme implied in *A Lie of the Mind*: machismo is seen as an artificial mask, a role adopted to stave off the male's – and in this case the nation's – terror of existential meaninglessness. The idea is enunciated repeatedly in the Colonel's ranting, in phrases which move from the mock-sublime to the patently ridiculous:

> Slowly, through my own diligence and perseverance, this pattern takes
> on a beauty and form that would have otherwise been incomprehensi-
> ble to my random, chaotic laziness. Now I become the master of my
> own destiny. (33)

> Aggression is the only answer. A man needs a good hobby. (39)

The brutal irony is that this kind of attitude has brought about the very
fate the Colonel fears. "These ones have not left us to wallow in various
states of insanity and self-abuse," he declares of his forebears, but insanity and self-abuse is – quite literally – what these characters are descending into. Picking up on the Colonel's exhortation that he "Become a man!"
Stubbs repeats the phrase louder and louder, climaxing just as the White
Man, who has been quietly simulating masturbation in a lap covered with
clam chowder, reaches orgasm.

Such moments, of course, always border on the self-indulgently gross,
but Shepard insists that "if theatre loses the ability to enjoy slapstick . . .
we've shot ourselves in the foot."[6] And it is through such grotesque theatricality that the play's disgust toward America's myopic arrogance is
most fully realized. Living up to its subtitle, "A Vaudeville Nightmare,"
the play steadily descends from quirky banter between the two double
acts into a slapstick depravity which exposes the facade of cozy domesticity even more ruthlessly than the war sounds outside. Indeed, in the premiere production, the various stage directions indicating food throwing
were expanded each night – with Shepard's blessing – into a full-scale
improvised food fight. America, it is implied, has been reduced to a kind
of decadent circus-society, gorging itself on sticky food while blindly
awaiting some sordid apocalypse: "It's too late for clam chowder," the
White Man announces gloomily (25).

What makes the play particularly pertinent to '90s confusion is this
sense that barbarity and violence is depicted as having come home to
roost in this consumer sanctuary of the American heartland. Glory Bee
reports that first the manager and then the chef have become casualties
of battle: "The thing I can't get over is, it never occurred to me that
'Danny's' could be invaded," she notes in distress: "I always thought we
were invulnerable to attack. The landscaping. The lighting. The parking
lot. All the pretty bushes. Who would touch us. Who would dare?" (40).
The ones who would dare, it seems, are Americans themselves, bewildered and outraged at the state of a nation that has failed to fulfill its
extravagant promises. The idea of violent death meeting the staff of a
family restaurant inevitably recalls the various incidents in the late '80s in

which gunmen-without-a-cause walked into fast-food outlets and mowed down whatever innocents stood in their way, and Glory's words have only acquired more poignancy since they were written: they seem almost pre-scient of the national soul-searching brought on by such incidents as the 1995 bombing in Oklahoma City, when it became clear that America faced an enemy within potentially far more disruptive to its sense of self than either Arabs or Russians. Shepard's final image suggests precisely that, as the shell-shocked Stubbs (having regained the use of his legs) seizes the Colonel's saber and stands frozen over him, holding it aloft as if ready to decapitate him. It is impossible to say whether this represents vengeance, revolution, or Oedipal patricide (he has already stolen Glory Bee, the Colonel's newly appointed brood mare), but as a naked image of America's future it is perhaps even more unsettling than the similar image of mutual masculine enmity which had closed *True West*. The freeze is held throughout the closing "vaudeville" act, as the entire cast (except Stubbs) sing Leadbelly's "Goodnight Irene": that quietly suicidal lament for unrecoverable dreams, juxtaposed starkly with that Damoclean sword hovering over Uncle Sam, wielded by his own "son," creates a chilling conclusion to an awkward but nonetheless provocative play.

A similarly uncompromising view of America's guilt and bewilderment is offered by the film *Silent Tongue*. Rather than using contemporary war-fare as the peg, though, Shepard opts to go right back to the historical roots of the problem by creating – unprecedentedly for him – a period piece. The desolate prairie of New Mexico functions as the frontier of Wild Western lore, complete with Indian war parties and trekking pio-neers. There is, however, nothing romanticized or heroic about any of this: the prairie is shot under harsh, starkly unglamorous sunlight, and its European colonizers are worn-out detritus. Moreover, in blunt contra-diction of the traditional frontier myths of heroic individualism, the film suggests that America, then as now, was characterized by corrupt and unprincipled profiteering. This is epitomized by Eamon MacCree, owner of a Medicine Show which tours around the territories looking for gullible customers to entertain and then fleece with sales of a supposedly mysti-cal cure-all which is clearly just cheap moonshine. The Medicine Show premise allows Shepard to build in a number of performative set pieces (a comic double act, dwarf acrobats, a trick-riding display, and elaborate rhetorical blarney), but the overall impression created is of run-down charlatanry. As in *States of Shock*, there seems to be a metaphorical equa-tion of American culture with sleazy vaudeville. And again, there is the

Claire Vousden, Jason Done, Michael Shaw, Charlotte Woolford, and Michael Wade in *States of Shock*, presented by Kay Messina at BAC, London, 1996. (Photo courtesy of BAC)

suggestion of a horrific violence underlying this veneer: the frontier land
into which the settlers are moving is already occupied by Native Americans, and Shepard alludes to a whole history of genocidal injustice
through his microcosmic tale of MacCree's casual brutality toward them.
He is seen, in flashback, raping a lone, defenseless Indian woman for
sport, and in the present as the father of her two daughters, whom he
treats as no more than slaves, chattels to be sold off for personal profit.

Shepard has described the Colonel in *States of Shock* as "a character
of such outrageous, repulsive, military, fascist demonism" that he is
beyond redemption, and MacCree is cast in the same mold.[7] Completely
without moral compunction, the only thing he feels attached to is
whiskey: "I can't just sever a connection like that. It's not like a woman"
(172). Latterly, it would seem, Shepard's determined attempt to understand even the most hopeless of his male characters has been replaced by
unequivocal horror and exasperation. MacCree, like the Colonel, is
haunted by guilty fears which he constantly denies to himself, and his
unease thus becomes warped into wild paranoia. It is perhaps refreshing
to find Shepard - in both these pieces - reducing the Great American
Male to an object of derision, but *Silent Tongue* also adds depth and
poignancy to the scenario by suggesting that even basically decent characters have been corrupted by the tainted mercantilism that MacCree
epitomizes. Prescott Roe, for example (played with painful dignity by
Richard Harris), is a desperate father who will seemingly sacrifice anything to save his only, sickly son, Talbot, from slipping into insanity. Yet
his idea of salvation involves buying a wife for him: when she (Awbonnie)
dies in childbirth, Prescott blindly believes that buying a replacement
(her sister Velada) will solve the problem, and when MacCree postpones
the sale, Prescott steals her by force. Meanwhile, Talbot (as lost and broken as that other son, Stubbs) is playing out a warped version of the same
misguided possessiveness by trying to hold onto the corpse of Awbonnie.
Awbonnie's Ghost – rather like the Chindi in *The Holy Ghostly* – materi-
alizes out of the desert night to try to force him to set her spirit free by
burning or burying the body: "You keep me bound here out of your selfish fear of aloneness!" (150). When he resists, she shifts from Antigone to
avenging Fury, traversing the prairie to terrorize not only Talbot, but also
MacCree and Prescott, as if taking retribution on their entire race. Certainly they all share the guilt: "You're not absolved!" MacCree yells at his
self-righteous son, Reeves, summing up the film's implication that
nobody is (187). The supernatural elements, and the overtones of Greek
tragedy, lend the film an air of apocalyptic judgment on the European
invaders of the wilderness. Silent Tongue, the woman whom MacCree

raped, watches the proceedings from afar, like a mute but all-seeing force of nature. Only, perhaps, when Prescott finally summons the strength to surrender the corpse to the flames, has some kind of atonement been enacted.

Shepard is playing a dangerous game here, in dividing his characters along binary fault lines not only of gender (selfish, possessive males versus brutally victimized females - beaten, sold, raped, lassoed, and mutilated) but also of race (white men versus Kiowa women). The film treads perilously close to reducing females and Native Americans alike to the status of mysterious, alien "other," whom the lost and lonely men can only wonder at. That danger was also compounded by the fact that the film came as a late addition to a mini-trend for Hollywood movies romanticizing Indian culture, such as *Dances with Wolves* (1990) and *Thunder Heart* (1992). Shepard, who himself appears in the latter as a corrupt FBI agent, suggested that this fad was grounded in a deeper truth: "we're haunted by the Native American religiousness, the true religiousness of a people who were in harmony with their environment, which we're completely not in touch with."[8] And yet whereas this theme had been treated crudely and tokenistically in *Operation Sidewinder*, *Silent Tongue* is far more mature, deftly avoiding the twin perils of romanticization its scenario opens itself to. For one thing, the film follows up on *A Lie of the Mind* by blurring gender traits across the binary divide (Velada, for example, is almost as mercenary as her father, while Prescott displays an unexpected degree of real tenderness). Still more significant, though, is that the native mystical dimension manifests itself not in the usual peace pipe visions and cinematic mumbo jumbo, but as an elemental expression of righteous outrage. Indeed, Awbonnie's ghost – played with both power and subtlety by Sheila Tousey – paradoxically emerges as the most sympathetically human figure in the film. Seen not as a wraith but as a three-dimensional physical presence, she is a frustrated but powerful woman with "an almost masculine physical strength" (150), urgently seeking a peace which is being denied her. As director Michael Almereyda notes, "a crucial sense of weirdness emerges from the sheer matter-of-factness of Shepard's approach."[9]

Prismatic Guilt

The underlying problem with both *States of Shock* and *Silent Tongue*, for all their various strengths, is that they strive rather too hard toward making these bold, symbolic statements about America's guilty past and complicit present. In so doing, they largely forfeit the kind of multilayered complexity, ambiguity, and – especially in the case of *Silent Tongue* – self-mocking irony which distinguishes Shepard's best work. *Simpatico*, however, abandons the attempt at a historical overview on the nation's present dilemma, returning instead to another version of the unsettled realism which he had been developing in the '80s, in order to explore questions of guilt, culpability, and retribution in a much more localized, personal context. In so doing, it actually seems to allude to far more: where *States of Shock* had at times seemed oddly dated in its sensibility, *Simpatico* is tuned in to the high-speed, high-tech 1990s, portraying America as a village which is steadily becoming smaller, and its bonds of guilt more tangled and incestuous.

At first glance, *Simpatico* looks like another variation on certain of the themes worked over in Shepard's family plays. Certainly the basic stage setup is virtually a carbon copy of *A Lie of the Mind*: the play dramatizes concurrent events in two states – this time California and Kentucky – by splitting the stage in two, and separating these locations with blackness ("No landscape of any kind. Just black").[10] Still more obviously, the basic premise of a dualistic relationship between the main characters Carter and Vinnie, portrayed in the play's opening and closing scenes, is highly reminiscent of Lee and Austin in *True West*. This is a complementary pairing of opposites, pitting the wealthy, sophisticated Carter (of the Kentucky country club fraternity) against the penniless, bum-like Vinnie (as transient and rootless as the area of southern California in which he is holed up). Clearly, too, there is again an autobiographical element to this double-headed pairing: it is difficult not to read Vinnie's mockery of Carter's current position ("Kissing ass with the gentry": 20) as being – at least in part – a self-mockery of Shepard's own life among his fellow landowners in rural Virginia. With Carter arriving to pay Vinnie a visit in his hovel at the play's outset, it opens like an inversion of Lee's invasion of Austin's comfortable suburban hideaway, and their quietly loaded conversation, always hinting at far more than it states, is also in the same mold. Over the course of the play a similar role-reversal is acted out, as Carter becomes bogged down in memories and alcohol at Vinnie's, while Vinnie trots off to Kentucky to hobnob with racing folk and with Carter's wife, Rosie - who used to be *his* wife, and whom Carter stole away in Vinnie's Buick. As Shepard acknowledges, the "two guys" scenario is "an old, old situation which I've been struggling with for years."[11] He claims that there are eight or nine unfinished manuscripts dealing with these same characters.

The pairing of Vinnie and Carter is, however, different from that of
Austin and Lee in certain vital respects. First and foremost, they are not
brothers, nor are they related in any way (other than sharing a wife). The
tangled questions of blood ties, heredity, and familial responsibility are
thus removed from the equation from the outset: Shepard's focus here is
on a pair of childhood friends whose ties are entirely of their own making. Despite years of separation caused by "some-schism," they are still so
close that they seem like "the right and left hand" of a single being (111).
This closeness signals what is perhaps the play's predominant concern, an
exploration of the webs of connection and entrapment which people
weave for themselves, without the need for some deterministic fate
descending from outside. Vinnie, Carter, and Rosie, it emerges, together
hatched a plot to frame and discredit the racing commissioner Simms,
who has since moved away and sought to take on a new identity as
"Ames." And Simms, too, knows he is no innocent victim, since the frame
included a sexual entrapment he willingly participated in. Likewise, in
the play's present, the notionally innocent Cecilia is drawn into the situation by her willingness to act as an emissary from Carter to Ames, effectively double-crossing her lover Vinnie in exchange for tickets to the
Derby. Though always treated with varying degrees of irony, Shepard's
vision here is nevertheless a moral one, as it clearly is in his other work of
the '90s. These characters are never portrayed as victims of their upbringing, or of uncontrollable passions, as are the characters in the previous
"realist" plays, but are entirely responsible for their own little American
hells.

Simpatico's emphasis on such webs of guilt also effectively inverts the
concern of his family dramas with the idea of separation and dislocation,
of blood being the only feeble justification for people staying together.
For while the characters here are very much separate people, embittered
toward each other and alone with their own fears, they are also bound
together by the past, whether they like it or not. The problem is less that
of overcoming existential aloneness by building new identities and a new
sense of solidarity, as it was in A Lie of the Mind, than of how to live knowing that one cannot truly be separate even if one wants to be.

That inversion – inextricable links rather than unbridgeable separation – is stressed again and again by the play. It is seen in minor key in the
fact that the human body itself, far from being the site of brokenness as
it was with Beth's aphasia and disconnected language, is repeatedly seen
as site of a crippling connectedness: Carter and Cecilia both display con-

vulsive physical reactions to emotional pressure ("a symptom of something much bigger. A much bigger pain": 43). On a broader scale, it also
seems as if Shepard's reprisal of *Lie*'s set arrangement is both quotation
and inversion, for far from suggesting tracts of endless distance between
the two set rostra, the play actually concertinas the distances so that they
seem like nothing. Mirroring the frequent textual allusions to the speed
of communications afforded by new technologies ("computer-read-outs
and what-have-you. Fax machines. Electronic mail": 52), Vinnie himself
is mysteriously transported (teleported?) from California to Kentucky in
less time than it takes Carter to drive between San Dimas and Cuca-
monga. The distances between people and places, the play thus suggests,
are frighteningly close together in this brave new world: "You've got no
concept of how things are hooked up these days" (12). Perhaps the black
void between the stages is the virtual void of cyberspace rather than the
existential void of the abyss. In the 1995 London production, a cable
strung around the blackness of the theatre's walls pulsed with light every
time Carter's cellular phone rang.

The London production also ingeniously extended Shepard's implication in the script that all of the set locations should somehow exist at once,
not only by presenting a split stage in the foreground, but by allowing
other locations to appear to the rear of the Royal Court stage. The performance gradually built up from the single set of act 1, to the point
where the three different sets required in acts 2 and 3 were simultaneously visible, with the trucks shifting between scenes so as to place one at
the center of attention for each scene. The effect suggested was that of a
rotating prism, with the audience viewing the entangled situation from
different angles. The production thereby perfectly complemented the
construction of the play itself, for what Shepard presents in *Simpatico* is
less a linear plot that acquires momentum toward a denouement, than a
kind of circularity: the Vinnie and Carter scenes represent simply the
entrance and exit points for the audience's exploration of a situation
which builds in complexity as it is viewed from new, different perspectives in each scene. Those scenes, moreover, are a succession of duologues, each time homing in on the particular dynamic created by rubbing any two of the characters up against each other (one scene has a
third character, but she is peripheral). Shepard seems to be seeking to
combine the kind of sustained exploration of character confrontation
seen in *True West* or *Fool for Love*, with the broader overview of situation
introduced by *A Lie of the Mind*. Moreover, this technique of examining

a complex of relationships as if it were a prism, to be viewed from different angles, represents a further development of his long-standing interest in the prismatic treatment of characters. At an individual level, Shepard draws figures who are as erratic and unpredictable as ever, tending to react violently at the tripping of hair triggers. But it is the sequenced combination of these various portraits of volatility which takes Shepard's writing into new territory here. "The thing about crisis," notes Cecilia, is that "it happens suddenly" (75), and the play as a whole shows crisis spreading contagiously from scene to scene, life to life: "Panic is a terrible thing. . . . It's like a disease" (78).

For an audience, moreover, this technique of viewing the situation from a range of different perspectives represents a new variation on Shepard's concern with confounding the attempt at a straightforward reading of the "truth" of a situation ("Aah! The Truth! The Truth! And one of us is supposed to have a handle on that I suppose!": 17). The characters are constantly dropping hints and suggestions as to what has happened to them in both past and present, but these are chronically unreliable. "You've got to pay close attention to this," Vinnie mocks Carter: "Try to grasp all the details" (11). But Vinnie, Carter suggests, is "a professional liar," and nothing he says can be taken at face value (49). The same is as true of the other characters: their motives seem lethally double-edged, their utterances conditioned variously by mendacity, denial, and distrust, and the audience is thus unable to come to clear conclusions about the situations depicted.

Take, for example, the central issue of the compromising photographs which Vinnie, we are told, took of Rosie and Simms in flagrante delicto. These were supposedly used to destroy Simms's career, and Vinnie now seems to think that giving them to him will allow him to redeem himself. Yet how is it that a sexual indiscretion would discredit a racing commissioner (who hardly has the same job description as a politician), and how is it that regaining these photographs would help Simms clear his name? Equally, why is Carter, who is not in them, and who claims that "all we did was document the truth" (19), so desperate to get them back himself? They "could destroy an innocent man's life," he tells Cecilia (51): how? There is some talk of written documents detailing a plot ("I have letters," says Vinnie, "correspondence. Absolute proof": 61), which might explain Carter's anxiety, but the exact nature of these documents is far from clear, and the focus of everybody's attention seems to be the photographs, which Vinnie carries about the country in a battered shoe box. In effect, Shepard is playing with the classic Hitchcockian "McGuffin": the con-

crete details of what the sought-after object will do are far less important
than the anxieties it sets in motion. Further ambiguities are generated by
the questions over who actually initiated this photographic frame-up, and
why (Vinnie and Carter both behave as if Rosie was dragged into a setup
of theirs, yet Rosie claims that the whole thing was *her* idea). And why
was it that Vinnie and Carter sought to discredit Simms in the first place?
They had apparently effected a switch between two similar racehorses
(just as they themselves seem to reverse roles): Simms had found out
about this, and – Carter tells Cecilia – had to be destroyed when he
refused to be bought off. Elsewhere, however, Carter suggests that he *did*
cut a deal with Simms ("I set him up with a bloodstock agency. . . . He's
doing all right for himself": 32), and their covert telephone calls during
the play reinforce the idea of some continuing collusion. How then to
explain the frame-up?

In short, the narrative details in *Simpatico* are every bit as bewildering
and unstable as in any of Shepard's other "realist" plays. Here, though, the
absence of other facade-subversion techniques suggests that the concern
is less with an interrogation of the subjective status of reality itself, than
with the moral mire this mass of confusions indicates. As more and more
details accumulate, it becomes evident that this is a hopelessly murky situation that defies clear understanding. What *is* clear is the culpability of
all involved: of all the possible motivations for these characters' actions in
past and present, none remains untainted.

Significantly, this shift of emphasis is also evident in Shepard's other
work during the 1990s. In *States of Shock*, for instance, no objective truth
is to be discovered regarding either the circumstances of Stubbs's maim-
ing or the question of whether or not the Colonel truly is his father: both
have very different takes on these subjects. Yet the play is clearly less concerned with the conflict of subjective perceptions per se than with the
question of the Colonel's denial of any responsibility, and with his desperate attempts to construct a narrative of Stubbs's fate which will allow
him to shore up that complacency. Similarly, Shepard's revisions of
Buried Child for Steppenwolf's 1995 revival (which moved to Broadway
in 1996) seem to have been angled toward playing down the more blatantly disruptive properties of the original text, thereby allowing an
emphasis on the more human questions of denial and responsibility.
While Gary Sinise's production maintained, and even scaled up, the
gothic-mystery dimensions of the play, the textual changes cut down
some of the more clearly "unrealistic" monologues (notably Dodge's
recital of his will, and Halie's speech about Ansel's wedding), and muted

the wilder ambiguities surrounding the buried child itself. For example, Shepard simultaneously removed the idea that Vince might in some way be the dead baby come back to haunt, *and* resolved some of the confusion over the child's paternity, through the addition of a new line for Dodge after Vince introduces himself as Tilden's son: "He had *two*, I guess."[12] Similarly, the likelihood of Dodge's third-act revelations being "true" is enhanced by his self-reflective observation, before telling the story, that "I wouldn't mind hearing it hit the air again, after all these years of silence" (46). Explaining these changes, Shepard noted simply that he wanted to "follow through . . . certain questions that were ignited" in the original play, including that of Tilden's incestuous paternity. The play's ambiguities, he insisted, "shouldn't be resolved," but at the same time "I didn't want anything to be gratuitously mysterious."[13]

Whether or not these alterations improve the play is obviously a moot point, but certainly they operate to shift its emphasis somewhat, moving it away from its original location as part of Shepard's work of the mid- to late '70s, when he was experimenting with destabilizing stage ontology in plays such as *Angel City*, *Seduced*, and *Suicide in B*^{b} (which is nothing if not "gratuitously mysterious"). Instead, *Buried Child* moves closer into line with a play like *Simpatico*: the realism is less overtly problematized, and the remaining ambiguities operate to emphasise the extent to which the characters are trapped within a state of present crisis dictated by the events of the past. In particular, Shepard's revisions in act 2 accentuate the very human sense of bewilderment felt by Vince in the face of his family's unwillingness or inability to recognize him. When he returns in act 3, he now responds to Halie's description of him as a murderer not with maniacal assent, but with bitter derision: "How could I be a murderer when I don't exist?" (46).

The ironic flip side of this argument is that *Simpatico* itself, in creating an air of murky mystery reminiscent of film noir, also revives various motifs which were central to those wilder pieces of the mid-'70s. The notion of hidden conspiracies, for example, is reprised here: the play is riddled with allusions to secret deals and underhand operations of all sorts, conjuring up the sense of an entire society up to its neck in layer upon layer of personal and commercial cloak-and-dagger. This is apparent in everything from the references to fixing horse races to the threats of personal violence: "I'm the wife of someone," Rosie tells her ex-husband: "Someone of tremendous power and influence. He could have you done in from a distance and you wouldn't even know what hit you" (102). Such schemes spiral wildly, Simms even suggesting that the absence of coherent narratives in the movies (and by extension in this play?) is a conspiracy in itself: "Who was it decided to do away with all the plots? . . . They must've had a meeting somewhere. Behind closed doors" (56). But Shepard's use of this theme suggests not so much the postabsurdist, Pynchonian paranoia of *Suicide* and *Seduced*, as a more pragmatic sense of the damage done to the most basic human relations by the predominant atmosphere of suspicion and distrust. Rosie will not even acknowledge that she knows Vinnie until the nanny is out of the room, apparently for fear that she might be a spy.

Another element revived from the '70s noir plays is the overt inclusion of a detective in the scenario, as though to highlight the audience's own struggle to piece together the various contradictory clues in search of the truth. Vinnie hops between locations, seeking out the connections, but like Pablo and Louis in *Suicide in B♭*, he discovers that nothing is what it seems. Nor, indeed, is Vinnie: the detective role itself is the source of yet more confusions. Carter insists that this is just fakery, a pose Vinnie has been using since his youth to impress women, and Vinnie accepts that assertion, only to insist elsewhere that "I've been working as a private investigator for the past five years" (55). Has fantasy really become truth, or is this another lie? When he finally dons badge and gun in the last minutes of the play, Vinnie's speech only serves to underline further the inaccessibility of any final truth. His words are reminiscent of Niles's at the end of *Suicide*, except that, again, they allude not to ontological bewilderment but to the consequences of bedrock vice: "I'm working on a new case," he says, having summarily failed to resolve this one: "the great thing about this business is that there's no end to it. It's bottomless. Just imagine that. Right now, right this very second, someone is cutting someone else's throat. It's amazing" (134).

Perhaps the most unsettling aspect here is that Vinnie himself is so actively involved in further entangling the webs of guilt which link these characters. Far from taking some coolly objective distance from the situation, he goes looking to create mischief, waving the photographs in the faces of Simms and Rosie. Perhaps, by extension, the audience members also are "detectives" in this same way, looking to make up stories where no "truth" is to be had. Certainly, one of the play's most ingenious strokes is to implicate the audience in the scenario: their wish to get to the bottom of this murky little tale makes them participants in the very culture of private investigations and tabloid sleaze which the play critiques. The photos in the shoe box, for instance, inevitably stir a desire in the viewer to see what all the excitement is about, and this voyeuristic engagement is implicitly exposed by the dialogue: "Did they arouse your prurient interest?" Simms asks Cecilia (113). An even more pointed moment is provided by the confusion over the nature of Vinnie and Cecilia's relationship: did they just casually date a few times, or were they intimate? The signals are mixed from both: "We were having an affair, for Christ's sake!" Cecilia insists to Carter (46), before later denying ever having slept with him. Curiosity is aroused, and the play uses this hook to draw the audience, through Carter, into a blatant invasion of privacy. "I - I don't understand," he tells her, innocently enough:

> CECILIA: He kissed me once.
>   *Pause*
> CARTER: He did?
> CECILIA: Yes. Just once.
> CARTER: Where?
> CECILIA: In my kitchen.
> CARTER: I mean on your body! Where on your body!
>   *Pause*
> CECILIA: That's private, Mr. Carter. (80)

Even as one is caught out, the appetite to know more is only whetted further. In contrast to conventional morally oriented realism, Shepard will not permit his audience to rest in the complacent liberal pretension that they somehow know better than, or remain above, the decadence he depicts. The practice of turning tables on the judgmental is even more directly applied by Simms. Knowing that his visitors are viewing him as a man who participated in perversion, he has a habit of biting back with unsettlingly blunt questions about their own proclivities: "You indulge in the odd blow-job from time to time?" (60).

Shifting Pasts

Simms is one of Shepard's most intriguing character creations, a figure who – having suffered the loss of everything he once had – has acquired some philosophical distance on the kind of scheming and dreaming that the other characters still seem intent on involving themselves in. He refuses Vinnie's covert suggestion that he use the photos and documents to clear his name, preferring instead to "let sleeping dogs lay" (66), and scorning the idea that embroiling himself afresh in such dealings will help him in any way. He sees the contemporary insistence on making personal interconnections ever closer and more tangled as inherently foolish and self-defeating: "the cloning of the phone," for example, is described as "another disease" – thereby adding further to Shepard's growing list of phenomena classified as such (106).

The question, however, is whether Simms's monklike distance on the world actually stems from enlightenment – from a sense of having atoned for his past errors and won peace – or from reliance upon an embittered victim complex he does not want to break free of. Both possibilities are presented: he declines Vinnie with calm dignity, and yet at other moments seems almost to enjoy wallowing in his sense of victimization, as if it is a drug which is all he has to live for now: "Loss," he states in one of the play's most tantalizing lines, "can be a powerful elixir" (65). Whichever is the case, Simms knows that the past is something that cannot simply be wiped away, and so there is no point in trying. Here in Kentucky he has a new name and a new identity, but still, everything he is has been conditioned by the events of a personal history he cannot escape.

Obviously there are wider implications to Simms's position: in contrast to *A Lie of the Mind*, *Simpatico* views the whole idea of self-reinvention with a cold and unromantic gaze. Things that one does in the present can indeed change one forever, as Cecilia discovers when she acts as Carter's agent: unwittingly seduced by lust for money (she vividly describes rolling naked on crisp notes on her hotel bed), she discovers with a shock - like so many Shepard characters before her - that "I didn't recognize myself at all" (117). And yet changing into someone new does not mean that you ever leave behind what you were or did before. Simms knows this, as indeed does Rosie, who scorns the naiveté of the old plan that she and Carter would sever all trace of connection between themselves and their old lives in California. Vinnie too has learned through bitter experience that no matter where he has gone, his baggage has gone with him: "I've changed my name a dozen times," he tells Carter, "and nothing came of it" (33). It seems that Carter himself is the one character who still believes that reinvention can be a positive move: his transformation into a Kentucky horse trainer has brought him fame and fortune, and distanced him – at least publicly – from the guilty secrets of his past. "You make a move like this," he tells Cecilia in persuading her to work for him, "just one little move and everything shifts. Everything falls into place behind it. It carries its own momentum" (86). Carter's phraseology here is significant: on the one hand it recalls the comments of previous Shepardian shape-changers like Rabbit and Weston ("You make an adjustment"), and yet on the other it begs questions. What if a point arrives when the teetering weight of all that baggage, shifting behind you, finally brings it crashing down? That is precisely what happens to Carter in the play: his pretense at having taken care of his past is exposed as self-deceit. As Cecilia pointedly asks him of his and Vinnie's role-playing games as children, "Did you fool everyone or just each other?" (70).

Carter, then, is the architect of his own self-destruction: the pressure of trying to keep a lid on the Pandora's box of his previous life finally proves too much. As Vinnie steps out of line, and as his own paranoid terrors of retribution and exposure begin to snowball, he hits the bottle and his mind begins to unravel (he thus duplicates MacCree's trajectory in *Silent Tongue*). Carter winds up a shivering mess in Vinnie's filthy bed, still trying to delude himself that one more reinvention will solve everything: "I'm going to change my name. . . . I'm going to disappear. . . . We could maybe start up with the claimers again. Start brand new." Vinnie's response (echoing Rosie's to his own suggestions) summarizes the play's exposure of America's oldest and fondest myth: "Those days are over, Carter. Long gone. Give it up" (131).

If *A Lie of the Mind* had appeared to place a tentative hope in the positive potential of remaking one's own identity, *Simpatico* does not so much contradict that idea as provide a rider to it: progress is perhaps possible, provided that such changes are made in the full knowledge of their implications, and full recognition of the ever-unstable weight of the past. Indeed, there is a clear sense in the play of Shepard himself looking back over his many past lives and trying to come to terms with what that means for him now. ("As you grow older," he noted in a 1996 interview, "the past looms a lot larger.")[14] Vinnie recalls the days of sleeping on floors in the 1960s, Cecilia looks back on the lessons of living in England in the 1970s, and Carter's move from California to Kentucky, a broken relationship in his wake, is likewise partly autobiographical. "How many lives do you think a man can live?" Simms asks Vinnie: "How many lives within this *one*?" (61). If the play suggests a hard-earned wisdom and clarity on Shepard's part, it also draws together elements from several previous stages of his writing, utilizing not only the "realistic" character explorations and confrontations of his family plays, but also the conspiracy theories, detective work, and national critique of his mid-'70s work, and even something of the sense of cliché and cultural debasement apparent in the rock/pop plays. This is the work of a mature writer weaving various of the threads of his earlier work into a dense, humanly complex new structure.

Simpatico's fascinating ambiguity is perhaps epitomized in the character of Vinnie, who (unlike Carter) seems fully aware of the weight of the past, the instability of identity, the cost of embroiling oneself in webs one can never escape from, and yet (unlike the coldly distanced Simms) continues to play with his life like a child embarking on new adventures. He even appears to stake his sense of self on a continued willingness to submerge himself ever further in human confusion: "It's a great feeling to embark on a case," he tells Carter at the end, "It fills me with purpose. I'm my own man again" (134). Does this make him the ultimate postmodernist trickster, willfully playing games with the shifting sands of reality; a "master-adapter" with hindsight; Crow with the blinkers off? Or does it make him a portrait of the artist as a not-so-young man, resolved to keep on weaving new connections, making up yet more never-to-be-resolved narratives? Or does it, perhaps, make him both? As Shepard remarked in an interview when *Simpatico* was about to open, it is the bottomlessness of the questions surrounding human identities and relationships which continues to motivate him to write: "I mean, you have these assumptions about somebody, and all of a sudden this other thing appears. Where is that coming from? That's the mystery. . . . That's what's so fascinating."[15]

Afterword

THE PROBLEM WITH CONCLUDING a book of this sort is knowing where to stop. In 1996, even as I have been making final adjustments to this text, there has been a whole new burst of activity from Shepard. In April, Steppenwolf's revised *Buried Child* began a critically acclaimed, if commercially unsuccessful, run on Broadway. May saw the publication of a remarkable new collection of prose writing, *Cruising Paradise*. *When the World Was Green: A Chef's Fable,* a brand-new play by Shepard and Joseph Chaikin, had its premiere performances at the Olympic Arts Festival in Atlanta in July, before reopening in New York in late fall, as part of a season of Shepard's work being mounted by the Signature Theatre Company (both productions were directed by Chaikin himself). The Signature season opened in November with an updated and overhauled version of *The Tooth of Crime*.

Although I am unable to deal with this new burst of activity in any detail here, it seems somehow appropriate that Shepard's output appears to be accelerating again just at the point that I am rounding this book off: as was stressed at the outset, I have no interest in trying to provide a finished judgment on a fixed body of work. Suffice to say that each of the new pieces suggests a further maturing of Shepard's writing, although in his case, as has been previously noted, "maturity" does not necessarily equate with greater accessibility. First reports on *The Tooth of Crime: Second Dance,* for example, indicate that much of the chaotic, pop-art-inflected brashness of the original has been stripped away in favor of a tighter, still darker focus on the underlying themes of murder and the loss of self. This more somber tone, however, has also resulted in a loss of

theatrical dynamism, while the play's newer intricacies have proved difficult for audiences to grasp. One wonders how wise it is for Shepard, of all
people, to attempt to rework material written in another era, by another
self.

By contrast, *Crusing Paradise* has a freshness about it that seems
indicative of a writer enjoying roaming into new territory while simultaneously keeping one eye on home ground. While it strongly resembles
Motel Chronicles both in its preponderance of autobiographical material
(much of it intensely personal), and in its spare, lucid, and subtly lyrical
prose style (the resemblance to Richard Ford's short stories is still more
pronounced here), these "tales" are generally longer and less fragmentary
than their predecessors, allowing their implications to resonate more
deeply with the reader. Though many of the pieces are reportedly the
fruits of various, unsuccessful attempts at writing a novel, they have been
ingeniously rearranged and intercut. The resulting impression is of reading a densely layered collage rather than simply picking one's way through
shards of memory and incidental whimsy.

When the World Was Green, likewise, is both a consolidation of and a
departure from earlier work.[1] More so even than Chaikin and Shepard's
previous, performance-poetry collaborations, the piece seems to fuse the
artistic preoccupations of both men into a true synthesis. Chaikin's long-
standing fascination with the fable form, previously most evident in his
work with Jean-Claude van Itallie, manifests itself in the fact that the
piece is neither temporally nor geographically specific in its setting, and
acquires overtones of universality through its presentation of a cycle of
fall and redemption. In a series of spare, direct dialogues between an ageing chef jailed for murder and a young female journalist who interviews
him about his life story, the play unfolds a simple story of a centuries-old
family feud being ended when the woman – apparently the daughter of
the man the chef poisoned – opts to break the cycle of vengeance and for-
give. (The play's title refers to a prelapsarian time before the feud began.)
Yet while it avoids Shepard's usual tangled complexity and cultural specificity, *When the World Was Green* also represents a crystalline distillation
of several of his recurring thematic concerns. His fascination with male
duality, for instance, resurfaces yet again, this time in the form of the
implication that the Old Man has been seeking to kill a figure who is, in
effect, his own alter ego. In completing the deed (if indeed he has), he
has in some sense – like Poe's William Wilson – ended his own life. That
he apparently had no choice in this, that it was his lifelong mission and
destiny (the ground zero of his *identity*), also recalls Shepard's concerns

with the cycles of masculine violence and retribution – handed down, inevitably, from generation to generation.

If Shepard's most recent work has implied that America's contemporary bewilderment stems from the weight of its past sins, the seeming universality of this piece allows its resonances to spill out to take in the wider anguish of the post–Cold War world in general. Although the play makes passing reference to various locations in America (most notably to that most European of its cities, New Orleans), there are also numerous allusions to unnamed horrors which suggest the ossified ethnic hatreds of old world Europe or Africa, the writers having drawn (by their own admission) on recent accounts of atrocities in war zones such as Bosnia and Rwanda. What is perhaps most remarkable about the piece, therefore, is that it manages, finally, to offer an image of hope and reconciliation which seems neither cheap nor sentimental in the light of these images. As in much of Shepard's more recent work, the healing is found in "the female side," in a woman who chooses to befriend a man she could have chosen so easily to hate. Yet the play's true hope for the future lies in its recurrent images of cooking, which are actualized in the last scene as the Interviewer brings the Old Man the equipment to make her one special dish. The sight, sound, and smells of the cooking, combined with the text itself (which ascribes symbolic properties to the various ingredients), create a remarkably sensual stage metaphor which suggests the blending of supposed incompatibles into a New Orleans, or even New World, gumbo. Again, there is the suggestion that lives, perhaps even cultures, can be reinvented for the better if past failures can somehow be faced up to and moved on from, rather than denied. The play, finally, feels like a kind of culinary prayer for the next millennium.

Moving on to a little cooking of my own, I want to remix some of the observations of the foregoing chapters into the form of an Afterword. This book, as I have stressed, is intended as an open-ended commentary, and these concluding remarks are not intended as a conclusion (a cooking of the books): they are simply some personal thoughts aimed at provisionally locating Shepard's work in the general context of American theatre and also of the wider cultural landscape.

In theatrical terms, Shepard undoubtedly belongs – to borrow the title of an international symposium on his work in Brussels in 1993 – somewhere "Between the Margin and the Center." The question remains opens as to exactly where "in between" he stands, and there is a case for

suggesting that he has effectively blurred that binary distinction too: insofar as he has been accepted by the mainstream, he has also brought the
margins with him, by infiltrating the conventions of domestic realism with
unsettling, destabilizing elements. My own feeling is that Shepard's work,
whatever the disguises it has worn, has always been far more in tune with
the experimental fringe than with the establishment. Indeed, there is a
sense in which it provides a kind of crazed, idiosyncratic route map
through the avant-garde trends of the last thirty years. It is not simply that
he has drawn on various nontheatrical innovations shortly after they have
occurred (action painting, pop art, and superrealism, to cite only the
examples from visual art): his playwriting also demonstrates noticeable
parallels with Michael Vanden Heuvel's generalized but nonetheless persuasive account (in his 1991 book *Performing Drama/Dramatizing Performance*) of American experimental theatre's overall transitions over the
last three decades. These general shifts, from the intuitive, antirational
modernism of the 1960s, through the disintegrative postmodern formalism of the 1970s, to the recovery in the 1980s of an ironized and provisional interest in character and narrative, are all matched by related
developments in Shepard's work. And if the alternative art of the early
'90s was characterized, as Carol Becker suggests in her book *The Subversive Imagination* (1994), by a renewed engagement with the political,
then Shepard, in his own way, echoed that direction too. It should come
as no surprise that, while mainstream critics have this decade largely
backtracked on the praise they heaped on him in the mid-'80s, his work
has continued to be received with interest and enthusiasm by fellow
artists. What *does* seem perverse is that Shepard should now have been
written so firmly into the canon of "major American playwrights."

The canonical line of descent is usually seen as originating with the
ostensibly single-handed innovations of Eugene O'Neill, and moving
through Thornton Wilder, Tennessee Williams, Arthur Miller, and
Edward Albee to Shepard and – latterly – David Mamet. This is a construction which has rightly been attacked for the unspoken prejudices
underlying it, including most particularly the way it reduces to a historical footnote a number of highly significant female and nonwhite dramatists – one of whom, Amiri Baraka (LeRoi Jones), Shepard himself
described in 1979 as "the greatest American playwright."[2] Shepard was
co-opted into this club as a result of his series of ostensibly realistic family dramas (the genre which embraces almost all the traditionally recognized "classics" of the American stage). Yet the tendency to view him as

part of a line of canonical descent has latterly resulted in the real strengths of his work being glossed over rather than celebrated. Admittedly, his plays share numerous thematic connections with those of his "forefathers": the loss of the frontier and the corruption of the "American Dream"; family dynamics; the pressures of urbanization; the denial of the past. But applied across the board, this list becomes little more than a set of clichés, functioning to create a homogenized frame of reference which simply obscures the distinctive contributions of each writer. This is particularly true in Shepard's case: certain relatively incidental features of his work have come to be viewed, retrospectively, as somehow characterizing it, with the result that many now view his plays with a set of woefully misconceived preconceptions. Take, for instance, Irving Wardle's bemused response to the farcical and grotesque elements of *Curse of the Starving Class*, when reviewing a 1991 revival: "Shepard, famed for his elegies to the shrinking desert, here seems to be parodying himself."[3] Wardle not only forgets that *Curse* actually predates the "famed" pieces he is alluding to (presumably *True West* and *Paris, Texas*); he also entirely ignores the fact that elements of pastiche, subversive irony, and savage humor were hallmarks of Shepard's writing long before the "shrinking desert" was even mentioned. Every mention of that desert, moreover, from Lee's story in *True West* through to the description of Gregory Peck riding across it in Shepard's lyrics for the Bob Dylan song "Brownsville Girl" (from Dylan's 1986 album, *Knocked Out Loaded*), is accompanied as much by self-mockery as it is by wistful regret.

Shepard's most notable connection to the work of the other canonized writers is not any common thematic concern but the distinctly unorthodox, experimental streak they all share. For example, he shares with O'Neill not only an obsession with the inescapable effects of heredity, but a ruthless insistence on exploring theatre's formal properties, in an attempt to tap into the terrors lying beyond the mask of rationality. Similarly, he shares with Tennessee Williams a defiant obsession with what the latter once called "the incontinent blaze of live theatre, a theatre meant for seeing and for feeling," and both have drawn on the inspiration of musical improvisation in the attempt to realize this. Williams's foreword to *Camino Real* (1953) predated Shepard's own jazz experiments by a decade, but his description of feeling "a new sensation of release, as if I could 'ride out' like a tenor sax taking the breaks in a Dixieland combo or a piano in a bop session" could come from any Shepard interview.[4]

Other connections could be drawn with Albee or even Miller, but the point is that highlighting Shepard's various similarities with these other "major" American playwrights succeeds only in pointing up the flaws inherent in the whole project of creating a coherent canon. Shepard is one of the most resolutely iconoclastic playwrights of recent decades: even by comparison with other experimentalists of his own generation, his work is unusually complex in terms of its decenteredness, its multiplicity of layers and perspectives. And while his writing rarely, if ever, displays the kind of self-conscious analytical rigor characteristic of the work of European postmodernist playwrights like Peter Handke, Howard Barker, and Heiner Müller, the restlessly chaotic spirit of Shepard's best plays captures the confusion of contemporary experience with a peculiar immediacy and intensity. Certainly it is hard to think of a dramatist whose blurring of the boundary between "high" and "low" culture has been quite so unapologetic and persistent: in fusing and often ironizing such a diverse range of cultural influences – jazz, rock and folk music, abstract and pop art, television serials and comic books, beat poetry, Jung and Freud, Greek tragedy, the well-made family drama, gothic horror and melodrama, Beckett, Handke, O'Neill, Laurel and Hardy, California kitsch, film noir, sentimental romance – Shepard has created theatrical conditions which are either overtly disorientating or, in his later work, covertly unsettling. Yet at the same time, his manic humor and colorful stage imagery give his plays the potential for an accessibility not often seen in such complex material. He has continued throughout his career to represent the spirit of Off-Off-Broadway, that peculiar mix of the populist and the avant-garde.

Turning to the question of Shepard's place in the wider cultural landscape, I would suggest that the unruly spirit of his writing is one of his most vital contributions, and a reply of sorts to those critics who have asked, in recent years, whether his avowed disinterest in politics masks a conservative, or even reactionary, perspective. For many in the theatre, Shepard's very refusal to compromise his own vision, his resistance to all conventions but his own, is itself an important statement. "Free is the operative word here," noted Toby Zinman in 1984, reporting on La Mama's retrospective Shepard season:

> Aesthetic freedom and psychological freedom are, for both [the director, George] Ferencz and [musical director, Max] Roach, clearly connected to political freedom. . . . Ferencz sees the plays as political in their progressive force, working against what he sees as a rising wave of conservatism in the theatre. Shepard "works with such a sense of freedom that it's hard to stay immune. It's contagious – it expands you."[5]

It can perhaps be countered that formal freedom in and of itself may be inspiring, but does not necessarily confront or change anything. What his work does achieve, however (and this, paradoxically, becomes most evident in the later, apparently more formally conservative, realistic work), is a profound subversion of established codes and assumptions, which leaves audiences unable to view the plays without comfortable patterns of expectation being disrupted. It is significant that this dimension of Shepard's work has proved an inspiration to some younger playwrights with more overtly ideological agendas. The Asian-American dramatist David Henry Hwang, for example, has cited Shepard as a primary influence, because of his prismatic, collage-like treatment of situation and character (particularly as elucidated in the "Note for Actors" prefacing *Angel City*).[6] Hwang's award-winning play, *M. Butterfly* (1988), adapts these techniques to his own concerns, cleverly juxtaposing different perspectives so as to expose and demystify the racial, sexual, and cultural prejudices inherent in the Western view of Far Eastern peoples.

Shepard's approach, of course, has never been as deliberate and preconceived as Hwang's: his concern has always been with the more or less open-ended investigation of tangled emotional experiences. Yet this emphasis on the personal also represents a political position of sorts. Shepard is a member of a generation of playwrights who grew up resisting the idea that a play should seek to teach, or direct its audience how to think. This was not because they wanted simply to divest themselves of any such responsibility, but because of a deep suspicion toward the idea of adopting such an authoritative position. Shepard himself once voiced this perspective in bluntly dismissive terms: "A lot of people think playwrights are some special brand of intellectual fruitcake with special answers to special problems that confront the world at large. I think that's a crock of shit."[7] His colleague Maria Irene Fornes put it more eloquently when she observed that whereas older writers like Arthur Miller and Edward Albee have usually seemed to be making some definite statement about society or the human condition, the writers who emerged from Off-Off-Broadway have tended toward depicting "a more personal vision, a personal experience" of sociocultural and psychological conditions in the late twentieth century. Such a vision might have no simple or easily apprehended "meaning," but it is "something that seems significant enough to want to present it."[8]

In Shepard's case, this emphasis on the exploration of intensely personal experience has meant that he has not delved deeply into the problematics of the more overtly politicized issues of his era, such as racial and sexual injustice, because unlike peers such as Fornes or Adrienne Kennedy, he has not seen them as impinging directly on his own personal struggles. The experiences which have shaped him, as a person and a writer, are those of a privileged white male, but Shepard has insisted relentlessly on picking apart the implications of that position. He avoids any resort to political metanarratives, but the various micronarratives of his plays accumulate to form a highly idiosyncratic, but nonetheless corrosive critique of the various popular mythologies which continue to prop up America's white-male-Anglo-centric system. Shepard's work insistently exposes flaws and fault lines in whatever material it tackles, from "rugged individualism" to the nuclear, patriarchal family, from boy-gets-girl romantic love to American military hegemony.

Frequently, the plays seem to suggest that such constructions have been set up in a collective or individual attempt to stave off fear of the void, of existential meaninglessness. Yet even as they point to the hollowness and destructiveness of such delusions, they remain visibly resistant to the brand of postmodern thought which casually dismisses the search for meaning and consonance as an outdated irrelevance. That is, Shepard's work demonstrates an awareness not only that these delusory myths still condition the way people behave and cannot be simply dismissed in a puff of abstract theory, but also that faith in a structure of some kind is vital if one is to retain a sense of one's own identity, and so remain sane. That faith, as implied by work as diverse as *The Mad Dog Blues* and *A Lie of the Mind*, will necessarily be a provisional one, involving contradictory ironies, but if one is aware of this from the outset, one can perhaps discover a new and better way forward.

It would be difficult, however, to view optimism as one of the more prevalent threads of Shepard's work, largely because his view of late-twentieth-century life is so uncompromising. As is evident in an article Shepard wrote for *Time Out* in 1974, his writing aims at being a relevant response to the world as he perceives it, a kind of warped mirror in which audiences will be made to see some uncomfortable truths, but the question – inevitably – is whether any such response is going to be adequate:

> Right now I'm wondering what kind of significance a play can have in the face of these last few days. . . . The news makes me empty. The news set next to an opening night or even a rehearsal. My values go swimming around. . . . When I wrote this play something was going on. Something urgent. At times I can still feel it. [*The Tooth of Crime* is about] this weird world of people playing a murder game. I dream

about L.A. In the middle of the Royal Court, in the middle of rehearsals, I dream about L.A. That burning house. Five hundred men shooting it out for two hours with an ex-con and some armed men. Five hundred cops at the same place at the same time firing on one little house in California.[9]

This sense of a world dominated by insanity and violence is, of course, as pertinent in the 1990s as it was in the 1970s (as Shepard's decision to update *Tooth* perhaps indicates). But what if – as the remarks above seem to fear – in reflecting the chaos of the world the artist succeeds simply in perpetuating and exacerbating that confusion? This is a familiar dilemma for contemporary artists. And yet it is precisely the point of Shepard's work that it refuses to try to bolster up preconceived ideas or dogmas, even if that means peering into the abyss. His pursuit of that distinctly modernist faith in the validity of rigorous and unblinking self-honesty – even to the vanishing point of confronting the postmodernist fear that there is no such thing as "self" – has meant there has never been any guarantee that his explorations will lead anywhere positive. Nevertheless, there remains for Shepard the constant possibility that the act of theatrical creation itself might somehow open up new directions. Though these plays are rarely "satisfying," in the sense of feeling whole or resolved, it is their imaginative power, and their stubborn refusal simply to let things lie, which make them so distinctive. In the bewildering contemporary environment, that response is surely not only a valid one, but also entirely necessary.

> WHEELER: It's going to open up the world. . . . It's going to reveal something. It's going to change everything from the way it is now to something else.
> RABBIT: Can't you stand the way it is?
> WHEELER: Can you? . . .
> WHEELER: (*pauses, staring at bundle*) What if it's worse than we can imagine?
> RABBIT: It couldn't be.
> WHEELER: No. I guess not.[10]

Notes

Preface

1 I am indebted to Leonard Wilcox's article "Modernism vs. Postmodernism: Sam Shepard's *The Tooth of Crime* and the Discourses of Popular Culture" (*Modern Drama* XXX [1987], 560–73), for providing me with the initial inspiration for this modernist/postmodernist line of inquiry.

2 Shepard interviewed by Irene Oppenheim and Victor Fascio, "The Most Promising Playwright in America Today Is Sam Shepard," *Village Voice*, 27 October 1975, 82.

3 Susan Sontag, "Against Interpretation," *A Susan Sontag Reader* (Harmondsworth, 1983), 104.

Introduction

1 David Mamet, *Writing in Restaurants* (London, 1988), 26, 132.

2 Robert Woodruff quoted by Michael Vermuelen, "Sam Shepard: Yes, Yes, Yes," *Esquire*, February 1980, 85.

3 Sam Shepard, "Language, Visualization and the Inner Library" (1977), reproduced in Bonnie Marranca (ed.), *American Dreams: The Imagination of Sam Shepard* (New York, 1981), 215.

4 Shepard interviewed by Amy Lippman, "Rhythm and Truths," *American Theatre*, April 1984, 11.

5 From Shepard's Introduction to *The Unseen Hand and Other Plays* (New York, 1986), x.

6 See Michael Almereyda's interview with Shepard, "Sam Shepard: The All-American Cultural Icon at 50," *Arena*, May/June 1994, 65.

7 Shepard interviewed by Naseem Khan, "Free-Form Playwright," *Time Out*, 7–13 July 1972, 31.

8 Shepard interviewed by Stewart McBride, "Sam Shepard," *Christian Science Monitor,* 23 December 1980, B2.

9 All references in this paragraph from Shepard's "Language . . . ," 215.

10 These papers held in Boston University's Mugar Memorial Library, Shepard archive, Box 3, File 2 ("White Slavery"), and Box 13, File 2.

11 Lippman interview, 9–10.

12 Shepard interview by Kenneth Chubb, "Metaphors, Mad Dogs and Old Time Cowboys" (1974), reprinted in Marranca (ed.), 198.

13 Shepard interviewed by Jennifer Allen, "The Man on the High Horse," *Esquire,* November 1988, 148.

14 Shepard, *The Rolling Thunder Logbook* (New York, 1977), 52. Subsequent references included parenthetically in the text.

15 Shepard interviewed by Carol Rosen, "Silent Tongues," *Village Voice,* 4 August 1992, 36.

16 Notes for January 1978, Boston University archive, Box 4, File 7.

17 Shepard interviewed in "A Long Ride," *Paris, Texas* press kit (ed. Jean Pierre Vincent; Paris, 1984), 16.

18 John Lion, "Rock and Roll Jesus with a Cowboy Mouth," *American Theatre,* April 1984, 8.

19 John Lion in an unpublished interview with the author, 7 August 1996.

20 Vermuelen interview, 86.

21 Shepard interviewed by Michiko Katukani, "Myths, Dreams, Realities – Sam Shepard's America," *New York Times,* 29 January 1984, 2.26. This opposition of personality and essence is, significantly, consistent with the terminology used by the Russian mystic G. I. Gurdjieff, whose ideas have long been of deep personal importance to Shepard. It is, however, difficult to relate Gurdjieff's often arcane writings to the details of Shepard's actual playwriting, and this is not a connection I shall be pursuing.

22 Chubb interview, 198.

23 Lion, "Rock and Roll Jesus," 8.

24 Shepard, *Motel Chronicles and Hawk Moon* (London, 1985), 45–6. Numerous other pieces in the book display similar automythologizing tendencies.

25 Boston University archive, Box 13, File 7 (1979 notes): "All my dreaming is in vain: a repetition of actors repeating themselves. Six Egomaniacs in Search of an Audience."

26 Shepard quoted in John Dugdale (ed.), *File on Shepard* (London, 1989), 62.

27 In *The Right Stuff,* Shepard (who is known to be afraid of flying) plays the fearless Yeager as unflinchingly cool and manly. This pose is exploited to the point where, in the final scene, he walks unharmed out of a wrecked and burning airplane. "Is that a man?," asks one of the salvage crew. "You're goddamn right it is!" comes the reply.

28 Letter from Shepard to Schechner, cited in the latter's book *Performance Theory* (London, 1988), 76.

29   Cf. Chubb interview, 202. Speaking in 1974, Shepard mercilessly parodies the
     environmental theatre approach which Schechner had recently applied to
     The Tooth of Crime: "If an audience walks into a building and people are swing-
     ing from the rafters and spaghetti's thrown all over them, it doesn't necessarily
     mean . . . that their participation in the play is going to be any closer. In fact it
     might very well be less so, because of the defences that are put up as soon as that
     happens."

30   I am indebted to Michael Vanden Heuvel for this concept of a dialogics of pro-
     duction, which he develops in his book *Performing Drama/Dramatizing Perfor-
     mance* (Ann Arbor, 1991).

31   Edward Albee, "Theatre: *Icarus's Mother,*" *Village Voice*, 25 November 1965, 19.

32   Jack Gelber, "The Playwright as Shaman," in Marranca (ed.), 47.

33   Shepard, "News Blues," *Time Out*, 31 May–6 June 1974, 17.

Chapter 1

1   Shepard interviewed by Kenneth Chubb, "Metaphors, Mad Dogs and Old Time
     Cowboys" (1974), reproduced in Bonnie Marranca (ed.), *American Dreams*
     (New York, 1981), 193.

2   Sam Shepard, *The Rock Garden*, in *The Unseen Hand and Other Plays* (New
     York, 1986), 43. Subsequent references for all plays discussed in this chapter are
     taken from this edition (unless otherwise stated), and included parenthetically in
     the text.

3   Jerry Tallmer, "Tell me about the morons, George," *New York Post*, 12 October
     1964, 16. The one known surviving copy of the *Cowboys* script was acquired
     from Ralph Cook by David DeRose and is described in his book *Sam Shepard*
     (New York, 1992).

4   Michael Smith, "Theatre: *Cowboys* and *The Rock Garden,*" *Village Voice*, 22
     October 1964, 13.

5   Shepard interviewed by Michiko Katukani, "Myths, Dreams, Realities: Sam
     Shepard's America," *New York Times*, 29 January 1984, 2.26.

6   Jacques Levy, quoted in Ellen Oumano, *Sam Shepard* (New York, 1986), 54.

7   Chubb interview, 191.

8   Elinor Lester, "The Pass-The-Hat Circuit," *New York Times* Magazine, 5
     December 1965.

9   Shepard interviewed by Sylvie Drake, "Sam Shepard: A Play for Every Life
     Style," *Los Angeles Times*, 21 October 1979, Calendar section, 58.

10   Katukani interview, 26.

11   Ferlinghetti became a long-term associate of Shepard's (almost twenty years
     later publishing the first edition of *Fool for Love* through his City Lights Book-
     store in San Francisco), as indeed did another key beat writer, Michael McClure.

12   It is no coincidence that in 1971, in her poetic mythologization of Shepard's
     career, "Nine Random Years," Patti Smith (his lover at the time) located him in

the same tradition of *art-brut* self-destruction as Pollock. The poem even envisages the playwright mimicking the painter's legendary death by dying at speed in a car crash.

13   Notes for *Jackson's Dance* in Boston archive, Box 26, File 5.

14   Shepard, "American Experimental Theatre: Then and Now" (1977), reproduced in Marranca (ed.), 212.

15   Shepard, "Language, Visualization and the Inner Library" (1977), reproduced in Marranca (ed.), 214.

16   Robert Pasolli, *A Book on the Open Theater* (Indianapolis, 1970), 21.

17   From interviews with Drake (62), and with Roger Downey, "Inside the Words," *Time Out*, 22–28 April 1977, 11.

18   Don Nielsen, "On Stage with a Jazz Great," New York *Daily News*, 9 December 1984, Leisure section, 15.

19   Shepard interviewed by Pete Hamill, "The New American Hero," *New York*, 5 December 1983, 80.

20   From Strindberg's Introduction to *A Dream Play*, in *Strindberg, Plays: One*, trans. Michael Meyer (London, 1976), 92.

21   Nancy Meckler in an unpublished interview with the author, 30 March 1992. Subsequent quotes are also from this source.

22   Shepard, *The Rolling Thunder Logbook* (New York, 1977), 135.

23   Shepard interviewed by Naseem Khan, "Free-Form Playwright," *Time Out*, 7–13 July 1972, 31.

24   C. G. Jung, *Aspects of the Masculine*, ed. John Beebe (London, 1979), 17.

25   Ralph Cook's Introduction to *Chicago*, in Shepard's *Five Plays* (Indianapolis, 1967), 10.

26   Shepard interviewed by Mel Gussow, "Sam Shepard: Writer on the Way Up," *New York Times*, 12 November 1969, 42.

27   Allen Ginsberg quoted by James Breslin in "Allen Ginsberg: The Origins of *Howl* and *Kaddish*," in Lee Bartlett (ed.), *The Beats: Essays in Criticism* (London, 1981), 88.

28   Shepard, "Language. . . ," 218

29   *La Turista*, in Shepard's *Seven Plays* (New York, 1981), 265. Subsequent references parenthesized in the text.

30   See Shepard's 1969 notebook. Boston archive, Box 26.

Chapter 2

1   Shepard interviewed by Mel Gussow, "Sam Shepard: Writer on the Way Up," *New York Times*, 12 November 1969, 42.

2   Boston University archive, Box 26: 1969 notebook. All archive references in this chapter are taken from this or from loose notes held in this box.

3   Shepard's *Melodrama Play*, in *Fool for Love and Other Plays* (New York, 1984), 117. Subsequent references to this play and to *Cowboy Mouth* are taken from this edition and included parenthetically in the text.

4 Shepard's *Cowboys #2*, in *The Unseen Hand and Other Plays* (New York, 1986), 141. Subsequent references to this play and to *Forensic and the Navigators, The Holy Ghostly, Operation Sidewinder, The Mad Dog Blues, Back Bog Beast Bait*, and *The Unseen Hand*, are all taken from this edition, and included parenthetically in the text.

5 Shepard interviewed by Michiko Katukani, "Myths, Dreams, Realities – Sam Shepard's America," *New York Times*, 29 January 1984, 2.26.

6 Shepard interviewed by Robert Goldberg, "Off-Broadway's Street Cowboy," *Rolling Stone College Papers*, Winter 1980, 43.

7 Shepard interviewed by Pete Hamill, "The New American Hero," *New York*, 5 December 1983, 80.

8 Shepard, *Motel Chronicles and Hawk Moon* (London, 1985), 157–8. Subsequent references included parenthetically in the text.

9 Shepard, "Autobiography," *News of the American Place Theatre* III, 3 (April 1971), 1.

10 Shepard, "Azusa Is a Real Place," *Plays and Players*, May 1973, special insert section, 1.

11 Shepard interviewed by Michael White, "Underground Landscapes," *The Guardian*, 20 February 1974, 8.

12 Shepard quoted by Richard Schechner in his account of their correspondence over the Performance Group's 1972 production of *The Tooth of Crime*. Bonnie Marranca (ed.), *American Dreams* (New York, 1981), 166.

13 White interview.

14 Shepard's *Shaved Splits*, in *The Unseen Hand and Other Plays* (Indianapolis, 1971), 179. Subsequent references are included parenthetically in the text. (*Shaved Splits* was the only one of Shepard's published plays not to have been reprinted by Bantam in its 1980s compilations.)

15 Shepard, "Azusa . . ."

16 Arthur Sainer, Theatre Review, *Village Voice*, 6 August 1970.

17 Shepard interviewed by Jennifer Allen, "The Man on the High Horse," *Esquire*, November 1988, 148.

18 Shepard interviewed by Kenneth Chubb, "Metaphors, Mad Dogs and Old Time Cowboys" (1974), reproduced in Marranca (ed.), 195.

19 For an extreme example, see Tavel's *Gorilla Queen* (1966), a gay/transvestite pastiche of Hollywood musicals and *King Kong*, in Albert Poland and Bruce Mailman (eds.), *The Off-Off-Broadway Book* (Indianapolis, 1972).

20 Fredric Jameson, *Postmodernism and the Cultural Logic of Late Capitalism* (London, 1988), 9.

21 Clive Barnes, Theatre Review, *New York Times*, 2 April 1970.

22 Michel Foucault, *The Order of Things: An Archeology of the Human Sciences* (New York, 1970), xviii.

23 Publisher Michael Roloff, quoted in Ellen Oumano, *Sam Shepard* (New York, 1986), 130.

24 Chubb interview, 208.

25   R. D. Laing, *The Politics of Experience and the Bird of Paradise* (Harmondsworth, 1967), 12, 20.

26   For a detailed account of Hopi mythology and a description of the Snake-Antelope ceremony in its original form, see Frank Waters, *Book of the Hopi* (New York, 1972).

27   Shepard quoted by Kenneth Chubb, "Fruitful Difficulties of Directing Sam Shepard," *Theatre Quarterly* IV, 15 (1974), 24.

28   Cf. Linda Hutcheon, *A Poetics of Postmodernism* (London, 1988), 39. "In a direct reaction against the tendency of our times to value only the new and the novel, [postmodernist nostalgia] returns us to a re-thought past to see what, if anything, is of value in that past experience."

29   Shepard interviewed by Kevin Sessums, "Geography of a Horse Dreamer," *Interview*, September 1988, 78.

30   Frederick Jackson Turner, *The Frontier in American History* (New York, 1920), 37, 33n.

31   Shepard interviewed by Robert Coe, "Saga of Sam Shepard," *New York Times Magazine*, 23 November 1980, 122.

32   Shepard quoted by Oumano, 11.

33   This was one of the effects Tom O'Horgan had to be particularly inventive with in the original La Mama production, using bolts of colored cloth as flames.

34   Gris-Gris's screeching strings were probably partly inspired by the atonal viola of the Velvet Underground's John Cale. The Velvets' leader, Lou Reed, also wrote one of the play's three darkly morbid songs.

Chapter 3

1   Shepard interviewed by Kenneth Chubb, "Metaphors, Mad Dogs and Old Time Cowboys" (1974), reprinted in Bonnie Marranca (ed.), *American Dreams* (New York, 1981), 198.

2   *Ibid.*, 208.

3   Shepard's *Geography of a Horse Dreamer*, in *Fool for Love and Other Plays* (New York, 1984), 286. Subsequent references to *Geography* and *Action* are taken from this edition and included parenthetically in the text.

4   Shepard, "Language, Visualization and the Inner Library" (1977), in Marranca (ed.), 216, 219.

5   Quoted by Richard Schechner in *Performance Theory* (London, 1988), 76.

6   Chubb interview, 204, 208.

7   T. E. Kalem, *Time* magazine, 27 November 1972, 73.

8   See Florence Falk on *Tooth*'s "perverse re-run" of the Ford film, "Men Without Women: The Shepard Landscape," in Marranca (ed.), 93.

9   Shepard, *The Tooth of Crime*, in *Seven Plays* (New York, 1981), 203. Subsequent references are included parenthetically in the text.

10   Shepard interviewed by Robert Goldberg, "Off-Broadway's Street Cowboy," *Rolling Stone College Papers*, Winter 1980, 44.

11 Shepard interviewed by Naseem Khan, "Free-Form Playwright," *Time Out,* 7–13 July 1972, 31.
12 Irving Wardle, Theatre Review, *The Times,* London, 18 July 1972, 11.
13 Charles Marowitz, "Sam Shepard: Sophisticate Abroad," *The Village Voice,* 7 September 1972.
14 Shepard interviewed by Roger Downey, "Inside the Words," *Time Out,* 22–28 April 1977, 11.
15 Shepard, "Autobiography," *News of the American Place Theatre* III, 3 (April 1971), 1.
16 Shepard, "Language . . . ," 216.
17 Richard Schechner, "The Writer and the Performance Group: Rehearsing *The Tooth of Crime,*" in Marranca (ed.), 163.
18 Stephane Mallarmé, *Poems,* trans. Roger Fry (New York, 1951), 51.
19 Khan interview, 31.
20 Peter Brook, *The Empty Space* (Harmondsworth, 1972), 65–6.
21 See Shepard's 1975 article "Time," reprinted in Marranca (ed.), 211, and his 1974 letters to Joseph Chaikin, printed in *Joseph Chaikin and Sam Shepard: Letters and Texts: 1972–1984,* ed. Barry Daniels (New York, 1989), 12.
22 See Jean-François Lyotard, *The Postmodern Condition,* trans. Bennington and Massumi (Manchester, 1984), xxiv.
23 Shepard, "Language . . . ," 216–17.
24 Shepard interviewed by Goldberg, 45, and by Stewart McBride, "Sam Shepard," *Christian Science Monitor,* 23 December 1980, B.3.
25 Handke's introduction to his play *The Ride Across Lake Constance,* trans. Michael Roloff (London, 1973), 5.
26 David Savran argues this line most coherently in his essay "Sam Shepard's Conceptual Prison: *Action* and the Unseen Hand," *Theatre Journal* XXXVI, 1 (March 1984), 57–74.
27 Cf. Zygmunt Bauman, *Intimations of Postmodernity* (London, 1992), xvii–xviii. "Denying belief does not, by itself, neutralize the awful, propelling force of the *fear of void*; and postmodernity has done next to nothing to support its defiance of past pretence with a new practical antidote for old poison . . . men and women have been left alone with their fears."
28 Cf. Bauman, xix.
29 Nancy Meckler interviewed by the author, 30 March 1992.

Chapter 4

1 Manuscripts of these pieces are held in the Shepard archive at Boston University, Box 1, File 4, and Box 2, File 15, respectively.
2 John Lion, in an unpublished interview with the author, 7 August 1996.
3 Shepard interviewed by Sylvie Drake, "Sam Shepard: A Play for Every Lifestyle," *Los Angeles Times,* Calendar section, 62.

4   Review of albums by Ornette Coleman and Little Brother Montgomery, quoted in Don Shewey, *Sam Shepard* (New York, 1985), 96.

5   See Brian McHale, *Postmodernist Fiction* (London, 1987), 1–9.

6   Shepard, *Suicide in B♭*, in *Fool for Love and Other Plays* (New York, 1984), 198. Subsequent references to this play and to *Angel City* and *Seduced* are taken from this edition, and cited parenthetically in the text.

7   Thomas Pynchon, *Gravity's Rainbow* (London, 1975), 434.

8   Boston archive, Box 3, File 6.

9   Shepard interviewed by Michiko Katukani, "Myths, Dreams, Realities – Sam Shepard's America," *New York Times*, 29 January 1984, 2.26.

10 Boston archive, Box 1, File 2. The first-draft manuscript has scrawled corrections by Shepard, which clearly add to the play's jaggedness. Rabbit's long speech, for example, is altered to make his sudden conversion to power hunger at the end less gradual, more abrupt. Miss Scoons' sudden "I look at the screen" speech was a wholesale addition to the first draft, thereby breaking up the flow of a scene she originally simply exited from. In act 2, various pronunciations of Wheeler's, which schematize the theme of the contemporary contempt for the sacred too obviously, are cut altogether. Many of the play's dialogue exchanges were also altered slightly to accentuate the abrasive aggression between the characters: Tympani's first scene with Rabbit, for instance, is marked by a greater degree of shortness and contempt in the redraft.

11 Robert Woodruff interviewed by Robert Coe in Bonnie Marranca (ed.), *American Dreams* (New York, 1981), 157.

12 *The Sad Lament of Pecos Bill on the Eve of Killing His Wife*, published as an afterpiece to Shepard's *Fool for Love* (London, 1984), 112.

13 See Frank Waters, *Book of the Hopi* (New York, 1972), 11–22.

14 Cf. C. G. Jung, *Jung: Selected Writings*, ed. Anthony Storr (London, 1983), 109. "She is the much needed compensation . . . the solace for all bitterness, and at the same time the great illusionist, the seductress."

15 See Waters, 222–30.

16 Cf. the apocalyptic marriage of the Sun King and Moon Queen in alchemical lore, a coming together so forceful that both partners die instantly.

17 See William Kleb, "Sam Shepard's *Inacoma* at the Magic Theatre," *Theater*, Fall 1977, 59.

18 See Boston archive, Box 2, File 4, which contains this and other textual fragments used in *Inacoma*.

19 Sam Shepard, *Seven Plays* (New York, 1981), 313.

20 *Joseph Chaikin and Sam Shepard: Letters and Texts, 1972–1984*, ed. Barry Daniels (New York, 1989), 158.

Chapter 5

1   Walter Kerr, "Sam Shepard: What's The Message?" *New York Times*, 10 December 1978, 2.3.

2　See Shepard's interviews with Kenneth Chubb, "Metaphors, Mad Dogs and Old-Time Cowboys," reprinted in Bonnie Marranca (ed.), *American Dreams* (New York, 1981), 208, and with Amy Lippman, "Rhythm and Truths," *American Theatre*, April 1984, 9.

3　Unfinished draft of a letter from Shepard to his mother, circa 1974, in a notebook in Boston University, Shepard achive, Box 26, File 7.

4　"Shepard interviewed by Richard Downey, "Inside the Words," *Time Out*, 22–8 April 1977, 11.

5　Manuscript of *The Last American Gas Station* held in Boston archive, Box 1, File 13.

6　An enlightening contrast can be made here with Arthur Miller's tendency to project his own voice through lawyer characters: Shepard's intuition and contingency versus Miller's earnest deliberation.

7　Shepard interviewed by Robert Coe, "Saga of Sam Shepard," *New York Times Magazine*, 23 November 1980, 58.

8　Shepard, *Seven Plays* (New York, 1981), 86. Subsequent references to both *Buried Child* and *Curse of the Starving Class* are taken from this edition and parenthesized in the text.

9　Shepard interviewed by Robert Goldberg, "Off-Broadway's Street Cowboy," *Rolling Stone College Papers*, Winter 1980, 44.

10　*Buried Child* production notebook, entry dated June 1978. Boston archive, Box 4, File 14.

11　Shepard interviewed by Jennifer Allen, "The Man on the High Horse," *Esquire*, November 1988, 148.

12　Coe interview, 122.

13　Michael Billington, "The dud avocados" (review of the Royal Shakespeare Company's revival at the Barbican Pit in London), *The Guardian*, 13 September 1991.

14　Robert Woodruff interviewed by Robert Coe, in Marranca (ed.), 153.

15　Shepard interviewed by Michael Vermuelen, "Sam Shepard: Yes, Yes, Yes," *Esquire*, February 1980, 85.

16　Irving Malin, *New American Gothic* (London, 1962), 9.

17　Shepard's growing frustration with *Gas Station* is evident in annoyed notations in the margins of the manuscript, and in the narrative's suicidal plunge into Grand Guignol, complete with cannibalism and transformations into animals.

18　Allen interview, 148.

19　For a more detailed account of the processes used in developing character for this production, see my article "Towards a Rhythm Method: Exploring 'Psychological Realism' in Sam Shepard's *Buried Child*," *Studies in Theatre Production* 10 (December 1994), 4–19.

20　Woodruff/Coe interview, 152, 154.

21　Nancy Meckler in an unpublished interview with the author, 30 March 1992. Subsequent quotes also taken from this interview.

22　Don Shewey, *Sam Shepard* (New York, 1985), 127.

23   See draft manuscript for *Curse of the Starving Class*, Boston archive, Box 1, File 5.

24   Allen interview, 148.

25   This image was unavailable for inclusion here, but see – for instance – the photograph reproduced in William W. Demastes's *Beyond Naturalism* (Westport CT, 1988), 96.

26   Woodruff/Coe interview, 156.

27   Goldberg interview, 45.

Chapter 6

1   Shepard's *True West*, in *Seven Plays* (New York, 1981), 3. Subsequent references noted parenthetically in the text.

2   Nancy Meckler in an unpublished interview with the author, 30 March 1992.

3   Shepard interviewed by Stewart McBride, "Sam Shepard," *Christian Science Monitor*, 23 December 1980, B.3.

4   Shepard interviewed by Amy Lippman, "Rhythm and Truths," *American Theatre*, April 1984, 40.

5   Shepard interviewed by Ann McFerran, "Poet of Post-War Americana," *Time Out*, 4–10 December 1981, 25.

6   Lippman interview, 13.

7   Shepard, *Fool For Love and Other Plays* (New York, 1984), 21. Subsequent references included parenthetically in the text.

8   John Lion, "Rock and Roll Jesus with a Cowboy Mouth," *American Theatre*, April 1984, 8.

9   All quotations in this paragraph from Shepard's unfinished article "Theatre of the Future." Boston University archive, Box 13, File 3.

10   Joseph Papp, the Public Theatre's producer-impresario, insisted on casting two movie actors, Tommy Lee Jones and Peter Boyle, in the lead roles, replacing the Magic Theatre cast of Peter Coyote and Jim Haynie against the wishes of Shepard and director Robert Woodruff. Woodruff resigned from the production before the opening, and Shepard issued a statement disowning the show. Papp went ahead with his chosen cast, completing the direction himself.

11   Shepard interviewed by Chris Peachment, "American Hero," *Time Out*, 23–9 August 1984, 16.

12   The label was coined by Bill Buford, editor of *Granta* literary journal, who published a collection of these new stories in *Granta 8: Dirty Realism* (Cambridge, 1983).

13   Lippman interview, 13.

14   Shepard interviewed by Stephen Fay, "Renaissance Man Rides Out of the West," *The Sunday Times*, 26 August 1984, magazine section, 19.

15   Shepard interviewed by Robert Coe, "Saga of Sam Shepard," *New York Times Magazine*, 23 November 1980, 122, and by McFerran, 25.

16 Cf. C. G. Jung, *Jung: Selected Writings*, ed. Anthony Storr (London, 1983), 343.

17 Shepard interviewed by Kevin Sessums, "Geography of a Horse Dreamer," *Interview*, September 1988, 73.

18 Shepard and Chaikin, *The War in Heaven*, in *Joseph Chaikin and Sam Shepard: Letters and Texts 1972–1984*, Barry Daniels, ed. (New York, 1989), 171.

19 Shepard interviewed by Jack Kroll, "Who's that Tall, Dark Stranger?" *Newsweek*, 11 November 1985, 74. Jessica Lange interviewed by Nancy Collins, "Full Tilt Jessica," *Vanity Fair*, October 1991, 128.

20 Manuscript of *California Heart Attack* is held in Boston University archive, Box 1, File 4.

21 Shepard interviewed by Bernard Weiner, "Shepard: Waiting for a Western," *San Francisco Chronicle*, 9 February 1983, 55.

22 See the account of *Jacaranda* in Jennifer Dunning's article "A Nagrin Dance to a Shepard Libretto," *New York Times*, 31 May 1979, C.13.

23 Shepard interviewed by Carol Rosen, "Silent Tongues," *Village Voice*, 4 August 1992, 36. See also Shepard's interview with Jennifer Allen, "The Man on the High Horse," *Esquire*, November 1988, 149.

24 Don Shewey, *Sam Shepard* (New York, 1986), 151.

25 Jean Baudrillard, *America*, trans. Chris Turner (London, 1988), 30.

26 Shepard interviewed by Michiko Katukani, "Myths, Dreams, Realities – Sam Shepard's America," *New York Times*, 29 January 1984, 2.26.

27 I am indebted to Toby Silverman Zinman for pointing out this connection in her article "Sam Shepard and Super-Realism," *Modern Drama* XXIX, 3 (1986), 423–31. However, I believe her attempt to place the more grotesquely theatrical *Curse* and *Buried Child* under the "superrealist" label is mistaken.

28 Shepard interviewed in "A Long Ride," *Paris, Texas* press kit, ed. Jean-Pierre Vincent (Berlin, 1984), 17.

29 Lippman interview, 41.

30 Manuscript of *Pictures* is in the Boston archive, Box 10, File 5.

31 "A Long Ride," 10.

32 Laura Mulvey, "Visual Pleasure and Narrative Cinema," *Screen* 16, 3 (Autumn 1975), 13. This article has become the touchstone for complex, ongoing debate about the filmic gaze.

Chapter 7

1 Shepard interviewed by Kevin Sessums, "Geography of a Horse Dreamer," *Interview*, September 1988, 78.

2 Previous discussions of possible plot resolutions included serious talk about hiring John Huston to play Travis's father, a role absent from the finished film. Conversely, there was at one stage doubt as to whether Jane (Nastassja Kinski) would ever actually need to appear.

3   Michael Almereyda, "Sam Shepard: The All-American Cultural Icon at 50," *Arena*, May/June 1994, 65.

4   Shepard interviewed by Ben Brantley, "Sam Shepard: Storyteller," *New York Times*, 13 November 1994, H.26.

5   Shepard interviewed by Ross Wetzsteon, "Unknown Territory," *Village Voice*, 10 December 1985, 56.

6   James Gammon interviewed by Nan Robertson, "The Multi-Dimensional Sam Shepard," *New York Times*, 21 January 1986, C.15.

7   Brantley interview.

8   Charles Mingus and Jimmy Knepper quoted by Ekkehard Jost, *Free Jazz* (New York, 1981), 38.

9   Brantley interview.

10 Wetzsteon interview, 55.

11 Sessums interview, 76.

12 Travis's brother, Walt, from Shepard and Wenders's screenplay to *Paris, Texas* (Berlin, 1984), 57. Subsequent references included parenthetically in the text.

13 Shepard, *A Lie of the Mind* (New York, 1987), ix. Subsequent references included parenthetically in the text.

14 Peter N. Carroll and David W. Noble, *The Free and the Unfree: A New History of the United States* (Harmondsworth, 1977), 422.

15 Sheila Rabillard, "Sam Shepard: Theatrical Power and American Dreams," *Modern Drama* XXX, 1 (1987), 68.

16 Sessums interview, 74.

17 Shepard, *States of Shock; Far North; Silent Tongue* (New York, 1993), 105–6. Subsequent quotes parenthesized in the text.

18 Sessums interview, 76.

19 Wim Wenders interviewed in *Paris, Texas* press kit, ed. Jean-Pierre Vincent (Berlin, 1984), 12.

Chapter 8

1   Shepard interviewed by Robert Coe, "Saga of Sam Shepard," *New York Times Magazine*, 23 November 1980, 58.

2   Michael Coveney, "Theatre: Epic Duet in the Wild West End," *The Observer*, 16 April 1995, Review section, 11.

3   Shepard, *States of Shock; Far North; Silent Tongue* (New York, 1993), 29. Subsequent references to these pieces noted parenthetically in the text.

4   W. J. Wetherby, "Rile 'em, Cowboy," *The Guardian*, 4 June 1991, Arts page.

5   Shepard interviewed by Carol Rosen, "Silent Tongues," *Village Voice*, 4 August 1992, 39

6   Rosen interview, 35.

7   Ibid., 39.

8   Shepard interviewed by Michael Almereyda, "Sam Shepard: The All-American Cultural Icon at 50," *Arena*, May/June 1994, 65.

9   Ibid., 69.

10 Shepard, *Simpatico* (New York, 1996), 3. Subsequent references noted paren-
    thetically in the text.

11 Shepard interviewed by Ben Brantley, "Sam Shepard: Storyteller," *New York
    Times*, 13 November 1994, H.26.

12 Shepard, *Buried Child* (revised version), published in *American Theatre*, Sep-
    tember 1996, 36. Subsequent references parenthesized in the text.

13 Shepard interviewed by Stephanie Coen, "Things at Stake Here," *American
    Theatre*, September 1996, 28.

14 Coen interview.

15 Brantley interview.

Afterword

1   At time of writing, *When the World Was Green* is unpublished. These comments
    are based on a typescript kindly supplied by Shepard's agent, Judy Boals.

2   Shepard interviewed by Robert Goldberg, "Off-Broadway's Street Cowboy,"
    Rolling Stone College Papers, Winter 1980, 45: "I don't think there's a playwright
    in this country who speaks with that kind of conviction and intensity."

3   Irving Wardle, "Theatre," *Independent on Sunday*, 15 September 1991.

4   Tennessee Williams, *The Rose Tattoo and Camino Real* (London, 1958), 119.

5   Toby Silverman Zinman, "Shepard Suite," *American Theatre*, December 1984,
    16–17.

6   David Henry Hwang interviewed by David Savran, *In Their Own Words* (New
    York, 1988), 120.

7   Shepard, "Autobiography," *News of the American Place Theatre* III, 3 (April
    1971), 1.

8   Maria Irene Fornes, in an unpublished interview with the author, 17 August
    1994.

9   Shepard, "News Blues," *Time Out*, 31 May–6 June 1974, 17.

10 Shepard, *Angel City*, in *Fool for Love and Other Plays* (New York, 1984),
    110–11.

Chronology

1943
5 November: Samuel Shepard Rogers born, Fort Sheridan, Illinois.

1949
Starts school in South Pasadena, California.

1961
Graduates high school. Trains in animal husbandry.

1963
Leaves home for New York. Gains work as busboy at Village Gate nightclub, Greenwich Village. Changes name to Sam Shepard.

1964
10 October: *Cowboys* and *The Rock Garden* premiere at Theatre Genesis, St. Mark's-in-the-Bouwerie (dir. Ralph Cook).

23 November: *Up to Thursday* premieres at the Village South Theatre, under the auspices of Edward Albee's Playwrights' Unit (dir. Charles Gnys).

1965
10 February: *Dog* and *Rocking Chair* premiere at Cafe La Mama (dir. John Banks).

16 April: *Chicago* premieres at Theatre Genesis (dir. Ralph Cook).

September: *4-H Club* premieres (Playwrights' Unit at the Cherry Lane Theatre, dir. Charles Gnys).

16 November: *Icarus's Mother* premieres at Caffe Cino (dir. Michael Smith).

1966
20 January: *Red Cross* premieres at Judson Poets' Theatre (dir. Jacques Levy).

Spring: *Fourteen Hundred Thousand* premieres at Firehouse Theatre, Minneapolis (dir. Sydney Schubert Walter). Subsequently filmed for National Educational Television (dir. Tom O'Horgan).

1967
Five Plays published by Bobbs-Merrill.

4 March: *La Turista* premieres at American Place Theatre (dir. Jacques Levy).

18 May: *Melodrama Play* premieres at Cafe La Mama (dir. Tom O'Horgan).

November: *Cowboys #2* premieres on multiple bill, "The Scene," at Mark Taper Forum, Los Angeles (dir. Edward Parone).

26 December: *Forensic and the Navigators* premieres (Theatre Genesis, dir. Ralph Cook).

1968

Shepard works on screenplay for Antonioni's *Zabriskie Point*. Resigns. Tours with Holy Modal Rounders and records *The Moray Eels Eat the Holy Modal Rounders* (Elektra).

1969

17 June: Kenneth Tynan's "erotic" revue *Oh! Calcutta* opens at Eden Theatre, New York, incorporating final scene of Shepard's *The Rock Garden*.

November: Shepard marries O-Lan Johnson at St. Mark's Church.

26 December: *The Unseen Hand* premieres at La Mama E.T.C. (dir. Jeff Bleckner).

1970

January: *The Holy Ghostly* receives U.S. premiere at McCarter Theatre, Princeton, N.J., in production by Tom O'Horgan's New Troupe (formerly the La Mama Troupe) following European tour.

12 March: *Operation Sidewinder* premieres (Lincoln Center for the Performing Arts, dir. Michael Schultz).

May: Jesse Mojo Shepard born.

July: *Shaved Splits* premieres (La Mama E.T.C., dir. Bill Hart).

1971

Shepard temporarily leaves O-Lan for Patti Smith, living with her at the Chelsea Hotel.

4 March: *The Mad Dog Blues* premieres (Theatre Genesis, dir. Robert Glaudini).

29 April: *Cowboy Mouth* (written with Patti Smith, dir. Robert Glaudini) and *Back Bog Beast Bait* (dir. Tony Barsha) premiere at American Place Theatre. *Cowboy Mouth* closes after one night as Shepard, playing Slim, goes AWOL.

Summer: Shepard, O-Lan, and Jesse move to London.

1972

17 July: *The Tooth of Crime* premieres (Open Space Theatre, London, dir. Charles Marowitz).

The Open Theatre presents its new collaborative work, *Nightwalk*, which includes fragments of text by Shepard.

1973

Spring: *Blue Bitch* screened by BBC Television.

Hawk Moon prose collection published.

Richard Schechner's Performance Group presents controversial U.S. premiere of *The Tooth of Crime*.

1974

21 February: *Geography of a Horse Dreamer* premieres (Royal Court Theatre Upstairs, dir. Shepard).

25 March: *Little Ocean* premieres (Hampstead Theatre Club, dir. Stephen Rea).

Summer: Shepard and family leave England for California.

October: *Action* premieres (Royal Court Theatre Upstairs, dir. Nancy Meckler).

1975

15 April: U.S. premiere of *Action* and *Killer's Head* (American Place Theatre, dir. Nancy Meckler). Shepard directs same double bill for San Francisco's Magic Theatre shortly afterward.

Fall: Shepard joins Bob Dylan's Rolling Thunder Revue tour as writer for prospective film.

1976

2 July: *Angel City* premieres (Magic Theatre, dir. Shepard).

15 October: *Suicide in B*$^\flat$ premieres (Yale Repertory Theatre, dir. Walt Jones).

22 October: *The Sad Lament of Pecos Bill on the Eve of Killing His Wife* premieres (Bay Area Playwrights' Festival, dir. Robert Woodruff).

1977

18 March: *Inacoma* premieres at Magic Theatre; devised by company of actors and musicians under Shepard's direction.

21 April: *Curse of the Starving Class* premieres (Royal Court Theatre, dir. Nancy Meckler).

Rolling Thunder Logbook published.

Director Jacques Levy acquires Shepard's draft manuscript for a play about Jackson Pollock, *Jackson's Dance* (written 1972), intending to mount it at the Public Theater, but is unable to obtain legal permission from Pollock's widow, Lee Krasner.

1978

April: *Seduced* premieres (Trinity Square Repertory Theatre, Providence, R. I., dir. Jack Gelber).

7–11 June: *Tongues* premieres in a brief run at the Magic Theatre. Both Shepard and Joseph Chaikin perform in it following a devising residency.

27 June: *Buried Child* premieres, also at the Magic Theatre (dir. Robert Woodruff).

Summer: Shepard makes movie acting debut in Terrence Malick's *Days of Heaven*.

1979

7 June: *Jacaranda* premieres (St. Clement's Church, New York): Daniel Nagrin dance piece, libretto by Shepard.

5 September: *Savage/Love* premieres in double bill with *Tongues* at Eureka Theatre Summer Festival, San Francisco, following devising residency.

Pulitzer Prize for Drama awarded to *Buried Child*.

1980

10 July: *True West* premieres (Magic Theatre, dir. Woodruff). Subsequent New York transfer to Public Theatre blighted by disputes with producer Joseph Papp.

Movie appearance: *Resurrection*.

1981

O-Lan Shepard and Overtone Theatre devise *Superstitions* from pieces in *Motel Chronicles*.

Movie appearance: *Raggedy Man*.

1982

Motel Chronicles prose collection published.

Chicago's Steppenwolf Theatre revives *True West*, with John Malkovich as Lee.

Movie appearance: *Frances*. Shepard begins relationship with its star, Jessica Lange.

1983

8 February: *Fool for Love* premieres (Magic Theatre, dir. Shepard).

Movie appearance: *The Right Stuff*. Shepard wins an Oscar nomination as Best Supporting Actor.

Shepard and Lange move to Santa Fe, New Mexico.

1984

March: Death of father, Sam Rogers.

July: Shepard concludes divorce from O-Lan.

Paris, Texas, directed by Wim Wenders from a screenplay by Shepard, is released and wins Palme d'Or at Cannes Film Festival.

Shepard working in Massachusetts with Chaikin and his Winter Project collaborators, when Chaikin suffers stroke. *The War in Heaven* subsequently written with Chaikin during his convalescence.

Movie appearance: *Country*, with Jessica Lange.

1985

8 January: *The War in Heaven* premieres on WBAI radio.

5 December: *A Lie of the Mind* premieres (Promenade Theatre, New York, dir. Shepard). Wins New York Drama Critics Circle Best Play Award.

Movie appearance in Robert Altman's version of *Fool for Love*.

1986

Shepard and Lange move to Scottsville, Virginia

Brownsville Girl, a narrative song written by Shepard and Bob Dylan, appears on the latter's album *Knocked Out Loaded*.

Movie appearance: *Crimes of the Heart* (with Lange, from play by Beth Henley).

1987

July: *Esquire* publishes "True Dylan," an interview with Bob Dylan conducted by Shepard and presented as a bizarre one-act play with added sound and light effects.

Movie appearance: *Baby Boom*.

1988

Shepard directs his screenplay, *Far North*, on location in Minnesota, with Lange.

1989

Movie appearance: *Steel Magnolias*.

1990

Movie appearance: *Bright Angel* (adapted from Richard Ford's short story collection *Rock Springs*).

1991

30 April: *States of Shock* premieres (American Place Theatre, dir. Bill Hart).

Movie appearances: in *Defenseless,* and in leading role in Volker Schlöndorff's *Voyager* (the filming of which is later detailed in *Cruising Paradise*).

1992

Shepard directs his screenplay *Silent Tongue,* on location in New Mexico.

Movie appearance: *Thunder Heart.*

1993

Movie appearance: Alan J. Pakula's *The Pelican Brief.*

1994

Shepard's mother dies.

1 November: *Simpatico* premieres (Joseph Papp Public Theatre, dir. Shepard).

Movie appearance: *Safe Passage.*

1995

4 October: Revised version of *Buried Child* opens at Steppenwolf Theatre (dir. Gary Sinise). Broadway transfer in April 1996.

Shepard, Lange, and family move to Minnesota.

Movie appearance: *Streets of Laredo.*

1996

May: *Cruising Paradise* published.

19 July: *When the World Was Green* (written with and directed by Joseph Chaikin) premieres at Olympic Arts Festival, Atlanta.

November: New York's Signature Theatre Company opens a season dedicated to Shepard's playwriting with the premiere of a revised version of *The Tooth of Crime* (now subtitled *Second Dance*) at the Lucille Lortel Theatre (dir. Bill Hart).

Movie appearance: *Lily Dale* (screenplay by Horton Foote).

Selected Bibliography

Plays and Screenplays by Sam Shepard

This book refers to the following editions, which are listed alphabetically by title:

Angel City and Other Plays. London: Faber, 1978.
Buried Child (revised version). *American Theatre*, September 1996, 29–48.
Five Plays. Indianapolis: Bobbs-Merrill, 1967.
Fool for Love and Other Plays. New York: Bantam, 1984.
Fool for Love and The Sad Lament of Pecos Bill on the Eve of Killing His Wife. London: Faber, 1984.
Joseph Chaikin and Sam Shepard: Letters and Texts 1972–1984. Ed. Barry Daniels. New York: New American Library, 1989.
A Lie of the Mind. New York: New American Library, 1987.
Paris, Texas, written with Wim Wenders. Berlin: Road Movies/Greno, 1984.
Seven Plays. New York: Bantam, 1981.
Simpatico. New York: Vintage, 1996.
States of Shock; Far North; Silent Tongue: A Play and Two Screenplays. New York: Vintage, 1993.
The Unseen Hand and Other Plays. Indianapolis: Bobbs-Merrill, 1971.
The Unseen Hand and Other Plays. New York: Bantam, 1986.

Prose Writing and Articles by Sam Shepard

"American Experimental Theatre: Then and Now." *Performing Arts Journal* II, 2 (Fall 1977), 13–14.
"Autobiography." *News of the American Place Theatre* III, 3 (April 1971), 1–2.
"Azusa Is a Real Place." *Plays and Players*, May 1973, special insert, 1.
Cruising Paradise. New York: Knopf, 1996.

"Language, Visualization and the Inner Library." *The Drama Review* 21, 4 (December 1977), 49–58.

"Less Than Half a Minute." *Time Out*, 12–18 July 1974, 16–17.

Motel Chronicles and Hawk Moon. London: Faber, 1985.

"News Blues." *Time Out*, 31 May–6 June 1974, 17.

The Rolling Thunder Logbook. New York: Viking, 1977.

"True Dylan." *Esquire*, July 1987, 57–68.

Interviews with Sam Shepard

Allen, Jennifer. "The Man on the High Horse." *Esquire*, November 1988, 141–51.

Almereyda, Michael. "Sam Shepard: The All-American Cultural Icon at 50." *Arena*, May/June 1994, 62–9.

Brantley, Ben. "Sam Shepard, Storyteller." *New York Times*, 13 November 1994, H.1, 26.

Chubb, Kenneth, and the editors of *Theatre Quarterly*. "Metaphors, Mad Dogs and Old Time Cowboys." *Theatre Quarterly* IV, 15 (1974), 3–16.

Coe, Robert. "Saga of Sam Shepard." *New York Times Magazine*, 23 November 1980, 56, 58, 118, 120, 122, 124.

Coen, Stephanie. "Things at Stake Here." *American Theatre*, September 1996, 28.

Downey, Roger. "Inside the Words." *Time Out*, 22–28 April 1977, 11.

Drake, Sylvie. "Sam Shepard: A Play for Every Lifestyle." *Los Angeles Times*, 21 October 1977, Calendar section, 1, 58, 62.

Fay, Stephen. "Renaissance Man Rides Out of the West." *Sunday Times Magazine*, 26 August 1984, 16, 19.

Goldberg, Robert. "Sam Shepard: Off-Broadway's Street Cowboy." *Rolling Stone College Papers*, Winter 1980, 43–5.

Gussow, Mel. "Sam Shepard: Writer on the Way Up." *New York Times*, 12 November 1969, 42.

Hamill, Pete. "The New American Hero." *New York*, 5 December 1983, 75–102.

Kakutani, Michiko. "Myths, Dreams, Realities – Sam Shepard's America." *New York Times*, 29 January 1984, 2.1, 26.

Khan, Naseem. "Free-Form Playwright." *Time Out*, 7–13 July 1972, 30–31.

Kroll, Jack. "Who's That Tall, Dark Stranger?" *Newsweek*, 11 November 1985, 68–74.

Lippman, Amy. "Rhythm and Truths." *American Theatre*, April 1984, 9–13, 40–1.

McBride, Stewart. "Sam Shepard." *Christian Science Monitor*, 23 December 1980, B.2–3.

McCrary-Boyd, Blanche. "True West." *The Face*, March 1985, 23–6.

McFerran, Ann. "Poet of Post-War Americana." *Time Out*, 4–10 December 1981, 24–5.

Oppenheim, Irene, and Victor Fascio. "The Most Promising Playwright in America Today Is Sam Shepard." *Village Voice*, 27 October 1975, 81–2.

Peachment, Chris. "American Hero." *Time Out*, 23–9 August 1984, 14–17.

Rosen, Carol. "Silent Tongues: Sam Shepard's Exploration of Emotional Territory."
    Village Voice, 4 August 1992, 34–42.

Sessums, Kevin. "Geography of A Horse Dreamer." *Interview*, September 1988,
    72–8.

Vermuelen, Michael. "Sam Shepard: Yes, Yes, Yes." *Esquire*, February 1980, 79–86.

Vincent, Jean-Pierre (ed.). "A Long Ride: Interview with Sam Shepard." *Paris, Texas*
    press kit. Berlin: Road Movies, 1984, 15–17.

Weiner, Bernard. "Waiting for a Western." *San Francisco Chronicle*, 9 February 1983,
    54–5.

Wetzsteon, Ross. "Unknown Territory." *Village Voice*, 10 December 1985, 55–6.

White, Michael. "Underground Landscapes." *The Guardian*, 20 February 1974, 8.

Selected Criticism and Biography on Shepard

Auerbach, Doris. *Sam Shepard, Arthur Kopit, and the Off-Broadway Theater.*
    Boston: Twayne, 1982.

Bigsby, C.W.E. *Critical Introduction to Twentieth Century American Drama.* Vol. 3:
    Beyond Broadway. Cambridge: Cambridge University Press, 1985.

Blau, Herbert. "The American Dream in American Gothic: The Plays of Sam Shep-
    ard and Adrienne Kennedy." *Modern Drama* XXVII, 4 (1984), 520–39.

Bottoms, Steve. "Towards a Rhythm Method: Exploring 'Psychological Realism' in
    Sam Shepard's *Buried Child.*" *Studies in Theatre Production* 10 (December,
    1994), 4–19.

Callens, Johan. "Memories of the Sea in Shepard's Illinois." *Modern Drama* XXIX, 3
    (1986), 403–15.

Carroll, Dennis. "The Filmic Cut and 'Switchback' in the Plays of Sam Shepard."
    Modern Drama XXVIII, 1 (1985), 126–38.

Chubb, Kenneth. "Fruitful Difficulties of Directing Shepard." *Theatre Quarterly* IV,
    15 (August–October 1974), 17–24.

Cima, Gay Gibson. "Shifting Perspectives: Combining Shepard and Rauschenberg."
    Theatre Journal 38 (March, 1986), 67–81.

Cohn, Ruby. *New American Dramatists: 1960–1980.* London: Macmillan, 1982.

Demastes, William W. "Understanding Sam Shepard's Realism." *Comparative Drama*
    XXI, 3 (Fall 1987), 229–48.

Demastes, William W. *Beyond Naturalism: A New Realism in American Theatre.*
    Westport, CT: Greenwood, 1988.

DeRose, David J. *Sam Shepard.* New York: Twayne, 1992.

Dugdale, John (ed.). *File on Shepard.* London: Methuen, 1989.

Glore, John. "The Canonization of Mojo Root Force: Sam Shepard Live at the Pan-
    theon." *Theater* 12 (Summer–Fall 1981), 53–65.

Grant, Gary. "Writing as a Process of Performing the Self: Sam Shepard's Notebooks."
    Modern Drama XXXIV, 4 (1991), 549–65.

Hart, Lynda. *Sam Shepard's Metaphorical Stages.* New York: Greenwood, 1987.

Hart, Lynda. "Sam Shepard's Pornographic Visions." *Studies in Literary Imagination* XXI, 2 (1988), 69–82.

King, Kimball (ed.). *Sam Shepard: A Casebook.* New York: Garland, 1989.

Kleb, William. "Sam Shepard's *Inacoma* at the Magic Theatre." *Theater* (Fall 1977), 59–64.

Lion, John. "Rock and Roll Jesus with a Cowboy Mouth." *American Theatre*, April 1984, 4–8.

Marranca, Bonnie (ed.). *American Dreams: The Imagination of Sam Shepard.* New York: Performing Arts Journal Publicatons, 1981.

Mazzocco, Robert. "Heading for the Last Round-Up." *New York Times Review of Books*, 9 May 1985, 21–7.

Mottram, Ron. *Inner Landscapes: The Theater of Sam Shepard.* Columbia: University of Missouri Press, 1984.

Oumano, Ellen. *Sam Shepard: The Life and Work of an American Dreamer.* New York: St. Martin's Press, 1986.

Parker, Dorothy (ed.). *Essays on Modern American Drama.* London and Toronto: University of Toronto Press, 1987.

Patraka, Vivian M., and Mark Siegel. *Sam Shepard.* Boise, Idaho: Boise State University Press, 1985.

Putzel, Steven. "Expectation, Confutation, Revelation: Audience Complicity in the Plays of Sam Shepard." *Modern Drama* XXX, 2 (1987), 147–60.

Rabillard, Sheila. "Sam Shepard: Theatrical Power and American Dreams." *Modern Drama* XXX, 1 (1987), 58–71.

Savran, David. "Sam Shepard's Conceptual Prison: *Action* and the Unseen Hand." *Theatre Journal* XXXVI, 1 (March 1984), 57–74.

Schlueter, June (ed.). *Feminist Rereadings of Modern American Drama.* London: Associated University Presses, 1989.

Shewey, Don. *Sam Shepard.* New York: Dell, 1985.

Tucker, Martin. *Sam Shepard.* New York: Continuum, 1992.

Vanden Heuvel, Michael. *Performing Drama/Dramatizing Performance: Alternative Theater and the Dramatic Text.* Ann Arbor: University of Michigan Press, 1991.

Wilcox, Leonard. "Modernism vs. Postmodernism: Sam Shepard's *The Tooth of Crime* and the Discourses of Popular Culture." *Modern Drama* XXX, 4 (1987), 560–73.

Wilcox, Leonard (ed.). *Rereading Shepard: Contemporary Critical Essays on the Plays of Sam Shepard.* London: Macmillan, 1993.

Wilson, Ann. "Fool of Desire: The Spectator to the Plays of Sam Shepard." *Modern Drama* XXX, 1 (1987), 46–57.

Zinman, Toby Silverman. "Sam Shepard and Super–Realism." *Modern Drama* XXIX, 3 (1986), 423–31.

Zinman, Toby Silverman. "Shepard Suite." *American Theatre*, December 1984, 15–17.

Index